SKETCHES

REFORMS AND REFORMERS,

OF

GREAT BRITAIN AND IRELAND.

BY HENRY B. STANTON.

NEW YORK:
PUBLISHED BY BAKER AND SCRIBNER,
145 NASSAU ST. AND 36 PARK ROW,
1850.

S. W. BENEDICT,
Stereo. and Print., 16 Spruce St.

PREFACE.

THIS Book aims to give a summary view of the most important general Reforms, which have been effected or attempted in Great Britain and Ireland, from the period of the French revolution down to the present time. Neither history nor biography has been attempted, but the work aspires to be only what its title indicates—*Sketches*. Large parts of it have recently appeared, from time to time, in the *National Era*, of Washington; no expectation being then entertained that it would assume any other form of publication. The present occasion has been embraced to revise and reärrange the whole, and by condensation and pruning off repetitions, to make room for considerable additions to the list of subjects discussed, and individuals noticed. It is even now incomplete, many men and things, which deserve a place here, being left out—some because I may underrate their relative importance—others because the limits of this work will allow only of selections. Still, it is believed that no important subject has been wholly omitted; though, on account of the vast number of those worthy to be called Reformers, it has been found impossible to make special mention of many able and excellent individuals. Though it may contain errors of fact and opinion, yet, as it is confined to those phases of events, and incidents in the lives of persons, which history too seldom dwells upon, it may be found not wholly valueless to those who would examine the most interesting and instructive period in the recent annals of England.

The chronological plan of the work is, generally, to notice prominent popular movements in their order of time, and, in connection with each, to give sketches, more or less full, of persons who bore a leading part in it. But such slight regard has been paid to chronological arrangement, that each subject stands by itself, having only a general connection with what precedes or follows it

As to my statistics, I have occasionally been compelled to reach conclusions much in the same manner as juries agree upon verdicts—consult a dozen authorities, each one differing with all the others—get the sum total of the whole, divide it by twelve, and adopt the result.

This Book is submitted to the reader as an humble attempt to make some of the Reformers of America better acquainted with some of the Reformers of the Old World—to show that the Anglo-Saxon love of liberty, which inspires so many hearts on both sides of the Atlantic, flows from the same kindred fountain—to prove that, though when measured by her own vaunted standards, Great Britain is one of the most oppressive and despicable Governments on earth, her radical reformers constitute as noble a band of democratic philanthropists as the world has ever seen—to induce candid Americans to make just discriminations in their estimate of "England and the English," and to draw distinctions between the privileged orders of that country and a small, but increasing, and even now powerful body of its people, who admire the free institutions of the United States, and are laboring with heroic constancy, and a zeal tempered with discretion, to secure for themselves and their fellow-subjects the rights and privileges enjoyed by trans-Atlantic republicans,—and, finally, to record my admiration of those rare and true men, who, during the past half century, and while struggling against difficulties and enduring persecutions, of which we have but the faintest conceptions, have achieved so much for the cause of Humanity and Freedom.

H. B. S.

SENECA FALLS, N. Y., October, 1849.

CONTENTS.

CHAPTER XX

CHAPTER XXI.

CHAPTER XXII.

CHAPTER XXIII.

CHAPTER XXIV.

CHAPTER XXXIII.

CHAPTER XXXIV.

CHAPTER XXXV.

CHAPTER XXXVI.

REFORMS AND REFORMERS.

CHAPTER I.

Introductory—The "Condition of England" Question.

THE People of the United States must ever be interested in the history of Great Britain. We have a common origin, and an identity of language; we hold similar religious opinions, and draw the leading principles of our civil institutions from the same sources. Reading the same historic pages, and while recounting the words and deeds of orators and statesmen who have dignified human nature, or the achievements of warriors who have filled the world with their fame, we say, "these were *our* forefathers." The sages and scholars of both nations teach the youth to cherish the wisdom of Alfred, the deductions of Bacon, the discoveries of Newton, the philosophy of Locke, the drama of Shakspeare, and the song of Milton, as the heir-looms of the whole Anglo-Saxon family. The ties of blood and lineage are strengthened by those of monetary interest and reciprocal trade; while the channels of social intercourse are kept open by the tides of emigration which flow unceasingly between us. And such are the resources of each in arts, in arms, in literature, in commerce, in manufactures, in the productions of the soil, and such their advanced position in the science of government, and such the ability and genius of their great men, that they must, for an indefinite period, exert a controlling influence on the destiny of mankind.

Nor when viewed in less attractive aspects, can America be indifferent to the condition and policy of her trans-Atlantic rival. She is enterprising, ambitious, intriguing. Whitening the ocean with the sails of her commerce, she sends her tradesmen wherever the marts of men teem with traffic. Belting the earth with her colonies, dotting its surface with her forts, anchoring her navies in all its harbors, she rules one hundred and sixty millions of men, giving law, not only to cultivated and refined States, but to dwarfed and hardy clans that shrivel and freeze among the ices of the polar regions, and to swarthy and languid myriads that repose in the orange groves or pant on the shrubless sands of the tropics. With retained spies in half the courts and cabinets of Christendom, she has for a century and a half caused or participated in nearly all the wars of Europe, Asia, and Africa, while by her arrogance, diplomacy, or gold, she has shaped the policy of the combatants to the promotion of her own ends. Ancient Rome, whose name is the synonym of resistless power and boundless conquest, could not, in the palmy days of her Cæsars, vie with Great Britain in the extent of her possessions and the strength of her resources. Half a century ago, her great statesman, sketching the resources of her territory, said, "The King of England, on whose dominions the sun never sets." An American orator, of kindred genius, unfolded the same idea in language which sparkles with the very effervescence of poetic beauty, when he spoke of her as "that Power, whose morning drum-beat, following the sun, and keeping company with the hours, encircles the earth daily with one continuous and unbroken strain of the martial airs of England." In a word, she embodies, in her history and policy, in large measure, all the virtues and vices of that alternate blessing and scourge of mankind, THE ANGLO-SAXON RACE.

Britain, once a land of savage pagans, was, long after the Norman Conquest, the abode of ignorance, superstition, and despotism. And though for centuries past she has witnessed a steady advance in knowledge, and civil and religious liberty—though her men of letters have sent down to their posterity works that shall live till science, philosophy and poetry are known no more—though her lawyers have gradually worn off the rugged features of the feudal system, till the common law of England has been adopted as the basis of our republican code—though her spiritual Bastile, the State Church, long since yielded to the attacks of non-conformity, and opened its gates to a qualified toleration—though all that was vital and dangerous in the maxim, "the King can do no wrong," fell with the head of Charles I, in 1649—yet it is only within the last fifty years that she has discovered at work on her institutions a class of innovators, designated as "REFORMERS."

Humanity will find ample materials for despair, when contemplating the condition of the depressed classes in Great Britain and Ireland. But philanthropy will find abundant sources of hope in studying the character and deeds of their radical reformers. The past half century has seen an uprising, not of "the middle class" only, but of the very substratum of society, in a peaceful struggle for inherent rights. No force has been employed, except the force of circumstances; and the result has been eminently successful. This "middle class" (and the term has great significance in England) discovered its strength during the revolution under Hampden and Cromwell, and received an impulse then which it has never lost. The nobility and gentry have too often silenced the popular clamor by admitting its leaders to the rank and privileges of "the higher orders." Still, concessions were made to the mass of middle men, which stimulated them to demand, and strengthened them to obtain more. But a truth, destined to be all-potent in the nineteenth century, remained to be discovered, viz: the identity in interest of the middle and lower classes. The lines which custom and prejudice had drawn between them grew fainter and fainter as the day approached for the full discovery of this truth. The earthquake shock of the

French Revolution overthrew a throne rooted to the soil by the growth of a thousand years. Britain felt the crash. Scales fell from all eyes, and the people of the realm discovered that subjects were clothed with Divine rights as well as kings. Englishmen said so, in public addresses and resolutions, not always expressed in courtly phrase, nor rounded off in the style of rhetorical adulation so grateful to regal ears. The king, not having duly profited by the lesson the American rebels had taught him, indicted Hardy, Thelwall, Tooke, and their compatriots, for sedition and treason. These men were the representatives of both the middle and lower classes. Their constituents—THE PEOPLE OF ENGLAND—combined for their mutual safety against the common oppressor. The wall of partition was partially broken down, and, from that hour to this, the struggle between Right and Privilege, between the Subject and the Crown, has gone on, distinguished by alternate defeat and victory, by heroic constancy and dastardly treachery—noble martyrs dying, valiant combatants living to continue the good fight.

"*The Condition of England*" *question* (as the Parliamentary phrase runs) was, a century ago, a matter of indifference to the masses. Lord Castlereagh but uttered the adage of a hundred years when he said, "the people have nothing to do with the laws, except to obey them." Parliament was opened with a dull King's speech, to be followed by the opening of the annual budget of the Chancellor of the Exchequer, proposing to raise a loan for foreign wars, or a fund to sink the interest of the public debt. An oracular response was given by the Minister now and then to some query touching the relations of the kingdom to continental Powers, or the resources of some newly-acquired colony. An occasional bill was introduced to pamper the landlord aristocracy, or to increase the resources of the clergy, and enforce the collection of tithes in the manufacturing districts. Untitled manhood was held "dog cheap;" and all legislation (excepting the throwing of a bone now and then to the Cerberus of "vulgar clamor") looked to the conservation of the privileged classes, the dignity of the nobility, the wealth of the church, and the prerogatives of the Crown. How different now! The representatives of THE PEOPLE have broken into the sacred inclosure of "the Government," and new men, with new opinions, have usurped the places of an ancient aristocracy, and its antiquated principles. Now, "the Condition of England" question takes cognizance of the rights and the wrongs of all, and involves searching examinations, and hot and irreverent discussions, in and out of Parliament, of poor laws, pension laws, game laws, corn laws, free trade, universal education, unrestricted religious toleration, standing armies, floating navies, Irish repeal, East and West India emancipation, colonial independence, complete suffrage, the ballot, annual Parliaments, law reform, land reform, entails, primogeniture, the life-tenure of judges, an hereditary peerage, the House of Lords, the Bench of Bishops, the Monarchy itself, with other matters of like import, about which the trader and the farmer of Queen Anne's time knew but little, and never dared to question above his breath, but which, in the days of Victoria, are the common talk of the artisan and yeoman. Ay, more than this: reforms not dreamed of in 1805, by Fox, the liberal, are proposed and carried in 1845 by Peel, the conservative. "Oh, for the golden days of good Queen Bess," when the common people paid their tithes and ate what bread they could get, and left law-making to the Knights of the Shire and the Peers of the Realm!

But he must superficially read history who supposes that the fruitful Reforms, which now strike their roots so deep into British soil, and throw their branches so high and wide over the land, were planted by this century. Their seeds were sown long since, and watered with the tears and fertilized by the blood of men as pure and brave as God ever sent to bless and elevate our race. From the conquest of William the Norman, down to the coronation of Victoria the Saxon, one fact stands prominently on the page of English history, viz: that there has been a gradual circumscribing of the powers of the nobles and the prerogatives of the Crown, accompanied with a corresponding enlargement of the liberties of the people. Omitting many, I will glance at some of the more conspicuous landmarks in this highway of reform.

The mitigation of the rigors of the feudal system by William Rufus, the son of the Conqueror, who established it.—The general institution of trial by jury, in the succeeding reign of Henry II, and the granting of freedom to the towns of the realm by royal charters.—Old King John, at Runnymede, affixing his sign manual to MAGNA CHARTA, with trembling hand, at the dictation of his haughty barons and their retainers. The establishment of the House of Commons, about the middle of the thirteenth century, thus giving the commercial men of the middle class a voice in the Government.—Edward I, "the English Justinian," encouraging the courts in those decisions which tended to restrain the feudal lords and protect their vassals; and approving a statute which declared that no tax or impost should be laid without the consent of the Lords and Commons.—The introduction into England, in the latter part of the fifteenth century, of the art of printing, and the consequent cheapness of the price of books, and the diffusion of that knowledge which is power.—The discovery of America, giving an impulse to British commerce, and increasing the importance of the trading classes, by placing in their hands those sinews of war which kings must have, or cease to make conquests. The Reformation, introduced into England in 1534, unfettering the conscience, and giving to the laity the Heaven-descended charter of human rights—the Bible.—The Petition of Right—the British Declaration of Independence—signed by Charles I, in 1628, by command of his Parliament, which materially curbed the royal prerogative.—His headless trunk on the scaffold at Whitehall, in 1649, when the aspiring blood of a Stuart sank into the ground, to appease the republican wrath of Deacon Praise-God Barebones and Captain Smite-them-hip-and-thigh Clapp, and their brother Roundheads—teaching anointed tyrants that, though kings can do no wrong, they can die like common felons.—The succeeding Commonwealth, when a Huntingdonshire farmer swayed with more than regal majesty the scepter which had so often dropped from the feebler hands of the Plantagenets and Tudors. The passage of the *Habeas Corpus* act, in 1678, in the reign of Charles II, who saved his head by surrendering his veto. The Revolution of 1688, which deposed one line of kings and chose another, prescribing to the elected monarch his coronation oath, and exacting his ratification of the new Declaration of Rights.—The American Revolution, with its Declaration of Independence, teaching the House of Hanover the salutary truth, not only that "resistance to tyrants is obedience to God," but it can be successful. These, and cognate epochs in English history, which preceded those Modern Reforms of which I am more particularly to speak, are links in that long chain of events which gradually circumscribed the power of the princes and nobles. Each was a concession to that old Anglo-Saxon spirit of liberty, which demanded independence for the American Colonies, and is now working out the freedom of the subjects of the Queen of Great Britain and Ireland.

The object of the following chapters will be, to briefly sketch some of these Modern Reforms, interspersed with notices of some of the prominent actors in each.

CHAPTER II.

British Cabinets from 1770 to 1830—Summary of the Efforts of the Reformers, from the War of 1793 to the Formation of the Grey Ministry in 1830.

BEFORE specially considering any one prominent Reform in English history, a general summary of events may be profitable. It will be *but* a summary, preliminary to a more general discussion, and will be mainly confined to the period between the French Revolution and the formation of the Grey Ministry in 1830.

From 1770 to 1830, the Government of Great Britain was, with the exception of a few months, swayed by the enemies of Reform. In the former year, Lord North, a name odious to Americans, who had previously led the Tories in the House of Commons, assumed the premiership. He retained his place, his principles, and his power, twelve years. In 1782, a *quasi* liberal ministry supplanted him, headed by Rockingham, Fox, and Burke, which was dissolved in three months, by the death of the former, when Fox, Burke, and their friends, refused to unite under Shelburne, the succeeding Tory Premier, who sought new supporters, giving young Pitt the seals of the Exchequer and the lead in the Commons. Stung by mortification at their exclusion from office, Fox and Burke united with North in forming the famous "Coalition," and in April, 1783, prostrated Shelburne. Thereupon, a new ministry was made up of those disaffected Whig and Tory chiefs, Fox, Burke, the Duke of Portland and Lord North being its leading spirits. This Coalition, which for years damaged the fame of Fox, struggled for its unnatural existence till the following December, when, failing to carry Mr. Fox's India bill, it expired, dishonored and unregretted. Pitt, "the pilot that weathered the storm," then took the helm of State, which he held eighteen tempestuous years, and was succeeded, not supplanted, in 1801, by the weak but amiable Mr. Addington. Lord Hawkesbury (the subsequent Lord Liverpool) took the pen of Foreign Secretary; Eldon (Sir John Scott) clutched the great seal of Chancery; and Perceval put on the gown of Solicitor General. This ministry leaned on Pitt for support, and was his puppet, having taken office to do what he was too proud to perform—make peace with France. The war demon smoothed his wrinkled front only for a short period, when his visage suddenly became grim, and the ship of State was, in 1803, again plunged in the waves of a European contest. The helm soon slipped from the feeble hands of Addington, and "the pilot" was recalled to his old station, where he remained till 1806, when his lofty spirit sinking under the shock of the overthrow at Austerlitz of the Continental Coalition against Napoleon, of which he was the animating soul, he hid his mortified heart in a premature grave.

A liberal ministry, clustering around Lord Grenville and Mr. Fox, took up the reins of power which had dropped from the relaxed hands of Pitt, abolished the slave trade, attempted to ameliorate the condition of the Catholics, encountered the bigotry of George III, failed, resigned, and were succeeded by an ultra Tory administration, of which Perceval, Liverpool, Eldon, Castlereagh, and Canning were the chief members. For six years they followed in the footsteps of Pitt, fighting Napoleon abroad and Reformers at home, propping up the thrones of continental despots, and fortifying the prerogatives of the English crown, till, in 1812, Perceval, who was then Premier, fell before the pistol of a madman in the lobby of the House of Commons. Simultaneously with putting the crazy assassin to death, almost without the forms of a trial, Liverpool, as Premier, and Castlereagh, as Foreign Secretary, came into power, and, pursuing the policy of Pitt and Perceval, the same ministry, with occasional modifications, retained its place until the death of Liverpool, in 1827. Castlereagh, its life and soul, and the evil genius of England, and the truckling tool of the Holy Alliance, perished by his own hand in 1823, and was succeeded in the Foreign Department by Canning, who infused a more liberal spirit into the Cabinet, especially in the attitude of England towards the Alliance.

Such had been the advance of free principles amongst the body of the people during the fifteen years of Liverpool's administration, that George IV had great difficulty in forming a new ministry. Wellington and Peel refused to become members if the friends of Catholic Emancipation were admitted, and Canning refused to join if they were excluded. After a long train of negotiations, the anger of the King exploded at the stubbornness of the Iron Duke, and he gave Canning his royal hand to kiss, with a *carte blanche* for the enrolment of a ministry. He formed a mixed Government, whose average quality was mollified Toryism. He brought into the compound Robinson and Huskisson, his recent associates in the Liverpool cabinet, whose liberal course on trade and finance, during the last four years, foreshadowed the repeal of the corn laws and the dawning of better days. Wellington and Peel spurned the amalgamation, whilst Eldon, with the shedding of many tears and the tearing of much hair, surrendered the great seal, which his strong hand had grasped for twenty-six years, to the great detriment of suitors with short purses, and the great profit of barristers with long wind. The country expected much from the new administration. But whether well or ill founded, its anticipations were extinguished in a few brief months by the death of the brilliant genius who had inspired its hopes. When the grave closed over Canning, Lord Gooderich (Mr. Robinson) organized a piebald ministry, of such incongruous materials that it broke in pieces almost in the very act of being set up. Wellington was then summoned to the King's closet, and in January, 1828, became Premier, giving the lead of the Commons to his favorite, Peel, he himself undertaking to control the House of Peers, much according to the tactics of the field of Waterloo. The Iron Duke, who was always adroit at a retreat, and the supple commoner, both of whom had refused to join Canning because he favored Catholic amelioration, now reluctantly granted, because they dared not withhold, the repeal of the Corporation and Test Acts, and the emancipation of the Catholics! The Wellington-Peel Government struggled bravely till late in 1830, when the tide of Parliamentary Reform, rising to a resistless hight, overwhelmed them, and the first liberal ministry (excepting a few distracted months) which England had witnessed for sixty-five years, was organized by Earl Grey. Fortunate man! He now saw the seeds of that reform, which, forty years before, in the fervor of youth, he sowed in Parliament, and had steadily cultivated under contumely and reproach from that day till this, about to yield an abundance which his matured and ennobled hand was to garner in, whilst the people "shouted the Harvest Home."

Begging the reader's pardon for introducing this dry detail of names and dates, it may be further noted, that in glancing over the dreary wastes which stretch between the elevation of North and the downfall of Wellington, but few verdant spots rise to relieve the reformer's eye. From the commencement of the French war, in 1793, till the repeal of the Corporation and Test Acts, in 1828, not a solitary important reform was carried, except the abolition of the slave trade, and the British empire exhibited a broad sea of rank Conservatism. But, though nothing was *perfected* in these thirty-five years, no period of British history teems with events more gratifying to a hopeful and progressive humanity. Foul and fetid as were the waters of the Dead Sea, they were constantly lashed by a healthful and purifying agitation. These fruitless years were the seed-time of a harvest to be reaped in better days; and all the reforms which from 1828 till now have blessed and are blessing England were never forgotten, but continually pressed upon the attention of Parliament and the country, by a resolute band of men illustrious for their talents and their services In proof of this, a few rude landmarks, before entering upon a more minute survey of this period, may be worth the erecting

The trials, at the Old Bailey, in 1794, of Tooke, Hardy, and their associates, prosecuted for high treason for their words and acts as members of a Society for Parliamentary Reform, were the first outbreak of the wide-spread alarm at the prevalence of the political opinions introduced into the kingdom by the French Revolution. The Government was foiled; the prisoners were acquitted; Erskine, their advocate, won unfading laurels; and the doctrine of "constructive treason" was forever exploded in England.

The foreign policy of Pitt and his successors, which sent England on a twenty-five years' crusade to fight the battles of Absolutism on the continent, encountered the fiery logic of Fox, the dazzling declamation of Sheridan, the analytical reasoning of Tierney, the dignified rebukes of Grey, the sturdy sense of Whitbread, the scholastic arguments of Horner, and the bold assaults of Burdett. And at a later period, when Castlereagh humbled the power of England at the footstool of the Holy Alliance, Brougham made the land echo with appeals to the Anglo-Saxon love of liberty, till Canning, in 1823, protested against the acts of the Allied Sovereigns, and in the following year declared in the House of Commons, while the old chamber rung with plaudits, that ministers had refused to become a party to a new Congress of the Allies.

In 1806–7, the slave trade fell under the united attacks of Wilberforce, Fox, and Pitt; Clarkson, Sharpe, and other worthies, supplying the ammunition for the assault. And the West India slave, long forgotten, was remembered when Canning, in 1823, introduced resolutions that immediate measures ought to be adopted by the planters to secure such a gradual improvement in the slave's condition as might render safe his ultimate admission to participation in the civil rights and privileges of other classes of His Majesty's subjects; and addressed a corresponding ministerial circular to the colonies.

In 1809, Romilly brought his eminent legal knowledge and graceful eloquence to bear against the sanguinary criminal code which a dark age had obtruded on the noonday of civilization. He subsequently exposed the abuses of the Court of Chancery, which, under the tardy administration of "that everlasting doubter," Lord Eldon, pressed heavily on the country. He laid bare the absurd technicalities and verbosities which blocked the avenues to the common law courts. Having removed some of this rubbish, and softened a few of the asperities of the criminal code, his benevolent heart sunk in the grave, when the philosophic and classical Mackintosh resumed the work, and carrying a radical motion for inquiry over the heads of ministers in 1819, pressed it nearer that tolerable consummation which Brougham, Williams, and Denman reached at a later day. The cause of law reform was powerfully aided by the closet labors of that singular person, Jeremy Bentham, whose world-wide researches and world-filling books, written in a style as consecutive and tedious as the story of The House that Jack Built, discussed everything pertaining to government, from the constitution of a kingdom to the construction of a work-house.

The condition of Ireland and the relief of the Catholics occupied much of the public attention during the period under review. The rebellion of 1798 turned all eyes towards that devoted island. The next year, Pitt proposed the Legislative Union. It encountered the fierce epigrams of Sheridan; and though it passed both Houses, it met with such vehement opposition from the Irish Parliament, that it was abandoned till the next year, when Pitt renewed the proposal. Grattan, the very soul of Irish chivalry, rained down upon it a shower of invective from the West side of the channel, and was seconded by the glittering oratory of Sheridan and the calmer reasoning of Grey and Lord Holland on the East. But Britain extended to Ireland the right hand of a Judas fellowship, whilst with the left she bribed her to accept the proffered alliance. In 1807, Lord Grenville, who was ever a firm friend of religious liberty and of Ireland, and Grey, in behalf of the Cabinet, proposed an amelioration of the bigoted code which made the worship of God by the Catholic a crime. They failed, and ministers resigned. The question of Catholic relief was pressed to a division, in various forms, fourteen times, without success, from 1805 to 1819. In the latter year, Grattan moved that the House take into consideration the matter of Catholic Emancipation, and failed by only two majority. In 1821, Plunkett, distinguished for his attainments and virtues, and a model of eloquence, whether standing at the Irish bar or in the British Senate, carried the motion which Grattan lost, Peel strenuously resisting, by a majority of six. He followed up his victory by pushing the Consolidation Bill (a measure of amelioration only) through the Commons; but it was thrown out by the Lords. Sparing further details for the present, suffice it to say, that at intervals during this period, Sydney Smith, with his Peter Plymley Letters, laughed to scorn the fears of high churchmen; a host of pamphleteers of all sizes sifted the question to its very chaff, and O'Connell and his "Associations" and "Unions," in spite of the suspension of the *habeas corpus* and the enactment of coercion bills, agitated from the Giant's Causeway to Cape Clear, and ultimately wrung from the fears of the oppressor what his sense of justice would not give.

The Protestant dissenters, with a less rude hand, knocked at the doors of Parliament, demanding the purification of the Established Church, and the opening of its gates to Toleration. The rich clergy were compelled by law to pay higher salaries to their poor curates—Hume's clumsy abuse fell on the heads of the lazy prelates who made godliness gain—and the "pickings and stealings," which the Establishment tolerated in a long train of sanctimonious supernumeraries, were exposed to the gaze of the uninitiated when Brougham carried his bill against ministers, in 1819, for a board of commissioners to investigate the abuses of public charities. The Corporation and Test Acts, which enslaved the consciences of dissenters, were denounced by Fox and Burdett, preparatory to their ultimate repeal (of which more anon) by Lord John Russell's bill in 1828.

Nor was the importance of educating the masses forgotten. Not content with aiding Romilly, Smith, Horner, Mackintosh, and Jeffrey, in instructing the higher circles by frequent contributions to the Edinburgh Review on domestic and European politics, Brougham wrote rudimental tracts for the lower orders—lectured to Mechanics' Institutes—contributed to Penny Magazines—and in 1820, after a speech which exhibited perfect familiarity with the educational condition of the unlettered masses, launched in Parliament his comprehensive scheme for the instruction of the poor in England and Wales; thus proving that *he* was entitled to the eulogy he bestowed on another, as "the patron of all the arts that humanize and elevate mankind."

Having seen this favorite scheme fairly afloat, this wonderful man turned to far different employments. The misguided but injured Queen Caroline landed in England in 1820, amidst the shoutings of the populace. Ministers immediately brought in their bill of pains and penalties; *i. e.*, a bill to degrade and divorce the Queen, without giving her the benefit of those ordinary forms of law which protect even the confessed adulteress. She appointed Brougham her Attorney General. In the midst of such a popular ferment as England has rarely seen, he promptly seized the royal libertine in his harem, and while giving one hand to the regulation of his new educational machine, with the other dragged him into the open field of shame, and concentrated upon him the scorn of Virtue and Humanity.

The corn laws were the subject of frequent debates and divisions. Waiving till another occasion their more particular consideration, it may here be stated, that the frequent recurrence of extreme agricultural and commercial distress always brought with it into Parliament the subject of the corn trade, provoking a discussion of the antagonistic theories of protection and free trade, and challenging to the arena the learning and experience of Burdett, Horner, Ricardo, Baring, Hume, Huskisson, and Brougham. It was on these occasions that the latter used to exhibit that close familiarity with the statistics of political economy and of domestic and foreign trade, and of the laws of demand and supply, which surprised even those acquainted with his exhaustless versatility. His only match in this department was Huskisson, to whose enlightened and steady advocacy of unrestricted commerce its friends are greatly indebted. As early as 1823, this generally conservative gentleman moved a set of resolutions providing for an annual and rapid reduction of the duties on foreign corn, till the point of free trade was attained.

Closely allied to this subject was that of budgets, sinking funds, loans, civil lists, and army and navy expenditures, all summed up in the word *taxes*. The means of paying the interest on the £600,000,000 debt Pitt had run up in reënthroning the pauper Bourbons (not to speak of the 240 000,000 pounds before existing) was to be provided for. The current expenses of the Government clamored for large sums. Under this annual load of taxation, a nation of Astors might have staggered. The liberal party plead for economy and retrenchment in the army and the navy, in the church and the state. Brougham, Ricardo, and other smaller ciphcrers, applied the pruning knife to the prolific tree of taxation and expenditure. But the chief annoyance of Ministers was Mr. Hume. After he entered Parliament, all schemes for raising or appropriating money encountered his scrutinizing eye and merciless *figurings*. With no more eloquence than the multiplication table, he as rarely made mistakes in his calculations. And whenever Mr. Vansittart, the foggy-headed Chancellor of the Exchequer, appeared on the floor with his money bills, his tormentor was sure to pin him to the wall by his skillful use of the nine digits, which he followed up by crushing that unfortunate gentleman between huge columns of statistics.

Parliamentary Reform, the enginery by which the people of England must work out a bloodless revolution, was repeatedly agitated, and with various results. Stormy debates, followed by divisions and defeats, did not discourage Grey, Mackintosh, Brougham, Lambton, and Russell, within doors, nor Tooke, Cartwright, Cobbett, Hunt, and a host of other good, bad, and indifferent men without, from seeking enlarged suffrage and equal representation. Nor did laws enacted to stop the circulation amongst the working classes of cheap publications, by laying a tax on them ; and to put down reformatory societies, under the pretext of prohibiting seditious meetings ; and to seize arms found in the hands of the lower orders, so that their assemblies might be dispersed at the bayonet's point without fear of retaliation ; nor the occasional searching of a library and demolishing a press, and sending a writer or lecturer to Botany Bay, deter the masses from demanding that "the People's *House* should be open to the People's *Representatives*." Passing by many noteworthy occurrences, we find Birmingham, in 1819, without a representative for its teeming thousands, while rotten Grampound, with scarce an inhabitant, had two, adopting the bold measure of electing "a Legislatorial Attorney" to represent it in the House of Commons ! The next year, a large and peaceable meeting of reformers at Manchester is dispersed by cavalry, with loss of much precious blood. The common people throughout the kingdom are deeply moved at this spectacle—riots follow—troops shed more blood —Ministers denounce the agitators—Burdett defends them—

Brougham defies Ministers, and Lord John Russell numbers the days of Grampound. The next session he moves to disfranchise that rotten borough, which had been convicted of bribery, and transfer its members to Leeds. He fails. The next session, Lambton (Earl Durham) brings in a bill for a radical reform, and is defeated by a scurvy trick of Ministers. Lord John renews the conflict with another bill—the People's petitions press the tables of the House—Ministers begin to give way—Grampound is disfranchised, and its members transferred to York county, and the first nail is driven! In 1823, Lord John leads on the attack by explaining a well-digested scheme of reform in a luminous speech. Canning makes a conciliatory reply, and, in his brilliant peroration, tells Russell he will yet succeed, but on his head be the responsibility. Russell is beaten, but the minority is swelled by the accession for the first time of several young members of the ancient nobility. The same year, Castlereagh cuts his throat, and falls into a grave which Englishmen will execrate till the crack of doom. The "radicals" (a name which the reformers received when Birmingham elected her attorney) take courage—Lord John beats ministers on an incidental question—Old Sarum trembles for her ancient privileges—the French monarchy is temporarily overthrown, and Earl Grey rises to power.

In this summary, which sets chronological order and historical symmetry at defiance, I have only aimed to show that, from 1793 to 1830, the fires on Freedom's Altar were kept burning by a band of worshipers, many of whose names find few parallels in English history, whether we consider the vigor of their understandings, the extent of their knowledge, the splendor of their genius, the luster of their services, and the fidelity and courage with which they followed the fortunes of the liberal cause through thirty-seven years of opposition to Court favor and Ministerial patronage.

A more particular notice of these events and persons will be pursued in future chapters.

CHAPTER III

Treason Trials of 1794—Societies for Reform—Constructive Treason —Horne Tooke—Mr. Erskine.

THE first conflict between Englishmen and their rulers, to which I will now more particularly refer, is the sedition and treason trials, near the close of the last century; more especially alluding to the trials of JOHN HORNE TOOKE, HARDY, THELWALL, and their associates, in 1794, for high treason. The victories then achieved heralded those subsequent reforms in Church and State which have so blessed the common people of England. It was the crisis of British freedom. Though failure then would not have uprooted the goodly tree, it would have blasted much of its sweet fruit, and retarded its luxuriant growth. Maj. Cartwright, ("that old heart of sedition," as Canning called him,) one of England's early reformers, in a letter written at the time, said: "Had these trials ended otherwise than they have, the system of proscription and terror, which has for some time been growing in this country, would have been completed and written in blood." The verdicts of "not guilty" not only pronounced the acquittal of the prisoners, but proclaimed the right of individuals and associations to examine and reprobate the acts of their King and Parliament; to discuss the foundations of government, and declare the rights of man and the wrongs of princes; and to arouse public opinion to demand such changes in the laws as would secure the liberties of the people. The crime charged against Tooke and his associates was, endeavoring to excite a rebellion, overthrow the monarchy, wage war on the king, and compass his death. Their real offense was, belonging to "the London Corresponding Society" and "the Society for Constitutional Information," better known as societies for Parliamentary reform, in which they canvassed the nature of government, the rights of the people, and the acts of their rulers, and specially advocated a reform in the Parliamentary representation and the electoral suffrage.

This was no new movement. Similar associations had existed for twenty years. The Society of "the Friends of the People" numbered among its members the imposing names of the Duke of Richmond, Pitt, Sheridan, Whitbread, Grey, and other men of rank. They had held meetings, published pamphlets, and petitioned Parliament. Discussions had taken place in both Houses. In 1770, the great Chatham advocated a moderate reform in the representation in the lower House. In 1776, Wilkes, the favorite of the London populace, made an able speech on moving for leave to bring in a radical bill to the same end. In 1783, Pitt, yielding to the generous impulses of his youth, moved for a committee to inquire into the same subject, and supported his motion in two eloquent speeches. In 1790, Flood, the celebrated Irishman, spoke with fervor on moving for a more equal representation in the Commons, and was replied to by Wyndham and Pitt, (who had become frightened by the French revolution,) and powerfully supported by Fox, then in the zenith of his fame, and by Grey, just giving earnest of those talents which, forty years after, carried the reform bill through the Lords. The discussion of kindred topics in Parliament during the same periods stimulated the popular party. The expulsion of Wilkes, the idol of the London mob, from the Commons; the seizure of his papers and the imprisonment of his person in the Tower for a seditious libel against the Tory Government; his repeated reëlection by his Middlesex constituency, and the votes of the House declaring his seat still vacant; the consequent debates in both Houses during the years 1768–'70 excited the populace to the verge of rebellion, and challenged inquiry into the relative rights of the people and their Parliament. The debates on the stamp act, the taxation of the colonies, and the American war, covering fifteen years, enlisted the best powers of Chatham, Burke, Fox, and Barre, and elicited from those high sources radical declarations of the rights of man. The denunciations of the test acts and of the Catholic penal code by Fox and his followers, from 1786 to 1790, as subversive of the rights of conscience, added fuel to the popular flame. All these agitations within the walls of Parliament were but the remoter pulsations of the great heart beating without—the faint shadows of that genius of reform, which, till recently, has numbered its representatives by units and its constituency by hundreds of thousands.

The political sea, ruffled by these winds, was soon to be tossed by violent storms. The French revolution produced a profound sensation in all classes of Englishmen. The fulminations of its *third estate* against monarchy, and the democratic doctrines of Paine's Rights of Man, (republished in England from the Parisian edition, and scattered far and wide,) found a response in thousands of British hearts. The people felt their grievances to be more intolerable than ever, and the example of France emboldened them to demand redress in firmer tones. The London Society for Constitutional Information, which had grown languid, suddenly felt a revival of more than its original spirit, and kindred associations sprang into existence all over the kingdom. Their orators declaimed upon the rights of man, painted his wrongs, extolled the merits of the people, and denounced the vices of bishops and nobles. The oppressions of the middle and lower classes, (of both which the societies were mainly composed,) by the privileged orders, afforded ample materials for these appeals to the best and worst passions of human nature.

The Government was alarmed. The events of France in

1792 had determined the English Ministry to crush in the bud the revolution they pretended they saw springing up at home Their real object was to prostrate the reformatory associations. Louis was deposed, and the Republic had decreed fraternity and aid to the people of all nations in recovering their liberties. Riots occurred in a few English manufacturing towns. The King suddenly convened Parliament, and declared in his speech, that conspiracies existed for overthrowing the Government, and that the kingdom was on the eve of a revolution. In the debate on the King's speech, the Minister said that seditious societies had been instituted, under the plausible pretext of discussing constitutional questions, but really to promote an insurrection of the people. Mr. Fox met the assertions of King and Minister with a denial, whose language borders on temerity. He declared, "there was not one fact stated in His Majesty's speech which was not false—not one assertion or insinuation which was not unfounded. The prominent feature in it was, that it was an intolerable calumny on the people of Great Britain; an insinuation of so gross and black a nature that it demanded the most rigorous inquiry and the most severe punishment!" Bold words, these; not unlike those of Cromwell, who declared "he would as soon put his sword through the heart of the King as that of any other man."

But the Government was not to be arrested in its course by the bold words of the Opposition leader. It continued to prosecute printers and lecturers for seditious libels and speeches, fining, imprisoning, cropping, branding, and transporting, at will. The progress of events in France was precipitating the crisis. In 1793, Louis and his Queen were guillotined, and the next year saw the Princess Elizabeth's head fall, while the bloody star of Robespierre loomed in the ascendant. At these scenes, the cheek of monarchical Europe turned pale. Pitt was alarmed. Prosecutions for sedition did not reach the seat of the disease. Royal proclamations did not silence the reformers. The constitutional societies still met and debated. Early in the session of 1794, he brought in bills to clothe the Government with extraordinary powers to detect suspicious persons, (*i. e.* reformers,) and to suspend the *habeas corpus* act. After a furious contest, in which Fox, Grey, and Sheridan, stood by the popular cause, the bills passed. The *habeas corpus* was suspended in May, 1794. The safeguard of English liberty being prostrated, a fell blow was aimed at the societies, through the persons of some of their leading members. Informations for high treason were filed in May by the Attorney General (Sir John Scott—Lord Eldon) against Tooke, Hardy, Thelwall, and nine others, and they were sent to the Tower to await their trials. Both parties now prepared for a death-struggle. The Ministers trusted for success to the power of the Crown, the subserviency of the judges, and the wide-spread panic among the higher classes. The common people, though alarmed at the strength of this combination, relied upon the innocence of the accused persons; but, at all events, (though the more timid erased their names from the roll of the societies,) the mass resolved to make a stand for the freedom of speech and the press, and the right of associating for a redress of grievances, worthy of the exigency. From the papers of the London Society, which had been seized, it appeared that the members contemplated holding a National Convention to promote Parliamentary reform; and this was regarded as a conspiracy to subvert the monarchy and establish a republic!

I have stated the crime with which these men were charged. Indicted for conspiring to subvert the monarchy, depose the King, and compass his death, it was only pretended that they had uttered and published seditious words with the intent to alter his Government; when, in fact, they had only advocated radical reforms in the two Houses of Parliament. The *existence* of the constitutional societies and their *doings* were clearly legal. No doubt, many unguarded and some unwarranted expressions about the King and Parliament had been used. But nothing had been said or done which, on a fair construction, exposed the parties to a just conviction of any crime. Most assuredly they were not guilty of high treason; and as surely their words and deeds were tame and puerile, compared with what the English press and people have since said and done in the ear of Ministers and under the eye of Majesty. In short, they were to be immolated on the judicial guillotine of "CONSTRUCTIVE TREASON."

The character and station of the prisoners excited the interest of different ranks of society. They had been shut up in the Tower six months, closely confined, and all access to them by their friends denied. Hardy was a shoemaker, and, with two or three others, was from the upper strata of the lower orders. Kyd was a barrister; Holcroft, a dramatic writer; Joyce, a minister; and Thelwall, a political lecturer. These belonged to the middle class. JOHN HORNE TOOKE, the most considerable person among them, held a debatable position in the higher circles. He was a gentleman of limited aristocratic connections, and a scholar of rare and varied learning. He had taken holy orders in his youth, but had long ago left the altars of the church for the closet of the student and the forum of the politician. He was the author of the profound philosophical treatise on the English language, called "*The Diversions of Purley.*" Many then supposed him to be the author of Junius. He had had a violent newspaper controversy, feigned or real, with that writer, and had worsted him. He was the ablest pamphleteer and debater among the ultra-liberals, and was ever ready, with his keen pen and bold tongue, to contend with the scribes of the Government through the press, or its orators on the rostrum, and he never gave cause to either to congratulate themselves on the results of the encounter. Nearly twenty years ago he had stood before the same tribunal, and defended himself with consummate skill, and a courage bordering on audacity, against a prosecution for publishing a defense of "the American rebels" at the battle of Lexington. He and his associates were now to make a stand for their lives.

The trials took place at the Old Bailey, in October and November, 1794, and extended through several weeks. The prisoners were defended by Erskine, whose name was a tower of strength, and Gibbs, the very embodiment of legal knowledge, (Tooke aiding in his own case,) whilst Scott, long-headed, learned, and unscrupulous, assisted by the Solicitor General, prosecuted for the Crown. The hall and the passages leading to it were densely thronged with persons of all ranks and conditions, eager spectators of or participants in, the most memorable struggle which the courts of the common law have witnessed. No overt *acts* of any moment could be proved against either of the accused, and the prosecution had to rely mainly on ambiguous words and writings of doubtful import. The whole power of the Court of the King, and the Judges of the King's Court, was brought to bear upon the doomed prisoners, aided by the multifarious lore and subtle reasoning of the Attorney General. Every doubtful word was distorted, every ambiguous look transformed into lurking treason. The rules of evidence were put to the rack, to admit bits of letters and conversations, written and uttered by others than the accused, and to hold them responsible for all that had been said and done by every man who, at any time and anywhere, had belonged to the societies, or taken part in their discussions. The friends of the prisoners spoke with bated breath, as the trials proceeded; for they knew, if the prosecution succeeded, a reign of terror had begun, in which the King was to enact the Robespierre, and they were to be his victims. But neither the ravings of the Court at Windsor, nor the partialities of the Court at London, could suffice against the learning, the logic, the skill, the vigilance, the eloquence, the courage, the soul, which Erskine threw into his cause. He battled as if his own life had been at hazard. He knew that twelve "good and true men" stood between the lion and his prey. The Court ruled that if the jury believed the discussions and writings of the prisoners, or of the societies to which they belonged, tended to subvert the monarchy and depose the King, or change the Constitution, they must find them guilty. But Erskine maintained, with a power of argument which, for the moment, shook the faith of the Court, that *for British subjects to utter their sentiments, in* ANY FORM, *concerning the Government of their country, was not* TREASON. So thought the jurors, (though the Court leaned heavily to the side of the Crown,) and one after another these hunted plebeians passed the terrible ordeal. The King lost; the People won. They shouted their triumph so loud, that he heard it within his palace, and the crowned lion growled, gnashed his royal teeth, and beat the bars of his constitutional cage, till his anointed head throbbed with anguish.

Hardy, whose case was extremely perilous, was first set to the bar. His trial lasted nine days. Tooke's came next, and Thelwall's next; when the prosecutors, frantic with rage and mortification at their signal overthrow, abandoned the contest. When Tooke was acquitted, the joy of the people knew no bounds. He was an old reformer, had ever been the steady advocate of popular rights, and was the idol of the Radicals. He had suffered much before in the common cause. His library had been repeatedly ransacked for treasonable papers, his family insulted, and his person again and again thrust into prison. And now they had seen him stand for six days, battling with the Court which lowered upon him, and bearing unruffled the taunts with which the Government witnesses had poorly withstood his searching cross-examination, contending for a life whose every pulsation had been given to the service of the people. When the foreman pronounced the words, "Not Guilty," the arches of Old Bailey rang with plaudits. After addressing a few words to the Court, he turned to Scott, and said: "I hope, Mr. Attorney General, that this verdict will be a warning to you not to attempt again to shed men's blood on lame suspicions and doubtful inferences." He then thanked the jury with much emotion for the life they had spared to him. The entire panel shed tears—the very men who had been so obviously packed to convict him, that at the opening of the trial Erskine said, "Mr. Tooke, they are murdering you!" The populace bore the old patriot through the passages to the street, where they sent up shout upon shout. It was a great day for Reformers, and its anniversary is still celebrated by the Radicals of England.

Erskine's speech for Hardy (whose case was very critical, and the first one tried,) is one of the most splendid specimens of popular juridical eloquence on record. Owing to the running contests on points of law and evidence, constantly kept up while the trial went on, he lost his voice the night before he was to address the jury. It returned to him in the morning, and he was able to crowd seven hours full of such oratory as is rarely heard in our day. He regarded Hardy's acquittal or conviction not only as the turning point in the fate of his eleven associates, but as settling the question whether constructive treason should for long years track blood through the land, or its murderous steps be now brought to a final stand. He made a superhuman effort for victory, and achieved it. Profound as was his legal learning, eminent as were his reasoning faculties, classical as was his taste, transcendent as were his oratorical powers, all conspiring to place him not only at the head of the English bar, but to rank him as the first advocate of modern times; yet all were overshadowed by the inflexible courage and hearty zeal with which he met this crisis of British freedom. With the combined power of the King, his ministers, and his judges, arrayed against his clients and against him as their representative, seeking their blood and his degradation, he cowered not, but maintained the home-born rights of his proscribed fellow-subjects with arguments so matchless, with eloquence so glowing, with courage so heroic, with constancy so generous, that his name will ever find a place in the hearts of all who prefer the rights of man to the prerogatives of power. But more than all; he exploded the doctrines of constructive treason, and established the law on the true foundation, that there must be some overt *act* to constitute guilt; and he reïnscribed upon the Constitution of England the obliterated principle, that Englishmen may freely speak and publish their opinions concerning the Government of their country without being guilty of treason—a principle, under whose protecting shield they now utter their complaints, their denunciations even, in the very ear of Majesty itself.*

* The text states only a *legal* truth. Practically there yet remain great obstacles in the way of the free utterance of opinions hostile to the Government—as witness the recent prosecutions of O'Connell, Jones, &c.

CHAPTER IV

Constructive Treason—The Law of Libel and Sedition—The Dean of St. Asaph—The Rights of Juries—Erskine—Fox—Pitt.

I TOOK occasion in the last chapter to speak at some length of the trials of Tooke, Hardy, and others, for high treason, in 1794, and of the successful attack then made by Mr. ERSKINE on the doctrine of constructive treason. Down to the period of these trials, the English law of treason was infamous. Among other things, treason was defined to be waging war against the King, or compassing and imagining his death, or the overthrow of his Government. The law evidently contemplated the doing of some *act*, designed and adapted to accomplish these ends. But the construction of the courts had subverted this principle, and declared the mere utterance of *words* high treason. In the reign of Edward IV, a citizen was executed for saying "he would make his son heir of *the crown*;" meaning, as was supposed, that he would make him the heir of his *inn*, called "the Crown." Another, whose favorite buck the King had wantonly killed, was executed for saying, "he wished the buck, horns and all, in the bowels of the man who counseled the King to kill it." The court gravely held, that as the King had killed it of his own accord, and so was his own counselor, this declaration was imagining the King's death, and therefore treason! So it had been held, that using words tending to overawe Parliament, and procure the repeal of a law, was levying war on the King, and therefore treasonable. At length the courts yielded to the doctrine that there must be some overt act to constitute the crime. But they also held that, reducing words to *writing* was an overt act, even though they were never read or printed! Peachum, a clergyman, was convicted of high treason for passages found in a sermon which had never been preached. The immortal Algernon Sidney was executed, and his blood attainted, for some unpublished papers found in his closet, containing merely speculative opinions in favor of a republican form of government. It was in allusion to this judicial murder by the infamous Jeffries, and to the fact that the record of the conviction had been destroyed, that Erskine, on the trial of Hardy, uttered the splendid anathema against "those who took from the files the sentence against Sidney, which should have been left on record to all ages, that it might arise and blacken in the sight, like the handwriting on the wall before the Eastern tyrant, to deter from outrages upon justice." It has already been said that this peerless lawyer exploded these dangerous doctrines, and made it safe for Englishmen to speak and write freely against the King and Government, without exposure to a conviction for treason.

But this is not the only salutary legal reform for which England is indebted to his exertions. Pernicious as is the existing law of CRIMINAL PROSECUTIONS FOR LIBELS AND SEDITIOUS WRITINGS in that country, it was vastly worse till his strong arguments and scathing appeals had shaken it to its foundations. A glance at the law. Any publication imputing bad motives to King or Minister; or charging any branch of Government with corruption, or a wish to infringe the liberties of the People; or which cast ridicule upon the Established Church; and any writing, printing, or speaking, which tended to excite the People to hatred or contempt of the Government, or to change the laws in an improper manner, &c., were seditious libels, for which fine, imprisonment, the pillory, &c., might be imposed. Nor was the truth of the libel any defense. Admirable snares, these, to entangle unwary reformers, and catch game for the royal household! And these bad laws were worse administered

The juries had no power in their administration—the only check in the hands of the People. The court withheld from the jury the question whether a writing was libelous or seditious, and permitted them only to decide whether the prisoner had published it. In a word, if the jury found that he *published*, they must convict; and then the judge growled out the sentence. These trials were ready weapons for State prosecution in the hands of a tyrannical King and Ministry, with pliant judges at their beck; and in the latter half of the last century they were used without stint or mercy. They struck down Wilkes, Tooke, Woodfall, Muir, Palmer, Holt, Cartwright, and other liberals, for publications and speeches in vindication of the People, which, at this day, would be held harmless even in England. Some were heavily fined, others imprisoned or transported, others set on the pillory, or cropped and branded, their houses broken open and searched, their wives and daughters insulted, their private papers rifled, their printing presses seized, their goods confiscated, their names cast out as evil, and they might regard their lot as fortunate if their prospects for life were not utterly ruined. The treatment of Muir and Palmer, in 1793, was barbarous. Muir was a respectable barrister, and Palmer a clergyman of eminent literary attainments. They had merely addressed meetings and associations for Parliamentary reform in Glasgow and Edinburgh, and reports of one or two of their speeches had been printed. Muir was sentenced to transportation for fourteen years, and Palmer for seven. They were shipped off to Botany Bay with a cargo of common felons! Several other persons, for attending a Reform Convention in Edinburgh the same year, shared a like fate. These are trials which sunshine politicians of the liberal school never contemplate, except to draw from them materials for rounding off fine periods about freedom and the rights of man. But they endear the sufferers to the struggling masses of their own time; and, in after years, when the sons of the persecutors garnish their tombs, those who then endure like trials swear by their memories and conjure with their names.

The times of which I write were prolific of these State prosecutions. Mr. Erskine was the ready counsel of the proscribed reformers then, as Mr. Brougham was at a later period. His great effort on these trials was to convince the court that the juries had the right to decide upon the character of the publication in making up their verdicts; or, in legal phrase, that they were "judges both of law and fact." In this effort, he had many a fierce conflict with the judges, when, with his usual courage, he braved their rebukes and challenged the execution of their hinted threats to commit him for contempt. He always argued this point fully to the court, in the presence of the jury; and such was his mastery over the reason and the feelings, that he sometimes prevented a conviction when he could not obtain an acquittal. It was in an affair of this sort that he had a quarrel with Mr. Justice Buller, a judge who coupled double the imperiousness of Mansfield with half his talents, and whose frown, glowering out from under his huge wig, has silenced many a barrister of more than common nerve. The respectable DEAN OF ST. ASAPH, who breathed the mountain air of Wales, published a clever political tract, under the guise of a dialogue between King George and a farmer. Erskine went down to defend him. Buller presided at the trial. Erskine argued his favorite topic with more than his accustomed ability. The jury listened with absorbing attention; the judge with impatient interruptions. He charged furiously against the Dean, and told the jury, if they believed he published the tract, they must render a general verdict of guilty. The words of reason and power of the great barrister, and his piercing eyes, which riveted everything within their gaze, went with them to their room. They returned a verdict in these words: "Guilty of publishing only." The astonished judge ordered them out again, with directions to render a general verdict of guilty. Erskine interposed, and insisted upon their right to render such a verdict as they had. The judge replied tartly, and the jury retired. Again they came in with the same verdict. The judge reprimanded them, while Erskine insisted that their verdict should be recorded. Buller retorted, explained his law to the refractory panel, and sent them out. The third time they appeared with the same verdict. The judge grew furious, and said, unless they rendered a general verdict, he should order the clerk to enter it "guilty." Erskine protested in strong terms. Buller ordered him to sit down. Erskine said he would not sit down, nor would he allow the court to record a verdict of guilty against his client, when the jury had rendered no such verdict. Buller hinted at commitment. Erskine defied him. The jury were frightened, and, in their panic, assented to a general verdict of guilty.* Erskine excepted, and carried the case to the full bench. But the day of triumph was at hand. So clearly had he in his great arguments exposed the iniquity of the rule, (if, indeed, it was law at all,) and so pertinaciously had he contested it on the trial of the Dean, that Parliament passed a declaratory act soon after, (thus admitting that Erskine was right,) giving jurors, in these prosecutions, the power to render a verdict upon the whole offense charged, *i. e.*, making them "judges of the law as well as the fact."† I need not say that, after this,

* This scene is given from memory—the report not being at hand.

† A like contest early arose in this country. Congress passed an act similar to that of the English, in 1798. In the State of New York, the case of *People vs. Croswell*, for a libel on Jefferson, attracted great attention. It was tried in 1803. The judge charged the jury according to the old English law, and the defendant was convicted. It was carried before the full bench, and argued in 1804. The speech of Alexander Hamilton, for the defendant, was one of the ablest ever delivered in America. The court being equally divided in opinion, the Legislature, the next year, passed a declaratory act, giving to juries the right to determine the law and the fact. This is now the prevailing law of the country. Croswell's case is reported in 3d Johnson's Cases.

prosecutions for seditious libels became less potent and frequent weapons in the hands of royal and ministerial persecutors, and reformers breathed freer.

It does the heart good to contemplate talents like Erskine's devoted to such purposes. To see the foremost lawyer of his time, in the midst of wide-spread aristocratic clamor, and despite the fulminations of kings and ministers and judges, take the side of humble men, who are denounced as incendiaries, agrarians, levelers, French Jacobins, traitors, and infidels, plotting to murder their sovereign, upheave his throne, and prostrate the altars of the church, (and these are but a tithe of the catalogue,) and for years perform prodigies of labor for poor clients and poorer pay, thus blocking up the avenues to preferment in his cherished profession, and all for the love he bears the common cause! Such a spectacle should go somewhat to blunt the edge of those taunts so constantly aimed at a profession which he adored and adorned, and which, in every struggle for human rights, has furnished leaders to the popular party among the bravest of the brave. The law, like every other profession, has its scum and its vermin, and yields its share of dishonest men. But they are dishonest not because they are lawyers, but because they are scoundrels, and would have been so had they chosen to be merchants, physicians, or horse-jockies. When reproaching the whole legal fraternity as a "pack of licensed swindlers," it might be well to remember that the most conspicuous rebels and martyrs of English freedom, in the olden times, were lawyers—that Erskine, Emmet, Romilly, Mackintosh, O'Connell, and Brougham, of later and milder days, were lawyers; and that Jefferson, Adams, Otis, Sherman, Henry, and Hamilton, with many other bold spirits who thundered and lightened during the storm of the American revolution, were lawyers.

But we must leave Mr. Erskine by saying, that he possessed ability and learning to maintain the boldest positions; eloquence for the most thrilling appeals; imagination to sustain the loftiest flights. He was graceful in action, melodious in elocution, and had an eye of whose fascinating power jurors were often heard to speak. He was a wit and a logician—a lawyer and a reformer—a man, cast in the noblest mold of his species.

Mr. Erskine was powerfully sustained in his efforts for law reform by the great liberal leader in the House of Commons. CHARLES JAMES FOX deserves a conspicuous place among the early Reformers of England. Entering Parliament in 1768, when just turned twenty-one, he rallied under the banner of Mr. Burke, then the chief debater on the Whig side, whose lead he followed through the doubtful contest on American questions; and when victory, and peace, and independence, crowned their efforts, the chief resigned the standard of opposition to the hands of his younger and more robust lieutenant. Fox is called "the disciple of Burke," and, after their unnatural estrangement, he gratefully said, "I have learnt more from Burke alone than from all other men and authors." He remained in the Commons till his death, in 1806; and though hampered by aristocratic connections and the leadership of his party, his generous nature and warm heart, through nearly forty years of Parliamentary life carried his great talents to the liberal side. He headed the forlorn hope of English freedom during the panic immediately following the French revolution, and in the darkest and stormiest nights of that gloomy period, his voice sounded clear and firm above the tempest, hurling defiance at his foes, and bidding the few friends of man and constitutional liberty who stood around him to be of good cheer, for the day of their redemption was drawing on. His speech against the stamp act, the taxation of the colonies, the American war, the test act, the suspension of the *habeas corpus*, the treason and sedition bills, the slave trade; and in favor of Parliamentary reform, religious toleration, Catholic emancipation, the rights of juries, and of peace, contain volumes of liberal principles which endear his name to the friends of humanity in both hemispheres. As Erskine was the first advocate that ever stood at the English bar, so Fox was the first debater that ever appeared in its Commons. Burke wrote of him, after their separation: "I knew him when he was nineteen; since which, he has risen to be the most brilliant and accomplished debater the world ever saw." His argumentative powers were of the highest order, and his wit, his invective, and his appeals to the judgment and feelings unrivaled. In the partisan warfare of extemporaneous debate, he bore down on his antagonists with an energy which, when fully roused, bordered on ferocity. But it was the ferocity of impassioned logic and intense reasoning. Not content with once going over the ground in controversy, he traveled it again and again, unfolding new arguments and adding additional facts, till his searching and vigorous eloquence had discovered and demolished every objection that lay in his track. The very embodiment of the reasoning element in man, he saw through his subject with rapid glances, grappled sturdily with all its strong points, despised mere ornaments, rejected all bewildering flights of the imagination, and shunned excursions into collateral fields which skirted his line of argument. In these latter respects he was totally unlike his great master. As his reasoning powers were cast in the most colossal mold, so his heart was of the finest and noblest quality. Mackintosh has justly said, that "he united in a most remarkable degree the seemingly repugnant characters of the mildest of men and the most vehement of orators." His appeals to magnanimity, to generosity, to integrity, to justice, to mercy, thrilled the soul of Freedom, while the tide of consuming lava which he poured on hypocrisy, meanness, dissimulation, cruelty, and oppression, made the grovelers at the footstool of power hide with fear and shame. He was a statesman of the broadest and most liberal views. His capacious mind was stored with political knowledge; he had deeply studied the institutions of ancient and modern States; and no man better understood the general and constitutional history of his own country, nor the delicate machinery which regulated its complicated foreign and domestic affairs. As bold as a lion, he never cowered before the King, his ministers, or his minions; but gloried in being the mouthpiece of out-door Reformers, whose radical principles and humble connections prevented their admission within the Parliamentary walls. He repeated the coarse opinions of Cartwright and his companions, in a place whose doors they were forbidden to darken, but in language worthy of the classic scion of Holland House. He was of invaluable service to the radical party, in gaining them favor with the aristocratic and learned Whigs, because he could throw over their principles the shield of argument, adorn them with the grace of scholarship, and dignify them with the luster of birth and station. In this regard his conduct might be profitably studied by his professed admirers on this side of the Atlantic.

Mr. Fox was totally unlike his great rival. Pitt was stately, taciturn, and of an austere temper. Fox was easy, social, and of a kindly disposition. Pitt was tall and grave, and, entering the House carefully dressed, walked proudly to the head of the Treasury bench, and took his seat as dignified and dumb as a statue. Fox was burly and jovial, entered the House in a slouched hat and with a careless air, and, as he approached the Opposition benches, had a nod for this learned city member, and a joke for that wealthy knight of the shire, and sat down, as much at ease as if he were lounging in the back parlor of a country inn. Pitt, as the adage runs, could "speak a King's speech off-hand," so consecutive were his sentences; and his round, smooth periods delighted the aristocracy of all parties. Fox made the Lords of the Treasury quail as he declaimed in piercing tones against ministerial corruption, while his friends shouted "hear! hear!" and applauded till the House shook. Pitt's sentences were pompous and sonorous, and often "their sound revealed their own hollowness." Fox uttered sturdy Anglo-Saxon sense; every word pregnant with meaning. Pitt was a thorough business man, and relied for success in debate upon careful preparation. Fox despised the drudgery of the office, and relied upon his intuitive perceptions and his robust strength. Pitt was the greater Secretary—Fox the greater Commoner. Pitt's oratory was like the frozen stalactites and pyramids which glitter around Niagara in mid-winter, stately, clear, and cold. Fox's like the vehement waters which sweep over its brink, and roar and boil in the abyss below. Pitt, in his great efforts, only erected himself the more proudly, and uttered more full Johnsonian sentences, sprinkling his dignified but monotonous "state-paper style" with pungent sarcasms, speaking as one having authority, and commanding that it might stand fast. Fox on such occasions reasoned from first principles, denouncing where he could not persuade, and reeling under his great thoughts, until his excited feelings rocked him, like the ocean in a storm. Pitt displayed the most rhetoric, and his mellow voice charmed, like the notes of an organ. Fox displayed the most argument, and his shrill tones pierced like arrows. Pitt had an icy taste; Fox a fiery logic. Pitt had art; Fox nature. Pitt was dignified, cool, cautious; Fox manly, generous, brave. Pitt had a mind; Fox a soul. Pitt was a majestic automaton; Fox a living man. Pitt was the Minister of the King; Fox the Champion of the People. Both were the early advocates of Parliamentary reform; but Pitt retreated, while Fox advanced; and both joined in denouncing and abolishing the horrors of the middle passage. Both died the same year, and they sleep side by side in Westminster Abbey, their dust mingling with that of their mutual friend Wilberforce; while over their tombs watches with eagle eye and extended arm the molded form of Chatham.

CHAPTER V.

The French Revolution—The Continental Policy of Mr. Pitt—The Policy of Mr. Fox and his Followers—The Continental Wars—Mr. Sheridan—Mr. Burke—Mr. Perceval.

In determining whether the policy which Pitt and his successors pursued towards France, from 1792 to 1815, was wise for England and beneficial to Europe, an American republican will remember that it was sustained by the party which ever resisted all social and political improvement among the people—that the enemies of change warred on the Directory, the Consulate, the Empire—that the patrons of existing abuses restored the Bourbons. Nor will he forget that this policy was steadily opposed by the friends of enlightened progress and useful reform—the champions of civil and religious freedom. The specious reasoning and showy declamations of a score of Alisons will never destroy these facts.

France, equally with Great Britain, had the right to enjoy the Government of its choice. But the latter, early in 1793, declined to negotiate or correspond with the former, because it was a republic; and refusing to receive the credentials of its minister, ordered him to quit the kingdom. France, sustained by the law of nations, declared war against the Power which had insulted her. Pitt asserted that the French revolution had no sufficient cause in the nature of the Government or the condition of the people, and was the offspring of a reckless spirit of innovation. He avowed his determination to put down the republic, restore the monarchy, and maintain the cause of legitimacy in Europe. This avowal was met by the declaration of the liberal party, that the true cause of the revolution was the undue restriction and limitation of the rights and privileges of the people; and that, however it might be perverted, its real object was to wrest from the Government what had been unjustly withheld from its subjects. They demanded, therefore, that the diplomatic representative of France should be received by the ministry; and they resisted all interference with its internal affairs, all attempts to suppress liberal movements in Europe, all efforts to uphold its crumbling thrones. They plead for peace and an armed neutrality. And, after Napoleon's schemes of conquest were disclosed, they contended that England ought not to unite in a coalition for his overthrow, so long as it was a battle among kings, but should wait till *the people* of the continent requested assistance; and even then, that it ought not to be given till the rulers of the endangered States were pledged to grant reasonable privileges to their subjects. On this elevated ground did the liberal party take its stand. But Pitt, representing only the monarchical and privileged orders, at the outset of the conflict pledged the power and resources of England to the accomplishment of his ends; and his policy was steadily followed, with ruinous and mortifying results, until the European combination of 1814–15 finally crushed Napoleon at Waterloo, and restored the Bourbon to his throne.

And what did England gain by her armies and fleets, her intrigues in foreign cabinets and subsidies of men and money? True, Napoleon was prostrated. But she had spent £600-000,000 in doing it. At the commencement of the war, her debt was less than £240,000,000. At its close, it had swelled to more than £840,000,000! Centuries of taxation to restore the Bourbons to a throne which they cannot retain, and to postpone for fifty years the general overthrow of monarchy in Europe! The seventh descending son of the youngest Englishman alive will curse the day that Pitt entered on this crusade against Destiny. When the unnatural fever of the contest abated, the reaction, the retribution, came. Peace had returned, but she was not accompanied by her twin-sister, Plenty. English trade, commerce, manufactures, agriculture, languished—laborers wandered through the provinces in search of employment—the country sunk exhausted into the arms of bankruptcy. The smoke of battle no longer blinding the eye, the people began to look about and inquire, "What have we gained by all this outgush of blood and treasure?" The wealthy saw before them ages of remorseless taxation—the poor clamored in the streets for bread—all but the extreme privileged classes regarded the result of the war as a triumph over themselves. At peace with all the world, (almost the first time for three-fourths of a century,) the nation was the scene of internal discords more threatening than foreign levy. Nothing but general lassitude, and the pressure of misfortunes common to all, prevented a revolution.

This contest was injurious to England in another way. It so *possessed* the public mind that there was little room left for domestic improvement. Meanwhile, the cause of reform was turned out of doors. The French Revolution was a God-send to Pitt and the Tories. Seizing upon its early excesses, they conjured with them thirty years, frightening the middling men from their propriety, and terrifying even the giant soul of Burke. The "horrors of the French revolution" were thrown in the face of every man who demanded reform. The clamors of the tired and fleeced suitors in Lord Eldon's court were silenced by "the horrors of the French revolution." Old Sarum and Grampound lengthened out their "rotten" exististence by supping on "the horrors of the French revolution." Point to the festering corruption of the Church Establishment, and it lifted up its holy hands at "the horrors of the French revolution." The Catholics were persecuted, the Irish gibbeted, and printers transported, to atone for "the horrors of the French revolution." The poor starved in damp cellars, whilst the landlord fattened his protected soil with "the horrors of the French revolution." In a word, these "horrors" constituted the chief staple of Tory argument and declamation, and were a conclusive answer to all who asked for cheap bread, religious toleration, law reform, reduced taxes, and an enlarged suffrage.

The lessons of wisdom, so dearly purchased by this scheme of Continental interference, have not been thrown away on a nation which spent so much to gain so little. The second French revolution was followed by England granting Parliamentary Reform, to prevent a revolution at home. The third revolution, which prostrated a monarchy, and reared a republic in a day, was promptly recognized and respected by England, whose Premier declared that she heartily accorded to the people of France the right to ordain for themselves such a system of Government as they might choose! Men may prate eternally about the virtues of Louis XVI, the grasping ambition of Napoleon, the far-seeing sagacity of Burke, and the wisdom and firmness of Pitt, and it will still remain true, that the principles thrown up with the fire and blood of the great French eruption will yet work out the regeneration of Europe.

Mr. Sheridan was as steady a supporter of freedom, and as inflexible an opponent of Pitt, as a man of so volatile a temperament could well be. This gentleman is best known on our side of the Atlantic as the author of the comedy the "School for Scandal," and of a speech on the trial of Warren Hastings. The comedy still holds a deservedly high place on the stage. The speech, which once claimed a position at the head of English forensic oratory, is no doubt much overrated. The intense interest pervading the public mind in respect to the impeachment of the conqueror and ruler of a hundred millions of the people of India—the august character of the tribunal, the peers and judges of the realm—the imposing talents of the committee by whom the Commons sent up the articles of impeachment, consisting of Burke, Fox, North, Grey, Wyndham, Sheridan, with other lights worthy to shine in such a constellation—the romantic branch of Hastings's administration, the opening of which was assigned to Sheridan—the gorgeous colors which he spread upon the oriental canvas—the theatrical style in which he pronounced his oration before a learned, fashionable, and sympathizing audience, all conspired to give to his effort a temporary fame alike extraordinary and undeserved. Nor was the immediate effect of his two days' coruscation diminished by the tragical manner in which he contrived, at its close, to sink backward into the arms of Burke, who, transported beyond measure, hugged him as unaffectedly as if his generous and unsuspecting nature had not been duped by a mere stage trick.

But though he occasionally used the clap-traps of the theater, Sheridan was a debater to be shunned rather than encountered. Pitt dreaded him. Lying in wait till the Minister had addressed the House, the Drury Lane manager used to let fly at him such a cloud of stinging arrows, pointed with sarcasm and poisoned with invective, that the stately Premier could not conceal his mortification, nor hardly retain his seat till the storm had passed away. No Parliamentarian ever inspired so much dread in his opponents, and won so much applause from his friends, with so scanty a stock of statesmanlike acquirements. His political knowledge was gathered from the columns of the current newspapers and the discussions in the club-rooms, and his literary stores were made up from the modern poetry and drama of England. True, he was educated at Harrow, but he threw aside Demosthenes and Cicero for Congreve and Vanburgh, and wrote comedies when he should have studied mathematics. He never claimed to be a statesman, and only aspired to be an orator. To shine as a dazzling declaimer, he bent all the powers of his intense and elastic mind. He attended debating clubs, and caught up the best sayings—practiced attitudes and tones in the green-room—set down every keen thought which occurred to him in a note-book

—conned his lesson—then entered the House, and rushing into the arena of debate with the bound and air of a gladiator, won the reputation of being the readiest wit, the most skillful off-hand disputant, and the most gorgeous orator of the day. And it was the day of Burke, Pitt, Fox, Erskine, Grattan, and Wyndham! Lord Chesterfield was not so very wrong when he told his son that, even in Parliament, more depended upon the manner of saying a thing, than upon the matter of which it was composed. Though his taste was formed on the flashy model of the modern drama, and in the composition of his numerous tropes and metaphors he did not always distinguish between tinsel and gold, between painted glass and pure diamonds, yet he generally succeeded in doing what he intended—producing a tremendous sensation. His rockets set the hemisphere in a blaze; nor was he always careful on whose head the sticks fell; for he spared neither friends nor foes, if he must thereby lose a good hit.

Though Sheridan regarded the color of the husk more than the character of the kernel, he uttered much that will perish only with the English tongue. In an attack on Ministers, who were attempting to carry a bill against the freedom of the press, he exclaimed, "Give them a corrupt House of Lords; give them a venal House of Commons; give them a tyrannical Prince; give them a truckling Court—and let me but have an unfettered press, and I will defy them to encroach a hair's breadth upon the liberties of England"—a passage worthy of Chatham. During the treason trials, in 1794, he poured a torrent of ridicule upon the proceedings, which did not a little toward restoring a panic-stricken public to its senses. An extract will give an idea of his sarcasm. In replying to Pitt, he said, "I own there was something in the case; quite enough to disturb the virtuous sensibilities and loyal terrors of the right honorable gentleman. But, so hardened is this side of the House, that our fears did not much disturb us. On the first trial, one pike was produced. This was, however, withdrawn. Then a terrific instrument was talked of, for the annihilation of his Majesty's cavalry, which, upon evidence, appeared to be a *te-totum* in a window at Sheffield. But I had forgot—there was also a camp in a back shop ; an arsenal provided with nine muskets ; and an exchequer, containing exactly the same number of pounds—no, let me be accurate, it was nine pounds and one bad shilling. * * * * The alarm had been brought in with great pomp and circumstance on a Saturday morning. At night, the Duke of Richmond stationed himself, among other curiosities, at the Tower, and a great municipal officer, the Lord Mayor, made an appalling discovery in the East. He found out that there was in Cornhill a debating society, where people went to buy treason at sixpence a head ; where it was retailed to them by inch of candle ; and five minutes, measured by the glass, were allowed to each traitor, to perform his part in overturning the State. In Edinburgh an insurrection was planned ; the soldiers were to be corrupted : and this turned out to be—by giving each man sixpence for porter. Now, what the scarcity of money and rations may be in that part of the country, I cannot tell ; but it does strike me that the system of corruption has not been carried to any great extent. Then, too, numbers were kept in pay ; they were drilled in a dark room, by a sergeant in a brown coat ; and on a given signal they were to sally from a back kitchen, and overturn the Constitution."

Though this celebrated orator was wayward in his pursuits, and habitually intemperate, yet, from the time he entered Parliament in 1780 till his sun began to decline, he ever sustained the liberal cause, and his rare talents bore with striking effect against the Continental policy of Pitt, and in favor of Irish Regeneration, Parliamentary Reform, the freedom of the press, and the rights of the people.

I have spoken of EDMUND BURKE, than whom, no man could afford a stronger contrast to Sheridan. He had an original, daring genius, but it was sustained by a broad and comprehensive judgment. His imagination was as gorgeous as ever plumed the wing of eloquence, but it was enriched and invigorated by learning vast and varied. Until his mind became engrossed, not to say *possessed* with the subject which occupied the latter years of his great life, (the French revolution,) he was the advocate and ornament of progressive freedom. He first led and then followed Fox in all the lines of policy which the liberal party pursued from 1765 to 1790, when they separated, and Burke became not so much the advocate of Pitt and his Tories, as the opponent of France and its Republicans; choosing thereafter, as he expressed it, to be a Whig, "without coining to himself Whig principles from a French die, unknown to the impress of our fathers in the Constitution." He left Parliament in 1794, and died in 1797. During the last six years of his life he seemed almost diseased by the excesses of the French revolution; and whatever subject he surveyed, on whatever ground he looked, he appeared to see naught but the convulsions of that tragedy. The vivid impressions which he received he transferred to publications which glowed with his fervid soul, and produced a prodigious sensation amongst the higher orders of his countrymen. But take him all in all, his was the most magnificent mind of modern England. If called to designate the most remarkable name which adorns its later annals, to whose would we so unhesitatingly point as to his? Is he not entitled to a place among the five most extraordinary men which that kingdom has produced—Bacon, Shakspeare, Newton, Milton, Burke? He possessed the multifarious learning of our Adams, the intellectual grasp of our Marshall, the metaphysical subtlety of our Edwards, the logical energy of our Webster, the soaring imagination of our Wirt, the fervid glow of our Clay; and he was the equal of each in his most cultivated field. As a Parliamentary leader, he was inferior to Fox and Pitt. His essay-like style was not adapted to so popular a body as the House of Commons. His speeches wore the air of the academy rather than the forum;

and much of his discourse was too elaborate, too learned, too philosophical, too ornate, to be appreciated by the general run of commonplace sort of men that drift into the halls of legislation. During the thirty years he participated in affairs, there fell from his lips and pen an amount of political sagacity, far-seeing statesmanship, philosophical disquisition, and oratorical display, all set off and adorned by an amplitude of learning, a majesty of diction, and a brilliancy of imagery, the fourth of which would have carried their author's name to posterity as one of the remarkable men of his time. He who thinks this eulogium extravagant has only to find its confirmation in the mines of intellectual wealth which lie embedded in the sixteen volumes of the works he has given to his country and the world, to his cotemporaries and to posterity. True, there will be found, mingled with these strata of pure gold, veins of impracticability, sophistry, prejudice, extravagance, and violence. His later writings, and in many respects his most grand and beautiful, are disfigured by a morbid dread of change, and obscured by a gloomy distrust of the capacities of man for self-government; proving, that though gifted with genius beyond most mortals, he was not endowed with the Divine spirit of prophecy. But it is equally true, that while the English language is read, the speeches and writings of Edmund Burke will be classed with the richest treasures of the statesman, the philosopher, and the scholar.

Next to the curse of a military chieftain attempting to adapt the tactics of the camp to the regulations of the cabinet, is the nuisance of a narrow-minded lawyer carrying the prim rules of the bar into the councils of the State, and aiming to be a statesman when he is only capable of being a pettifogger. On the downfall of the Grenville-Fox ministry, Mr. Perceval took the leading place in his Majesty's Government. He was a lawyer with a keen intellect, and a soul shriveled by the most limited views and bigoted prejudices. When ruling England, he looked upon her position in reference to Continental affairs, and the part she was to perform in the drama of nations, much as he was wont to regard the ten-pound case of a plaintiff whose brief and retainer he held. He argued the great questions which nightly agitated the House of Commons, and whose decisions were to affect not only his own time, but coming ages, like a mere lawyer struggling for a verdict. His weapon was sharp, and he applied its edge in the same way, whether analyzing the title of James Jackson to a ten-acre lot in Kent, or of Louis XVIII to the throne of France. He discussed a financial scheme in Parliament to raise twenty millions sterling to carry on the war, just as he argued the consideration of a twenty-pound note before a jury of Yorkshire plowmen. Yet he was a good tactician; saw a point readily and clearly, though he saw nothing but a *point;* knew how to touch the prejudices of bigots; was great at beating his opponents on small divisions; rarely lost his temper under the severest provocations; was quick at a turn and keen at a retort; and spoke in a lively, colloquial, straight-forward style, which pleased the fat country gentlemen much better than the classical allusions and ornate periods of Mr. Canning. He kept on the even tenor of his way till assassinated by a madman in the lobby of the House, in 1812.

And this is the man who shaped the financial policy of England during six of the most eventful years of her existence, and whom she permitted to plunge her into debt to the amount of £150,000,000! "How could this be?" The answer is plain. Mr. Perceval stood firmly by the King and the Bishops, flattering the prejudices of the one and the bigotry of the other; and never flinched from eulogizing royalty, when the rude hand of popular clamor drew the vail from the immoralities of the Prince Regent and his brother of York. Then he was a thorough business man; never alarmed "Church and State" by wandering, like Canning and Peel, out of the beaten Tory track; and, so far from giving up a bad cause in the worst of times, he raised his voice the more sternly as the storm of public discontent whistled louder, and cheered his flagging comrades to their daily round of degrading toil. Such a minister was fit to be beloved by a bigoted king and his profligate heir.

CHAPTER VI.

Pitt's Continental Policy—Mr. Tierney—Mr. Whitbread—Lord Castlereagh—Lord Liverpool—Mr. Canning.

In examining a little further among the statesmen who opposed the continental policy of Mr. Pitt and his successors—though by no means intending to notice all who thus distinguished themselves—a less notorious person than Mr. Sheridan attracts the eye; but one who, when we regard the solid, every-day qualities of the mind, greatly surpassed the showy blandishments of that celebrated orator. I allude to Mr. Tierney. Like Mr. Perceval, he was bred to the bar; but unlike him, he was not a mere lawyer, nor was his comprehension hemmed in by narrow prejudices, nor his soul shriveled by bigotry. Though his reputation in this country is dim when compared with other luminaries that shone in that Whig constellation in the dawn of the present century, yet it would be difficult to name one who shed a more steady and useful light along the path of the liberal party, during the first ten years of that century—always excepting Mr. Fox. Mr. Tierney was foremost among the reformers in the perilous times of the treason trials, in 1794—was a prominent member of the society of "Friends of the People"—penned the admirable petition to Parliament, in which that association demonstrated the necessity and safety of an enlarged suffrage, and an equal representation—and, having attained a highly respectable standing at the bar, entered Parliament in 1796, the year before Fox and the heads of the Opposition unwisely abandoned their attendance upon the House, because they despaired of arresting the course of Pitt. Mr. T. was at once brought into a prominent position. He took up the gauntlet, and during two or three sessions was the main leader of the remnant of the Whigs, who stood to their posts ; and he showed himself competent to fill the occasion thus opened to him. Night after night he headed the diminished band, arraying the rigid reasoning powers and tireless business habits which he brought from the bar, against the haughty eloquence of Pitt and the dry arguments of Dundas, blunting the cold sarcasms of the former with his inimitable humor, and thrusting his keen analytical weapon between the loose joints of the latter's logical harness. He was solicitor general of Mr. Addington's mixed administration ; but the dissolution of that compound soon relieved him from a cramped position, whence he gladly escaped to the broader field of untrammeled opposition. Here he did manful service in the popular cause, effectually blocking up all avenues to advancement, both in the comparatively secluded walks of the profession which he ornamented, and the more rugged and conspicuous paths of politics, which he delighted to tread. During a part of the dark night of the Continental Coalition, he guided the helm of his party with a skill and vigilance which its more renowned chiefs might have profitably imitated. His ability to master the details, as well as trace the outlines, of a complicated subject, (so essential to success at the bar,) induced his colleagues to devolve upon him the labor of exposing those exhausting schemes of finance by which Pitt and his successors drained the life-blood of England's prosperity, and swelled a debt which the sale of its every rood of soil could hardly discharge. Thus he acquired a knowledge of trade and finance, second only to that of the later Mr. Huskisson. It is meet that the unassuming talents and services of such a man, "faithful among the faithless," should not be overlooked when naming the modern reformers of England.

I have spoken of Mr. WHITBREAD. Some who have not

looked into the Parliamentary history of the times we are now glancing over, suppose him to have been merely a great brewer, purchasing an obscure seat in the House of Commons by his ill-gotten wealth, who held his tongue during the session, and sold beer in vacation. But he possessed an intellect of the most vigorous frame, which had been garnished by a complete education, and liberalized by extensive foreign travel. He was the companion and counselor of Fox, Erskine, Sheridan, Grey, Mackintosh, Romilly, and Brougham—a frequent visitor at Holland House—a ready and strong debater, always foremost in the conflicts of those violent times—for a short period the trusted leader of his party in the House—and in 1814, when the quarrel between the imprudent Caroline and her lewd husband came to an open rupture, he was selected, with Brougham, to be her confidential adviser and friend. Generous in the diffusion of his vast wealth—gentle and kindly in his affections—the warm friend of human freedom, and the sworn foe of oppression in all its forms—he gave his entire powers to the cause of progress and reform, and resisted, in all places, at all seasons, and when others quailed, the foreign policy of Pitt, Perceval, and Castlereagh. The return of Napoleon from Elba alarmed all classes of Englishmen, and for the moment swept all parties from their moorings. An Address to the Throne for an enlargement of the forces was immediately moved by Grenville in the Lords, and Grattan in the Commons, (both Whigs,) and supported by a large majority of the panic-struck Opposition. Whitbread stood firm; and, though denounced as a traitor and a French Jacobin, made an able speech in favor of his motion that England ought not to interfere for the restoration of the Bourbons. Such a fact illustrates the inflexible metal of the man, more than a column of panegyric. His political principles approached the standard of democracy; and this, with his plebeian extraction and rather blunt manners, gave him less favor with some of the full-blooded patricians of his party than with their common constituency. He died in 1815, and like Romilly and Castlereagh, fell by his own hand.

Many worthy and not a few illustrious names might find a place here. Grey, the dignified and uncompromising—Romilly, the sagacious and humane—Mackintosh, the classical and ornate—Grattan, the chivalrous and daring—Burdett, the manly and bold—Horner, the learned and modest—Holland, the polished and generous—Brougham, the versatile and strong—all of whom, with others scarcely less notable, sustained the drooping cause of freedom against the policy of Pitt and his followers, and kept alive the sacred fires, to break out brightly in happier times. But, each may be noticed in other connections. We will now speak of three statesmen of a different school.

Lord Castlereagh was the life and soul of Pitt's continental policy during the six years before Napoleon fell. Like Sheridan, he was an Irishman. But, unlike him, he resisted every measure which promised to bless his native country, with the skill of a magician and the venom of a fiend. Ever ready to bribe, bully, or butcher, he plunged England deeper and deeper into debt and into blood, and seemed to regret when there was no more money to be squandered, and no more fighting to be done. As the best atonement he could make for permitting her to come out of the conflict with a free Government, and without being utterly ruined, he went to the Congress of Vienna, and humbly begged leave to lay her constitution and her honor at the feet of the allied despots whom she had impoverished herself in sustaining against the arms of France. It has been contended that Perceval was an honest bigot; at least as honest as any man could be who performed so many bad deeds. But, beyond all question, Castlereagh is one of the most atrocious and despicable Englishmen of the nineteenth century. The name of no other modern statesman is so cordially and so justly detested by the mass of the people. With no more eloquence than a last year's almanac—

utterly incapable of cutting even a second-rate figure as a Parliamentary debater—yet, because of his intimate acquaintance with the affairs of that vast kingdom, his blunt sense, promptness in council, unflinching courage, and his unfaltering attachment to the Throne, and his unscrupulous execution of its decrees, he led the Tory party in the Commons, and controlled the counsels of the King through eleven of the most turbulent years in England's recent history. Though not the nominal Premier, he was the real head of its ministry during the war with this country, and in the times which preceded and followed the overthrow of Bonaparte, and bore a leading share in the subsequent despotic transactions which assumed the soft name of "the pacification of Europe." At the Congress of Vienna he represented the Power which had staked all, and nearly lost all, in restoring the Bourbons. This gave him the right to demand, in her name, that the victories she had bought or won should redound to the advancement of constitutional liberty. But this cringing tool of anointed tyranny, so far from bearing himself in a manner worthy of his great constituency, succumbed to the dictation of Russia and Austria —aided them in forming the diabolical Holy Alliance, that politico-military Inquisition for "the settlement of Europe" —and, decked out in his blazing star and azure ribbon, seemed to take as vulgar a satisfaction in being permitted to sit at the council-board of these monarchs, as did Mr. Tittlebat Titmouse, when admitted to the table of the Earl of Dreddlington. His subsequent course in endorsing the military *surveillance* which this Holy Inquisition exercised over the people of Europe, encountered the tireless hostility of the liberal party of England, whose leaders made the island ring with their protests. At length, this bold, bad man, this "*ice-hearted dog*," as Ebenezer Elliott called him, having opposed the abolition of the slave trade, the amelioration of the criminal code, the modification of the corn laws, Catholic emancipation, Parliamentary reform, and every other social and political improvement, during twenty-five years, suddenly finished a career which had been marked at every step by infamous deeds. Immediately thereupon, Mr. Canning, who succeeded to his place as Foreign Secretary, filed his protest against certain proceedings of the Holy Alliance, and England withdrew from that conspiracy of royal rogues.

Throughout the period just mentioned, LORD LIVERPOOL was the nominal head of the Ministry. He was a very respectable nobleman, with a large purse and few talents; an easy, good-for-nothing, James-Monroe sort of a body, whom every Whig and Tory made a low bow to, but whom nobody feared or cared for; a pilot that could steer the ship of state tolerably well in quiet waters, but who quit the helm for the cabin the instant the sky was overcast, or the waves raged. He was in office so long that he became a sort of ministerial fixture—a kind of nucleus around which more ambitious, showy, and potent materials gathered. People had become so accustomed to see him at the head of affairs, where he did so little as to offend no one, that they looked upon him as almost as necessary to the working of the governmental machine as the King himself. This commonplace man, under the successive names of Mr. Jenkinson, Lord Hawkesbury, and Lord Liverpool, held important stations in the Cabinet more than thirty years, nearly half of which he was Premier.

As has been remarked, MR. CANNING succeeded Lord Castlereagh as Foreign Secretary in 1823, and Lord Liverpool as Premier in 1827. Like Castlereagh, Canning was of Irish descent; but, unlike him, he had some Irish blood in his veins. Like him, he sustained the continental policy of Pitt; but, unlike him, he did not desire to degrade England, after she had destroyed Napoleon. Like him, he exercised great sway in the councils of the country; but, unlike him, it was not so much the influence of mere official station, as the voluntary tribute paid to a splendid and captivating genius. For thirty-five years, this remarkable man participated in public affairs:

and whatever opinion may be formed of his statesmenship, he was undoubtedly the most brilliant orator (I use the term in its best and in its restricted sense) which has appeared in the House of Commons the present century.

Canning's father was a broken-down Irish barrister, who, having little knowledge of law, and less practice, quit Ireland for London, where he eked out a scanty existence by writing bad rhymes for the magazines, and tolerable pamphlets for the politicians. He died the day George was a year old—April 11, 1771. The mother, left penniless, listened to the flatteries of Garrick, went upon the stage, tried to sustain first-rate characters, failed, sunk silently into a secondary position, married a drunken actor, who then had two or three wives, and who, after strolling about the provinces a few years, died in a mad-house, when she married a stage-smitten silk mercer, who had a little more money than her late husband, and a rather better character. Failing in business soon after, he tried the stage in company with his wife, where he speedily broke down, and she continued for some years to figure in third-rate characters at the minor theaters. In such company as would naturally surround such guardians, the future Prime Minister of England spent the first nine or ten years of his life. He had a respectable paternal uncle in London—a merchant of some wealth. An old actor, by the name of Moody, detected the glittering gem of genius in the unpromising lad, went to this uncle, and urged him to take his nephew (whom he had never seen) under his care. He complied, sent him to a grammar school, then to Eton, and, dying, left the means of educating his ward at Oxford. Young Canning shone conspicuously at the University, as a wit, an elocutionist, and a poet, and contracted some aristocratic friendships which served his turn in subsequent life, especially that with Mr. Jenkinson, afterwards Lord Liverpool.

After he left the University, he became intimate with Sheridan, who knew something of his mother and his own history, and by him was introduced to Fox and other leading Whigs. Though impregnated with liberal principles, his ambitious eye saw that Whigism was an obscured luminary, and so he turned and worshiped the ascendant star of Pitt. Entering Parliament in 1793, just at the bursting of the continental storm, he at once took his seat on the Treasury benches, and soon became a polished shaft in the quiver of the great anti-Gallican archer. In or out of office, he followed the fortunes of Pitt and his successors, till he quarreled and fought a duel with Castlereagh, in 1809, when they both left the Cabinet, and Canning remained under a cloud till 1814, when he was banished as minister to the Court of Lisbon. From this time, he never had the full confidence of the old school Tories, though he was their most brilliant advocate in Parliament, and generally shared office with them, and sustained their measures. After Castlereagh died, Mr. Canning drew closely around him the more liberal Tories—such as Lords Melbourne, Palmerston, Glenelg—and made up, in conjunction with Mr. Huskisson, a "third party," called "Canningites," who, through the auspices of Brougham, in 1827, formed a *quasi* coalition with the Whigs. After the death of their chief, many of his followers went completely over to the Whigs, aided Earl Grey in carrying the reform bill, took office under him, and subsequently, in an evil hour, became the leaders of that party.

With the exception of giving a hearty support to the abolition of the slave trade, and advocating the cause of Catholic emancipation, Mr. Canning sustained the worst Tory measures from his entrance into Parliament to the death of Castlereagh—a period of thirty years—bringing to bear against the People's cause all the resources of his classical learning, vivid wit, vigorous reasoning, captivating manners, and unrivaled oratory. Undoubtedly, he despised the truckling course of Castlereagh towards the Holy Alliance ; and, either because he wished to escape from "a false position," or because his colleagues desired to cripple his influence, he was just about to go out to India as Governor General, when the suicide of Castlereagh altered his destination, and he exchanged a subordinate foreign station for the chief control of that department of affairs. Immediately, England took a nobler position toward the continental alliance in which she had been entangled by his wily predecessor. The new Secretary protested against the interference of the Allied Sovereigns with the popular movements in Spain, and early the next year (1824) stated in his place that Ministers had refused to become parties to another Congress. This was the longest stride toward progress for thirty years, and well might the House of Commons ring with enthusiastic plaudits. This was promptly followed by the virtual recognition of the independence of the new South American Republics—another blow at the Holy Military Inquisition. Calling Mr. Robinson to his aid as Chancellor of the Exchequer, and Mr. Huskisson as President of the Board of Trade, the reörganized ministry (good, easy Lord Liverpool being its nominal head) adopted a more liberal policy in commerce and finance, which, coupled with its course in foreign affairs, drew to it a large share of confidence in the middle classes, and softened the asperities of the Opposition. During the four years that Canning controlled Liverpool's ministry, taxes were reduced, several restrictions removed from trade, the endless delays in chancery inquired into, the death penalty curtailed, resolutions passed looking toward slave emancipation, the corn laws slightly modified, and a bill for the relief of the Catholics was carried in the Commons, but thrown out by the Lords. Liverpool died early in 1827. After a quarrel with Wellington and Peel, Canning, in May of that year, reached the culminating point of his ambition, the Premiership of England. But, at the end of four months of vexed and troublesome rule, he died, much lamented by the people, who were expecting good things from his administration.

Viewed from one point of observation, Mr. Canning's later policy was favorable to the cause of reform; but, in another aspect, it may be doubted whether his half-way measures were not, in the long run, detrimental to that cause. He was raised up to save the Tory party, if they would have consented to be saved by him; for, had he lived, he would have continued gradually to yield to the advancing spirit of the age, and kept them in power many years. But their distrust of him after the peace of 1815 crippled his genius, mortified his pride, and determined him in due time to rend the party which would not permit him to rule. Through the aid of his personal adherents, his "third party," he did for the Tories in 1826–7, what Peel did for them twenty years later—yielded to liberal opinions—split the party in twain—and formed a *quasi* coalition with his ancient opponents. Though by this means some measures, such as Catholic emancipation and Parliamentary reform, were sooner carried (though only to a partial extent) than they otherwise might have been, yet it is hardly to be doubted that the liberal cause is now more depressed than it would have been, had no such coalition been formed and no such resulting concessions made. Though the secession of the Canningites weakened the Tories, the accession diluted the Whigs. It ultimately gave them such leaders as Melbourne and Palmerston—men who, down to 1828, had been among the most strenuous opponents of reform—men who have made Whigism popular at Court, by arraying it in purple and fine linen, and other soft clothing—who have stripped it of its rugged aspect, and decked it in the high-bred airs which it wore in the days of the elder Georges and the Walpoles, when a few noble families controlled its affairs. But, on the other hand, Mr. Canning broke the power of old-fashioned John Bull Toryism—the remorseless, insolent, *statu-quo* Toryism of French revolutionary times—and introduced the more complying, civil, progressive Toryism, which emancipates Catholics and repeals corn laws.

Mr. Canning was like Mr. Fox in one respect. Each introduced a new era in his party. The aristocratic Whigism of the last century, to which I have alluded, is graphically hit off by Brougham, when he says the heads of the few great families who controlled the party "never could be made to understand how a feeble motion, prefaced by a feeble speech, if made by an elderly lord and seconded by a younger one, could fail to satisfy the country and shake the Ministry!" Fox, the Jefferson of English liberalism, opened the door for men without ancestry or wealth to enter the party, and find the place to which their talents assigned them, whether at its head or its foot. He introduced the Whigism of the type of Grey, Brougham, Romilly, Russell, and the Edinburgh Review. It has served its day and generation, and has become so like modified, *Canningized* Toryism, that the chief distinction between them is in the different modes of spelling their names. Within the last twenty years, the people of England have advanced a century, while the Whig leaders have not kept pace even with the calendar. English liberalism looks with longing eye for "the coming man;" and when he appears, he will be as far in advance of the Palmerstons and Russells of to-day, as they are before the Pitts and the Percevals of past times.

To return to Mr. Canning. During the last five years of his life, he occupied a sort of middle-ground between the ancient and the modern *regime;* or, rather, was the connecting-link between the old and the new order of things. Having served under Pitt in his youth, he formed an alliance with the disciples of Fox in his maturity. Having advocated the complete destruction of the Irish Parliament in 1799 and 1800, he proposed a qualified emancipation of its Catholics in 1823 and 1827. Having sustained the European coalition for the overthrow of Napoleon, he repudiated its legitimate offspring, the Holy Alliance. Having drained England of her wealth to nourish and maintain absolutism on the continent, he shrunk from permitting her to pluck the fruit of her own culture. In these latter years, he might have been properly called either a liberal Tory or a Conservative Whig. He was the friend of Catholic emancipation ; but though public sentiment was not ripe enough during his administration to accomplish this reform, his efforts tended to bring it to that maturity which, soon after his death, enabled this proscribed sect to gather the fruit from that tree of religious toleration which his hand had aided to plant in the breast of English Protestantism. But, on the vital subject of Parliamentary reform, he would yield nothing. It was in reference to this that he had his famous quarrel with Brougham, who, by the bye, was for many years the pitted antagonist of Canning. The point in controversy was the disfranchisement of a rotten borough, which had been convicted of bribery. Both girded themselves for the contest. Never was the rugged intensity of the one, nor the polished strength of the other, more conspicuous than on that occasion. Brougham's attack was compared to the concave *speculum*, in which every ray was concentrated with focal intensity, and poured in a burning stream upon his shrinking victim. Canning's, to the convex mirror, which scattered the rays, and showered them down upon his foe with blinding fervor.

Turning from the statesman to the orator, we find him occupying a place equaled by few of his cotemporaries ; surpassed by none. He was the Cicero of the British Senate ; and, using the term *oratory* in its precise sense, he shines unrivaled among the English statesmen of our day. He is an admirable refutation of the somewhat popular error, that a *reasoner* must necessarily be as dull and uninteresting as the Rev. Dr. Dryasdust—that wit, raillery, vivid illustration, and suggestive allusions, are incompatible with sound argument—that to be convincing, one must be stupid—that logic consists in a lifeless skeleton of consecutive syllogisms, divested of the flesh, blood, and marrow of eloquence—and that the profundity of a speech is to be measured by the depth of the slumbers into which it precipitates the auditory. It is thus that many a man has gained the reputation of being a great reasoner, when he was only a great bore ; or been accounted wiser than his more vivacious associates, because he wore a stolid visage and held his tongue—completely putting to rout the venerable maxim of "nothing venture, nothing have."

Though few public speakers of his time dealt more with the lighter graces of oratory—wit, fancy, epigram, anecdote, historical illustration, and classical allusion—so, few excelled him in the clearness of his statements, the solidity of his arguments, and the skill with which he brought all his resources to bear upon the point to be reached, and the power with which he pressed it home to the conviction of his hearers. A burst of laughter from all sides, excited by his infectious wit, or a round of applause from his friends when some galling sarcasm pierced the mailed harness of the Opposition, relieved the tedium of a currency debate, intolerably dull in most hands, but which he, by mingling figures of speech with the figures of the budget, always made interesting, and thus kept his party in good humor while he drove these wearisome topics through the thick skulls of knights of the shire and country squires, of which material the Tories were largely made up. Throwing around the path where he led his auditors a profusion of flowers, gathered in all climes and refreshing to all tastes, he was ever carrying forward the heavy chain of argument, delighting while he convinced, and amusing that he might convert.

But these rare qualities produced their drawbacks. So skillful a master of so bewitching an art could not be sparing in the exhibition of his peculiar powers. His pleasantry and by-play, when handling momentous questions, offended graver men, who could not believe that so much levity was consistent with sincerity. He excited the jealousy of plainer understandings, who saw things as clearly as he, but could not set them in so transparent a light. His coruscations were not only glittering, but they often dazzled and confounded less ornate minds. His sarcasms stung his enemies to madness; and, not content merely to drive his opponents to the wall, he hurled them there with such force, that they rebounded into the arena, to become in turn the assailants; and his friends found that a brilliant attack led on by him often resulted in a counter assault, which summoned to the rescue all the forces of his party. And more than this, his port and bearing left the impression upon most minds that a consummate artist was acting a part, and not a sincere man speaking from the heart. His obscure origin, (obscure for one who aspired to be a Tory Premier,) and his early coquetry with the Whigs, affixed to him the epithet of "an adventurer;" and he never shook off the epithet, nor effaced the impression that it was fitly bestowed. The people of England, whether he was Treasurer of the Navy, Foreign Secretary, Prime Minister, or Parliamentary orator, never wholly escaped from the suspicion that the son was following the profession of the mother, but had chosen the chapel of St. Stephen's rather than the theater of Drury Lane, for the display of his genius.

Turning from the orator to the man, we find much to delight the eye. George Canning never forgot the humble mother that bore him. So soon as his resources would permit, he made ample provision for her support; and for years after he entered Parliament, and even when a foreign ambassador, he wrote her a weekly epistle, breathing the kindliest affection. Though he could never elevate her tastes and associations above the connections of her youth, he used to throw aside the cares of office, that he might visit her, and the humble cousins with whom she dwelt, at Bath; and there, when in the zenith of his fame, would walk out with his plebeian relatives, and receive the homage of the lordly visitants at that fashionable resort, in their company. This marks him a noble man. He delighted in literary pursuits—would drop the pen when preparing a diplomatic dispatch, to talk over the classics with his university acquaintances—was a brilliant essayist, and wrote Latin and English verses with grace and beauty.

CHAPTER VII.

Abolition of the African Slave Trade—Granville Sharpe—Wilberforce—Pitt—Stephen—Macaulay—Brougham.

In tracing the foreign policy of Pitt, we have been led beyond the period of the great philanthropic achievement of 1806-7—the Abolition of the African Slave Trade. I shall not trace the origin and growth of this traffic, nor describe its horrors, nor detail the measures, in and out of Parliament, which led to its legal prohibition. They are familiar to those who will be likely to read this chapter.

Thomas Clarkson was the father of the movement for the abolition of the slave trade, and, consequently, for the destruction of negro slavery itself, of which it is but an incident. The circumstances which turned his attention to it are novel. In 1785, he was a senior bachelor of arts of St. John's College, Cambridge. The vice chancellor, impressed with the iniquity of the slave trade, announced to the seniors as a subject for a Latin dissertation, (I translate it,) "Is it right to make slaves of others against their will?" He little thought of the far-reaching consequences of this proposal. Young Clarkson, having secured the Latin prize the previous year, was anxious to obtain it again. He went to London, and procured all the books relating to the subject he could find. His sensitive mind was shocked beyond measure at the horrors of "the middle passage," which they disclosed. Sleep often left his pillow, while digesting the materials for his essay; and during its preparation he resolved to devote his life to the destruction of so appalling an evil. Noble resolution! Little did the young philanthropist then imagine that he should live, not only to see this trade abolished by Great Britain, and declared piracy by all Christian Powers, but to witness the abolition of slavery itself in those islands of the West, around which his warm sympathies clustered; that he should see the humanity of the world roused in arms to put down the crime of chattelizing mankind; and should himself, after a lapse of fifty-five years, preside, "the observed of all observers," in the metropolis of England, at a large Convention assembled from the four quarters of the globe, to devise means to achieve a final victory in this war upon the "wild and guilty phantasy, that man can hold property in man." But, I anticipate. Clarkson finished his essay, won the prize, and, true to his vow, commenced, friendless and without resources, the work of abolition. He translated and enlarged his essay, and committing it to press, started on a pilgrimage through the kingdom, in search of facts to illustrate the character of the traffic, and friends to aid him in its destruction. A singular instance of his patient zeal may be stated. He was anxious to ascertain whether slaves were *kidnapped* by the traders in the interior of Africa. He was told by a gentleman, that about a year before, he had conversed with a common sailor, who had made several excursions up the African rivers, in pursuit of slaves, and presumed he could inform him on this subject. He knew not the sailor's name, nor his residence, nor where he sailed from, and could only say, that when he saw him he belonged on board some man-of-war in ordinary. Clarkson started on the forlorn hope of finding this sailor. He successively visited Deptford, Woolwich, Chatham, Sheerness, Portsmouth, and Plymouth—boarding, during the tour, which occupied several weeks, 317 ships, and examining several thousand persons. I give the result in his own words: "At length, I arrived at the place of my last hope, (Plymouth.) On my first day's expedition I boarded forty vessels, but found no one who had been on the coast of Africa in the slave trade.

One or two had been there in King's ships, but they had never been on shore. Things were now drawing to a close ; and my heart began to beat. I was restless and uneasy during the night. The next morning I felt agitated between the alternate pressure of hope and fear ; and in this state I entered my boat. The fifty-seventh vessel I boarded was the Melampus frigate. One person belonging to it, on examining him in the captain's cabin, said he had been two voyages to Africa ; and I had not long conversed with him before I found, to my inexpressible joy, that he was the man." This long-sought witness confirmed his suspicions in regard to kidnapping. In 1786, Clarkson published a tract, embodying a summary of the various information he had obtained, and in June 1787, organized, in London, the first committee for the abolition of the slave trade, and was appointed its secretary and agent. When visiting this patriarch of humanity, at Playford Hall, in 1840, he showed me the records of this committee. There were the original entries, in his own handwriting, made more than fifty-three years before ; and he was alive to read them to me, accompanied by many lively anecdotes of the early friends whose names and deeds were there recorded. In 1787, he had his first interview with Mr. Wilberforce, and found a ready access to the heart of that great and good man. In 1788, he published his important work, "The Impolicy of the Slave Trade." The next year he visited France, to enlist the friends of liberty in that country in favor of his scheme. He had interviews with Mirabeau, Neckar, and others. He was denounced as a spy, and came near being seized. Owing to the revolutionary storm then rising over the kingdom, he accomplished little by this tour, except to present copies of his printed works to the King, and obtain promises from Mirabeau and Neckar to call public attention to the subject when the agitations of the period had subsided. These promises were soon engulfed in the earthquake which shook, not only France, but Europe to its center.

Previous to 1788, such progress had been made in public sentiment and feeling in England, through the indefatigable labors of Clarkson and the committee he had founded, that it was determined to bring the subject of Abolition before Parliament. Mr. Wilberforce was selected to open the question; but, owing to his ill health, Mr. Pitt, on the 9th of May, 1788, moved that the House do resolve to take into consideration the state of the slave trade early in the next session. In 1790, Wilberforce introduced a proposition for the total abolition of the traffic, and sustained it with eminent ability, Pitt, Fox, and Burke giving him their support. The West India interest took fire, insisting that the trade was sanctioned by the Bible, and its abolition would ruin the commerce of London, Bristol, Liverpool, and other large marts. The session of 1792 saw the tables of both Houses loaded with influential petitions. Wilberforce led off, as usual, followed closely by Fox and Pitt. Dundas, "the right hand of Pitt," opposed the measure, and was scathed by Fox in reply. In the Lords, the Duke of Clarence denounced Wilberforce as a "meddling fanatic," who ought to be expelled from Parliament. But the object of his censure lived to see his royal traducer, as King William IV, sign a bill appropriating £20,000,000 for the abolition of slavery in the West India islands! Omitting details, suffice it to say, that the friends of Abolition pressed its consideration upon the public attention from year to year, with increasing fervor, Clarkson being the out-door manager, and Wilberforce the Parliamentary, (always sustained by Pitt and Fox,) till, on the downfall of Pitt, and the coming in of a liberal administration, with Fox for its leader, in 1806, a condemnatory vote was obtained, which, in the next year, was followed by the total abolition of the trade.

I will not stop to state why this measure, since adopted from time to time by all Christian nations, has not fulfilled the expectations of its friends; nor why the number of victims of the slave trade in our day is double that of the time when Clarkson commenced his labors. In a word, so long as the existence of slavery makes a demand for fresh "cargoes of human agony," so long wretches will be found to brave heaven, earth, and hell, to furnish the supply. But the failure to attain complete success should not lessen our admiration of those early toils, which, like an oasis in the wide desert of human selfishness, refresh the eye of all who recognize the common brotherhood of man.

Mr. Clarkson was greatly aided in his labors by GRANVILLE SHARPE. This singular person had already become known for his advocacy of the rights of negro slaves when Clarkson commenced his work. He was born of humble parents, in 1735. He had a mind peculiarly fond of probing everything to the bottom. While an apprentice, a controversy with a Socinian led him to study Greek, that he might read the New Testament in the original. A dispute with a Jew induced him to obtain a knowledge of Hebrew. In 1767, his interference in behalf of a West India slave, whose master, then in London, had whipped him nearly to death, cost him a lawsuit. He must be beaten, if the master could hold his slave in England. Eminent counsel told him he must fail, for the right of the master was not invalidated by bringing his slave to England. Repudiating this advice, Sharpe, with his usual diligence and bent of mind, devoted himself to the study of the law, preparatory to his own defense. The "law's delay" gave him ample time to explore the subject to its foundations. He published a tract "On the injustice and dangerous tendency of tolerating slavery, or even of admitting the least claim to property in the persons of men, in England." His rare authorities and profound reasoning converted to his views many leading members of the bar. After a delay of two years, the plaintiff abandoned the case, paying Sharpe heavy costs. While further prosecuting his legal researches, he had another affair of a similar kind, in which he was partially successful. By this time, though comparatively an obscure man, he was better read in the law of slavery, and the restrictions upon the system in England, than any barrister or jurist in Westminster Hall. In 1772 came on the hearing, before Lord Mansfield, in the matter of the negro Somersett, a West India slave, who claimed his freedom on the ground that his master had brought him into England. The ablest counsel were employed on both sides; the case was argued twice or thrice, and was under consideration several months. Sharpe took deep interest in the issue, frequently conferred with Somersett's counsel, and wrote in his behalf for the newspapers. At length, on the 22d of June, 1772, Mansfield, with great reluctance, (for he leaned to the side of the slaveholder,) pronounced the celebrated judgment, that slavery, being contrary to natural law, was of so odious a nature that nothing but positive law could support it, and that every slave, on touching English soil, became free, and "therefore the man must be discharged!" This rule has ever since been recognized as law in all climes where England bears sway, and is so regarded in America and most of the civilized States of the world. For three-fourths of a century it has pursued the Evil Spirit of slavery with uplifted weapon, ready to cleave it to the earth the moment it passed the boundaries of its own odious and unnatural law; and in our day it stands like the flaming sword of Paradise, turning every way, to guard the tree of Liberty. For the early announcement of this far-reaching and deep-sounding principle, the world is indebted to the labors of one who commenced his career as a humble London apprentice. Having fought the good fight of Abolition with Clarkson and Wilberforce, and gained considerable distinction by his philanthropic deeds and writings, numbering Sir William Jones among his intimate friends, he died in 1813. A monument, with suitable devices and inscriptions, was erected to his memory in the Poet's Corner of Westminster Abbey, to mark the public sense of his merits.

Mr. WILBERFORCE has not been over-estimated, but, in my

judgment, he has been mis-estimated. Entitled to less relative praise for his Abolition services than is generally bestowed, he is worthy of a higher position as a statesman and orator than is usually assigned to him. This common error is readily accounted for. The commanding place he so long occupied, as the Parliamentary leader in this Reform, rendered him more conspicuous at home, and especially abroad, than any of his coadjutors, though no man was more ready than he to acknowledge that his services were meager, compared with those of some of his less noted colaborers. So, on the other hand, such is the luster of Mr. Wilberforce's undoubted achievements in the Abolition cause, that to the public eye they have thrown into the shade his very superior talents in other and more general aspects. He would have stood in the front rank of Parliamentary orators, (and those were the days of Burke, Fox, Pitt, Erskine, Wyndham, and Sheridan,) had he never thrown a halo round his name by consecrating his powers to humanity. Thoroughly educated, and furnished with general information, his eloquence was of a high order—fervid, instructive, persuasive; his diction classical and elegant; his voice musical and bland; and though his figure was diminutive, and not graceful, his countenance was remarkably expressive. He possessed a lively imagination, a keen sense of the ludicrous, a ready wit, and powers of sarcasm which Pitt might envy. These latter, however, he kept in subjection, mainly from his strong religious susceptibilities and kindly spirit, which impelled him to avoid giving pain, choosing to disarm personal assailants by winning appeals to their calmer judgments. On one occasion, after being repeatedly and coarsely alluded to, as "the honorable and very religious member," he turned upon his antagonist, and poured upon him a torrent of contempt, sarcasm, and rebuke, which astonished the House, not more for the ability it displayed, than that so great a master of indignant declamation should so rarely resort to its use. These intellectual elements combined with the spotless purity and winning beauty of his character, to give him great weight in the House, and contributed not a little to sustain the general policy of Mr. Pitt, whose supporter he usually was, though he ever maintained a position of comparative political independence. He had much personal influence over that minister, whose repeated offers to take office under his Administration he steadily declined. He retired from Parliament in 1824. His last public appearance was in 1830, when, on motion of his old friend Clarkson, he took the chair at a large meeting of delegates, in London, assembled to promote the abolition of slavery in the West Indies.

Mr. Pitt's advocacy of Abolition is now believed to have been hollow-hearted—a mere trick to gain popular applause in unwonted quarters, and retain his hold upon Wilberforce. During the twenty years which this question agitated Parliament and the country, Pitt, with the exception of two or three, reigned supreme, and never failed to carry any scheme he set his heart upon. At the wave of his hand, he could have driven from the House half the members, who steadily voted against Abolition, whilst with a dash of his pen he could have swept from the offices of the kingdom every occupant who dared oppose his will on this measure. By his personal advocacy of it, he lost nothing, and gained much.

We turn with more pleasure to contemplate for a moment the services of two very different coadjutors of Wilberforce and Clarkson—James Stephen and Zachary Macaulay. It has already been said that the more imposing character of Mr. Wilberforce's services threw into the shade those of many not less worthy colaborers. Of these, Messrs. Stephen and Macaulay were among the most eminent.

Mr. Stephen was a barrister. On being called to the bar, he emigrated to St. Kitts, and attained such distinction in the colonial courts as to be called "the Erskine of the West Indies." Impaired health induced his return to England in 1794, where he urged his way to a respectable standing in

Westminster Hall. Soon after his return, he procured an introduction to Wilberforce, and immediately entered, with characteristic zeal, into the great work to which the former had devoted his powers. He was prepared for this from the fact, that such was his abhorrence of slavery, that he never owned a slave during his protracted residence in the West Indies. He subsequently married the sister of Mr. Wilberforce. He consecrated his vigorous pen to the cause of Abolition, and contributed much to create that public sentiment which demanded the abrogation of the traffic. At the solicitation of Mr. Perceval, he entered Parliament in 1808, where he remained seven or eight years. Always conscientious in the discharge of his political duties, he refused to support the administration which followed that of Perceval, in consequence of their neglect to promote a measure, which he had anxiously pressed upon them, for the registration of slaves in the West Indies. He soon after resigned his seat, and devoted himself more exclusively to the duties of a master in chancery, to which office he had been appointed in 1811, and which he held twenty years. He was the means of introducing several reforms in the practice of the court of chancery, though by so doing he essentially lessened his own emoluments. As an instance of his disinterestedness, it may be mentioned that he forbade his clerk to take the ordinary gratuities, and remunerated him for his loss out of his own pocket to the amount of about £800 a year. What time he could spare from his official duties was devoted to the abolition of the slave trade by foreign States, and of slavery in the West Indies. Besides numerous pamphlets, occasional speeches, and an extensive correspondence on these subjects, he published an admirable legal work, entitled, "Slavery of the British West India Colonies Delineated," the plan of which has apparently been followed by Judge Stroud, of Philadelphia, in a work of equal ability, on American slavery. Mr. Stephen descended to his honored grave in 1832, at the advanced age of 75.

Mr. Macaulay is the father of the brilliant essayist and historian whose writings are so well known in this country. And it is high praise to say that, as a writer, he is the worthy progenitor of such a descendant; for, though his publications fall short in beauty and splendor of those of his celebrated son, they are equal to his in logical acumen and argumentative power. Though younger in years than Stephen, Macaulay's services in the abolition of the slave trade were equal to his, while those in the cause of West India emancipation far transcended his.

The Life of Wilberforce, published by his sons, in 1838, was thought to have done injustice to the early labors of Clarkson in the abolition of the slave trade. An unpleasant controversy at once arose, as to the relative merits of these philanthropists, and especially in reference to their agency in promoting the abolition. An anecdote was told to me in London respecting the matter, which illustrates one of the idiosyncrasies in the mental constitution of another early and steadfast Abolitionist—Henry Brougham—who, though young at the period of the abolition, had, while traveling on the continent, assisted Wilberforce by pursuing various inquiries in Holland, Germany, Poland, and other countries, in regard to the traffic. Some of the particulars of the story are forgotten, but enough are remembered for the present purpose. Soon after the appearance of the Life, the friends of Clarkson caused a book to be prepared, vindicating his services and claims, to which Brougham agreed to furnish an introduction. The body of the work was in press before the ex-chancellor, pressed with multifarious labors, had prepared his paper. The committee having the matter in charge waited upon him, and stated that the publication was delayed for want of his introduction; that country booksellers and anti-slavery societies were impatient to have their orders filled, &c. Brougham told them he had not written a line of it, but would have it completed by a given day of the same week. At the appointed time the committee called, and he read the paper. What was their mortification to find incorporated into the middle of it a ferocious attack on Daniel O'Connell, the very man upon whom they were relying to help carry through the Commons the bill then pending for the abolition of the apprenticeship in the West Indies, and with whom they had had an interview on the subject that very morning. Here was a dilemma! They expostulated with Brougham; explained the ruinous consequences to the cause, of their sanctioning such an attack on O'Connell; and while they did not wish to interfere with the controversy between him and O'Connell, assured him that for them to issue such a publication at that crisis might seal the fate of the apprenticeship bill—nor could they send out the work without his introduction, without disappointing the public. After rather an exciting interview, Brougham dismissed them by peremptorily declaring, "they must take it as it was, or not at all." They left in despair. The next day, one of the committee called, to see if something could not be done to get over the difficulty, when lo, his lordship handed him the paper with the offensive passage omitted. The secret of the alteration was this: The night after the first interview, Brougham went down to the House of Peers, and "pitching into" the debate, castigated some half dozen of the lords spiritual and temporal to his heart's content, and, having thus worked off "the slough of his passion," returned home in a calmer mood, and blotted the obnoxious paragraph from his Introduction.

CHAPTER VIII.

Law Reform—Jeremy Bentham—His Opinion of the Common Law—His "Felicity" Principle—His Universal Code—His Works—The Fruits of his Labors—His Talents and Character.

THE father of Modern Law Reform was JEREMY BENTHAM. This singular person has been often sneered at by Americans, who knew nothing of him or his writings, except that he lived somewhere in Europe, and was called "a visionary foreign philosopher" by the North American Review. He was the constant theme of ridicule for a large class of Englishmen, who only cared to know that he was said to be an eccentric old man, who shunned the world, admitted his guests to dine one at a time, wore an uncouth garb, was an abominable sloven, turned wooden bowls on a lathe and run in his garden for exercise, relieved the tedium of study by playing now on a fiddle and then on an organ, heated his house by steam, slept in a sack, looked very much like Ben. Franklin, did not believe in rotten boroughs or rotten creeds, did believe in free trade in corn and money, thought the common law the perfection of absurdity, Lord Eldon's court a libel on equity, and wrote codes for all creation to use in the twenty-ninth century.

Mr. Bentham was one of the most remarkable men that has appeared in our age. He was born in 1747, and was descended from a race of attorneys. At the age of five, the family called him "the philosopher;" at eight he played well on the violin, on which he afterwards became a proficient; and at thirteen went to Oxford, where he excited admiration and wonder by his acute observations, logical skill, and precision of language. When he took his degree, he was esteemed the first reasoner and philosophical critic in the University. He was at Oxford when Wesley and the "Methodists" were expelled, and his generous soul took up arms against this tyranny. This induced him to examine the thirty-nine articles of the Church, one by one; and when it became necessary for him to subscribe them, long was the struggle before Bentham could bring his hand to do it. He has left on record a rebuke of this test, which ought to consign it to universal condemnation. At Oxford, he attended the law lectures of Blackstone, (being the substance of his Commentaries,) and his clear mind detected the fallacies in his reasoning, and his humane and honest spirit revolted at many of his eulogiums on the Common Law of England.

The Bar, to which he was admitted in 1772, opened a brilliant prospect before him. His precise and acute method of drafting equity and law pleadings was much extolled, and his refusal to receive the usual fees excited no less attention. A sharp solicitor swelled a swindling bill of costs in a case in which Bentham had succeeded—he protested—"Quirk" told him it was made up according to the rules, and he would lose caste if he altered it. Bentham was disgusted, resolved to quit the profession, and spend his life in "endeavoring," as he expressed it, "to put an end to the system, rather than profit by it." To the grasping pertinacity of this solicitor, the world is indebted for the sixty years' labor of Jeremy Bentham in the cause of law reform. Soon after this, he published his first work, "A Fragment on Government; being an examination of what is delivered on that subject in Blackstone's Commentaries." He then visited Paris, where he became intimate with Brissot, through whose agency, and without his knowledge, he was subsequently made a citizen of the French Republic, and elected a member of the second National Assembly.

His father died in 1792, leaving him a moderate fortune,

which enabled him entirely to abandon his profession, and devote himself to the preparation of those works on Law and Government which have celebrated his name in the Four Quarters of the Globe. During the truce of Amiens, he again visited Paris, accompanied by Sir Samuel Romilly, where he found himself famous. M. Dumont was then publishing his works in French. Of his "*Traites de Legislation Civile et Penale*," in 3 vols., about 4,000 copies were sold in Paris. At this time, there happened to be three vacancies in the French Institute, one of which was reserved for Bonaparte. Bentham was chosen to fill one of the vacancies. From elective affinity, no less than through the agency of Romilly, he soon after became intimate with the young men, known as "the Edinburgh Reviewers," Brougham, Jeffrey, Smith, Horner, Mackintosh, and their associates, and from that time was the Mentor of that galaxy of talent on the subject of Law Reform.

When Bentham was admitted to the bar, he found the English law, its principles and its practice, entrenched behind the interests of powerful classes, and embedded in the prejudices of all. Though called the perfection of reason, to his penetrating eye it was the offspring of a barbarous age, and, though a noble production for the times that gave it birth, had obtruded into the light of an infinitely milder and more liberal civilization the harsh features which stamped its origin. To him it was the patchwork of fifteen centuries—a chaos of good and evil—an edifice exhibiting the architecture of the ancient Briton, the Gaul, the Goth, the Dane, the Saxon, and the Norman, all jumbled together, and to which, in order to render it tenantable, modern hands had made numerous additions and improvements, till the whole had become a huge, shapeless, and bewildering pile. He saw that it contained masses of material to aid in the erection of a new edifice, adapted to the enlarged wants and cultivated tastes of the present age. And he entered upon the elucidation of his plans for a judicial structure worthy of the noon of the nineteenth century. He was the first man who sat down to the task of exposing the defects of the English law. Heretofore, its students and ministers had been content to sift its principles from a chaotic mass of statutes and decisions, and collect and arrange the perplexing details of its form of procedure. Commencing at the bottom, he worked up through all its ramifications, bringing everything to the test of expediency, and inquiring whether the parts were homogeneous with the whole, and whether the whole was suited to the wants of existing society, and the promotion of human well-being. Probably not intending, when he started, to do more than improve the system by amending it, he soon aimed at its complete reconstruction, branching out into an exhausting discussion of the principles on which all human laws should be based, nor stopping till he had surveyed the nature of Government in its widest relations.

The test-principle of his system may be explained briefly thus: The only proper end of the social union is, the attainment of the maximum of the aggregate of happiness; and the attainment of this maximum of the aggregate of happiness is by the attainment of the maximum of individual happiness. The standard for determining whether a law is right or wrong, is its conduciveness to the maximum of the aggregate of happiness, by conducing to the maximum of individual happiness. This was known in his day, and in ours, as "the greatest-happiness principle," or "the principle of felicity"—which latter term he much preferred to that by which it is more commonly known, "the doctrine of utility." This was the keystone of Bentham's system. With this principle in his hand, he traversed the entire field of legislation, dividing it into two great parts—internal law, and international law. Internal law included the legislation which concerns a single State or community; international, that which regulates the intercourse of different States with each other. His chief attention was devoted to preparing a code of internal law, under the Greek name of *Pannomion*, (the whole law.) This he divided into four parts—the constitutional, the civil, the penal, and the administrative. The *constitutional* defined the supreme authority, and the mode of executing its will. The *civil* defined the rights of persons and of property, and was termed the "right-conferring code." The *penal* defined offenses and their punishments, and was termed "the wrong-repressing code." The *administrative* defined the mode of executing the whole body of the laws, and was termed "the code of procedure." Some of these codes he run out into details. Others he left unfinished. They all bore the stamp of great research, learning, and symmetry, and were supported by vigorous reasoning, and elucidated by a comprehensive genius. Many a *codifier* of our day has been indebted, directly or indirectly, to these labors of Jeremy Bentham, to an extent of which he was perhaps not aware.

His system struck at the very root of the English law. Of course, such a "wild enthusiast," such a "reckless innovator," was laughed at, misrepresented, and abused. Not a single tile or crumbling pillar of "the perfection of reason" must be touched. The rubbish that blocked up the avenues leading to it, the dust which choked its passages, must not be removed. Venerable for its age, hallowed as the legacy of our ancestors, the work of wise men and dead men, it must be worshiped at a distance and let alone. All classes deified it, and denounced such as would sneeze at its consecrated dust. The king as he placed the golden round on his anointed head, and the noble as he gazed on his stars and ribbons—the fat bishop as he pocketed his tithes, and the lean dissenter as he paid them—the judge in his scarlet robes, and the barrister in his wig of horsehair—the merchant as he paid his onerous duties to the government, and the yeoman as he liquidated the ruinous rents of his landlord—the clodhopper as he took his shilling for twelve hours of exhausting toil, and the culprit as he hung on a cross-tree for killing the hare which poached on his beans—all, high-born and low-born, patrician and plebeian, rich and poor, wise and foolish, were ready to make oath that the common law of England was the perfection of reason, and to swear at Jeremy Bentham for doubting it. If Bentham had done nothing more than dispel this delusion, he would deserve the thanks of the millions in both hemispheres who submit to the sway of the common law ; and this he did most effectually.

Bentham brought to his work reasoning faculties which did not so much probe subjects to the bottom as begin there, and work upwards to their surface—a patience which no amount of drudgery could weary—a taste whose light reading was Bacon and Beccaria—a memory retentive as tablets of brass—a boldness which shrunk from looking no institution in the face, and questioning its pretensions to utility and its claims to homage—an honesty which never averted the eye from conclusions legitimately born of sound premises—a conscience which followed truth wherever it led. Lord Brougham, who knew him intimately, has happily said : "In him were blended, to a degree perhaps unequaled in any other philosopher, the love and appreciation of general principles, with the avidity for minute details ; the power of embracing and following out general views, with the capacity for pursuing each one of numberless particular facts." He was an adept in numerous modern languages, as French, Italian, Spanish, and German, and he extended his linguistical knowledge into the Swedish, Russian, and other northern tongues. These acquisitions facilitated his study of the history of all countries and times, with whose philosophy, legislation and jurisprudence he was acquainted beyond most men.

His numerous writings all bore some relation to his "Felicity" principle, and the topics discussed were almost as multifarious as human exigency and action. Including his larger pamphlets, they must number some fifty volumes. They chiefly relate to Government, law, and jurisprudence ; but he also wrote extensively on morals, politics, and ecclesiastical establishments. Nor did science wholly escape his searching pen, for he treated of chemistry and anatomy. He wrote against Blackstone's Commentaries, and attacked Burke's plan for economical reform. He wrote on prison discipline and penal colonies, and illustrated the anti-Christian tendency of oaths. He advocated free schools, and denounced church establishments. He attacked rotten boroughs, and drafted plans for work-houses. He vindicated free trade, and showed the impolicy of the usury laws. He prepared a constitutional code to be used by any State, and drew up a reform bill for the House of Commons. He wrote separate volumes or pamphlets on bankruptcy, poor laws, primogeniture, escheats, taxation, jails, Scotch reform, the French judiciary, the criminal code of Spain, juries, evidence, rewards and punishments, oaths, parliamentary law, English reform, education, Church-of-Englandism, &c., &c., &c. He wrote for or offered codes to France, Spain, Greece, Russia, and the South American States—sent a letter to each Governor of the United States, proposing to prepare for them an entire code of laws—was intimate personally or by correspondence with Howard, Lafayette, Wilberforce, the Emperor Alexander, Napoleon, Brissot, Mirabeau, Neckar, Benezet, Franklin, Jefferson, Bolivar, Jean Baptiste Say, Toussaint L'Ouverture, and in fact with most of the men of his times, who were celebrated in any part of the world for their services in the cause of liberty, humanity and reform.

Of course no man, unless endowed with all the wisdom of the ancients and the moderns, could write so much on such a variety of subjects, without committing to paper a good deal of nonsense. Yet he wrote no page but contains some profound thoughts, whilst many of his volumes are replete with wisdom. And if any one mortal man could have written codes for all the nations on earth, that man was Jeremy Bentham.

His defects were partly the result of his peculiar mind, and partly of those idiosyncrasies which germinate in all speculators who mingle little with men and things. Bold and original to a fault, he rather suspected that an old thing was necessarily a bad thing. His exhaustless patience, and fondness for abstractions and theorizing, which grew by what they fed on, led him to carry everything out, out, out, till he sometimes trenched on absurdity or sunk in obscurity. In vulgar phrase, he was prone to "run a thing into the ground." He mixed so little with the world, and had such limited experience in the every-day business of life, that he often forgot that his codes must be executed by and upon mortal men. He lived fifty years in the house immortalized as the dwelling-place of Milton, in the very heart of London; and yet nine-tenths of the inhabitants, about whom he was thinking, and writing, and printing for half a century, never knew that he lived at all. Habits induced by this recluse life, were not improved by his being the head and oracle of a school, whose immoderate puffings, which he must hear, were not counterbalanced by denunciations from without, to which he never listened. He tried to reduce everything to a system, and wrote as if the human mind were a curious little wheel, to be put into a vast engine, which, when regulated according to his system, would run without jarring or friction. He made too little allowance for the individualities, eccentricities, *crooked-stickednesses* of mankind. But in this he did not differ from many other philosophers—men wiser and better than their generation—men so far beyond and above their times, that they look like dwarfs to their cotemporaries.

Then, he undertook so much that he left a great deal incomplete; so that, in many of his works, while he has finished one side of a subject, he seems not to have touched or seen the other side. His style, especially in his latter years, was rough, involved, uncongenial; often obscure from its very verbosity; and, when clear, fatiguing the reader by so thoroughly exhausting the subject as to leave nothing for him to do but read. He called his style of reasoning "the *exhaustive* mode," and he crowded it full of crabbed words of his own invention. He wrote many of his works in French, and they were given to the world by Dumont, a Genevan. Hazlitt has wittily said: "His works have been translated into French; they ought to be translated into English." Sydney Smith, when reviewing his "Book of Fallacies," remarks, in his quaint way, "Whether it is necessary there should be a middleman between the cultivator and the possessor, learned economists have doubted; but neither gods, men, nor booksellers, can doubt the necessity of a middleman between Mr. Bentham and the public. * * The mass of readers will choose to become acquainted with him through the medium of Reviews, after that eminent philosopher has been washed, trimmed, shaved, and forced into clean linen."

Bentham invented the words *Codify* and *Codification*, now in such general use. But let it not be supposed that he was guilty of the absurdity of imagining that the entire laws of a Commonwealth could be compressed into a single volume; nor of that other absurdity, that the laws can be written so plain that the meanest capacity can understand them fully, and apply them, without mistakes, to all the varieties of human rights and wrongs, and the ever-shifting vagaries and exigencies of society. He never had wit enough to see how it was, that what never could be true in regard to any other science or species of writing, must be true in regard to jurisprudence and legislation. He left that discovery for penny-a-liners, who believe all the law the world needs can be printed between the yellow covers of a twenty-page pamphlet.

Bentham labored without any apparent success at home for years. He was famous in France, and appreciated in Russia, before he was known in England. At length, his reiterated blows made an impression. He won converts in high places, and they became his "middlemen" with the public. Brougham and Smith spread out his great ideas in attractive colors on the pages of the Edinburgh, and they sparkled in brilliant speeches from Romilly and Mackintosh on the floor of Parliament. One after another, the champions for the inviolability of the ancient system were prostrated, till reasonable men admitted that, whether or not Jeremy Bentham was right, the common law was certainly wrong, and must be materially altered. Though he took no part in actual legislation, his was the master mind that set other minds in motion; his genius, the secret spring that operated a vast reformatory machine. He did not live to see his whole system adopted, (and would not, had he lived till the millennium,) but he saw parts of it incorporated into the jurisprudence of his country, whilst other parts were postponed rather than rejected. He saw the fruits of his labors in the amelioration of a sanguinary criminal code, and especially in the abridgment of the death penalty—in the improvement of the poor laws and penitentiaries, and the kindlier treatment of prisoners—in the softening of the harsher features of imprisonment for debt, of the bankrupt laws, and the general law of debtor and creditor—in lopping off some excrescences in chancery, and cutting down costs and simplifying the modes of procedure in other courts—in the abolition of tests, and the emancipation of the Catholics—in the greater freedom of trade, the enlargement of the suffrage, and the partial equalization of representation in Parliament—in the appointment of commissioners to revise the whole mass of statute law, and reduce it to a uniform code—and, more than all, in the conviction, penetrating a multitude of intelligent minds, that a large portion of the English law, as administered, so far from being the perfection of reason, was a disgrace to the human understanding, and the homage paid to it a degrading idolatry.

Nor did he see these fruits in England alone. As he labored for the world, so he saw the products of his toil in both hemispheres. France and Russia published his writings, and they were read in Germany and Switzerland. His works were circulated at Calcutta and the Cape of Good Hope; at

New York, and New South Wales; in the Canadas, and the Republics of South America. This country profits by his culture in the simplification of its laws, and their revision and codification in many of its States—in the comparative humanity of its criminal codes and prison discipline—and especially in the recent sweeping reforms in the practice of its courts in three or four States, and the abolition of the monopoly of the legal profession—a monopoly worthless to those whom it protected, and galling to those whom it excluded. By no means do I intend to say, that to him we are solely indebted for these reforms. But his hand planted the tree whose fruit is now being gathered. His chief glory is the emancipation of the Anglo-Saxon mind from a blind idolatry of the English common law; and for this he deserves unmeasured praise.

Mr. Bentham was kind, cheerful, simple-hearted, witty, and greatly beloved by his friends. Frank, so frank that he was bluff, he refused a costly present from the Emperor of Russia, lest he should be tempted to praise when he ought to blame. A great husbander of moments, he took air and exercise while entertaining ordinary visitors; and, when conversing on his favorite themes with such as Romilly and Brougham, kept his secretaries busy in noting down their remarks. The ridicule and abuse of which he was the subject rarely reached its aim, for he avoided personal controversies, discussing principles, and not men. He died in 1832, in the 85th year of his age; and gave a singular evidence of his attachment to his principles, by bequeathing his body to the surgeon's knife, for the advancement of medical science.

CHAPTER IX.

Law Reform—The Penal Code of England—Its Barbarity—The Death-Penalty—Sir Samuel Romilly—His Efforts to Abolish Capital Punishment—His Talents and Character.

THE earliest mouth piece of Jeremy Bentham in Parliament, and his "middleman" with the public, was Sir SAMUEL ROMILLY. This accomplished lawyer, from the period he entered Parliament, in 1806, till his death, in 1818, directed his main efforts to Law Reform; especially the amelioration of the Penal Code, and the diminution of the number of capital offenses.

The present criminal code of England is a disgrace to civilization. When Romilly commenced his labors, it would have disgraced barbarism. Blackstone had said in his Commentaries, (and it was substantially true in 1806,) "Among the variety of actions which men are liable daily to commit, no less than one hundred and sixty are declared by act of Parliament to be felonies, without benefit of clergy; or, in other words, to be worthy of instant death." I will specify a few items in this bloody catalogue. Treason, murder, arson, and rape, were of course capital crimes. So was counterfeiting coin; refusing to take the oath of allegiance under various circumstances; falsifying judicial records; taking a reward for restoring stolen goods, when accessory with the thief; obstructing the service of legal process; hunting in the night disguised; writing threatening letters, to extort money; pulling down turnpike gates; assembling to produce riots, and not dispersing at the order of a magistrate; transporting wool or sheep twice out of the kingdom; smuggling; fraudulent bankruptcies; marrying a couple except in "a church," without the license of the Archbishop of Canterbury, and making false entries in relation thereto in a marriage register; wandering as gipsies thirty days; burglary, in the night; stealing, from the person, property above the value of twelve pence, or, from a dwelling-house, above five shillings, or a vessel above forty shillings; stealing fish, hares, and conies; robbing on the highway to the value of a farthing; forgery in all its multiplied forms; sundry mere trespasses to personal property, such as tearing down fences, opening fish-ponds, destroying trees in parks and gardens, maiming cattle—and the list might be swelled through a chapter.

The legal mode of inflicting punishment, in many of these cases, was equally barbarous with the penalties. Not content with killing the wretch, he might be dragged to the place of execution at the heels of horses; or emboweled while alive; or burnt to death; or beheaded, quartered, and the parts nailed up in conspicuous places; or his skeleton left to rot on the gallows; or his hands and ears cut off, and his nostrils slit; or be branded on the cheek or hand, before execution. And down to the reign of William III, counsel were not allowed to prisoners, even in cases of high treason, when the whole power of the Government was brought to crush them; and it was not till the recent reign of William IV, that, in other capital cases, counsel for the accused were allowed to do more than state points of law to the court.

Such a Penal Code would disgrace the Fejee Islands. Yet, it was, in its main features, the law of England in 1806; and, notwithstanding the lucubrations of Bentham, the dashing essays of Brougham, and the lucid speeches of Romilly and Mackintosh, sustained by the protests and the petitions of churchmen and dissenters, Catholics and Quakers, it remained the law, with slight modifications, till the reign of George IV;

and much of it is law to this day! And this code could be eulogized by the classical Blackstone; whilst Paley, the archdeacon, could congratulate the readers of his Moral Philosophy on the fact, that torture to extort confessions had been excluded "from the mild and cautious system of penal jurisprudence established in this country!" Such mildness *is* a "caution!" The same author, alluding to those who might happen to be convicted and hung through mistake, counsels their surviving friends not to repine, but "rather to reflect that he who falls by a mistaken sentence, may be considered as falling for his country."

No one will suppose that such laws, the offspring of the dark ages, could be enforced against all offenders after the sunrise of the nineteenth century. Still, capital convictions under them were frightfully numerous. The statistics of English criminal jurisprudence afford abundant illustrations of the doctrines, that the severity of the law does not diminish crime, and that the certainty rather than the severity of punishment is the surest preventive. These doctrines had been maintained with great power by Lord Bacon, by Stiernhook, the Swedish Blackstone, by Blackstone himself, by the Marquis of Beccaria, by Voltaire, by Montesquieu, by Bentham; and even Paley had admitted their truth. Romilly enforced them in Parliament; and it may be safely affirmed, that the history of crime proves nothing if it does not establish their truth. Larcenies, burglaries, robberies, and forgeries, had increased in England during the eighteenth century, much beyond the advance of population and commerce, notwithstanding the severity of the law and its frequent execution. But these obvious facts were assigned to other causes than defects in the penal code, and these doctrines were scouted as the dogmas of visionary enthusiasts, by nearly the whole of the bench, the bar, and the leading influences in Church and State, at the dawn of the present century. They admitted that the unvarying execution of the law would be barbarous; but insisted that its frightful penalties ought to be suspended over the heads of offenders, to deter from crime; whilst they trusted to indirect modes of softening its rigors. So, judges undertook to bend the law to suit the merits of particular cases; and the humanity of juries, outrunning the injunctions of their oaths, opened the door of escape in cases of peculiar severity. The latter would frequently find that the value of the property stolen did not reach the capital point; as, that a shilling piece was worth but eleven pence farthing; or a crown, but four shillings and sixpence; or goods for which the thief had asked £8, and refused £6, were worth but thirty-nine shillings; thus stultifying their senses to save a life which the law clamored to sacrifice.

Another evil resulting from the severity of the English code, was felt, not only in that country, but has reached us and our times, and will afflict us so long as we are governed by the common law. Merciful judges, during the trial of offenders for minor crimes punishable with death, would lend a greedy ear to the ingenious cavils and absurd quirks of counsel, and quash the indictment—or refine away the plain words of a statute, so as to exclude the offense from its operation—anything to save the life of a fellow-creature whose crime deserved a ten days' commitment to the House of Correction. And *we* are now reaping the fruits of this; for, be it known to the uninitiated, that all these cavils, refinings, quibbles, quirks, and quiddities, are recorded in books, and have come down to us as authoritative parts of "the perfection of human reason," making convenient holes for sturdy rogues, with the help of sharp-pointed lawyers, to creep through the meshes of our comparatively mild criminal code.

Sir Samuel Romilly found the penal law of England thus sanguinary on the statute book; thus abused in its administration by the courts; thus entrenched behind the authority of judges, lawyers, statesmen, and divines, when he commenced the humane but apparently hopeless task of softening its penalties to the milder civilization of the present age. He brought to this work professional eminence the most exalted, talents of the rarest order, learning varied and accurate, eloquence captivating and powerful, and a zeal and courage surpassed only by the benevolent warmth of his heart. Having previously secured some reforms in the civil law, he carried a bill, in 1808, repealing the capital part of the act against stealing property of above twelve-pence value. This horrid law had existed more than a thousand years, and probably in a thousand cases in which it had been executed, the hangman's rope cost more than the stolen property for which a life was forfeited. Even then Romilly could induce the legislature to fix the death-limit no higher than £15. This and another repealing act had slipped through Parliament in a very quiet way, without exciting the attention of the country. In 1809, Romilly proposed two bills, repealing the laws making it capital to steal to the value of above five shillings from a shop, or forty from a dwelling-house. He sustained them by a speech, which exhibited great research into the statistics of crime, comprehensive views of the philosophy of rewards and punishments, lofty appeals to humanity, and a just appreciation of the benevolent and liberal tendencies of the times. Both bills failed. But the friends of the halter had become alarmed at these reiterated attempts to restrict the death-penalty. The gallows-toad, touched by the spear of Ithuriel, started up a devil. It was the first time the mask had been torn from the penal code of England, and its visage, grim and bloody, exposed to the public eye. The excitement caused by this attempt to narrow the scaffold is at this day incredible. The chancellor in his robes, and the bishop in his lawn; the barrister in his silk gown, and the attorney in his threadbare coat; the reviewer in the aristocratic quarterly, and the obscure pamphleteer in Grub street; all entered the lists to crush the disciple of Jeremy Bentham, and demolish his dangerous heresies. If Romilly had attacked the monarchy itself, or declared that the horse-hair wig of the Archbishop of Canterbury was not a part of the British Constitution, he could hardly have produced more indignation among judges and hangmen ; more consternation among the old women of both sexes. Jack Ketch was no longer to hang men for stealing a cast-off coat or petticoat worth five shillings and six pence, and what would become of England ! Sir Samuel published a pamphlet containing the substance of his great speech, with additional statistics, which Brougham made the basis of an able essay in the Edinburgh. The pamphlet and the essay produced a profound impression upon liberal and humane minds throughout the country.

But, for two years, he was able to accomplish nothing in Parliament. In 1811, he took advantage of some favoring circumstances to carry a law abolishing capital punishment in the cases of soldiers and sailors found begging, without having testimonials of their discharge from the service. Grateful country ; to consent not to hang a sailor, who lost his arm at Trafalgar, or a wooden-legged soldier who stormed Badajos, for begging a loaf of bread ! Through the seven following years, though Romilly and his coadjutors thundered on the floor of the Commons, and lightened from the pages of the Edinburgh, and rained down pamphlets upon the country, charged with appalling facts, unanswerable arguments, and glowing appeals to the heart of the nation, they fell on the iron-mail of the Tory party only to rebound in their own faces ; and this great man having bequeathed the prosecution of the work to Mackintosh, sunk into his grave, in 1818, without seeing one lineament of relenting in the grim visage of the Penal Code.

But, not alone to reforms in the criminal code did this excellent man give his hand. He probed the Court of Chancery, and hove up to the sun some of the abuses which festered under the stagnant administration of Eldon—exposed the huge masses of rubbish which so blocked up the common law courts, that the difficulty of suitors to get in was only surpassed by the impossibility of their getting out; and though the reforms which he proposed were very moderate, and aimed only at glaring defects, they encountered the same bigoted attachment to ancient abuses which assailed him in the other field of his exertions. Lord Eldon especially construed every insinuation that the system of Equity was not perfect, into a personal attack on its head. He regarded a peep into his court as Jack Ketch did a side-glance at the gallows, and repelled every insinuation that he was not competent to do for men's property what Jack did for their lives—suspend animation by stopping the circulation.

Nor was it law reform alone which enlisted the sympathies of Romilly. As Solicitor General he brought in the bill for the abolition of the slave trade, in 1806–7; and in 1814, when the European treaty of Peace, negotiated by Castlereagh on the part of England, and which provided for the revival of the traffic by France, came before Parliament, he led the friends of humanity to the attack upon that article of it in a speech of the loftiest rebuke, breathing the purest philanthropy and attired in the richest garb of eloquence. His eulogium on Wilberforce and Clarkson was beautiful, and his appeal to the former, as he turned and addressed him personally, thrilling.

Romilly's mind was cast in the rarest mold, and his heart was attuned to the liveliest emotions. He could master the understanding with his reason, and sway the will by his persuasion. He frowned down meanness with the dignity of a judge sentencing a culprit, and his sarcasm was too keen to be often provoked. Standing at the head of the Equity bar, his professional attainments covered the widest field, and were only equaled by the extensive practice to which they were applied. His character was beautifully pure, and he was the delight, almost the idol, of his intimate friends. Yet, his modesty always held him back from assuming in the courts and the Commons the place that was assigned to him by the universal homage of his party, and the all but unanimous verdict of his opponents.

Romilly was the grandson of a French mechanic, who, with his wife, fled to England, on the revocation of the Edict of Nantes. His father married the daughter of a refugee, and Samuel was, therefore, of pure French blood. He was born in 1757. His father, who was a watchmaker, articled him to a commercial house, the death of whose head soon threw him back into his father's shop, where he kept the books for two or three years. During this time, he marked out for himself, and pursued with avidity and success, a course of classical study. Leaving the shop, he entered as an apprentice the office of one of the clerks in chancery, and for several years devoted all the leisure hours he could snatch from the drudgery of business, to the cultivation of general literature. Arriving at his majority, he studied law, and was called to the bar at the age of twenty-five—an admirable specimen of "a self-made man"—the only sort of MAN, by the bye, that is made. The following anecdote shows how his sensitive mind was, in mere childhood, bent toward the work which engrossed his mature years. He says: "A dreadful impression was made on me by relations of murders and acts of cruelty. The prints which I found in the Lives of the Martyrs, and the Newgate Calendar, have cost me many sleepless nights. My dreams, too, were disturbed by the hideous images which haunted my imagination by day. I thought myself present at executions, murders, and scenes of blood; and I have often lain in bed, agitated by my terrors, equally afraid of remaining awake in the dark, and of falling asleep to encounter the horrors of my dreams. Often have I, in my evening prayers to God, besought him, with the utmost fervor, to suffer me to pass the night undisturbed by horrid dreams." And it may be that these childish terrors had something to do with his painfully tragic fall. The death of a wife to whom he was fondly attached, and over whose bed he had watched with agonizing solicitude, threw him into a paroxysm of insanity, and he terminated with his own hand a life which England could not afford to lose. He was proud to acknowledge himself the disciple, in law reform, of Jeremy Bentham, and the friendship between him and Henry Brougham was as strong as the cords of a brotherly affection.

CHAPTER X.

Law Reform—The Penal Code—Restriction of the Penalty of Death in 1823-4—Appointment of Commissioners to reform the Civil Law in 1828-9—Sir James Mackintosh—Brougham—Robert Hall.

On the death of Romilly, the leadership in the reformation of the criminal code devolved on Sir James Mackintosh. At the election just before his decease, the liberal party largely increased its members of Parliament. Early in the session of 1819, Sir James carried a motion against Ministers for a committee to revise the penal code. He was appointed its chairman; and in 1820-1, in pursuance of its doings, introduced six bills for the abrogation of capital punishment in certain cases of forgery, larceny, and robbery, and amending the law in other important particulars. The bills were defeated. A partial effort at reform was made the next session, and one or two feeble triumphs achieved. But the day was dawning. In 1823, Sir James proposed nine resolutions, providing for radical reforms in the penal code. Mr. Peel, the Home Secretary, caused these propositions to be rejected, only that Ministers might introduce bills of their own, which largely restricted the death-penalty, and prepared the way for other repealing acts, till capital punishment was abrogated in some fifty cases. Thus the dark and sanguinary system which had so long reared its front over the jurisprudence of England, received a fell blow.

In 1828, Mr. Brougham made his celebrated speech in favor of remodeling the whole civil branch of the common law. Near the close he said: "It was the boast of Augustus—it formed part of the glare in which the perfidies of his earlier years were lost—that he found Rome of brick, and left it of marble—a praise not unworthy a great prince. But how much nobler will be the sovereign's boast, when he shall have it to say, that he found law dear, and left it cheap—found it a sealed book, left it a living letter—found it the patrimony of the rich, left it the inheritance of the poor—found it the two-edged sword of craft and oppression, left it the staff of honesty and the shield of innocence!" This speech, one of the greatest Mr. Brougham ever delivered, was followed by an address to the throne for the appointment of commissioners to inquire into the origin, progress, and termination of actions in the courts, and into the state of the law regarding real property. Two commissions were immediately instituted; one of general common law inquiry; the other, of inquiry into the law of real estate. Afterwards, the subjects of codification, consolidation of the statutes, and reform of the criminal law, were referred to other commissions. The commission to inquire into abuses in courts of equity had previously been appointed. Some twenty or thirty of the ablest lawyers in the kingdom were placed on these commissions, several of whom have since been elevated to the bench. Their elaborate reports, presented during the past twenty years, have displayed vast research and learning, and the numerous reforms recommended by them, exhibiting a cautious but steady advance in the path of improvement, have generally been adopted by the legislature. Though the prevailing law of England still continues a chaos of absurdities and excellences, the reforms introduced by these commissioners will be appreciated by all who have occasion to explore the intricate windings and gloomy chambers of the huge structure. The reports alluded to have been the text-books of revisers and codifiers in other countries where the common law prevails, and were frequently cited, and their recommendations often adopted, by the able revisers of the New

York Statutes—which last have served as the model for revisers in other States of the American Union.

I am now to speak more particularly of Sir James Mackintosh, one of the brightest ornaments of the liberal party of Great Britain. This eminent Scotsman was born of humble parentage, in 1765. At the University of Aberdeen he met Robert Hall, the celebrated Baptist divine, to whom he became warmly attached, "because," as Sir James says, "I could not help it." He adds, that he "was fascinated by his brilliancy and acumen, in love with his cordiality and ardor, and awe-struck by the transparency of his conduct and the purity of his principles." Their class-mates called them Plato and Herodotus. They traveled the whole field of ancient and modern metaphysics and philosophy hand in hand, debating every point as they went, till in Plato and Edwards, in Aristotle and Berkley, in Cicero and Butler, in Socrates and Bacon, there was scarcely a principle they had not examined, and about which they had not enjoyed a keen encounter of their wits. The heat engendered by these friendly controversies fused more completely into one their congenial natures. Such an attachment, formed in the spring-time of youth, was sure to endure; and though, in subsequent life, they moved in widely different spheres, their intimacy continued throughout their long career.

Being destined for the medical profession, Mackintosh took his degree at Edinburgh, and went up to London to practice. George III. then exhibiting symptoms of insanity, the subject of his illness and of making his son Regent was agitating Parliament when Mackintosh arrived in the metropolis. *Doctor* Mackintosh, instead of prescribing for the diseases of the king, wrote a pamphlet in favor of the claims of the prince; leaving the constitution of the monarch to take care of itself, while he attended to the constitution of the monarchy. The king suddenly recovered, when, it being no longer necessary to administer medicine either to the Crown or the Constitution, the Prince of Wales returned to his mistresses, and Mackintosh went to Leyden to complete his studies, where he lounged away a few months, reading Homer and Herodotus, to the great neglect of Galen and Hippocrates. Returning to England, he plunged into matrimony before he had sufficient practice to buy an anatomical skeleton for his office. Happily, his wife sympathized in his literary tastes, and, at once detecting the defects of his character, "urged him to overcome his almost constitutional indolence."

The French revolution, which ruined so many fortunes, made his. In 1791, he published a volume entitled "*Vindiciæ Gallicæ*, or, a Defense of the French Revolution and its English Admirers against the Accusations of the Rt. Hon. Edmund Burke." The very title-page immediately carried off the first edition, and the acute reasoning, brilliant declamation, and classic style of this vigorous but immature production gave currency to three editions at the end of four months. There was a great deal of *heady* strength in both these essays. Mackintosh's was like a river sweeping to the ocean, covered with sparkling foam. Burke's like the long, heavy swells of that ocean, whose crests are pelted by the winds and dance in the sun. Both authors set up for prophets; and, like other inspired and less famous men, they mistook the illusions of their fancy and the suggestions of their imagination for the visions of the seer and the teachings of the divine *inflatus*. Burke was nearer right as to the result of the then pending revolution; but Europe would now account Mackintosh the best prophet. This volume gave Mackintosh an introduction to Fox and the other Whig chiefs, and he became their warm friend. Soon after, falling into the captivating society of Burke, his teachings combined with the sanguinary turn of French affairs to considerably modify the views put forth in his *Vindiciæ*.

Throwing physic to the dogs, Mackintosh entered Lincoln's Inn, and was called to the bar in 1795. But, though the study of the law was more congenial to his tastes than medicine, his practice in his new profession was scarcely more extensive than in the old. In truth, he was too indolent, too desultory in his efforts, too fond of literature and abstract speculation, to excel in any pursuit requiring close application and orderly habits, rendering his whole life a series of brilliant but mere inchoate performances. In 1798, he proposed to deliver a series of lectures in Lincoln's Inn, on the Law of Nature and of Nations. The doors were closed against him, because of his supposed Jacobinical principles—the Benchers of that conservative corporation not wishing to have the doctrines of the *Vindiciæ Gallicæ* promulgated in their halls. Mackintosh published his introductory lecture to refute the charge of Jacobinism, and it was so tinctured with Burkeism, and so philosophical and eloquent, that it captivated Pitt, who persuaded the Chancellor to recommend the opening of the Inn. It was done, and Mackintosh entranced a learned audience throughout his gorgeous course.

His next attractive performance was the defense of Peltier, a French refugee, the editor of the *Ambigu*, for an alleged libel on Napoleon, the First Consul. His oration (for it partook little of the character of a speech at the bar) in vindication of the liberty of the press was pronounced by Lord Ellenborough, the chief justice, to be the most eloquent address ever delivered in Westminster Hall. Madame de Stael sent it through Europe in a French translation, and it secured for its author a continental reputation. And in our day and country it is read by thousands who have hardly heard of any other production of his tongue or pen. His lectures and his oration not only gave him celebrity, but, what he needed quite as much, a little money; and they brought him an offer of a judicial station at Bombay. Still pressed by pecuniary embarrassments, after much reluctance, he consented to be banished, with his wife and children, from his native land, to an inhospitable clime amongst a strange people. For nearly eight years he discharged his judicial duties with fidelity, but through every month of those years he sighed for his country and its healthy breezes, his associates and their brilliant society. He relieved the tedium of his expatriation by making some researches into Oriental institutions, by founding a literary club at Bombay, and by indulging, in his desultory way, in classical and philosophical pursuits. His study and administration of the criminal laws of India turned his attention to the subject which occupied so large a share of his subsequent Parliamentary life—the penal code of England.

The generous and philanthropic mind which had prompted the extension of the right-hand of fellowship to the emancipated masses of France, in 1791, and which, forty years later, was stretched forth to break the chains from the limbs of the West India bondmen, was not slow to see that the criminal code of his own country was the legitimate offspring of a black and bloody age. Returning to England in 1811, he entered Parliament in 1813, where he remained until his death, in 1832. He promptly took his seat by the side of his friends, Brougham and Romilly, and threw his great soul into the contest of the People with the Crown. The important questions growing out of the European and American wars, in regard to the rights of neutrals, were then pending, and he joined Brougham in advocating liberal measures. And, to the end of his legislative career, on all questions of foreign policy and continental combinations, on the alien bill and the liberty of the press, on Catholic emancipation and the abolition of slavery, on the recognition of South American independence and the settlement of Greece, on the education of the poor and the freedom of trade, on the relief of the Dissenters and Parliamentary reform, he was ever found on the side of justice and humanity. For a short period he was the leader of the liberal party in the Commons, but he soon relinquished the post to the more daring and robust Brougham. Indeed, Sir James had not the capacity for leading a popular body like the House of Commons. He was too indolent in mastering dry details, too little of a business man, and his style of oratory was too philosophical, classical, and refined, to produce the best effect on such an assembly. He spoke over the heads of country squires and men of the 'change, who could not translate his Greek and Latin quotations, nor catch the point of his learned allusions, nor see precisely what these had to do with the traffic in corn or negroes, or the overthrow of the Holy Alliance abroad, or the uprooting of rotten boroughs at home. When Hume figured before the House, with his bales of statistics, these plain men could arrive at the sum total of what he was at. When Canning's arrows whirled about the heads of the Opposition, they could see them quivering in the flesh of his antagonists. When Romilly's eloquence wafted gently over them, they were refreshed and delighted. And even when Brougham shook the walls like an earthquake, they understood why they held so fast to their seats. But Mackintosh's Plato and Priam, his Homer and his Helicon, were "Greek" to them. His speeches were better adapted to be read in the library of the scholar than to be heard in the Commons House of Parliament. It was these defects in his oratory, and his utter want of all taste for business, and his indolent and immethodical habits, which kept him behind men of inferior talents and acquirements while his party was in opposition, and gave him no prominent place in its counsels when it assumed the reins of Government. Sydney Smith, in a characteristic letter to Sir James's son, writes thus: "Curran, the Master of the Rolls, said to Grattan, 'You would be the greatest man of your age, Grattan, if you would buy a few yards of red tape, and tie up your bills and papers.' This was the fault or misfortune of your excellent father. He never knew the use of red tape, and was utterly unfit for the common business of life."

Mackintosh was a man of the purest benevolence and the liveliest philanthropy. He held all his vast literary and philosophical attainments cheap in comparison with his labors in the cause of humanity. The friendless criminal, shuddering in the dock under the frown of some heartless judge—the imbruted slave, writhing under the lash of a task-master in the islands of the West—the yeoman at his plow, deprived of the electoral rights which the very sods he tilled could enjoy—the educated Dissenter and Catholic, shut out from stations of honor and trust for refusing a test which stained their consciences, were all advanced to a higher civilization and a broader field of civil and religious freedom, by his aid. He was the zealous co-worker of Wilberforce and Clarkson, of Brougham and Buxton, of Sturge and Lushington, in the work of negro emancipation. His last, greatest, speech in Parliament was on the Reform Bill. Bulwer says of it: "I shall never forget the extensive range of ideas, the energetic grasp of thought, the sublime and soaring strain of legislative philosophy, with which he charmed and transported me." Before such services as he rendered to the cause of MAN, how all the acquisitions and displays of the scholar and the metaphysician grow pale!

I have spoken of his intimacy with ROBERT HALL. There was a striking similarity in the structure of their minds and in their literary tastes. The politician was a classical, philosophical lawyer and Parliamentarian. The divine was a classical, philosophical theologian and preacher. Each was fond of abstract speculation—each was a profound and original reasoner and thinker—each reveled in the literature of the ancients—each was a writer of whom any nation or age might be proud. Hall much excelled his friend in the high walks of oratory, and the power of riveting, of transfixing an auditory, and holding them spell-bound while he played with their passions and emotions with masterly skill. The first pulpit orator of his day, in the zenith of his fame he could attract a greater crowd of rare men than any other preacher in the metropolis or the country. The same cannot be affirmed of Mackintosh in the theater where he displayed his forensic powers. The speech which so transported Bulwer *in* the House of Commons, because of defects in the delivery transported half the members *out* of it. Each shone no less in the social circle than in the forum. While Mackintosh was the more ornate and classical talker, Hall surpassed him in keen sarcasm and solid argument. The conversational talents of Hall were more appreciable by ordinary capacities, his style being racy, off-hand, bold. Mackintosh was fitted to be the companion of polite scholars and learned critics, and his conversation was more showy, dazzling, and prepared. The wit of Hall, when in full play, approached to drollery, and his sarcasm cut to the bone. The wit of Mackintosh was Attic, and his sarcasm refined and delicate. Hall crushed a pedantic fool with a single blow of his truncheon. Mackintosh tossed him on the end of his lance. Hall made no effort to shine in society, and all his good things seemed to bubble up naturally from a full fountain, whilst his strength was reserved for public exhibitions, where he shone in splendor. Mackintosh elaborated his social effusions, (and it was his weakness,) and his best things gushed like *jet d'eaus* from prepared reservoirs; and if he failed to win applause at St. Stephen's, he was sure to be the center of attraction at Holland House. Hall put down upstartism like a judge at *nisi prius* rebuking a shallow barrister for contempt of court. Mackintosh pricked the gas-bag with the delicate instrument of his irony. Hall was loved by his friends. Mackintosh was admired by his associates. Each was a philanthropist and reformer, and each in his sphere was in advance of his times in catholicity of spirit, boldness of speculation, and freedom from the cant of party and sect.

The works of Mackintosh are numerous—though some of his best writings hardly deserve to be called *works*, in the incomplete state in which he left them. Besides those already mentioned, there may be noted many rich contributions to the Edinburgh Review and other periodicals—some Parliamentary and anniversary speeches—a beautiful life of Sir Thomas More—an acute and eloquent dissertation in the Encyclopedia Britannica on the General View of the Progress of Ethical Philosophy—and a Fragment of English History concerning the Revolution of 1688.

During his lifetime, Sir James was abused by the Tories; nor did the tirade cease at his death. Somewhat covetous of fame, and utterly reckless of gold, he left little to his children, except a brilliant reputation and principles that can never die.

CHAPTER XI.

Religious Toleration—Eminent Nonconformists—The Puritans—Oliver Cromwell—The Pilgrims—The Corporation and Test Acts—Their Origin—Their Effects upon Dissenters and others—Their virtual Abandonment and final Repeal—The first Triumph of the Reformers.

For centuries it was a settled maxim in England, that the only sure way to convert a heretic was to put him to death. All dominant sects have been persecutors in their turn. The Papists burnt the Episcopalians, the Episcopalians decapitated the Puritans, and the Puritans hung the Quakers. With the advancing light of civilization, the dungeon and the pillory were substituted for the scaffold and the stake. Then, as each sect had the power, it imprisoned, scourged, and cropped the others. At length, bigotry was satisfied with imposing pecuniary fines and civil disabilities on schismatics. Though it is long since the nostrils of a dominant sect in England have been regaled with the incense of a roasting heretic, it is only twenty years since the Established Church of that country erased from the statute book the grosser penalties against the exercise of the rights of conscience, leaving a sufficient number unrepealed to operate as a terror to evil doers, and a praise and a profit to them that do not "dissent."

The struggle between Right and Prerogative, which has agitated the kingdom for the past half century, has not been confined to civil institutions. The miter of the archbishop has not been deemed more sacred from scrutiny than the crown of the monarch. The Church as well as the State has been shaken by the earthquake tread of Reform. Prominent among the divines of our time, who have materially contributed to these results, stand Robert Hall, John Angell James, Ralph Wardlaw, Thomas Chalmers, and Baptist W. Noel. But the tree of Toleration, whose fruits the people of England are now gathering, was planted long ago by hallowed hands. Distinguished among those who, in the expressive phrase of Burke, early preached and practiced "the dissidence of Dissent, and the protestantism of the Protestant religion," are Baxter, Owen, Calamy, Howe, Flavel, Henry, Bunyan, Bates, Doddridge, Law, Watts, and Fuller; names illustrious in the annals of Nonconformity, whose writings exerted a wide influence among their cotemporaries, and in our day are the text books of the profoundest theologians, and the solace and guide of the most humble and devout of the unlearned classes.

In tracing the origin of recent reforms in the ecclesiastical institutions of England, due credit should be given to the Puritans of the times of Cromwell. In the convulsions of 1642–9, the English Church establishment, the power which had held the national conscience in awe for more than a century, was overthrown, and Puritanism became the prevailing religion of the Commonwealth. The professors of the new faith were distinguished for a strange mixture of austere piety and wild fanaticism—the natural product of the times in which they lived. No wonder they were guilty of excesses. The tightest band breaks with the wildest power. Their extravagances were the spontaneous out-gush of the soul, when freedom of opinion, suddenly let loose from the thraldom of ages, found itself in a large place. Our Puritan fathers of the seventeenth century, by the recoil of the revolutionary wave, found themselves standing on the *terra firma* of the rights of conscience, high above the reach of the returning surge. They must have been more than mortal, had they not roamed far and wide over the fair country which spread its tempting landscape around them

No wonder they indulged in wild speculations, and made extravagant investments, in those then unexplored regions. They were like captives suddenly released from the galling chains and stifling atmosphere of the slave ship, who tread Elysian fields and inhale the intoxicating air of God's unfettered winds. It is an evidence of their sincerity that they carried their religion into everything, even their fighting and their politics. Bodies of their troops, often dispensing with what they denominated the carnal drum and fife, marched to the harmony of David's Psalms, sung to the tunes of Mear and Old Hundred. Sermons, extending in length to six and eight mortal hours, were preached to the regiments, by chaplains mounted on artillery carriages. The camp of the revolutionists was not more the scene of rigid military drilling, than of warm discussions on the five cardinal points of their faith. The Roundheads in Parliament engaged in debates on original sin, and the scriptural mode of baptism, as well as upon laws concerning the civil and military affairs of the State. The very names which figure in the transactions of those times indicate the spirit of the age. There was Praise-God Barebones, Kill-sin Pimple, Smite-them-hip-and-thigh Smith, Through-much-tribulation-we-enter-into-the-kingdom-of-heaven Jones—names as familiar as those of John Hampden and Harry Vane. What happier illustration of Cromwell's intuitive knowledge of the men he commanded, than his brief bulletin, pronounced at the head of his army, on the eve of one of the decisive battles of the revolution, fought under a drizzling rain, "*Soldiers! trust in God; and keep your powder dry!*" Faith and works.

Oliver Cromwell, *the* man of his age, and whose impartial biography is yet unwritten, was the soul of old Puritanism, and the warrior-apostle of religious toleration. He maintained this priceless principle in stormy debate, on the floor of Parliament, against the passive obedience of the Churchman, and the uniformity of the Presbyterian, and defended it amid the blaze and roar of battle against the brilliant gallantry of Rupert and the fiery assaults of Lesley. The "Ironsides" of the revolutionary forces, composed of the Independents of Huntingdonshire, constituting the "Imperial guard" of the republican army, were raised and disciplined by Cromwell. Through long training, in the camp and the conventicle, he had fired them with a hatred of kingly and priestly tyranny, which, in after years, on many a field, under his leadership, swept to ruin the legions of an arrogant court and hierarchy. The historic pen of England has done injustice to him and to them. The reason is obvious. That pen has not been held by their friends, but their enemies. For a hundred years succeeding Cromwell's time, the English scholar and historian was dependent on the rich and noble, in Church and State, for patronage and bread. He must have been a rare man who coveted opprobrium and penury, by writing against civil and ecclesiastical institutions, hoary with age and venerated by the great mass of his countrymen. And these very institutions Cromwell and his followers had temporarily overthrown. He assisted at the death of the monarch—they aided to prostrate the church—bringing kings and subjects, bishops and curates, to a common level. Can we expect the leveled to do justice to the leveler? English historians have written of him and them as the beaten always write of the beaters—as the scattered of the scatterers—the vanquished of the victors. Admitting their extravagances and their austere sectarianism, the impartial pen will record of the Puritans of 1645, that they exhibited many of the fruits of a sincere piety, and fostered the germ of that toleration which blends the dignity of free thought with the humility of Christian charity. Their descendants have exhibited all the heroic virtues of their fathers, tempered with the liberalizing influences of succeeding generations. Eminent for learning and piety, they have been the patrons of all the arts which adorn and purify mankind, and, in the darkest hours of the party of progress and reform, have been true to the good cause. The scion from the parent stock, planted by the Pilgrims at Plymouth, in

1620, struck its roots deep into our American soil, and myriads of master minds in all the States of the Confederacy now repose under its overshadowing foliage, and pluck the fruits of civil and religious freedom from its spreading branches.

The power of the Established Church received a blow in the civil wars, from which it never fully recovered. At the Restoration, under Charles II, it took advantage of a real or fancied dread of the increase of Popery in the kingdom, to seduce Dissenters into an acquiescence in the adoption of laws favoring Episcopal supremacy, and which were subsequently employed to oppress Protestant Nonconformists. The chief of these were the *Corporation* and *Test Acts*, to the enactment, operation, and final repeal of which, the reader's attention is invited.

Says the complacent Blackstone, "In order the better to secure the Established Church against perils from Nonconformists of all denominations; Infidels, Turks, Jews, Heretics, Papists, and Sectaries—there are two bulwarks erected, called the Corporation and Tests Acts. By the former, (enacted in 1661,) no person can be legally elected to any office relating to the government of any city or corporation, unless, within a twelvemonth before he has received the sacrament of the Lord's Supper according to the rites of the Church of England; and he is also enjoined to take the oaths of allegiance and supremacy at the same time that he takes the oath of office; or, in default of either of these requisites, such election shall be void. The other, called the Test Act, (enacted in 1683,) directs all officers, civil and military, to take the oaths and make the declaration against transubstantiation, in any of the King's courts at Westminster, or at the quarter sessions, within six months after their admission; and, also, within three months to receive the sacrament of the Lord's Supper, according to the usage of the Church of England, in some public church, immediately after divine service and sermon, and to deliver into court a certificate thereof, signed by the minister and churchwardens, and also to prove the same by two credible witnesses, upon forfeiture of £500, and disability to hold the same office." The disabilities operated still further. By subsequent enactments, if any person held office without submitting to the tests, he was not only fined £500, but was forever incapacitated from prosecuting any action in the courts of law or equity, from being the guardian of a child, or the executor or administrator of a deceased person, or receiving a legacy. By subsequent legislation, the same tests, except the sacrament, were exacted of various classes of persons not holding civil or military offices, such as dissenting ministers, practitioners of the law, teachers of schools or pupils, members of colleges who had attained the age of eighteen, &c.

As has been stated, the Corporation and Test Acts were passed when England was alarmed at a threatened invasion of Popery, and their penalties were intended to be aimed chiefly at Papists, though their sweeping provisions included all classes of Nonconformists. The Protestant dissenters, through fear or hatred of the Catholics, consented to be placed under the general anathema, with a sort of understanding that, when the danger was over, they should be relieved from its pressure. They lived long enough to repent of their folly.

These acts were not only a gross violation of the rights of conscience, but were injurious to the public weal in many respects, and beneficial in none. Whilst they never made one Christian, they deprived the State of the services of many of its best and bravest citizens, drove much of learning and piety from the pulpit, and genius and promise from the university. By making the profession of a particular creed a necessary qualification for office, and the reception of the Lord's Supper according to a prescribed ritual the passport to civil and ecclesiastical advancement, they degraded the holiest rites of religion, brought annually to the communion-table of the Establishment thousands of hypocrites, and placed constantly at its altars hundreds of horse-racing and fox-hunting clergymen.

They were a perpetual source of annoyance to dissenters who would not barter their faith for place and pelf, by subjecting them to prosecutions for refusing to qualify themselves for offices to which they had been maliciously elected, to be followed by ruinous fines or long imprisonments. In a single year (1736) £20,700 were raised from fines imposed on dissenters, who conscientiously refused to serve in the office of sheriff; and for a long time it was the custom of municipal corporations to elect dissenters to office, and then enrich their coffers from fines levied upon them for refusing to receive the qualifying tests. At length, the common oppression drove Protestant and Catholic dissenters into a formidable union for the restoration of their common rights, and engendered a hatred of the Established Church, its clergy, its creed, and its ordinances, which twenty years of qualified toleration have not been able to abate or scarcely to mitigate.

Repeated efforts were made for the repeal of these acts. Protestant dissenters, having suffered their penalties for nearly a century, grew numerous and influential, when Parliament, instead of boldly meeting the question of repeal, began to exercise that temporizing cunning so characteristic of British legislation, and grudgingly ameliorated a grievance which it had not the grace to wholly abrogate. It commenced the practice of passing, at the close of each session, amnesty bills, exempting dissenters, who had violated the acts, from the operation of their penalties; and so framing the bills as to cover not only past offenses, but all which might be committed before the close of the next session, when another bill would be enacted. This relieved dissenters from practical oppression under these acts, for some eighty years previous to their final repeal.

But, so intelligent and high-minded a portion of the State were not content to receive rights inherent and immutable, as an annual boon from the legislature. The struggle for unqualified repeal never ceased till the disgraceful acts were blotted from the statute book. On the 26th of February, 1828, was struck the first successful blow against the supremacy of the Church of England since the Restoration. Lord John Russell moved that the House resolve itself into a Committee to take into consideration the regulations of the Corporation and Test Acts. A stormy debate followed, in which Bigotry and Power made a desperate stand for victory. A division showed 237 for the motion, and 193 against it. In oommittee, Ministers entreated earnestly for delay, but a resolution was adopted for the instant repeal of the acts. A bill, based on this resolution, was introduced, and passed its second reading. The Bishop of Oxford rent his robes, and Lord Eldon shed many tears—but all in vain. After witnessing the temper of the House, Mr. Peel declared that he was prepared to dismiss from his mind every idea of adhering to the existing laws, and only asked for some slight modifications in the pending bill. His request being complied with, Ministers withdrew from the contest, and speedily the Corporation and Test Acts, the offspring of a grim and bigoted age, ceased to be the law of the realm.

This was the first cardinal measure which the modern reformers had carried through Parliament (the abolition of the slave trade and the melioration of the criminal code were advocated by the chiefs of both parties) during a conflict of nearly half a century. It was hailed as an era in the contests of the People with the Crown; the harbinger of better days to come; and was the first in a series of still more glorious achievements.

CHAPTER XII.

Ireland—The Causes of its Debasement—Dublin—Mementoes of the Captivity of the Country—Movements toward Catholic Emancipation—Its Early Champions—Mr. Grattan—Mr. Plunkett—Reverend Sydney Smith.

Before specially considering Catholic Emancipation, I will notice two or three persons who participated in the long struggle which prepared the way for this great measure of religious toleration. The act of Emancipation extended to Catholics alike in all parts of the United Kingdom. But, as the large majority of the professors of that faith dwelt in Ireland, and as they composed nearly seven-eighths of its people, and as it was there that the long and fierce conflict was waged which ultimately compelled English Protestants to yield to their Catholic fellow-subjects the rights of toleration which they themselves enjoyed, this was regarded as emphatically an Irish reform.

Ireland! What a throng of associated ideas start to life at the mention of that name! How varied their aspect—how contradictory their character—how antagonistic the emotions they kindle, the sentiments they inspire. Ireland, the land of genius and degradation, of vast resources and pinching poverty, of noble deeds and revolting crimes, of valiant resistance to tyranny and obsequious submission to usurpation. Ireland, the land of splendid orators, charming poets, and brave soldiers; the land of ignorance, abjectness, and beggary; measureless in its capacities, stinted in its products, a strange anomaly, a complication of contradictions.

Though this portraiture, sketched by no unfriendly hand, be but a rude outline, does it not shadow forth the original? Why are its darker colors no less faithful delineations of the prominent features than the brighter? The very problem which a whole century has not been able to solve! The British Tory will point to what he calls "the malign character of the Irish," as the prime cause of the debasement and wretchedness which exist among them. The British Whig, whose zeal for Protestantism, as a mere *ism*, has clouded his judgment, will assign the general prevalence of the Catholic religion in the island, as the source of most of the evils which afflict it. The genuine Irishman, who regards his native isle as the greenest and fairest the sun ever smiled to shine upon, will tell you that, giving due weight to many obvious but secondary influences, the degradation and misery which debase and crush such masses of his countrymen must be ascribed to the fact that Ireland, which could once boast of national independence, a regal sovereign, and a royal Parliament, is now a mere appendage to the English Crown, without a name, a flag, or a Senate; an oppressed colony crouching under a hated yoke of vassalage; a captive province paying tribute to a conqueror, who, having robbed it of nationality, appoints its rulers, dictates its laws, prescribes its ritual, plunders its wealth, tarnishes its reputation, and scoffs at its complainings.

Waiving till another occasion the question whether the prime cause of Ireland's miseries does not lie deeper than her compulsory and unnatural union with Great Britain, let us enter a little further into the feelings of the struggling Irishman. Go with him to Dublin. A beautiful city—one of the fairest in the United Kingdom. But, its beauty is that of the fading flower nipped by the untimely frost—the beauty of the chiseled marble, rather than of the living, acting, speaking man. Consumptive, pale, listless, it lacks the bloom, the freshness, the vivacity of conscious health. Its manufactures, its domestic trade, its foreign commerce, since the union with

England, have dwindled under the shadow of its towering rival beyond the channel, until its market days are as somber as a London Sabbath. Its dull streets and slumbering wharves, yea, the very gait and air of its populace, give token that its prosperity is arrested by the hand of decay, whilst its magnificent public edifices seem to stand only as tame and melancholy monuments of its departed greatness and glory. From the proud capital of an independent nation, Dublin has degenerated to the chief mart of a dependent province, whose owners are "absentee proprietors," whose husbandmen pay their rents to foreign landlords, whose merchants are the mere agents of distant capitalists, and whose nobles are proud to hide their Irish stars under English ribbons.

Everything in Dublin reminds the Irishman of the captivity of his country. He feels a blighting shame when he conducts a stranger through the stately halls of the Bank of Ireland; for there the Lords and Commons of the Emerald Isle once legislated. He is pained when you extol the grandeur of this noble building; for, to his eye, its glory has faded and fled. Walk with him through that broad and beautiful avenue, Sackville street, and your praise of its elegant mansions only reminds him that the Irish nobility that once resided there have gone to swell the brilliant pageant of the conqueror at Hyde Park and St. James's Palace. Wander with him amidst the filth and squalor of the lanes of the city, and he points to wretchedness and want as the fruits of English legislation. Go with him to the Castle, and, as the soldiery file through its turreted gate, clad in the uniform of the Saxon, he regards them not as the troops of a legitimate ruler, but as the trained assassins of an alien despot.

With such mementoes of the departed power and present captivity of Ireland, meeting his eye at every turn, was it not natural that the genuine Irishman, who submitted to the rule of England for the same reason that the slave wears the chain of his master, should, with the free blood which his Creator gave him boiling in his veins, twenty years ago present to his oppressor the alternative of civil war or unqualified toleration in the exercise of his hereditary religious faith—that nine years ago he should rush to Conciliation Hall, and agitate for his civil rights under the motto, "No People, strong enough to be a Nation, should consent to be a Province"—and that in the past year, when the last hope of civil emancipation by peaceful means had died out, and all Europe was in arms, casting away the chains of ages, he should light the fires of revolution on the hights of Tipperary, resolved to strike one despairing blow for the deliverance of a long-oppressed country? He who would brand Washington a traitor, may sink the iron into the foreheads of Mitchel, O'Brien, and Meagher.

Prominent among the early champions of Catholic Emancipation, stood MR. GRATTAN. To prove that, for nearly a century past, Ireland has constantly exhibited on the floor of the British Commons some of the most eloquent men who have swayed the councils of the United Kingdom, I only need mention the names of Burke, Flood, Sheridan, Grattan, Plunkett, O'Connell, and Shiel. Perhaps Canning may be included in the list. Both his parents were pure Irish, and he was, as it were, accidentally born in England. In this galaxy, Grattan shone unrivaled, except by Burke and Canning. He was the equal of the latter in many respects—his superior in some. As a practical Parliamentarian, he ranks scarcely below the former. And he stands at the head of all of his countrymen who have been strictly *Irish* members, representing Irish constituencies.

Graduating at Dublin, and entering the Middle Temple, London, in 1767, when just turned 21, Grattan was an eager observer, from the galleries of the Lords and Commons, of the fierce struggles of North, Grenville, Chatham, and Burke, then in the zenith of their fame. Throwing Coke and Plowden on the dusty shelf, he employed his leisure hours in writing sketches of these "Battles of the Giants," for the perusal of his Irish friends. He became enamored of politics, and resolved to shine in the Parliament of his native island. Some of his sketches found their way into the Dublin newspapers, and their point and power gave plausibility to the charge at one time made, that he was the author of Junius. In answer to a direct application to him, in 1805, to know if he were the famous author, he laconically replied :

"SIR : I am not 'Junius,' but your good wisher and obedient servant, HENRY GRATTAN."

On his permanent return to Ireland, he immediately connected himself with the opposition to the Vice-Regal Government, opening the attack by a series of newspaper articles in vindication of Irish rights, which attracted much attention, and came near subjecting him to a royal prosecution. From that moment, he gave his whole mind and soul to public affairs, and, during the subsequent fifty years, every page of Irish history records his name, associated with some measure for the amelioration of Irish wrongs. He is the author of what is miscalled "Irish Independence." On the accession of George III to the throne, the government of Ireland was then, as it is now, the chief difficulty of Ministers. During the American Revolutionary war, intestine commotions, from the incendiary proceedings of the "Whiteboys," (a rabble band which fired the houses of the landlords, and now and then put to death a non-complying tenant,) and the danger of invasion from France, impelled the middle classes to petition Government for succor and protection. They were frankly told that no aid could be afforded them, and they must take care of themselves. Acting on this license, a volunteer militia was enrolled in all parts of the island, the Government furnishing arms, which swelled till it numbered 100,000 men, of the bone and sinew of Ireland. The "Whiteboys" shrunk into the caves, the threatened invasion was abandoned, and the popular leaders, who had been active in mustering the volunteers, took advantage of their strong position to demand the removal of onerous restrictions on Irish commerce, and the amelioration of the Catholic penal code. The British Government essentially modified the commercial regulations between the two countries, and though some of the darker features of the code were relaxed, it still remained a disgrace to civilization. The greatest burden yet existed—*the supremacy of the British Parliament over Irish affairs.* Emboldened by success, an attempt was made to procure its repeal. Flood, the rival of Grattan, demanded a distinct disavowal, by the British Parliament, of the right to govern Ireland. Grattan, who had the hearts of his countrymen in his hand, avowed that he would be satisfied if Britain would repeal all existing laws interfering with Irish rights. The measure was adopted, and the Irish Parliament became the supreme legislature of Ireland, subject to the supervision of the King in Council. Hibernia was intoxicated with joy, and, in the fervor of their gratitude, the countrymen of Grattan voted him £50,000. Thus, in 1782, was *quasi* legislative independence granted to Ireland. But British gold and intrigue were ever able to seduce the integrity and distract the counsels of its legislators, till, eighteen years afterward, all was obliterated in the Act of Union. It was in allusion to the rise and fall of legislative independence that Grattan, years subsequently, so beautifully said, "I watched its cradle; I followed its bier." During these eighteen years, he did all that great talents and vigilant patriotism could to secure the prosperity and save the honor of his native land. The leader of the liberals in the Irish Parliament, he resisted the oppressions of the Saxon, and spurned his bribes, and appealed to Hibernia to be true to herself, and to maintain her national identity. Exasperated beyond endurance, Irish patriotism fomented the rebellion of 1798–9, which precipitated upon the heads of the "United Irishmen" the whole weight of British hatred and revenge. The scaffold ran blood, and the cheek of Ireland turned pale. In 1799, Pitt proposed the Union. Undaunted by the defection around him, Grattan, in the Irish Commons, resisted it with such vehement eloquence, that it was postponed till the next year. In the mean time, British gold proved more potent than its bayonets. Half the Irish Parliament was bribed into compliance with England's base proposals, and in 1800, after a last effort to rally the drooping spirits of his countrymen, Grattan followed the bier of Hibernian Independence to its resting place in St. Stephen's Chapel. Said his compatriot, young Emmet, the martyr, about to perish upon the scaffold, "When Ireland becomes a nation, let my epitaph be written!" Forty years afterward, in the midst of an excited throng, in the Dublin Corn Exchange, I heard O'Connell say, "Men of Ireland! I swear by your wrongs that Ireland shall yet become a nation!" Those wrongs are yet unavenged, the vow is yet unredeemed, the epitaph unwritten. BUT THEY WILL BE!

Grattan entered the British Parliament in 1805, where he remained till his death, in 1820. Ever in the front rank of Reformers, he was the special champion of Catholic emancipation, divided the House almost every year, and frequently two or three times in a session, on various propositions looking to ultimate emancipation, but without success; and in his last effort was defeated by only two majority—an earnest that the "good time" was coming. He met with the common misfortune of displeasing the ultras of both parties. He asked too little to please the extreme Catholics—too much to win the favor of the extreme Protestants. He asked for a part, and got nothing. At a later day, O'Connell demanded the whole, and got the greater part. History is philosophy teaching by examples.

Grattan was a model orator. His style had the genius, the enthusiasm, the brilliancy, the pathos, which mark Hibernian eloquence, and was divested of many of those peculiarities which often mar the forensic displays of a country where, as an accomplished Irishman says, "you may kick an orator out of every bush." If he was fertile in illustrations, he was redundant in principles—if his speech was replete with epigram, it abounded in terse reasoning—if it sparkled with wit, it was luminous in its calmer statements—if it blighted with its sarcasm, it mellowed with its pathos—if it was charged with the lightning of invective, it was freighted with the most ponderous argument—if it could wither a groveling enemy with its scorn, it could persuade a manly opponent with its logic. Nor did he overlay the solid parts of his oratory with the lighter graces of declamation, nor smother them under a redundancy of poetical illustration. He was a master of the compressed, nervous, rapid, racy style of argumentation—the very perfection of the art.

On the death of this great man, the cause of Catholic emancipation fell under the guidance of MR. PLUNKETT, who, next to him, was the ablest Irish representative in the Commons. Sir James Mackintosh sketches him, in one of his dashing conversational profiles, thus: "If Plunkett had come earlier into Parliament, so as to have learned the trade, he would probably have excelled all our orators. He and Counselor Phillips (or O'Garish, as he is nicknamed here) are at the opposite points of the scale. O'Garish's style is pitiful to the last degree. He ought, by common consent, to be driven from the bar." Plunkett brought to his work a true Irish heart, talents of the first class, eloquence cast in a rare mold, and a reputation unsurpassed at the Dublin bar. He bore a conspicuous part in all those violent throes, in and out of Parliament, in regard to Catholic emancipation, which convulsed the country from 1820 to 1829, and drove Ireland to the borders of rebellion. He won several partial triumphs over Ministers, preliminary to the granting of the great boon in the latter year, when the kingdom held its breath while O'Connell, the dreaded "Agitator," appeared at the bar of the Commons, to demand his seat for the county of Clare. When the Whigs rose to power, in 1830, Mr. Plunkett was made Lord Chancellor of Ireland.

Even this meager notice of the early friends of Catholic emancipation would be incomplete without the name of SYDNEY SMITH, the founder of the Edinburgh Review. Of all English Protestants, out of Parliament, he rendered the most effective aid to that cause. In six or eight articles in that influential periodical, in an equal number of speeches and sermons, and as many pamphlets, he pressed the Catholic claims upon public attention during twenty-five years, in a style which no mortal man but Sydney Smith could do. He did not so much argue the claims of the Catholics as ridicule the fears of their opponents. And never were wit, drollery, humor, irony, and sarcasm, rained down upon a bad cause in greater variety or rarer quality. He fairly drowned the High Church party in their own absurdities. His ten letters, signed Peter Plymley, addressed to "My Brother Abraham, who lives in the country," are the very effervescence of ridicule. They will be read when test acts are remembered only to be execrated. They will preserve them from the rottenness of oblivion. They are inimitable—capable of driving the blues from the cloister of an Archbishop. In the preface to his works, Mr. Smith says: "I have printed in this collection the letters of Peter Plymley. The Government of that day took great pains to find out the author. All that they *could* find was, that they were brought to Mr. Budd, the publisher, by the Earl of Lauderdale. Somehow or other it came to be conjectured that I was that author. I have always denied it. But finding that I deny it in vain, I have thought it might be as well to include the letters in this collection. They had an immense circulation at the time, and I think above 20,000 copies were sold." This is cool. But the letters were *cooler*. They gibbeted the absurd opposition which his Episcopal brethren made to emancipation, "without benefit of clergy." The services of Mersrs O'Connell and Shiel will be noticed in the next chapter.

CHAPTER XIII.

Catholic Emancipation—Antiquity and Power of the Papal Church—Treaty of Limerick—Catholic Penal Code of Ireland—Opinions of Penn, Montesquieu, Burke, and Blackstone, concerning it—Its Amelioration—Catholic Association of 1823—The Hour and the Man—Daniel O'Connell elected for Clare—Alarm in Downing Street—Duke of Wellington's Decision—Passage of the Emancipation Bill—Services of O'Connell and Shiel—The latter as an Orator.

THE subject-matter of this chapter will be, the Catholic Penal Code, and its repeal by act of Parliament, in 1829.

The antiquity and power of the Roman Hierarchy, and the sway it now holds over 150,000,000 of people, diffused through all quarters of the globe, is one of the most extraordinary facts in the history of the Christian era. Whether the combined efforts of Protestanism to overthrow it, during the next three centuries, will be more successful than during the three since the Reformation, time only can show. In his review of Ranke's History of the Popes, speaking of the Catholic Church, Macaulay says: "She saw the commencement of all the governments, and of all the ecclesiastical establishments, that now exist in the world; and we feel no assurance that she is not destined to see the end of them all. She was great and respected before the Saxon had set foot on Britain—before the Frank had passed the Rhine—when Grecian eloquence still flourished at Antioch—when idols were still worshiped in the temple of Mecca. And she may still exist in undiminished vigor when some traveler from New England shall, in the midst of a vast solitude, take his stand on a broken arch of London Bridge, to sketch the ruins of St. Paul's."

Amongst the adherents to the Papal faith, none have shown a steadier attachment to it, through all vicissitudes, than the Catholics of Ireland. For centuries it has been the dominant, and at times almost exclusive, religion of that country. Persecutions the most bigoted and bloody have not abated the zeal and tenacity with which the Irish have practiced and clung to their hereditary creed. The battle of the Boyne, in 1690, was followed by the Treaty of Limerick, by which William of Orange guaranteed in the most solemn terms religious toleration to his Irish Catholic subjects. The treaty was to be binding upon him, his heirs, and successors. But, a fear of the return of the banished Catholic princes of the house of Stuart, mingled with a propagandist zeal to convert Ireland to the doctrines of the Reformation, induced England to disregard the stipulations of the Treaty of Limerick. Partly by the direct legislation of the British Parliament, and partly through the medium of the Pale, a *quasi* Legislature of Ireland, the Catholic Penal Code was introduced into that country. Like other branches of British law, it was a piece of patchwork, the contribution of many reigns. It received its worst features within twenty years after the Treaty of Limerick. I will give a summary of its main provisions.

FIRST, *as to persons professing the Catholic religion.* No Papist could take the real estate of his ancestor, either by descent or purchase; nor purchase any real estate, nor take a lease for more than thirty-one years; and if the profits of such lease exceeded a certain rate, the land went to any Protestant informer. The conveyance of real estate in trust for a Papist was void; nor could he inherit any, nor be in a line of entail, but the estate descended to the next Protestant heir, as if the Papist were dead. A Papist who turned Protestant succeeded to the family estate; and an increase of jointure was allowed to Papist wives on their turning Protestant; whilst, on the other hand, a Protestant who turned Papist, or procured another to turn, was guilty of high treason. Papist fathers were debarred, on a penalty of £500, from being guardians of their children; and a Papist minor, who avowed himself a Protestant, was immediately delivered to a Protestant guardian. No Papist could marry a Protestant, and the priest celebrating the marriage was to be hanged. Papists could not be barristers; and being Protestants, if they married Papists they were to be treated as Papists. It was a felony for a Papist to teach a school; to say or hear mass subjected him to fine and a year's imprisonment; to aid in sending another abroad, to be educated in the Popish religion, subjected the parties to a fine, and disabled them to sue in law or equity, to be executors and administrators, to take any legacy or gift, to hold any office, and to a forfeiture of all their chattels, and all real estate for life. No Papist could hold office, civil or military, sit in Parliament, or vote at elections. Protestants, robbed by privateers in a war with a Popish prince were to be indemnified by levies on the property of Catholics alone.

SECOND, *as to Popish recusants*, i. e., persons not attending the Established Church. Such Papists could hold no office, nor keep arms, nor come within ten miles of London, on pain of £100, nor travel above five miles from home without license, on pain of forfeiting all goods, nor come to court on pain of £100, nor bring any action at law or equity; and to marry, baptize, or bury such an one subjected the offending priest to heavy penalties. A recusant married woman forfeited two-thirds of her dower or jointure, nor could she be the executrix of her deceased husband, nor have any part of his goods; and during coverture she might be imprisoned, unless her husband redeemed her at the rate of £10 per month. All other recusant females must renounce Popery or quit the realm; and if they did not leave in a reasonable time, or afterwards returned, they could be put to death.

THIRD *as to Popish priests*. Severe penalties were inflicted on them for discharging their ecclesiastical functions anywhere, and if done in England they were liable to perpetual imprisonment. Any such priest who was born in England, and, having left, should come in from abroad, was guilty of treason, and all who harbored him might be punished with death. Rewards were given for discovering Popish clergy, and any person refusing to disclose what he knew of their saying mass, or teaching pupils, might be imprisoned a year. A Popish priest who turned Protestant was entitled to £30 per annum. Besides this, they were subject to all the penalties ana disabilities of lay Papists.

FOURTH. Papists were excluded from grand juries; in all trials growing out of the Penal Code, the juries were to be Protestants; and in any trial on statutes for strengthening the Protestant interest, a Papist might be peremptorily challenged.

In surveying the lineaments of such a Code, the blood of a statue might glow with indignation, or chill with horror. It was inflicted on Catholic Ireland by Protestant England, in the name of that Church which claims to be the pillar and ground of the Christian faith. Well might the mild William Penn be aroused to denounce it as inhuman, when pleading before the House of Commons for toleration to the Quakers. Well might the sagacious Montesquieu characterize it as cold-blooded tyranny. Well might the philosophic Burke describe it "as a machine of wise and elaborate contrivance, noted for its vicious perfection; and as admirably fitted for the oppression, impoverishment, and degradation of a people, and the debasement in them of human nature itself, as ever proceeded from the perverted ingenuity of man." Even Blackstone, who usually selected his choicest eulogies for the darkest features of the English law, was forced to say of this Code: "These laws are seldom exerted to their utmost rigor; and, indeed, if they were, it would be very difficult to excuse them." Yes, though in the times when the "No-Popery" cry was at its hight, these laws were rigorously enforced, yet, as the mellowing light of civilization increased, the more cruel lay a dead letter on the statute book. But the whole hung over the head of the Catholic, like the sword of Damocles, ready to drop at the breath of any persecuting zealot or malicious informer.

This Code was essentially ameliorated in 1779, and again in 1793. Among other concessions, the electivef ranchise was extended to Catholics, though they were still excluded from Parliament. But, he who would bring himself within the pale of these ameliorations, must submit to many degrading and annoying requisitions, in the form of registrations, oaths, subscriptions, declarations, &c. In a word, down to 1829, when it was finally repealed, many of the worst features of the Code remained, making it an offense for seven-eighths of the people of Ireland to worship God according to the dictates of their consciences; subjecting them to degrading tests or heavy penalties for exercising precious civil and social rights; goading them with athousand petty and provoking annoyances, till they had come to be regarded as heathens while bowing at Christian altars, and aliens to a Government under which they were born, and to whose support they were compelled to contribute their blood in war, and their money in peace. To all this, one may enter his protest, while holding at arm's length the Catholic ritual. To worship God according to the dictates of his own conscience, without human molestation or earthly fear, is the divine right of every man, whether he be Irish Catholic or English Protestant, Massachusetts freeman or Louisiana slave.

Notwithstanding the important amendments made in the Catholic Code, in 1779 and 1793, its remaining disabilities and penalties hung over Ireland like a dark cloud, shutting out the sun of civil and religious freedom. In the latter year, an association was organized in Dublin, to agitate and petition for Repeal. Though ultimately rent in pieces by internal commotions, it was the germ of all subsequent organizations for the same objects. During the succeeding thirty years, this question frequently convulsed Parliament and the country. The remedies which the British Government usually prescribed for the political and religious diseases of Ireland were insurrection acts, coercion acts, suspensions of the *habeas corpus*, capital trials, hangings, and transportation, administered by the batons of the police and the bayonets of the soldiery.

The year 1823 saw a bright star of promise arise on the dark and troubled horizon of Hibernia. The exigencies of the times had healed the feuds of hostile factions among the Emancipationists, and they closed hands in defense of their common liberties. In May, of that year, Daniel O'Connell and Richard Lalor Shiel, who had long been estranged from each other, accidentally met among the mountains of Wicklow, at the house of a friend. A reconciliation took place, and they resolved to form a league for the deliverance of their enslaved Catholic countrymen. The same month they organized the "Catholic Association," in Dublin, on the plan of admitting all persons, of whatever sect or party, who approved its objects. It early enrolled some of the first minds in the island, who commenced an agitation which was soon felt in the fartherest corner of the kingdom, nor stopped till it brought back responses from France, Germany, the United States, Canada, the East Indies, and other distant countries. It made the realm vocal with its orators, crowded Parliament with its petitions, and scattered its tracts over the Continent. O'Connell and Shiel were the life and soul of the Association; the former being its chief manager, the latter its most brilliant advocate.

Undoubtedly some of the transactions of this almost omnipotent body were of an inflammatory character. But it gave concentration and rational aim to the efforts of the oppressed Irish, and, by exciting the hope of relief, withdrew from them the temptation to illegal acts of violence. The justice of its object, and the contempt which its petitions received from Parliament, ultimately rallied to its standard the whole of the Catholics and an influential portion of the dissenting Protestants of Ireland. Alarmed at its power, the session of March, 1825, after a stormy debate, passed an act terminating its existence. Immediately after the adjournment of Parliament, the Association was reörganized, with a constitution which did not come within the law. At the session of 1826, finding that the agitation could not be silenced, various efforts were made to ameliorate the condition of Ireland. After spending five months in vehement discussion, Parliament abandoned the country to the rage of party spirit, and it was left for the well-directed labors of the Association to prevent it from plunging into anarchy and revolution.

At the general election in the summer of 1826, the friends of Emancipation took the field and achieved some signal triumphs in returning members to Parliament. The Irish tenantry, the "forty-shilling freeholders," who had generally been supple instruments in the hands of the Protestant landlord, to perpetuate his domination and their chains, had, by the labors of the Association, been converted into an engine to overthrow the oppressors. They now voted with the Emancipators.

Canning rose to power in 1827. His professed regard for Catholic relief induced Ireland to wait and see what would come from his ministry. His early death quenched all hope of succor from his administration. After the repeal of the Corporation and Test Acts the next year, a struggle for partial relief to the Catholics, which resulted successfully in the Commons, but was defeated in the Lords, only stimulated the friends of Emancipation to take a bolder step. The hour to strike the decisive blow had come, and it brought with it the man.

In 1828, Mr. Fitzgerald, the member for Clare, received a place in the cabinet, thus vacating his seat in the Commons. He was a candidate for reëlection. The Catholic Association requested Mr. O'Connell to become a candidate for the vacancy, and in his own person seek to establish the right of Catholics to sit in Parliament. He immediately issued an address to the electors of Clare, in which, among other things, he said: "Fellow-countrymen, your county wants a representative. I respectfully solicit your suffrages, to raise me to that station. * * * * You will be told I am not qualified to be elected. The assertion is untrue. I am qualified to be elected, and to be your representative. It is true that, as a Catholic, I cannot, and of course never will, take the oaths at present prescribed to members of Parliament. But the authority which created those oaths can abrogate them. And I entertain a confident hope that, if you elect me, the most bigoted of our enemies will see the necessity of removing from the chosen representative of the people an obstacle which would prevent him from doing his duty to his king and to his country."

The address fell like a thunderbolt upon the enemies of Emancipation. The friends of Fitzgerald would not believe it was the intention of O'Connell to seriously contest the canvass. The speedy arrival of two of his agents in Clare dispelled their doubts. The county was in a boil of excitement. The day of election approaches. Shiel addresses a concourse of electors. His eloquence inspires a wild enthusiasm in their hearts. The time for the arrival of the great agitator himself is fixed. An immense throng hails him, with banners, music, and shoutings. The trial day comes, and the candidates appear before assembled thousands of the electors. Fitzgerald delivers an able speech. O'Connell rises and pronounces a magnificent harangue, which sways the passions of the peasantry as forests wave when swept by the wing of the tempest. A violent contest ensues, and at its close the high-sheriff declares that "Daniel O'Connell, Esq., is duly elected a member of the Commons House of Parliament for the county of Clare."

This unexpected result carried dismay into the councils of Downing street; for they knew that O'Connell was soon to appear in London and demand his seat in Parliament. His fame was no stranger to the place where his person was unknown. His reputation had long ago penetrated every mansion and cabin in the realm. The agitation of the past five years, whose tread had shaken Ireland from Cape Clear to the Giant's Causeway, had ever and anon caused the walls of St. Stephen's to tremble. And now, what seemed so terrible in the distance, was to be brought to its very doors. Parliament was not in session; but it had been announced that ministers would oppose Mr. O'Connell's entrance into the Commons. The declaration drove Ireland to the brink of civil war. The commander of the forces conveyed to the ministry the alarming intelligence, that the troops were fraternizing with the people, and their loyalty could not be relied on in the event of an outbreak. All minds not besotted with bigotry felt that the great right for which the Association had contended must be conceded. The Duke of Wellington, then at the head of the government, saw that the hour had come when either his prejudices or his place must be surrendered. He decided that the former must yield. Parliament was convened on the 5th of March, 1829. On the first day of the session, Mr. Peel moved that the House go into committee, "to take into consideration the civil disabilities of his Majesty's Roman Catholic subjects." After two days' debate, it prevailed. A bill of Emancipation was introduced. Ancient hatred was aroused, and in five days sent in a thousand petitions against its passage. The bill passed, after a severe struggle, and Mr. Peel carried it to the Lords. A fierce contest ensued, but it was forced through by the Iron Duke. On the 13th of April it received the royal assent, and was hailed with joy by the friends of religious freedom, whilst bigotry went growling to its den.

Mr. O'Connell appeared in the House to claim his seat. Having been elected before the act of Emancipation, the ancient oaths were tendered to him. He declined to take them. After tedious hearings before the Committee of Elections, extending through several weeks, and a powerful address at the bar of the House in support of his own right, his seat was declared vacant. He returned to Ireland, and was everywhere hailed as "the Liberator of his country." After walking over the course of Clare, he repaired to Westminster, and "the member for all Ireland" took his seat in the British House of Commons.

For this great concession to the Genius of Toleration, the age is indebted to the Catholic Association, organized and sustained by O'Connell and Shiel, the Castor and Pollux of Emancipation. No two men were more perfect antagonisms in the prime elements of their characters, and no two more harmoniously blended in the accomplishment of a common object. Each supplied what was wanting in the other. O'Connell was unsurpassed in planning, organizing, and executing, and his unique and vigorous eloquence could stir to its bottom the ground tier of Irish society. Shiel was rich in the highest gifts of oratory, ornate, classical, impassioned, and could rouse the enthusiasm and intoxicate the imaginations of the refined classes of his countrymen. The one contributed to the work, the learning and skill of an acute lawyer, the knowledge of a well-read historian of his country, an intimate acquaintance with all the details of the great question at issue, and business capacities of the first order. The other gave to it a transcendent intellect, adorned with the genius of a poet, the graces of a rhetorician, and the embellishments of a polite scholar. Both consecrated to it intense nationality of feeling, quenchless perseverance, and indomitable courage. Each yielded to the other the exclusive occupancy of the peculiar field of labor to which his talents were best adapted.

Mr. Shiel was born in 1791. In his youth, he won a high literary reputation as the author of two tragedies, *Evadne* and *The Apostate*, and some beautiful essays in the periodicals. He early acquired an enviable reputation at the Dublin bar as an advocate. But "the guage and measure of the man" were known to a comparatively small circle till his splendid oratorical displays in defense of the principles and objects of the

Catholic Association made his fame coëxtensive with the empire. The result of his services has been recorded. To apply to himself what he so graphically said of Grattan, "The people of Ireland saw the pinnacles of the Establishment shattered by the lightning of his eloquence." The Emancipation bill opened to him the doors of Parliament. He entered its hall in 1831, heralded by a reputation surpassing that with which most orators have been content to leave that field of their triumphs. It is the highest proof of the solidity of his reputation, that in this new arena he increased the brilliancy of his fame, being a marked exception to the rule, that orators who have become famous at the bar, or the hustings, or on the platform, have failed to meet the public expectation on encountering the severer tests of the House of Commons.

Several years ago I heard Mr. Shiel deliver a speech in Parliament, and I retain a vivid impression of his powers. He seemed the very embodiment of all that was gorgeous and beautiful in the arts of rhetoric and oratory. His sentences rushed forth with the velocity of a mountain torrent, while for an hour and a half he poured down upon the House a ceaseless shower of metaphor, simile, declamation, and appeal, lighted with the brilliant flashes of wit, and mingled with the glittering hail of sarcasm. He belongs not to the best school of oratory, but is master of that in which he was trained: There is no rant or fustian in his speeches, for they are eminently intellectual. Though polished in the extreme, they are pure ore, and sparkle with real gems. His ornaments are lavishly put on, but are never selected from the tinsel and mock diamond mine. His defect is, that he too much discards logic, and revels in rhetoric. In discussing even an appropriation bill, his figures are drawn less from the annual budget of the Chancellor of the Exchequer than from the perennial springs of Helicon. He aims to reach the heart, not through the reason, but the reason and the heart through the imagination. While his oratory lacks the logical power and majestic strength which bear aloft the poetic imagery and affluent illustration of Choate, it partakes largely of those embellishments that give brilliancy and grace to the eloquence of our distinguished countryman. He is no more like Brougham or Webster, than a dashing charge of Murat at the head of his cavalry is like a steady fire from a park of artillery.

As a specimen of his oratory, I subjoin an extract from one of his speeches. In 1837, Lord Lyndhurst declared, in the Upper House, that the Irish were "aliens in blood and religion." Shortly after, Mr. Shiel thus repelled the charge in the Commons. Lord L. was a listener.

"Where was Arthur, Duke of Wellington, when those words were uttered? Methinks he should have started up to disclaim them.

'The battles, sieges, fortunes that he passed'

ought to have come back upon him. He ought to have remembered that, from the earliest achievement in which he displayed that military genius which has placed him foremost in the annals of modern warfare, down to that last and surpassing combat which has made his name imperishable—from Assaye to Waterloo—the Irish soldiers, with whom your armies were filled, were the inseparable auxiliaries to the glory with which his unparalleled successes have been crowned. Whose were the athletic arms that drove your bayonets at Vimiera through the phalanxes that never reeled in the shock of war before? What desperate valor climbed the steeps and filled the moats of Badajos? All, all his victories should have rushed and crowded back upon his memory: Vimiera, Badajos, Salamanca, Abuera, Toulouse—and, last of all, the greatest. Tell me, for you were there—I appeal to the gallant soldier before me, (pointing to Sir Henry Hardinge,) who bears, I know, a generous heart in an intrepid breast—tell me, for you must needs remember, on that day when the destinies of mankind were trembling in the balance; while death fell in showers upon them; when the artillery of France, leveled with the precision of the most deadly science, played upon them; when her legions, incited by the voice, inspired by the example of their mighty leader, rushed again and again to the contest; tell me if for an instant, when to hesitate for an instant was to be lost, the 'aliens' blanched? And when, at length, the moment for the last decisive movement had arrived; when the valor, so long wisely checked, was at last let loose; when, with words familiar but immortal, the great captain exclaimed, 'Up, lads, and at them!'—tell me if Catholic Ireland with less heroic valor than the natives of your own glorious isle precipitated herself upon the foe! The blood of England, Scotland, Ireland, flowed in the same stream, on the same field. When the chill morning dawned, their dead lay cold and stark together. In the same deep pit their bodies were deposited. The green spring is now breaking on their commingled dust. The dew falls from heaven upon their union in the grave. Partakers in every peril, in the glory shall we not participate? And shall we be told, as a requital, that we are estranged from the noble country for whose salvation our life-blood was poured out?"

Though approaching the verge of good taste, conceive of the present effect of such an outburst gushing from the lips of Shiel, the perspiration standing in drops on his knotted locks, his eye kindled with Milesian fire, every feature of his expressive countenance instinct with passion, every limb of his small but symmetrical frame trembling with emotion, his shrill but musical voice barbing every emphatic word!

Since he entered Parliament, Mr. Shiel has acted with the liberal Whigs, has held office under Lord John Russell, and generally declined the lead of Mr. O'Connell. He stood aloof from the Repeal agitation, though he defended O'Connell, when on trial for Conspiracy some four years ago, with the ability and eloquence of his brightest days.

CHAPTER XIV.

Movements toward Parliamentary Reform—John Cartwright—The Father of Parliamentary Reform—His Account of the Trials of Hardy and Tooke—Lord Byron's Eulogium of him—His Opinions of the Slave Trade—The First English Advocate of the Ballot—His Conviction for Conspiracy—His Labors for Grecian and Mexican Independence—William Cobbett—His Character, Opinions, and Services—His Style of Writing—His Great Influence with the Middling and Lower Orders of England—Sir Francis Burdett—His Labors for Reform—His Recantation.

GRANT to the people of England universal suffrage and equal Parliamentary representation, and all other reforms will ultimately follow. The present century has taught the masses and the statesmen of that country, that, to wield influence over its Government, it is not necessary to occupy official stations. I am about to note some occurrences in the life of one who taught and illustrated the truth, that power and place are not synonymous terms—one who exerted much sway over public affairs for fifty years, one whose services were wholly of a popular character, he never having held office. I allude to JOHN CARTWRIGHT. His name is appropriately introduced previous to noticing the passage of the Reform Bill, for, no man did more than he to create a public opinion which demanded that great measure. By universal consent he was called "THE FATHER OF PARLIAMENTARY REFORM."

Mr. Cartwright was born in 1740. He entered the navy as a midshipman, saw a great deal of hard fighting, reached the post of first lieutenant, became distinguished for his science and skill in the service, and at the age of thirty-four abandoned the seas, and turned his mind to politics. In 1774, he published *Letters on American Independence*, addressed to the House of Commons, in which he took radical ground in favor of the rights of the Colonies. "It is a capital error," says he, "in the reasonings of most writers on this subject, (the rights of man,) that they consider the liberty of mankind in the same light as an estate or chattel, and go about to prove or disapprove the right to it, by grants, usage, or municipal statutes. It is not among moldy parchments that we are to look for it; it is the immediate gift of God; it is not derived from any one, but it is original in every one." Here we have the pioneer idea of our own Declaration of Independence, uttered by an unknown Englishman two years before that immortal paper saw the light. In 1776, an event occurred which put Major Cartwright's principles (he had been appointed major in the Nottinghamshire militia) to a severe test. He was always proud of the navy, and ambitious of promotion in the service. Lord Howe, who had witnessed his courage and skill, having taken command of the fleet to act against the American Colonies, urged Cartwright to take a captaincy of a line-of-battle ship. He was then paying his addresses to a lady of high family, whose friends would consent to her accepting his hand if he would accede to the proposal of Lord Howe. He declined, thereby losing the favor both of Mars and Hymen. This led to an acquaintance with the gallant Lord Effingham, an officer of the army, who proved himself a genuine nobleman by resigning his commission rather than act against "the rebels."

Cartwright now (1776) commenced the work to which he devoted the remaining years of his laborious and useful life—*Parliamentary Reform.* At the outset, he took the ground now occupied by the Chartists. In his first two pamphlets—and they were the earliest English productions on reform in the House of Commons—he maintained that equal representation, universal suffrage, and annual elections, were rights inherent in the body of the people. His system closely resembled that engrafted upon the United States Constitution twelve years later. This shows him a man of rare sagacity for the times, far in advance of his cotemporaries, and not a whit behind the most radical American patriots. The next year he presented an address to the King, urging peace with his Colonies, and a union with them on the basis of independent States. He organized, the same year, England's first association for promoting Parliamentary reform, called the " Society for Political Inquiry." Soon after, Cartwright stood twice for Parliament, but was unsuccessful, partly on account of his radical principles, and partly because he would not stoop to any form of bribery, not even " treating," declaring that "he would not spend a single shilling to influence the electors."

He continued to agitate for reform, by pamphlets, speeches, and correspondence, till, in 1781, he organized the celebrated " Society for Constitutional Information," which enrolled many of the first names in the kingdom, and to which Tooke belonged when tried for treason in 1794. Cartwright wrote the first address of the Society. It received the high encomiums of Sir William Jones, who said it ought to be engraven upon gold. The ship of Parliamentary Reform now glided smoothly, Cartwright being the chief pilot, when the French revolution burst upon the world. He hailed it as the dawn of a political millennium, and, filled with joy, he addressed a congratulatory and advisory letter to the French National Assembly. But, the skies of France, so bright at the rising of the revolutionary sun, soon became darkened, and the clouds poured down blood and fire upon the land, covering the friends of liberty in England with sorrow and dismay. The Reign of Terror in France was followed by a Reign of Terror in England. In the former, the victims were royalists. In the latter, radicals. In the former, Robespierre and the guillotine executed vengeance. In the latter, George III and the Court of King's Bench. Large numbers erased their names from the proscribed roll of the Society. Cartwright, Tooke, and a resolute band, resolved to stand by their principles and pledges, and brave the royal anger, come life, come death. The particulars of the treason trials which followed, I have already given.

Some of Cartwright's friends besought him to stand aloof from Tooke and his "brother traitors." He was too brave and true a man to desert his associates in the ordeal hour. He addressed a letter to the Secretary of State, asking permission to visit Tooke in the Tower, avowing that it had been the greatest pleasure of his life to coöperate with him for Parliamentary reform; and if his friend was a felon, and worthy of death, so was he. He has left interesting memoranda of the trials at the Old Bailey. He says, "Gibbs spoke like an angel" in Hardy's case, and that Erskine became so exhausted, toward the close of the trial, that, in arguing incidental points to the court, an intermediate person had to repeat what he said to the judges. He conveyed intelligence of the result of Hardy's case to his family in the country, in terms as terse as Cæsar's celebrated military dispatch: "*Hardy is acquitted. —J. C.*" He was a witness in Tooke's case. On the cross-examination of the Attorney General, though cautioned by the court not to criminate himself, he scorned all concealment, avowing that the objects of the Constitutional Society were to obtain equal representation, universal suffrage, and annual Parliaments, and replying to the caution of the judges, that "he came there not to state what was prudent, but what was true." When questioned about some expressions of his, as to "strangling the vipers aristocracy and monarchy," he said he had no recollection of using the terms, but, if he had, and they were applied to aristocracies and monarchies hostile to liberty, he thought them well deserved. He says Tooke grappled with the prosecuting counsel with the strength and courage of a lion. When a paper was produced, and Tooke was asked to admit his handwriting, the Chief Justice cautioned him not to do so hastily. Turning to his Lordship, he said, "I protest, before God, that I have never done an action, never written a sentence, in public or private, never entertained a thought on any political subject, which, taken fairly, with all the circumstances of time, occasion, and place, I have the smallest hesitation to admit." How the stout-hearted integrity of such men, in such a trying hour, puts to eternal shame the servile tricks and fawning arts of the common scum of office-hunting politicians.

The treason trials of 1794 being over, Cartwright resumed his work, and for some eight years seems to have been the only active man of character and standing in the enterprise—the others having cowered before the persecuting spirit of the times. In 1802, a ludicrous occurrence showed the suspicious state of the Governmental mind. The Major had a brother, Dr. George Cartwright, who was celebrated as a mechanician, being the inventor of the power-loom, and other valuable machines. He had taken out patents for them—these had been extensively infringed—and he had commenced suits against the violators. The Major was assisting him in procuring evidence; and for that purpose he had dispatched an agent to Yorkshire, with a letter of instructions, which had a good deal to say about *levers*, *cranks*, *rollers*, and *screws*. The messenger was arrested as a joint conspirator with the Major for the overthrow of his Majesty's Government, by means of some "infernal machine"—the phrases in the letter being interpreted to cover a dark design to "put the screws" on the King. Ascertaining that his agent was in *limbo*, Cartwright wrote to the Attorney General, offering to explain the matter. The Crown officer was not to be caught so. Indict and hang the conspirator he would, in spite of power-looms and militia majors. At length the facts became known, and the astute Attorney was glad to back out of the ridiculous scrape by an apologetic letter to the parties.

It would require a volume to record all that our patriot did for Parliamentary reform from 1804, when it had a limited revival, till 1824, when he died. Though he was sixty-four years old at the commencement of this period, and eighty-four at its close, he did more during these twenty years to procure for Englishmen their electoral rights, than any other ten persons in the kingdom. He published scores of pamphlets, written in a style, bold, lucid, and going to the roots of the controversy; convened hundreds of meetings in all parts of the country, to which he addressed able speeches; sent thousands of petitions to Parliament; formed numerous societies; and conducted a never flagging correspondence with the leading friends of liberty and reform. In 1810, he sold his farm and removed to London, that "he might be near his work." Brave old heart of oak, of threescore years and ten! The next year, thirty-eight persons were seized at Manchester while attending a reform meeting, and sent fifty miles to prison, on a charge of sedition. Cartwright went down to aid in preparing their defense and attend the examination. Having procured their release, he took a circuitous route home, getting up meetings and petitions on the tour. He was arrested, taken before a magistrate, his papers and person searched, when, finding nothing worthy of death or bonds upon him, he was discharged. Vainly endeavoring to obtain a copy of the warrant on which he was arrested, he subsequently presented the case by petition to the House of Peers. Lord Byron, the poet, in supporting the petition, said of him: "He is a man, my lords, whose long life has been spent in one unceasing struggle for the liberty of the subject, against that undue influence of the Crown which has increased, is increasing, and ought to be diminished; and, whatever difference of opinion may exist as to his political tenets, few will be found to question the integrity of his intentions. Even now, oppressed with years, and not exempt from the infirmities attendant on age, but unimpaired in talent, and unshaken in spirit, *frangas, non flectes*, he has received many a wound in the combat against corruption; and the new grievance, the fresh insult, of which he now complains, may inflict another scar, but no dishonor."

In 1814, he addressed a series of letters to Clarkson on the slave trade—he having taken an active part in the contest for its abolition—in which he argued that it should be punished as piracy, a doctrine which he was the first to broach. He also wrote against bribery at elections, and in favor of voting by ballot, being the first English advocate of that measure. A year or two after this, a mercenary widow of one of his old Scotch correspondents wrote to him that the Government had offered her a large sum if she would give up his letters—adding, significantly, that the circumstances of her family were such, that she thought she should comply with the offer. He extinguished her hopes of extorting money from him by informing her, that "it gave him great satisfaction to find that any of his letters were esteemed so valuable, and begged her to make the best bargain she could of their contents." In 1816, the great number and imposing character of the demonstrations in favor of Parliamentary reform alarmed the Government. Canning, in the House of Commons, denounced Cartwright as "that old heart in London, from which the veins of sedition in the country are supplied." The kingdom was in a flame—the *habeas corpus* act was suspended—and the "Six Acts," aimed at the Irish Catholic associations, and the English reform meetings, were adopted. Cobbett, the editor of the Register, fled to America. Others left their ears on the pillory at home, or carried them at the request of the Government to Botany Bay. Cartwright, who never flinched from friend or foe, stood his ground, and contrived new modes to keep up the agitation, evading the recent law against "tumultuous petitioning," by getting up *petitions of twenties*, and in various ways avoiding the prohibitions of the "Six Acts."

So far, he had kept out of the fangs of the law, excepting in the affair of searching his person. But, the Attorney General had his eye upon him. In 1819, he participated in the famous Birmingham proceedings, which resulted in the appointment, on his suggestion, of a "Legislatorial Attorney" for the town, who was to present a letter to the Speaker of the Commons, as its representative. This measure of "sending a petition in the form of a living man, instead of one on parchment," as he called it, precipitated the long-expected crisis. He was indicted for conspiracy and sedition, in Warwickshire. So soon as he heard of it, he set off by post to meet the charge, traveling one hundred miles in a single day, though then bowed down with the weight of fourscore years. Putting in bail, he returned to London, and resumed his work. Soon after, he presided at a reform meeting, drew up a petition, couched in the most energetic terms, signed it, sent it to the Commons, and then set about exposing the attempts of the Crown officers to pack the jury which was to try him. The trial took place in August, 1820. He called no witnesses; addressed the jury mainly in defense of his principles; was convicted; was not called up for sentence till the next May; when the judge, after eulogizing his general character, condemned him to pay a fine of £100, and stand committed till it was paid. He immediately pulled out a canvass bag, counted down the money in gold, slily remarking to the sheriff, that they were all "*good sovereigns.*"

When the heroic struggles of Greece, South America, and Mexico, resounded through Europe, they had no more attentive listener than Major Cartwright. Seizing his never-idle pen, he wrote "Hints to the Greeks"—a letter to the President of the Greek Congress—and another to the Greek Deputies. About the same time, he opened his doors to two of the liberal leaders in the Spanish Revolution, who had sought refuge in England. His sun was now declining. He had attended his last reform meeting in 1823; he wrote his last political pamphlet in 1824. In July of this year, he received a letter from Mr. Jefferson, who said, "Your age of eighty-four and mine of eighty-one years, insure us a speedy meeting;

we may then commune at leisure on the good and evil which, in the course of our long lives, we have both witnessed." He had taken a deep interest in the Mexican struggles for liberty, and frequently conferred with General Michelena, its envoy then in London, upon its affairs. On the 21st of September, 1824, the General sent to inform him that the scheme of Iturbide had failed, and that the liberty of Mexico might be considered as established. Two days afterward, "the father of Parliamentary reform" died, retaining his faculties and his fervent love of freedom to the last. He cheerfully resigned himself into the hands of his Maker, exclaiming, "God's will be done!"

Among the remarkable men who, like Cartwright, helped to prepare the public mind for the Reform Bill, and like him illustrated the truth, that power and place are not necessarily synonymous terms, is WILLIAM COBBETT, whom the "Corn-law Rhymer" calls England's

"Mightiest peasant-born."

His name is familiar on both sides of the Atlantic, and is much mixed up with good and evil report. He was no negation or neutral, but a man of mark, that left his impress on the age. He was not only one of the most voluminous, but one of the boldest and most powerful writers of the present century. Ever in the thickest of the strife, his "peasant arm" dealt goodly blows in the contests of the People with the Crown, during the last thirty years of his turbulent life. Cobbett was born in 1762. His father was a poor yeoman, who brought his son up to hard work and Tory principles. He never went to school, but was literally self-taught, learning even the alphabet without a teacher. He says: "I learned grammar when I was a private soldier on the pay of sixpence per day." Having committed Lowth's Grammar to heart, he used to make it a rule to recite it through from memory every time he stood sentry. He enlisted in the army when he was twenty-one, and served eight years in the British American colonies. He was discharged, returned to England, married, made a short tour in France, whence he embarked for the United States, arriving in New York in 1792. He was a violent Tory—joined the anti-French party—commenced publishing—attacked with ferocity Priestley, Franklin, Rush, Jefferson, Dallas, Monroe, Gallatin, Fox, Sheridan, Bonaparte, Talleyrand, and a score of other great men—was arrested, and compelled to give bail in a heavy sum for his good behavior—was sued for a libel by Dr. Rush, who recovered five thousand dollars damages—fled from Philadelphia to New York, where the execution overtook him—was thrown into prison—the judgment was paid by his admirers—he left the country, and arrived in England in 1801. While in America, he wrote under the name of "Peter Porcupine," and on his return to England published his writings in twelve volumes. They had a large circulation among the Anti-Jacobins, who received him with open arms. He had previously sent an account of his trans-Atlantic "persecutions" to the "Loyal Society" of London, "to be used as a panacea for the reformists, and the whole gang of liberty-men in England."

He started a paper in London in 1801, called "The Porcupine," which supported Pitt and the Tories, and attacked Fox and the Whigs, much after the style of his Philadelphia writings. He suspended the publication of "The Porcupine," and commenced his celebrated "Weekly Political Register" in 1802, which he continued till his death, a period of thirty-three years. This journal has given him an enduring name among the political writers of his times. For two or three years, it advocated High Toryism. Wyndham was enamored of it, and stated in the House of Commons, that its editor deserved a statue of gold. Wyndham promised to introduce Cobbett to Pitt. The latter declined to see him. The editor was deeply mortified at this rebuff of the aristocratic minister. Immediately thereafter, and probably *therefore*, Cobbett changed his politics, and from a high Church and King man, turned to be a radical reformer and champion of the people. The first public demonstration of the somerset was a violent philippic against the Irish Tory administration. He was prosecuted for libels, both at London and Dublin, on the Lord Lieutenant, Chancellor, Chief Justice, and Under Secretary for Ireland, and was fined a thousand pounds. This prosecution only stimulated his new-born zeal for liberalism. He sharpened his weapons, and plunged them into the bowels of his old friends as vigorously as he had before done into those of their enemies, sparing neither Church nor State, Ministry nor King. The Register soon became the terror of evil-doers. Its denunciations of profligate statesmen and rotten institutions were so bold and hearty, and its columns breathed such an air of defiant independence, that it was sought for with avidity by the radicals of the middling and lower orders, and the income as well as the fame of its editor became largely increased.

But Cobbett never could sail long in smooth water. Like the petrel, he loved the storm. In 1810, he was prosecuted for a libel on the Government, contained in an article reflecting in indignant terms on the brutal flogging of a company of the local militia, under the *surveillance* of a regiment of German mercenaries. He defended himself, was convicted, and sentenced to pay a fine of one thousand pounds, be imprisoned two years, and give sureties for his good behavior for seven years in five thousand pounds. He never forgot or forgave this injury. Two other prosecutions of editors grew out of the same transaction. They were defended by Brougham in two splendid speeches, which introduced the rising barrister to a first place among the forensic orators of the kingdom. The circulation of the Register had increased steadily from year to year; and soon after this trial, Cobbett continuing to edit it while in prison, it reached an unprecedented sale, some weeks numbering one hundred thousand copies. Its vigorous assaults on the Government conspired with the other reform move-men s of the times to cause the repeal of the *habeas corpus*, and the passage of the infamous "six acts," by which the ministry hoped to crush the agitators.. To avoid the blow aimed at him, Cobbett fled to America early in 1817, where he remained nearly three years. He regularly remitted "copy" across the Atlantic for the Register, which continued a pungent thorn in the side of Castlereagh and his friends, though the hand which wielded it was three thousand miles away.

Returning to England in 1820, he established a daily paper, which failed—tried to introduce the cultivation of Indian corn into the country, which failed—stood a candidate for Parliament for Coventry, and failed—defended himself against two prosecutions for libel, and failed, paying fines to the amount of nearly two thousand pounds—plunged into the Queen Caroline controversy with his brother liberals, and did *not* fail—advocated Catholic emancipation, and saw it succeed—made an attempt to enter Parliament for Preston, and was defeated—took an active part in all the agitations for Parliamentary reform—defended himself in a speech of six hours against a prosecution for sedition, growing out of an article in the Register in favor of the Reform Bill, the jury being discharged because they could not agree—and finally was reprimanded by the Speaker, for giving three cheers in the gallery of the Commons, when the bill passed the House. In 1832, he reached the acme of his ambition, by being returned to the first reformed Parliament for the borough of Oldham. But it is a rare tree that will bear transplanting in the sere and yellow leaf of advanced age. Cobbett was threescore years and ten when he took his seat in the House of Commons. Though he made a few vigorous speeches, he did not fulfill the expectations of his friends, nor exhibit the power and originality in debate which the public anticipated from the editor of the Political Register. He closed his stormy life in 1835.

Cobbett has been called "a bold, bad man." Bold he was; but, he was not as bad as the times in which he lived, nor the institutions he assailed. He was a man to be feared rather than loved—to be admired rather than trusted. But he was a MAN, "for a' that." He never croaked or *canted*—never whined or repined—was proud, self-willed, self-reliant—knew his strength, and asked no favors and showed no quarter. His idiosyncrasies, his egotism, his self-dependence, rendered it next to impossible for anybody to work with him even to attain a common end. He was the victim of prejudice, conceit, passion, and seemed not to advocate a cause so much from love of it, as from hatred of its opposite. He bent his great energies to tear down existing institutions, whilst he lent but feeble aid in building up others in their place. He hated all that was above him in birth and station, and his appeals usually being to the prejudices and passions of the class from which he sprang, he wielded a vast influence over the common people of England. They were proud of his attainments, because they regarded him as one of themselves, who had risen, by his own strength, to a commanding position among the leaders of public opinion, and they witnessed with pride his ability to grapple with and hurl to the earth, the titled champions of the privileged orders. Thus, more than any other writer, he was, for thirty years, looked up to as the representative, the oracle, of the "base born" of his countrymen. It contributed not a little to his influence with the ground tier of British society, that he was a practical farmer, in a moderate way—the great sale of his writings affording him the means of gratifying his cultivated tastes for agricultural pursuits. Taking it for granted that established systems, opinions, and institutions, were necessarily wrong, he attacked everything that was old, and everybody that was popular. He avowed that he attacked Dr. Rush's system of medical practice, because it originated with a republican—he called Washington "a notorious rebel and traitor"—nicknamed Franklin "Old Lightning-rod"—denounced Lafayette as "a citizen-miscreant"—and abused Jefferson because he was a popular democrat. But this was in the days of his toryism. However, when a radical, he showered ridicule on Shakspeare, Milton, and Scott, because all the *literati* praised them, and eulogized O'Connell, because all Englishmen anathematized him.

But, the objects of his assaults were not always so undeserving of it, nor so ill assorted. He exposed the land monopoly of England, and vindicated the rights and dignity of labor—he laid bare the rapacity of the Established Church, and maintained the rights of Catholics and dissenters—he denounced the game laws, the corn laws, and the penal code—he advocated the abolition of the House of Lords, and the bestowment of universal suffrage upon the people. It was impossible for a man of such giant powers and rooted prejudices, who had received the iron of persecution so often in his own person, and who was always in the thickest of the fray, to speak calmly or with measured words. Consequently, his writings abound in malevolent epithets, unmitigated vituperation, and coarse ridicule of men and measures. So do they abound in right good sense, cogent reasonings, elevated appeals to justice and humanity, interspersed with racy humor, graphic descriptions, happy illustrations, and lively anecdotes. The basis of his style was the old Saxon tongue, and it was as idiomatic and lucid as that of Franklin or Paley. He wrote on numerous subjects besides politics; and, in addition to the eighty-eight volumes of the Register, and the twelve of his Peter Porcupine, he put to press nearly fifty volumes. He was kind to his family, hospitable to the poor, and had a great deal of sunshine in his soul. He will be gratefully remembered by enfranchised Englishmen, when milder and meaner men, who affected to look down upon him with contempt, are forgotten, or are recollected only to be despised.

I close this notice of the great English peasant, by quoting the closing stanza of a beautiful tribute to his memory, by Ebenezer Elliott, the author of "Corn Law Rhymes."

"Dead Oak, thou liv'st. Thy smitten hands.
The thunder of thy brow,
Speak with strange tongues in many lands,
And tyrants hear thee NOW!"

Sir FRANCIS BURDETT has been mentioned as a friend of Parliamentary Reform. Few Englishmen did more for the cause than this bold advocate of liberal principles. Few titled Reformers have suffered more for opinion's sake than he. It was his good or bad fortune to be frequently caught in the net of legal prosecution. In 1809, Sir Francis then being a member of Parliament, a Mr. John Gale Jones, whose name would never have got beyond his shop had it not become associated with that of Burdett, published a handbill animadverting, in terms of clumsy abuse, upon some proceedings of the House of Commons; whereupon, that body of honorables committed him to Newgate. Sir Francis brought forward a motion for his liberation, based on the ground that the House had no right to imprison him for such an offense. Being defeated, he published an address to his constituents, in which he applied some contemptuous epithets to this contemptible proceeding. A furious debate sprang up, which terminated in a resolution to commit Burdett to the Tower. The Sergeant-at-Arms went to his house with the warrant of committal, but Sir Francis refused to accompany him to his new abode. The next day he repeated his visit; but by this time the populace had assembled in great numbers around the dwelling of the Baronet, and drove away the officer. Early the following morning, he broke into his apartments, seized Burdett, put him into a carriage, and bore him to the Tower, accompanied by several regiments of dragoons, where he remained in close confinement till the end of the session. The day of his release, all London was out of doors, and he was welcomed home with shoutings, flags, and salutes of cannon. In 1819, Sir Francis having continued to fight the good fight during the intervening ten years, a great reform meeting was held at Manchester, in the open air. All was orderly till a regiment of cavalry rode in upon the multitude, and, with drawn swords, cut down men, women, and children, leaving many dead and wounded on the field. Sir Francis published a manly letter to the electors of Westminster, (he being the representative of that great constituency,) commenting in eloquent terms on this infamous transaction. He was indicted for a seditious libel; and after contesting the prosecution, inch by inch, through all the courts—not so much for his own sake as for that of the great cause with which he was identified—he was fined £2,000 and imprisoned three months. To read the case, as reported in the English law books, will make the cheek of a republican lawyer tingle with indignation. These, and some other like occurrences in his life, have led candid observers to regard Sir Francis Burdett as something of a demagogue. He had a spice of that element in his composition. He was a bold, straight-forward man, who told plain truths in a plain way, whether addressing letters to his constituents, or speeches to the Commons House of Parliament. He often stood alone among his colleagues, cheered by the conviction that, though no member voted with him, he was supported by the voices of hundreds of thousands of the people. He was a great reader, a sound thinker, an able debater, and always exerted a controlling influence over the more radical portions of the House. His frequent letters to his constituents were dignified and pungent, cost him a good deal of persecution and money, and were worth all they cost. In 1818, he was chosen, with his friend Romilly, to represent the important borough of Westminster, after one of the bitterest contests modern England has known. He retained the seat through many years. In all the onsets upon corruption and prerogative, down to the era of the Reform bill, he was with the head of the liberal column, and stood where the blows fell thickest and heaviest, the idol of the people, the target of the crown. He was a Wilkes, without so large a measure of cowardice, meanness, turbulence, or rottenness of character and principle.

One regrets to be compelled to record of such a man, that in his old age he grew timid and conservative. After the passage of the Reform bill, he ceased to act with the radicals, and on the occasion of the attempt to deprive the Irish Church of a portion of its temporalities, he went wholly over to the Tories, since which he has sunk into comparative obscurity. Some years ago, in reply to a speech of Lord John Russell, he spoke of "the cant of reform!" Lord John electrified the House when he retorted with cutting emphasis, that "there was such a thing as the *re*-cant of reform!"

CHAPTER XV.

Parliamentary Reform—Old House of Commons—Rotten Boroughs—Old Sarum—French Revolution of 1830—Rally for Reform—Wellington Resigns—Grey in Power—Ministerial Bill Defeated—New Parliament Summoned—Commons Pass the Bill—Brougham's Speech in Lords—Peers Throw out the Bill—Mrs. Partington—Riots—Again Bill Passed by Commons, and again Defeated by Peers—Ministers Resign—Are Recalled—The Bill becomes a Law.

The House of Commons was instituted in the thirteenth century, when Henry III summoned the counties of the realm to send knights, and the principal cities and boroughs to send citizens and burgesses, to Parliament. This was done rather to afford him a check upon his arrogant barons, and to procure the sanction of "*the Commons*," (as the untitled property-holders were called,) to certain subsidies, than to vest in them any independent functions. But, this "third estate" continuing to be summoned in subsequent reigns, its influence increased with the wealth and intelligence of the middle classes, whom it represented, till what was long regarded by them as a burden came to be cherished as a right and a privilege; and a supple instrument, originally used by the monarch to strengthen his prerogative, gradually became the weapon of the democracy, to cripple its powers and limit its boundaries.

At first, all the counties, and the largest cities and boroughs, were summoned. Subsequently, as other towns rose to importance, they were added to the list. In process of time, as trade fluctuated, drying up old channels and opening new, many of the ancient cities and burghs fell into decay. Still, they sent representatives to Parliament. In 1509, the House consisted of 298 members, many of them even then representing very small constituencies. From that period, down to the passage of the Reform bill, no place was disfranchised, (except two or three for bribery,) while 255 members were added (including Scotland and excluding Ireland,) by the creation of new and the revival of old burghs. During the six centuries which the House had existed, what changes had passed over the kingdom, sweeping away the foundations of once populous marts, and causing others to rise on barren wastes!

Here we have the origin of "*rotten boroughs*;" i. e., towns which, centuries ago, had a flourishing existence, continuing to send representatives to Parliament long after any human being had made his local habitation therein, and whose very names would have perished from the land, but that they were annually recorded on the Parliamentary rolls. One of these has been immortalized by the discussions on the Reform bill—Old Sarum. Not a soul had dwelt there since the Tudors ascended the English throne—not a tenement had been seen there since Columbus discovered America—nor could the vestiges of its ruins be traced by the antiquarian eye of a Champollion or a Stephens. This sand-hill, in 1832, sent as many members to Parliament as Lancashire, with a population of a million and a half. Other represented boroughs were nearly in like condition; others could display their half score or more of decayed hovels. In the case of these rotten boroughs, the owner of the land, or of the old franchises, who was generally a wealthy Peer, sometimes an aspiring London attorney, occasionally an avaricious stock-jobbing Jew, by virtue of his single vote designated the representatives. Subject to the mutations of other real estate and franchises, they were transferable by private bargain, or auction, or sheriff's sale, or will, or assignment of a bankrupt's effects, or as security for a gambling debt. Not only were they instruments of corruption, but ludicrous libels on the claim of the House of

Commons to represent the people, and striking illustrations of extreme inequality in the distribution of political power.

An East India Prince, the Nabob of Arcot, once owned burghs entitled to twenty members of Parliament; and through his English agent, who held the parchment titles, he sent that number to the Commons. A waiter at a celebrated gaming-house sat for years in Parliament in this wise. He loaned money to a "noble" gambler, who gave him security for the loan on a rotten borough, which sent a member. The waiter elected himself to the seat. In the debates on the Reform bill, it was stated that certain places, with an aggregate population of less than 5,000, returned one hundred members. Old Sarum, Gatton, Newtown, and other decayed boroughs, exerted a controlling influence on British legislation, long after some of them had ceased to be the abodes of humanity; whilst Manchester, Birmingham, Leeds, and other important towns, swarming with life, and rich in arts and manufactures, had not a single representative. The elective franchise was very restricted, and generally based on absurd qualifications. Scores of members were chosen by close corporations, while others were designated by single individuals. The essence of the system is concentrated in the general fact, that, in 1832, less than two hundred persons, mostly of the "privileged orders," actually returned a majority of the House of Commons.

So enormous an evil was not without an occasional mite of good. Though these coroneted traffickers in Parliamentary seats usually bestowed them on favorites of their own class, there were some notable exceptions to this rule. John Horne Tooke, the most radical of all reformers, sat for Old Sarum, the rottenest of all rotten boroughs. Brougham entered the Commons through the narrow door of a "nomination borough," though he left it with the plaudits of the largest constituency in the kingdom. Burke, Romilly, Mackintosh, and other illustrious and liberal names, were indebted to close corporations for their introduction to Senatorial fame.

This system, the slow growth of centuries, was in full play at the ascension of William IV. It was destined to a speedy overthrow. Early in 1830, a simultaneous movement towards the long-deferred reform was made throughout Great Britain and Ireland. George IV died, and William IV ascended the throne, on the 26th of June, 1830. In the following month, the people of France rose and drove the Bourbons from their kingdom. The news descended upon the already excited mind of England like an animating spirit. The mass heaved with the throes of new life. The reformers held meetings in every important town, to congratulate their brethren of France on the expulsion of the elder Bourbons. Drawn together by the bonds of a common sympathy, they realized how numerous and powerful a body they were. The election for a new Parliament occurred in September. Liberal candidates sailed with the popular current. The result showed a great diminution of the supporters of Wellington and Peel. Parliament met in November. The cry of "Reform!" was ringing from the "unions" and "associations," which the last four months had seen established in every considerable town and village in the country. The king's speech made no allusion to the subject that absorbed all minds. In the exciting debate on the address to the throne, Earl Grey came out boldly for a radical reform in Parliament. Wellington, in reply, assumed the most hostile ground, declaring that, "so long as he held any station in the Government, he should resist to the utmost any such measure." The announcement that ministers were determined to cling to a system whose rotting props had been for years falling away, astonished and inflamed the Opposition. Fifteen days afterwards, ministers were brought to their senses, by being placed in a minority in the lower House, on a financial question. The next day, the Iron Duke in the Peers, and the supple Peel in the Commons, announced that they had relinquished the helm of affairs!

The Duke of Wellington resigned on the 16th of November,

1830. The King immediately authorized Lord Grey to form an administration, upon the basis of Parliamentary reform—the first liberal ministry, with the exception of a few turbulent months, for sixty-five years! Lords Grey, Durham, John Russell, Althorp, Lansdowne, Holland, and Mr. Brougham, were its leading spirits; its subordinates being made up of the Melbournes, the Palmerstons, and other converted Canningites. Parliament adjourned till February, to afford the new Cabinet time to perfect its plan. While Downing Street was anxiously cogitating the details of the great measure, its friends stimulated public sentiment in every part of the empire. On the 1st of March, 1831, Lord John Russell brought forward, in the House of Commons, the ministerial plan for a reform in Parliament. A summary of its leading provisions, as finally adopted, is subjoined.

It was a compromise between representation and prescription, on the three principles of disfranchisement, enfranchisement, and extension of the suffrage. The number of members, 658, was not altered, but their distribution was changed. The ultra rotten borough system was exploded. In England, 56 burghs were wholly disfranchised, 31 others partially, whilst 41 new towns were enfranchised, part receiving two members, others one. The large cities and counties received an increase of members. The same principles were less extensively applied to Scotland and Ireland.

The qualifications of electors were essentially modified, and the aggregate more than doubled. Property, in most cases, still continued to be the basis of the right of suffrage The greatest change was in the cities and burghs. In those, throughout the United Kingdom, the occupier of a building of the yearly value of £10, whether he owned or rented it, could vote for the local members. The ancient rights of voters, in burghs not disfranchised, were partially preserved, but provision was made for their gradual extinction. It was supposed that the bill added more than half a million to the number of

Parliamentary electors. In 1838, the number of electors registered was 978,816. It has since exceeded a million.

The sweeping character of the bill surpassed public expectation, and produced an electric effect upon the country; the reformers hailing it with enthusiasm, whilst the champions of old abuses were stricken with horror. Mr. Hume, the leader of the radicals, declared that "it far exceeded his highest hopes." Sir Charles Wetherell, the oracle of the legal formalists, denounced it as "a corporation robbery." Mr. Macaulay, the organ of the philosophic reformers, pronounced it "a great, noble, and comprehensive plan." Sir R. H. Inglis, the representative of the bigotry of Oxford University, said, "the plan of ministers meant revolution, not reformation."

All parties girded themselves for such a conflict as England had not witnessed for a century. After an inveterate contest of three weeks, the English bill (one for each kingdom was introduced) passed its second reading in the House by a majority of only one. A day or two afterwards, an amendment was carried against ministers, by a majority of eight. Immediately thereupon ministers announced that they should dissolve Parliament, and appeal to the people. At this suggestion, the Opposition broke through all restraint, and denounced them as revolutionists and traitors. They dreaded the appeal, for they knew the country was with the ministry. The Tory Peers resolved on the desperate measure of preventing the dissolution, by arresting the reading of the king's speech. The day came, and brought with it a scene of uproar in both Houses, which baffles description. A cotemporary writer says:

"A hope had remained, that the project of stopping the king's speech, and interposing an address, might succeed. That hope rested entirely upon the speech being read by the Chancellor, (Brougham,) and not by the king in person. Suddenly the thunder of the guns was heard to roar, breaking the silence of the anxious crowds without, and drowning even the noise that filled the walls of Parliament. In the fullness of his royal state, and attended by all his magnificent Court, the monarch approached the House of Lords. Preceded by the great officers of state and of the household, he moved through the vast halls, which were filled with troops in iron mail, as the outside courts were with horse, while the guns boomed, and martial music filled the air. Having stopped in the robing chamber in order to put on his crown, he entered the House and ascended the throne, while his officers and ministers crowded around him. As soon as he was seated, he ordered the usher of the black rod to summon the Commons; and his Majesty, after passing some bills, addressed them. By those who were present, the effect will not soon be forgotten, of the first words he pronounced, or the firmness with which they were uttered, when he said that 'he had come to meet his Parliament in order to prorogue it, with a view to its immediate dissolution, for the purpose of ascertaining the sense of his people in regard to such changes in the representation as circumstances might appear to require.' He then, with an audible voice, commanded the Lord Chancellor to prorogue; which being done, the Houses dispersed, and the royal procession returned amidst the hearty and enthusiastic shouts of thousands of the people."

Great praise is due to the "Sailor King" for the firmness with which he stood by his reform ministers in this crisis, despite the clamors of alarmists in Church and State.

At the elections, the friends of the bill swept the country. They carried nearly all the counties, and all the cities and large towns. Its opponents obtained their recruits chiefly from close corporations and rotten boroughs. The English bill was proposed in the New House on the 24th of June, and, after a running fight of three months, passed the Commons by 109 majority, and was sent to the Lords. The greatest anxiety was felt for its fate in that refuge of ancient conservatism. The debate on the second reading continued four nights. On the last evening, October 7th, Lord Brougham spoke five hours in its support, making the great effort of his remarkable life. His speech was an era in the history of that House.

He replied *seriatim* to the opponents of the measure, dissecting this lord with keen logic, scathing that marquis with impassioned rebuke, holding this duke's ignorance up to ridicule, putting down the effrontery of that viscount, basting this earl with the oil of flattery while he roasted him with intense reasoning, and bringing to the defense and elucidation of the bill those rich stores of learning, argument, eloquence, wit, sarcasm, denunciation, and appeal, which have given him an undying name. The radical boldness of his doctrines, and the *abandon* with which he demolished "illustrious dukes," or tore the drapery from "noble lords," were no less remarkable features of this speech, than its transcendent ability. Lord Dudley, probably the first scholar and the most polished orator in the House, had sneered at "the statesmen of Birmingham, and the philosophers of Manchester." Brougham repelled the sneer, and, in a passage of keen severity, contrasted Lord Dudley's accomplishments with the practical sense of the men he had traduced, closing it by saying, "To affirm that I could ever dream of putting the noble earl's opinions, aye, or his knowledge, in any comparison with the bold, rational, judicious, reflecting, natural, and, because natural, the trustworthy opinions of those honest men, who always give their strong sense fair play, having no affectations to warp their judgment —to dream of any such comparison as this, would be, on my part, a flattery far too gross for any courtesy, or a blindness which no habits of friendship could excuse."

He brought his great speech to a close, by uttering this solemn warning:

"My lords, I do not disguise the intense solicitude I feel for the event of this debate, because I know full well that the peace of the country is involved in the issue. I cannot look without dismay at the rejection of this measure. But, grievous as may be the consequences of a temporary defeat—temporary it can only be—for its ultimate, and even speedy success, is certain. Nothing can now stop it. Do not suffer yourselves to be persuaded that, even if the present ministers were driven from the helm, any one could steer you through the troubles which surround you, without reform. But our successors would take up the task in circumstances far less auspicious. Under them, you would be fain to grant a bill, compared with which, the one we now proffer you is moderate indeed. Hear the parable of the Sybil; for it conveys a wise and wholesome moral. She now appears at your gate, and offers you mildly the volumes, the precious volumes of wisdom and peace. The price she asks is reasonable; to restore the franchise which, without any bargain, you ought voluntarily to give. You refuse her terms, her moderate terms. She darkens the porch no longer. But soon, for you cannot do without her wares, you call her back. Again she comes, but with diminished treasures. The leaves of the book are in part torn away by lawless hands; in part defaced with characters of blood. But the prophetic maid has risen in her demands—it is Parliaments by the Year—it is Vote by the Ballot—it is Suffrage by the Million! From this, you turn away indignant, and for a second time she departs. Beware of her third coming; for the treasure you must have; and what price she may next demand, who shall tell? It may be even the mace which rests upon that woolsack. What may follow your course of obstinacy, if persisted in, I cannot take upon me to predict, nor do I wish to conjecture. But this I well know—that, as sure as man is mortal, and to err is human, justice deferred enhances the price at which you must purchase safety and peace; nor can you expect to gather in another crop than they did who went before you, if you persevere in their utterly abominable husbandry, of sowing injustice and reaping rebellion. . . You are the highest judicature in the realm. It is a judge's first duty never to pronounce sentence, in the most trifling case, without hearing. Will you make this the exception? Are you really prepared to determine, but not to hear, the mighty cause upon which a nation's hopes and fears hang? You are! Then beware of your decision! Rouse not a peace-loving but resolute people. Alienate not from your body the affections of a whole empire. I counsel you to assist with your uttermost efforts in preserving the peace, and upholding and perpetuating the Constitution. Therefore I pray and exhort you not to reject this measure. By all you hold dear—by all the ties that bind every one of us to our common order and our common country, I solemnly adjure you, I warn you, I implore you, yea, on my bended knees, I supplicate you, reject not this bill!"

The warning and the appeal were in vain. The bill was thrown out on the second reading by 41 majority. The struggle for the mastery between the people and the nobility had now come. The Commons adopted a strong vote of confidence in ministers, and ministers resolved to stand by the bill. Parliament was prorogued till December. In the vacation, reform meetings assembled in unprecedented numbers. On one of these occasions, at Taunton, Sydney Smith first brought to notice a venerable matron whose name is likely to be immortal in both hemispheres. In the course of his speech, the witty divine said:

"I do not mean to be disrespectful, but the attempt of the Lords to stop the progress of reform reminds me very forcibly of the great storm of Sidmouth, and of the conduct of the excellent Mrs. Partington on the occasion. In the winter of 1824, there set in a great flood upon that town—the tide rose to an incredible hight—the waves rushed in upon the houses, and everything was threatened with destruction. In the midst of this sublime and terrible storm, Dame Partington, who lived upon the beach, was seen at the door of her house with mop and pattens, trundling her mop and squeezing out the sea-water, and vigorously pushing away the Atlantic Ocean. The Atlantic was roused. Mrs. Partington's spirit was up; but I need not tell you that the contest was unequal. The Atlantic Ocean beat Mrs. Partington. She was excellent at a slop, or a puddle, but she should not have meddled with a tempest. Gentlemen, be at your ease—be quiet and steady. You will beat Mrs. Partington."

A few riots gave diversity to the scene. At Derby, the mob demolished the property of some anti-reformers—they terribly frightened Sir Charles Wetherell, at Bristol—they burnt the

Duke of Newcastle's turreted seat, at Nottingham—they smashed the windows of Apsley House, the town residence of the Duke of Wellington. The country was profoundly agitated, and the firmness of ministers averted a revolution.

Parliament met in December. The king's speech urged reform. Lord John introduced the English bill, slightly improved. A factious opposition, and an adjournment for the holidays, kept it suspended till the 22d of March, 1832, when it passed the Commons, and was sent to the Lords. After a hot debate, it passed the second reading, when a hostile amendment, which destroyed its utility, was sprung upon the House and adopted, on the 7th of May. The next day, Lord Grey asked, according to a previous understanding, for the creation of a sufficient number of Peers to carry the bill. The King declined. Ministers instantly resigned. The Commons addressed the King in behalf of ministers, with rare boldness. The people assembled *en masse*, and petitioned the Commons to stop the supplies. Many meetings resolved to pay no more taxes till the bill became a law. The King requested Wellington to form a compromise administration. At this proposal, the popular indignation was kindled afresh. Things were approaching a fearful crisis. The Duke tried to execute the royal wish—the ultras of both parties were not invited to seats in the Cabinet—the half-and-half reformers would not come through fear—and he gave up the task in despair. The King recalled Grey, with a pledge to create new Peers, if necessary. This brought the refractory Lords to terms. Dreading the introduction of so large a body of liberals into their ancient hall, whose votes would avail the reformers in future contests, a sufficient number of Tories absented themselves from the Peers to insure the passage of the bill. Those who remained concentrated, in their dying denunciations, the venom of the entire opposition. The English bill received the royal assent on the 7th of June, 1832. The Scotch and Irish bills speedily followed, and the month of July, after a two years' contest, which had shaken the empire to its center, saw the new Constitution of the House of Commons established.

Though the Reform bill has not proved to be so large a concession to the popular demands as was intended, nor as beneficial to the country as was anticipated, it was the greatest tribute to the democratic principle which the nation had paid since the Commonwealth. Its defects will be discussed when we examine the Chartist movement.

CHAPTER XVI.

Henry Lord Brougham—His Life, Services, and Character.

In connection with the passage of the Reform bill, it is proper to notice one of the foremost Englishmen of this century—Henry Brougham. Nothing strikes one more forcibly in the life of this extraordinary person than the number and variety of the subjects upon which he has exerted his powers. His published speeches and writings on either one of several of the political measures he has advocated, if viewed merely as intellectual efforts, might satisfy the ambition of an honorable aspirant after forensic or literary fame. The aggregate constitutes hardly a tithe of his achievements in the cognate departments of public affairs. From his entrance into the House of Commons down to the present time, his name glows on every page of England's parliamentary history; and his posterity will permit but few of the myriad rays that encircle it to be effaced or obscured. As an advocate and a jurist, many of his speeches at the bar and opinions on the bench will live long after the law of libel and the court of chancery cease to oppress and vex mankind. His services in the cause of popular education, whether we regard the time expended, the ability displayed, or the results attained, surpass the labors of many persons who have been assigned to a foremost place among the eminent benefactors of their age. His contributions to the Edinburgh Review, covering its whole existence, and a large circle of literary, scientific, political, social, legal, and historical subjects, would class him with the highest rank of periodical essayists. His more substantial works, as Sketches of Eminent Statesmen, History of the French Revolution, Lives of Men of Letters and Science, Discourse on Natural Theology, Political Philosophy, composed amidst the cares of public official station, would suffice to give him an enduring name in the republic of letters.

Great as are his mental achievements, it is as the early advocate of social progress and political reform—the champion of liberty and peace, the friend of man—that he is worthy of all his cotemporaneous fame, and all the applause which coming generations will bestow on his memory. Inconsistency, the common infirmity of mortals, has checkered his course—eccentricity, "the twin brother of genius," has been his frequent companion—independence, whose adjacent province is obstinacy, he has largely exhibited ; but, while the history of England, during the first third of the nineteenth century, remains, it will display to the impartial eye few names to excite more grateful admiration in every lover of his race than that which, from the abolition of the slave trade in 1806, to the abolition of slavery in 1834, was synonymous with intelligent progress and useful reform.

I believe Brougham was born about the year 1779. We first hear of him, when twenty years old, in Edinburgh, communicating some papers on geometry to the Royal Society in London, which were highly applauded, and translated into foreign tongues. In 1808, he appeared as counsel at the bar of Parliament, in behalf of the commercial and manufacturing interests, against the celebrated *Orders in Council*, which followed the Berlin Decree of Napoleon, and preceded the American Embargo. His examination of witnesses, extending through several weeks, and his closing argument, gave him a high reputation in England, and a name both in Europe and the United States. In 1809–10, he entered the theater where, for forty years, he has displayed his extraordinary gifts. His first published speech in Parliament, delivered in 1810, was a powerful appeal in favor of addressing the Throne for more effectual measures to suppress the slave trade. His next great effort was in 1812, when, assisted by Mr. Baring, (Lord Ashburton,) he examined witnesses for several weeks before the House of Commons, to prove that the still unrescinded Orders were ruining the trade and manufactures of the country, and provoking a war with the United States. At the close, he supported an address to the Throne for their repeal, in a speech replete with information, ably defending the policy of unrestricted commerce, and eloquently vindicating the superiority of the arts of peace over the glories of war. The motion prevailed—but too late to avert hostilities. Congress declared war the very day the speech was delivered.

His services in the cause of the people from this time downward, have been referred to in these chapters, as various subjects have passed under consideration. During the long and almost hopeless struggle of Liberty with Power, from 1810 to 1830, when he was removed from the theater of his greatest fame, he led the forlorn hope in the House of Commons. Unlike his great prototype, Fox, he never for a moment retired from the field in disgust and despair, but was ever at his post, stimulating the drooping spirits of his friends, hurling defiance at his foes, and rising from every defeat with renewed courage and strength. Though classified among the heads of the Opposition in the House, he never was—he never would be, in the strict sense, a party "leader." Nor, on the contrary, did he surround himself with a "clique" or "interest," whose oracle he was. Supporting the measures of the Whigs, he was ever in advance of them, cheering on the masses, as the Tribune of the people, and fighting the partisan battles of Reform as the guerrilla chief of Liberty.

In an evil hour, he was transplanted from his "native heath" to the conservatory of the aristocracy. Though surrounded by uncongenial spirits, and haunted with the nightmare of conservatism, the soul of McGregor retained for years much of its original fire in a place whose chilling atmosphere made the lion blood of a Chatham to stagnate and curdle. Some of his mightiest efforts in the good cause were put forth after he *descended* to the upper House of Parliament.

Had Brougham coveted and obtained "leadership" in its party sense, in either House, he must have failed. Too original, independent, wayward, and dogmatical, to be implicitly trusted and obeyed by his equals; too incautious and pushing; too impatient of dullness; too much of a genius, to be always appreciated and confided in by his inferiors, though he would have been applauded by the masses; yet his premiership, had he accepted the offer of King William, could not have long survived the passage of the Reform bill. With the exception of taking the great seal, he has chosen to be what he is—a rare comet, created to move in no orbit but its own—beautiful and lustrous in the distance, but grand and terrible in proximity.

The public measures with which he is most closely identified are—the advocacy of the manufacturing and commercial interests, as opposed to Orders in Council and other restrictions on trade; hostility to the continental combinations of the successors of Pitt, and their legitimate offspring, exhausting wars and the Holy Alliance; the vindication of Queen Caroline, in the struggle with her libertine husband; the freedom of the press, attempted to be overawed by prosecutions for libels on the Government and the church; the education of the middle and lower orders; religious toleration for dissenters and Catholics; reform in the civil and criminal law; parliamentary reform; municipal reform; poor laws reform; the abolition of the slave trade and slavery; retrenchment in Government expenditures; the independence of the Canadian Legislature, and the repeal of the corn laws. What a catalogue have we here! Upon all these measures, each of which was an era in British history, Brougham has acted a leading, and upon many, a controlling part. His speeches upon most of them surpassed those of any other of their advocates, whether we consider the extent of the information displayed, the depth and energy of the reasoning, the scope and vigor of the style, the eloquence of the appeals to justice and humanity, or the majesty and splendor of the higher passages.

Lord Brougham's fame, as an orator, has filled two hemispheres. We will look at him in the two aspects of matter and manner.

The four volumes of his speeches, with others gleaned from the Parliamentary reports, prove that his reputation is well founded. Their leading characteristic is power—crushing power—as distinguished from beauty and grace. They are not so gorgeous as Burke's, nor so compact as Webster's. But they contain more information and argument, and less philosophy and fancy, than the former's—more versatility and vigor, and less staid grandeur and studied method, than the latter's. As *speeches*, rather than *orations*, addressed to a deliberative body of friends and foes, who are to *act* upon the subject under discussion, they are more practical and to the matter in hand than Burke's; more hearty and soul-stirring than Webster's. Their style is a mixture of Burke and Webster—less extravagant anywhere than some passages of the former; frequently more slovenly than any passage of the latter; with more of bitter personal taunt and lofty rebuke of fraud, meanness, and oppression, than either. Viewed as literary productions, regardless of the immediate fruits they produced, they will hardly stand the test of posthumous fame like Burke's. Less universal in their application, less penetrated with principles adapted alike to all times, they often betray the advocate instead of the statesman, the partisan rather than the philosopher, the leader and champion of cotemporaries rather than the instructor and mentor of posterity. But it still remains a question, whether they were not the more valuable on that very account. Their immediate effect in moving masses of men, and molding public measures, far surpassed that of Burke's. And though the *words* of the latter may outlive those of the former, we have the highest authority for saying, blessed are those whose *works* survive them.

Lord Brougham's speeches deal little in mere declamation, even of the highest order, but are pregnant with apposite facts and arguments, giving the reader or hearer an unusual amount of information upon the matters under discussion. He excels, when he tries, in a plain, lucid statement of his subject; as witness, his speech on law reform, in 1828, when, for seven hours, he held the close attention of the unprofessional House of Commons, while he sketched the absurdities and abuses of every branch of the common law, and detailed the amendments he proposed in its principles and administration. But this is not his *forte*, and for that very reason his dexterity and self-control excite our admiration the more. If you would see him in his greatest moods, you must give him a person or a party to attack, which shall arouse his combative propensities, and bring his invective and sarcasm into full play; or some giant abuse to anathematize and demolish, which shall inflame his indignation and abhorrence.

We gather from his own statements that the garb and colors in which he attires the main body of a speech—the mere style and diction—are the impulse of the occasion; as most of the sarcasms and rebukes are flung out in the heat of delivery. But, where time for preparation is afforded, no speaker is more careful in arranging the general drift of the argument, and digesting the facts to illustrate and sustain it; whilst certain passages, such as the exordium or peroration, are the result of the most pains-taking labors of the closet. He has recorded that the peroration of his speech in the Queen's case was written no less than ten times before he thought it fit for so august an occasion. The same is probably true of similar passages in Webster's speeches; it is known to be so of Burke's.

No orator of our times is more successful in embalming phrases, full of meaning, in the popular memory. The well-known talismanic sentiment, "*The schoolmaster is abroad*," is an instance. In a speech on the elevation of Wellington, a mere "military chieftain," to the premiership, after the death of Canning, Brougham said: "Field Marshal the Duke of Wellington may take the army—he may take the navy—he may take the great seal—he may take the miter. I make him a present of them all. Let him come on with his whole force, sword in hand, against the Constitution, and the English people will not only beat him back, but laugh at his assaults. In other times, the country may have heard with dismay that 'the soldier was abroad.' It will not be so now. Let the soldier be abroad if he will; he can do nothing in this age. There is another personage abroad—a personage less imposing—in the eyes of some, perhaps, insignificant. The school-master is abroad; and I trust to him, armed with his primer, against the soldier in full military array."

Turning from the matter to the manner of the orator, (if we have not already passed the boundary,) Brougham stood unrivaled as a debater in the House of Commons. For twenty years he swayed the intellect and passions of the House, by his muscular and courageous eloquence, whilst Castlereagh, Canning, and Peel controlled its majorities and dictated its measures, by the wave of their official wand. Castlereagh was more self-possessed and matter-of-fact than he; Canning more brilliant and classical; Peel more dexterous and plausible. But, in weight of metal, he surpassed them all. His oratory was not the brawl and foam of a dashing mountain torrent, but the steady roar of the deep, broad cataract. In ability to inflame friends and foes, and shake the House till it quaked, he equaled either Chatham or Fox. When thoroughly roused, with all his elements in full play, he thundered and lightened till the knights of the shire clung to the Benches for support, the Ministers cowered behind the Speaker's chair for shelter, and the voting members started from their slumbers in the side galleries, as if the last trump were ringing in their ears.

Chatham introduced the style of the House of Commons into the debates of the House of Lords. Brougham's appearance there constituted almost as new an era in its oratory as the advent of Chatham. It was my good fortune to hear him two or three times in the Lords, several years ago—once when his best powers were put in action for a brief hour.

We enter the House of Peers. The lions—Brougham, Grey, Wellington, Lyndhurst, Melbourne—are in their places. An exciting debate is going forward, which has taken rather a personal turn. Yonder is Brougham, stretched out half his length on one of the Ministerial benches ; now listening to a clumsy Earl on the floor, whom he eyes with a portentous scowl ; anon whispering a hurried word to the Peer at his elbow. What an ungainly figure ! Those long legs and arms, loosely hung in their sockets, give him a slouching air. Human face could hardly look more ugly or intellectual. His iron-gray hair bristles over his forehead like the quills of the fretful porcupine. His restless eye peers through eyebrows that seem alive with nerves. He must be agitated with the debate, for he writhes as though his red cushion were a sheet of hot iron. He suddenly starts up, (who ever knew him to sit still five minutes ?) walks with long strides toward the door, and while chatting with the ladies, his tormentor stops, and the ex-Chancellor cries, with startling emphasis, (lest some one get the floor before him,) "My Lords !" and slowly advances to the table in front of the woolsack. An audible *hush* runs round the chamber ; for they had been anticipating a reply from the mercurial lord. Every whisper ceases, and all eyes are fixed on the towering intellect before them. The Peeresses leave their damask chairs, and approach the bar, to get a better view of the orator. Members of the House of Commons, till now chatting round the bar, lean forward in silence. The loungers in the lobbies enter the Hall, the word having passed out, "Brougham is up !" The untitled spectators rise from their seats on the carpet, where fatigue had sunk them, and stand on tiptoe, to catch every glance of the eye and wave of the hand of the scholar and statesman, whilst the crowded galleries forget their lassitude in listening to one whose name and fame are the property of mankind.

But to the speech. Listen to that first sentence! How it plunges into the very center of the subject. Every word is an argument—every period a demonstration. The first blow knocks the keystone from his last antagonist's speech, and tumbles the whole structure on his affrighted head and shoulders. And the dandy young Lord, over in the corner, who, in the puny oration he recited so prettily an hour ago, went out of his way to sneer at Brougham—see the blood fly from his cheeks when his nice little piece of rhetoric comes rattling in bits round his ears. As the lion fixes his eye on him, he would give his coronet and his curls if he could slink into a nutshell. A fiery glance or two having withered him, the monarch of the debate grapples with worthier antagonists. What a sweep does he give to the argument—what redundancy of facts—what fertility of illustration. How large the field of his comprehension—how exhaustless and varied its resources. What execution is done by those long-drawn sentences, with parenthesis within parenthesis, each a logical syllogism, or a home-thrust fact, or a blighting sarcasm, wound round and round his victims, till they are crushed in their folds! Great in matter, his speech is equally powerful in manner; violating every law of rhetoric and oratory promulgated by the schools, he is a law unto himself—original, commanding, majestic.

Brougham, having demolished his antagonists, took a seat at the clerk's table, and began to write a letter, when the Chancellor (Cottenham) rose and commenced a conciliatory speech. His calm, slow, cool manner contrasted strongly with the tempest which had just passed over our heads, reminding us of those dewy showers which follow smilingly in the trail of a dark cloud, after its thunder and lightning and torrent have raged and blazed and poured, and passed away.

This great man has been described so often, that not only his public history and mental character, but his personal peculiarities—yea, the nervous twitching of his eyebrows—are as familiar to Americans as to the reporters in the gallery of the House of Lords. As an orator or debater, he is sometimes compared to Webster. The very attempt is unjust to both. You might as well compare the repose of Lake Erie to the thunder of Niagara. Each has his own sphere of greatness. The Bostonian rarely enters the arena of debate, unless clad in mail to his fingers' ends—a safe and strong debater. Not so the Londoner. He sometimes rushes, sword in hand, without scabbard or shield, into the thickest of the fight, and gets sorely galled. Little arrows do not pierce Webster, nor do ordinary occasions summon forth his heaviest weapons. But Brougham, why, he will fight with anybody, and on any terms. The smallest Lilliput in the House can sting him into paroxysms with his needle-spear. But wo to the assailant! The bolt which annihilates the Earl of Musketo is equally heavy with that which strikes down the Duke of Wellington. As a whole, Brougham is unlike any of our public men. Could we mix into one compound the several qualities of Webster, Clay, Choate, Benton, and the late John Quincy Adams, and divide the mass into four or five parts, we might, by adding a strong tincture of John C. Calhoun, make four or five very good Henry Broughams.

I have spoken of the versatility of Brougham's talents and acquirements. Sir E. B. Sugden was arguing a cause before him in chancery. The Chancellor was not very attentive to the argument, employing part of the time in writing letters. This greatly piqued Sugden; and on retiring from the court, he drily said to a friend, "If Brougham only knew a little of Chancery law, he would know a little of everything." Undoubtedly he knows something about everything, and much about most things. Somebody has compared him to a Scotch Encyclopedia, without alphabetical arrangement. If he has not reached the highest place in any department of knowledge, it is because, in traversing so vast a field, he must here and there be necessarily only a gleaner. His success in so many departments proves that had he cultivated but one or two, he might have surpassed all cotemporary competition. Looking to the variety and extent of his acquisitions and labors, posterity will regard him as one of the most extraordinary men of his time. He reached his eminent position by no royal road. He is among the most laborious and diligent of men. Well known facts attest his wonderful activity.

His able work, " Practical Observations upon the Education of the People," published in 1825, was composed, he says, during hours stolen from sleep. Combe states of him, that he was once engaged in a court of law all day, from which he went to the House of Commons, and mingled in the debate till two o'clock in the morning ; he then retired to his house, and wrote upon an article for the Edinburgh Review till it was time to go to the court, where he was actively employed till the hour for the assembling of the Commons ; thither he went, and participated in the discussion as vigorously as usual till long after midnight—taking no rest till the morning of the third day ! The witty Hazlitt, alluding, at the time, to his speeches on commercial and manufacturing distress, said, " He is apprised of the exact state of our exports and imports, and scarce a ship clears out its cargo from Liverpool or Hull, but he has a copy of the bill of lading." It will be remembered, that while performing his political and miscellaneous labors, he was surrounded by a large circle of professional clients. His inaugural discourse, as Lord Rector of the University of Glasgow, thickly strown with Greek and Latin quotations, was, as the preface informs us, written during the business of the Northern Circuit. Sydney Smith says, in one of his graphic Reform speeches, " See the gigantic Brougham, sworn in at twelve o'clock, [as Chancellor,] and before six, has a bill on the table abolishing the abuses of a Court which has been the curse of the people of England for centuries."

A full share of the preparation and defense of the measures of Earl Grey's Administration devolved on him; while at the same time he did the work of an ordinary man in writing rudimental articles for the Penny Magazine, and scientific tracts for the Society for the Diffusion of Useful Knowledge, lecturing to Mechanics' Institutes, and contributing essays to the Edinburgh Review. An English friend informed me that during one of the busiest periods of his official life, a fatal accident happened to some laborers in excavating a deep well. Forthwith, out came a tract from the Lord Chancellor, on the best and safest mode of digging wells! Though his numerous publications and addresses on learned subjects, and his participation in the proceedings of the Royal Society and French Institute showed their author to be a scientific man, his later Lives of Men of Letters and Science exhibited an acquaintance with the sciences in his old age, for which his friends were hardly prepared. In the particulars here mentioned, no public man of our country can be compared with him, except the late John Quincy Adams, for whose wonderful exploits in his declining years Lord Brougham expressed the highest admiration.

The great political error of his life was his acceptance of the Chancellorship, and consequent removal from the House of Commons. It may be remarked, in passing, that it is a mistake to suppose he diminished his reputation as a lawyer by his judicial administration. He was never a first-rate technical lawyer. His mind was too broad, his ambition too high, to be a *mere* lawyer, tied down with red tape to *nisi prius* precedents and the *dicta* of cases. The profession to him was not an end, as it was to Scarlett and his school, but a subsidiary means to attain political eminence and influence. A great cause, like that of Queen Caroline, or of Williams, indicted for a libel on the Durham clergy, showed what he could accomplish when he bent his powers to professional work. His speeches on Law Reform prove his minute acquaintance with and utter contempt for the great body of the common law, as administered by the courts; and when presiding in a tribunal whose currents had been brought to a dead stand by the "everlasting doubts" of Lord Eldon, the best service he could render suitors and the country was to clear out the channels, and set the streams flowing, even though he might make mistakes in acting on the expedient maxim, that "it is better to have a case decided wrong, than not at all."

No man laments his removal to the upper House more keenly than himself. Speaking of Chatham's removal, he says, "No one ever did it voluntarily without bitterly rueing the step, when he found the price paid to be the loss of all real power." Grey first offered him the gown of Attorney General. Feeling it to be beneath his position in the Reform party, he contemptuously rejected it. The great seal was then placed in his hand. He should rather have taken the pen of one of the Secretaries of State, and remained on his "native heath." There he would have been at home, and there he would have been now. By superiority of intellect, or his "managing" or "pushing" propensity, the chief defense of the ministry in the Peers devolved on him instead of the Premier. He was in a false position. His native element was opposition. He was unequaled at tearing down—he had no skill for building up. The Reformers expected much from the new Administration, and everything from Brougham. All went smoothly till the Reform bill passed. Large quantities of ripe fruit were expected thereupon to be immediately gathered. Sydney Smith foreshadowed this, in his droll way. Said he, in a speech during the struggle, "All young ladies will imagine, as soon as this bill is carried, that they will be instantly married. Schoolboys believe that gerunds and supines will be abolished, and that currant tarts must ultimately come down in price; the corporal and sergeant are sure of double pay; bad poets will expect a demand for their epics; fools will be disappointed, as they always are; reasonable men, who know what to expect, will find that a very serious good has been obtained."

Much was done for Reform by the Grey ministry, after the passage of the bill. In less than two years, West India slavery was abolished—the East India Company's monopoly destroyed—the poor laws amended—the criminal code softened—the administration of the Courts essentially improved—the Scotch municipal corporations totally reformed—and many abuses corrected in the Irish Church Establishment. But young ladies, bad poets, and fools of all sorts, clamored for more; and many reasonable men were disappointed. The dead weights on advance movements were the Melbournes, the Palmerstons, the Grants, who, having bitterly opposed Reform all their days, were converted at the eleventh hour of the recent struggle, and brought into the Cabinet. The fatal measure of the Administration was an attempt to suppress agitation in Ireland, by a Coercion bill, which excited a quarrel with O'Connell, and divisions in the Cabinet, and finally led to the resignation of Grey. Glad to escape from an uneasy position, Brougham soon followed. Would that he could have got rid of his title, like Mirabeau, by opening a shop, and gone back to the Commons! But it stuck to him like the tunic of Nessus. Though consigned to perpetual membership in a body possessing no original influence in the State, and hemmed in by the usages of a mere revisional council, he has now and then shown himself "Harry Brougham" still. His speeches in the Lords on Parliamentary, legal, municipal, and poor laws Reform; on popular education; abolishing subscription in the universities; retrenchment; abolition of negro apprenticeship, and the African and Eastern slave trade; Canadian independence; repeal of the corn laws; and other topics, exhibit no abatement of intellectual power, or, so far as concerns those subjects, of regard for popular rights and social improvement Indeed, some of them rank among his greatest and best forensic displays. The speech on the education of the people in 1835 contains as much valuable information, and that on negro apprenticeship in 1838, as many eloquent passages, as any he ever delivered.

The conflict with Melbourne in 1837–8, which threw him out of Court and Whig favor, was a matter of course, if not premeditated. In a speech at Liverpool, just after his resignation in 1835, he declared that "his position of absolute political independence" would not be abandoned to join or sustain any Ministry that did not stand by the people, and go for large measures of reform. In 1837–8, on the Canada question, he first assailed the Melbourne Cabinet; he being for restoring peace to the colony, by granting the petition of its Legislature for an elective council, they for crushing disaffection by a dictator and the sword. His defense of the Canadian reformers was generous, bold, radical, and eloquent; worthy of the times when the young Commoner shook the Tory chiefs from the point of his lance, and fulminated living thunders at the crowned despots of the Holy Alliance. Pointing his long finger at the quailing Melbourne, he said, "Do the Ministers desire to know what will restore me to their support, and make me once more fight zealously in their ranks, as I once fought with them against the majority of your lordships? I will tell them here! Let them retract their declaration against Reform, delivered the first night of this session; and their second declaration, by which, to use the noble Viscount's phrase, they *exacerbated* the first; or let them, without any retraction, only bring forward liberal and constitutional measures, and they will have no more zealous supporter than myself. But, in the mean time, I now hurl my defiance at their heads!"

But, the truth of history requires that another view be taken of these transactions of 1835–8, and a far less eulogistic strain be employed in noticing the course of Lord Brougham for the last ten or twelve years. Early taught to admire him as the gallant leader of English reformers, it is painful to say, that during this period his conduct has been frequently such as to forfeit the esteem and confidence of his friends on both sides of the Atlantic, and to give currency to the charge that his line of action has been caused by chagrin at being left out of the Melbourne ministry, and to strengthen the suspicion that his denunciations of that Administration for faltering in the work of reform were dictated by mortified pride and thwarted ambition. For five or six years subsequent to 1835, he frequently attacked men and principles which he had won all his fame by previously advocating. But, it must not be forgotten, that, though supported by neither party and assailed by both, and set upon by Tory terriers and Whig whipsters, which betrayed him into losses of temper and dignity, it was in these years that he carried through Parliament several valuable reforms; whilst his writings—those records for the perusal of posterity—exhibited no marked change in his regard for liberal institutions.

On the return of the Tories to power, in 1841, he made a still wider departure from his early path. He has since shown much acerbity of temper, given his vote quite as often to the opponents as to the friends of reform, and has succeeded in alienating the affections of many of those who adhered to him during the Melbourne Administration. He has been alternately wayward, sour, vindictive, bold, brilliant, noble; exciting the contempt and fears of his enemies, and the disgust and admiration of his friends; now cracking a joke on the Duke of Wellington, that set the House in a roar, and then pounding the head of Melbourne till its chambers rang again; playing off eccentricities on some railway bill for the amusement of Punch, while sending to press a work on Voltaire and Rousseau that astonished Paris; giving his cheering voice to the repeal of the corn laws, and his growling "non-content" against the repeal of the navigation laws ; making himself ridiculous by trying to force his way into the French National Convention, and being received with loud plaudits as he entered the hall of the French National Institute ; now losing and then winning the favor of the people ; and ever and anon silencing the cry that "his powers were failing," by pronouncing a speech that startled the walls of St. Stephen's, and made every hilltop and valley in the land echo back the shout, "Brougham is himself again!"

It was a remark of Madame de Stael, that "Foreigners are a kind of cotemporaneous posterity." Americans may therefore pass an unbiased judgment upon the character of Lord Brougham. When his imperfections are forgotten in the grave, and the mists of prejudice and of party are cleared away, Posterity, which generously throws a vail over the follies and frailties of genius, will not willingly withhold from his tomb the epitaph he coveted in one of his earliest speeches —"HERE LIES THE DEFENDER OF LIBERTY, THE ADVOCATE OF PEACE, THE FRIEND OF THE PEOPLE!"

CHAPTER XVII.

Charles, Earl Grey—Advocates Abolition of the Slave Trade His Rise to Power—His Aid in Carrying the Reform Bill—Sydney Smith's Eulogy—His Two Great Measures, Parliamentary Reform and Abolition of Slavery—The Old and New Whigs—The "Coming Man."

A SKETCH of Modern English Reformers, which should omit special mention of CHARLES, EARL GREY, would be defective. For fifty eventful years, he took an active part in public affairs, and, with scarcely an exception, was found on the liberal side. With a mind cast in a highly polished, but not extraordinarily capacious mold, and in the attributes of originality and genius dwindling by the side of Fox and Brougham, he fully equaled either of these great men in calm sagacity and firmness of purpose. And if his oratory was not of the bold and vigorous type which marked theirs, it was of a high order; graceful, flowing, and classical, and set off by a manner always dignified, and in his younger days peculiarly fascinating.

Entering Parliament in 1786, when he had just reached majority, he immediately distinguished himself by a speech in opposition to the policy of Mr. Pitt. His rapid rise in the House is attested by the fact, that two years after his entrance, he was thought fit to occupy a place on the committee for the impeachment of Warren Hastings, by the side of Burke, Fox, Wyndham, and Sheridan. The year before, he had given a remarkable exhibition of the firmness and integrity which formed so striking a feature in his future life. In the debate on the Prince of Wales' (George IV) debts, Mr. Fox, by direction of the Prince, had denied, in his place, the marriage of the Prince with Mrs. Fitzherbert. The lady was sorely offended. She must be appeased by a public explanation. Wales applied to Grey to make some ambiguous statement in the House, which, without contradicting Fox, might seem to her to do so. Grey contemptuously refused to be the instrument of the royal debauchee, which ever after made him his enemy.

In 1792, he joined with Whitbread, Erskine, Francis, Sheridan, and Cartwright, in organizing the society for Parliamentary reform, called "The Friends of the People," and the same year sustained their petition in the House by a radical speech, in which he declared, rather than submit to the existing system of representation, he would adopt universal suffrage.

He was a member of the Grenville-Fox ministry—ably advocated its great measure of the abolition of the slave trade—and, on the death of Fox, assumed his post as Foreign Secretary, with the lead of the Commons. An attempt to carry a bill to open the army and navy to Roman Catholics provoked a quarrel with the bigoted old King, which threw out the ministry, and brought forth Sydney Smith's immortal Peter Plymley Letters. The death of his father the next year (1807) removed him to the House of Lords, where, during the following twenty-three years of royal proscription, his voice was ever heard defending the drooping cause of human freedom.

His rise to power, and the circumstances under which his ministry carried the Reform bill, have been detailed. The calm courage of the Premier steered the Government safely through this unprecedented tempest. Nerves less firm would have relinquished the helm in trepidation—an eye less steady would, by some precipitous movement, have whelmed all in destruction. On that memorable night, when the galleries, and lobbies, and every passage leading to "the tapestried chamber," were crowded with anxious spectators, and the venerable building itself was besieged with excited throngs, representing all stations in society and all shades in politics, who had come up to the metropolis from every part of the kingdom, to witness the decision of the long-pending struggle between the people and the patricians, Earl Grey, with a dignity and solemn earnestness befitting the august occasion, told the ancient nobility of Britain, that "though he was proud of the rank to which they in common belonged, and would peril much to save it from ruin, yet if they were determined to reject that bill, and throw it scornfully back in the faces of an aroused and determined people, he warned them to set their houses speedily in order, for their hour had come!" History has recorded the result of that appeal. The vassal rose up a man—the man stood forth an elector. The majesty of the subject was asserted, and the hereditary rulers of England swore allegiance to the principle, "the People are the legitimate source of Power." Never did popular agitation, wielding the peaceful weapons of truth, more brilliantly display its superiority over physical force, and the enginery of war, in accomplishing a great and salutary revolution.

Sydney Smith, speaking of Earl Grey, at a Reform meeting, while the bill was pending, said: "You are directed by a minister who prefers character to place, and who has given such unequivocal proofs of honesty and patriotism, that his image ought to be amongst your household gods, and his name to be lisped by your children. Two thousand years hence it will be a legend like the fable of Perseus and Andromeda; Britannia chained to a mountain—two hundred rotten animals* menacing her destruction, till a tall Earl, armed with Schedule A,† and followed by his page, Russell, drives them into the

* Rotten Boroughs. † The List of disfranchised boroughs.

deep, and delivers over Britannia in safety to crowds of ten-pound renters, who deafen the air with their acclamations. Forthwith, Latin verses upon this—school exercises—boys whipt, and all the usual absurdities of education."

This is rather rapturous; but it is only Smith's way of expressing the unquestionable fact, that Earl Grey was the very man who could, if mortal man could, carry such a measure in the face of the aristocracy of England. The people trusted him, and the sane portion of the hostile factions opposed him less obstinately than they would some more boisterous member of the liberal party, whom they could stigmatize as a "fanatic," or a "revolutionist." And even "the radicals" well knew, that to make a brilliant onslaught upon a strong Tory ministry, while the Reform party was weak, and it mattered little *what* was said and done, if *something* was only said and done, was a very different mission from attempting to lead that party when its swelled ranks required to be consolidated under a graver chieftain, with experience ripened by once having been a leading minister of the Crown, who might plant the conquering flag on the walls of the citadel. Such a chieftain was Earl Grey.

The two measures of Earl Grey's administration, which made it honorably conspicuous through the world, and will give it an enduring name with posterity, are Parliamentary reform, and the abolition of negro slavery. The defects in the former will be hereafter alluded to. The latter was clogged by the ill-contrived apprenticeship system. But, defective though they were, had his administration done nothing more for reform, the glory of those would atone for all its errors of omission and commission. The measure by whose magic touch eight hundred thousand slaves leaped to freedom, and bestowed the munificent gift of twenty millions sterling upon their masters, gave his Government greater renown abroad than the reform in Parliament. But the latter was much the more important event to the British nation. It was an era in its politics, big with present and future consequences. By bestowing the elective franchise on half a million of small traders and artisans in the cities and towns, it struck a blow at the landed monopoly from which it can never recover—subjected the Government more directly to the influence of public opinion—and opened the doors of Parliament to a new class of men, like Cobden, Bright, and Thompson, springing from and sympathizing with the people, who, by their services within and beyond the walls of the legislature, have left their enduring mark on the policy of the country. By recognizing the principle of representation, as opposed to prescription, it took the first step toward complete suffrage for the people, uniform representation in the House of Commons, and the election of the House of Peers. It was as worthy to be called a *revolution* as the event that deposed the Stuarts and enthroned William of Orange.

It is a singular fact in political and personal history, that the man, who, in the freshness of youth and in the face of popular clamor, broached the measure of Parliamentary reform, should, forty years afterwards, in the maturity of age, be selected to lead the people in its consummation. The fitting counterpart is the no less striking fact, that the very Prince by whose choice he completed this work, and who, about the period of its commencement, denounced Wilberforce as worthy of expulsion from Parliament for proposing the abolition of the slave trade, lived long enough to give his royal assent, in the presence of that Wilberforce, to a bill for the abolition of slavery itself.

Earl Grey may be regarded as the last of his political school. He was a singular compound of the aristocracy of the old Whigs, with the liberality of the new. The trusted leader of the popular party, in the hour of its first triumph, cherished an exalted opinion of what he termed "his order," and though he never shrank from any duty or peril in support of the common cause, and voluntarily shared in the long exclusion of all grades of reformers from office and court favor, his pride and austerity were so habitual as to cool his friends while they ex asperated his foes. In exclusiveness and aristocratic bearing, he seemed to belong to the Whigs of the times of the first two Georges. On the other hand, he exhibited, in his political sympathies, associations, and conduct all the democratic tendencies of the Whigs of the Fox and Russell school.

The old Whigs, of whom Walpole and Grafton were the type, were distinguished by large possessions, long titles, and "a landed air." By arrogance, gold, and skill, they ruled England from the death of Queen Anne to the ascension of Lord North. Then arose the new Whigs, whose type was Fox and Grenville. Their chief supporters came from bustling manufacturing towns and flourishing seaports, as those of the old came from rural districts and rotten boroughs; the sign of the one being the broadcloth of the stock exchange; of the other, the broad acres of the agricultural counties. Indeed, on the coming in of the younger Pitt, parties might be said to have changed places without changing names; the Tories assuming the power of the old Whigs, and like them ruling *over* the people; whilst the old disappeared, and the new arose in the place of the ascendant Tories, and assuming the Tory attitude of opposition, and basing it on *quasi* democratic principles, struggled for power *with* the people.

Grey's administration was the reign of the new Whigs. It was continued by Melbourne; but the species is now almost extinct. Another party has gradually arisen, from seeds sown long ago by liberal hands. It knew not the ancient Whigs; it regards not the modern. Its type is Cobden and Hume, with symptoms of affinity in such noblemen as the present Carlisle and Grey. It once looked forward to the day when its leader and Premier would be Earl Durham. What remained of this hope after his unlucky Canadian administration, was soon quenched in his grave. It had now better select its chief man from the ranks of the people, and put him in training; for, after a lapse of time, and John Russell, it must rule England.

CHAPTER XVIII.

Abolition of Negro Slavery—Canning's Resolutions of 1823—Insurrection in Demerara—"Missionary Smith's Case"—Immediate Abolition—Elizabeth Heyrick—O'Connell—Brougham's Celebrated Speech of 1830—Insurrection and Anarchy in Jamaica, in 1832—William Knibb—Parliamentary Inquiry—Buxton—The Apprenticeship Adopted, August, 1833—Result of Complete Emancipation in Antigua—The Apprenticeship Doomed—The Colonies themselves Terminate it, August 1, 1838.

DICKENS, in his Martin Chuzzlewit, records, that Miss Charity Pecksniff, being told her side face was much better-looking than the front view, ever after, when visited by her not very numerous suitors, presented her profile to their admiring gaze. The tribute which Great Britain has paid to the genius of Humanity, by her efforts and sacrifices for the abolition of the African Slave Trade and Negro Slavery, is the aspect in which she delights to be contemplated by other nations. The humblest Englishman is proud to reiterate the sentiment, uttered half a century ago by Curran: "I speak in the spirit of our Constitution, which makes Liberty commensurate with and inseparable from our soil; which proclaims, even to the stranger and the sojourner, the moment he sets his foot upon our native earth, that the ground he treads is holy, and consecrated by the genius of Universal Emancipation. No matter in what language his doom may have been pronounced; no matter what complexion, incompatible with freedom, an Indian or an African sun may have burnt upon him; no matter in what disastrous battle his liberty may have been cloven down;

no matter with what solemnities he may have been devoted on the altar of slavery: the first moment he touches our sacred soil, the altar and the god sink together in the dust; his soul walks abroad in her own majesty; his body swells beyond the measure of his chains, that burst around him; and he stands redeemed, regenerated, and disenthralled, by the irresistible genius of Universal Emancipation." The services and victories of Sharpe, Clarkson, Wilberforce, Stephen, Brougham, Macaulay, Buxton, Cropper, Lushington, Gurney, Sturge, O'Connell, Mackintosh, Thompson, Wardlaw, Scoble, and their fellow-laborers, in this department of philanthropy, mitigate the abhorrence with which Christendom views the continued oppressions of millions of British subjects in both hemispheres.

After the abolition of the slave trade, the attention of a few thoughtful and humane persons was turned toward slavery itself, of which the trade was only an incident. Public sentiment was gradually enlisted, till, in 1823, it had become sufficiently aroused to cause the passage, in Parliament, of Mr. Canning's celebrated resolutions, declaring the expediency of adopting decisive measures for meliorating the condition of the slave population in the Colonies, preparatory to their complete emancipation. A ministerial circular was sent to the Colonies, directing the authorities to act upon those resolutions in the future treatment of the slave population. But, as was predicted by those who had studied the genius of Slavery, the resolutions and circular were either contemptuously defied, coolly disregarded, or courteously evaded by the Colonies.

The latter part of the same year, an insurrection broke out in Demerara. The infuriated planters undertook to trace its origin to the religious teachings of a venerable English missionary of most pure and exemplary character, Rev. John Smith. He was seized, and, after resisting some attempts to extort confessions, and going through a trial in which the very semblance of justice was outraged, was convicted, and sentenced to death. In feeble health, he was thrown into a small and loathsome dungeon, where, after several weeks of intense suffering, he died. This attempt to

> " ——— bring back
> The Hall of Horrors, and the assessor's pen
> Recording answers shrieked upon the rack,"

produced a tremendous sensation in England. Early in June, Mr. Brougham introduced into Parliament a motion to censure the Government and Court of Demerara. A debate of surpassing interest followed, in which he supported his motion by two powerful speeches. It was on this occasion that Mr. Wilberforce made his last speech in Parliament. The motion was lost by a small majority.

These proceedings, touching a case of individual outrage, are worthy of special note, because they aroused a spirit in England that would never "down," till the last chain was stricken from the last slave. "The Missionary Smith's Case" became a rallying cry with all the friends of religious freedom, and all the enemies of West India slavery. The measures of the Abolitionists became more bold—their principles commanded a more general concurrence—those who voted against the motion of Mr. Brougham were either excluded from the next Parliament, or obtained their seats with extreme difficulty; and, to quote from the preface to Mr. B.'s speeches, "All men now saw that the warning given in the peroration of the latter, though sounded in vain across the Atlantic Ocean, was echoing with a loudness redoubled with each repetition through the British isles; that it had rung the knell of the system; and that at the fetters of the slave a blow was at length struck, which must, if followed up, make them fall off his limbs forever."

The year 1830 was memorable for a great advance in the principles of the Abolitionists, and the influence they exerted on public opinion. The doctrine of *immediate* as opposed to *gradual* abolition, had been set forth in a well-reasoned pam-

9*

phlet, published anonymously, in 1824, which was afterward found to have been written by Elizabeth Heyrick, of Leicester. It now became the watchword of the Anti-Slavery Societies, their publications and orators. The anniversary meeting of the metropolitan association in this year was addressed by some of the most distinguished men in the kingdom. It was on this occasion that Daniel O'Connell uttered the noble and comprehensive sentiment—" I am for speedy, immediate abolition. I care not what caste, creed, or color, Slavery may assume. I am for its total, its instant abolition. Whether it be personal or political, mental or corporeal, intellectual or spiritual, I am for its immediate abolition. I enter into no compromise with Slavery; I am for justice, in the name of humanity, and according to the law of the living God."

In July of the same year, Mr. Brougham introduced his motion in the Commons, just before the dissolution, pledging the House to take the subject of Abolition into consideration early the next session. His speech in its support, and which essentially contributed to his election for Yorkshire a few weeks afterward, as the successor of Wilberforce, contains the oft-cited passage: " I trust that at length the time is come when Parliament will no longer bear to be told that slave-owners are the best lawgivers on Slavery; no longer allow an appeal from the British public to such communities as those in which the Smiths and the Grimsdalls are persecuted to death for teaching the gospel to the negroes; and the Mosses holden in affectionate respect for torture and murder: no longer suffer our voice to roll across the Atlantic in empty warnings and fruitless orders. Tell me not of rights—talk not of the property of the planter in his slaves. I deny the right—I acknowledge not the property. The principles, the feelings of our common nature rise in rebellion against it. Be the appeal made to the understanding, or to the heart, the sentence is the same that rejects it. In vain you tell me of laws that sanction such a crime! There is a law above all the enactments of human codes—the same throughout the world—the same in all times—such as it was before the daring genius of Columbus pierced the night of ages, and opened to one world the sources of power, wealth, and knowledge; to another, all unutterable woes: such as it is at this day. It is the law written by the finger of God on the heart of man; and by that law unchangeable and eternal, while men despise fraud, and loathe rapine, and abhor blood, they will reject with indignation the wild and guilty fantasy, that man can hold property in man! In vain you appeal to treaties, to covenants between nations: the Covenants of the Almighty, whether the Old Covenant or the New, denounce such unholy pretensions. To those laws did they of old refer, who maintained the African trade. Such treaties did they cite, and not untruly; for by one shameful compact you bartered the glories of Blenheim for the traffic in blood. Yet, despite of law and of treaty, that infernal traffic is now destroyed, and its votaries put to death like other pirates. How came this change to pass? Not, assuredly, by Parliament leading the way; but the country at length awoke; the indignation of the people was kindled; it descended in thunder, and smote the traffic, and scattered its guilty profits to the winds. Now, then, let the planters beware—let their Assemblies beware—let the Government at home beware—let the Parliament beware! The same country is once more awake—awake to the condition of negro slavery; the same indignation kindles in the bosom of the same people; the same cloud is gathering that annihilated the slave trade; and, if it shall descend again, they on whom its crash may fall, will not be destroyed before I have warned them; but I pray that their destruction may turn away from us the more terrible judgments of God!"

The French revolution of 1830, the turning out of the Wellington and the coming in of the Grey Ministry, and the protracted contest for Parliamentary reform, absorbed a large share of the public attention for the next eighteen months

Meanwhile, the Abolitionists, taking advantage of the liberal tendencies of the times, gathered strength by agitating the country through numerous publications and addresses, from some of the most able pens and eloquent tongues in the kingdom.

In 1831–2, an outbreak in Jamaica inflamed the already excited mind of England to an unusual pitch. An attempt to deprive some of the negroes of their wonted Christmas holidays, conspired with a report that Parliament had abolished slavery, to provoke a revolt. The masters fled, the troops interfered and slaughtered a large number of the insurgents, leaving the courts to put to death a few hundred in a more leisurely way. Not content with this, the planters glutted their vengeance by pulling down several chapels of the Baptist and Independent missionaries—forbidding meetings for religious worship in which slaves participated—driving some of the ministers to the mountains, and hunting them like beasts of prey—throwing others into prison—whilst a more fortunate few escaped to England. Among the latter was the Rev. William Knibb, a Baptist preacher of heroic courage, commanding person and vigorous eloquence. Arriving in the mother country in June, 1832, he perambulated the island, and in conjunction with the more learned and brilliant George Thompson, now member of Parliament, who was then employed as an Anti-Slavery lecturer, stirred the national heart to its core.

Parliament was not idle. In May, of this year, the West Indian interest in the House of Lords procured the appointment of a committee of inquiry into the state of the islands. It was mainly composed of opponents of Abolition. The friends of liberty in the Commons, alarmed at this hostile proceeding, obtained, through their leader, Mr. T. Fowell Buxton, a committee to consider the expediency of abolishing slavery in the islands. Mr. Buxton was chairman of the committee. These two committees were in session when the exiled

Jamaica missionaries arrived. They were examined as witnesses, with some sixty others, representing both sides of the question—the inquiry extending through nearly three months. The result was, an overwhelming case against slavery. Both parties now girded themselves for the contest. The Ministry of Earl Grey had recently carried the Reform bill. It was a favorable moment for the friends of freedom to strike. Early in the session of 1833, Mr. Buxton was about to bring forward a motion for the immediate abolition of slavery, when Mr. Stanley, the Colonial Secretary, superseded him, by pledging ministers to introduce a measure, without delay, which "should be safe and satisfactory to all parties."

Mr. Stanley brought out the Government plan of abolition, on the 14th of May, 1833. Good, genial, and unsuspecting Mr. Buxton now wished he had kept the work in his own hands. Stanley's bill bore the stereotyped ministerial stamp. It was a compromise between what justice demanded and what oppression would grant. It immediately emancipated all slaves under six years of age ; and subjected house servants to an apprenticeship of four years, and agricultural servants of six years, to their former masters ; and gave to the latter a compensation of £20,000,000. At the end of the apprenticeship, the negroes were to be completely free.

Leading Abolitionists denounced the scheme, compelled ministers to reduce the period of apprenticeship from twelve (as first proposed) to four and six years, protested against compensation ; but, fearful of losing the boon, the majority finally yielded their opposition. In Parliament, the measure was discussed to its dregs ; the friends of immediate Abolition striving to remedy its defects—the West India interest contesting every clause and comma with heroic pertinacity. After vast rhetorical displays on all sides, with much patience and philanthropy on one, and a good deal of bad temper and bad ethics, mingled with prophecies of bankruptcy and bloodshed on the other, the bill became a law on the 28th day of August,

1833. Mr. O'Connell voted against it, on the two grounds, that it did not give immediate freedom to the slaves, whilst it gave compensation to the masters.

In its actual workings, the apprenticeship realized most of the objections made to it by the Abolitionists, and few of the horrible forebodings of their opponents. The instant transition of 800,000 slaves into *quasi* freemen was not attended by any disorder whatever. And during the four years which the ill-contrived scheme lasted, not a drop of blood was shed; crimes of all grades diminished; vagrancy seldom showed its head; property was respected; the adults banished many of those domestic vices incident to a state of slavery; the children filled the schools; and this class of West India society rose in the scale of civilization and morals. And even after the forts were dismantled, and the troops sent away to prevent an insurrection among the whites of Canada, the Anglo-Saxons in the Caribbean Isles slept on quiet pillows.

But, though a heaven-wide remove from slavery, the apprenticeship was not a paradise to the parties. The dissonance was inherent in the nature of the plan. Looking to harmonious results, it gave the planters too much power, or too little; the negroes too much liberty, or too little. The consequence was, interminable disputes between masters and apprentices; between planters and special justices; between the Home Government and the Colonial authorities. The majority of the justices, who had the chief agency in executing the Abolition act, endeavored to do it in its humane spirit. But too many of them could not withstand the seductive wit and wine of a class, whose chivalry and hospitality are proverbial wherever unpaid labor has shed its liberalizing influences.

Antigua and the Bermudas discarded the apprenticeship, and adopted complete abolition, the Act giving to the Colonies the alternative. Experience justified the wisdom of their choice. They reaped all the good fruits of the apprenticeship, and none of the bad. Messrs. Thome and Kimball, of this country, visited Antigua, Barbadoes, and Jamaica, in 1837. From their admirable "Six Months Tour," I quote the following description of the "immediate" conversion to men, of 30,000 slaves of Antigua, on the 1st of August, 1834:

"For some time previous to the 1st of August, forebodings of disaster lowered over the island. The day was fixed! Thirty thousand degraded human beings were to be brought forth from the dungeon of slavery, and 'turned loose on the community,' and this was to be done 'in a moment, in the twinkling of an eye!' Gloomy apprehensions were entertained by many of the planters. Some timorous families did not go to bed on the night of the 31st of July; fear drove sleep from their eyes, and they awaited with fluttering pulse the hour of midnight, fearing lest the same bell which sounded the jubilee of the slaves might toll the death-knell of the masters. Several American vessels which had lain for weeks in the harbor weighed anchor on the 31st of July, and made their escape, through actual fear that the island would be destroyed on the following day. * * * The Wesleyans kept 'watch night' in all their chapels on the night of the 31st. At St. John's, the spacious building was filled with the candidates for liberty. All was animation and eagerness. A mighty chorus of voices swelled the song of expectation and joy, and, as they united in prayer, the voice of the leader was drowned in universal acclamations of thanksgiving, and praise, and blessing, and honor, and glory to God, who had come down for their deliverance. In such exercises the evening was spent until the hour of twelve approached. The missionary then proposed that, when the clock on the cathedral should begin to strike, the whole congregation should fall upon their knees, and receive the boon of freedom in silence. Accordingly, as the loud bell tolled its first note, the immense assembly fell prostrate on their knees. All was silence, save the quivering half-stifled breath of the struggling spirit. The slow notes of the clock fell upon the multitude; peal on peal, peal on peal, rolled over the prostrate throng, in tones of angels' voices, thrilling among the desolate chords and weary heart-strings. Scarce had the clock sounded its last note, when the lightning flashed vividly around, and a loud peal of thunder roared along the sky—God's pillar of fire and trump of jubilee! A moment of profoundest silence passed—then came the *burst*—they broke forth in prayer ; they shouted, they sung, ' Glory,' ' alleluia ;' they clapped their hands, leaped up, fell down, clasped each other in their free arms, cried, laughed, went to and fro, tossing upward their unfettered hands ; but high above the whole there was a mighty sound, which ever and anon swelled up ; it was the utterings in broken negro dialect of gratitude to God."

The experiment of immediate abolition in Antigua and the Bermudas, and of the apprenticeship in the other Colonies, has established the following facts : That, while melioration is a great improvement on chattel slavery, yet immediate and complete emancipation is far preferable : That either change is safe to the person and property of the master : That, for either, it is rather the master than the slave who needs preparation.

Considerations of principle, uniting with a mass of facts showing the superiority of immediate emancipation over the apprenticeship, induced the Abolitionists of England, in 1836–7, to take a final stand for the complete disenthralment of the negro. A numerous Convention of delegates met in London, in November, 1837 ; resolved that the apprenticeship should cease on or before the first of August, 1838 ; memorialized the Government against its continuance ; and, through a deputation, waited on the Colonial Secretary, to enforce their appeal. They were coldly, not to say contemptuously, treated by Lord Glenelg. After selecting a Central Committee, to watch the Ministry and Parliament, the delegates went home to agitate the country. Thompson, Wardlaw, Smeal, and their coadjutors, aroused Scotland ; whilst Sturge, Buxton, Scoble, and their friends, shook England. In the course of the fall and winter, petitions poured into Parliament in unprecedented numbers, whilst seven hundred thousand women presented their prayer to the Queen in behalf of her oppressed female subjects in the Western isles.

Parliament began to move. On the 20th of February, 1838, Lord Brougham, in presenting a petition from Glasgow and vicinity, signed by upwards of 100,000 persons, moved a series of resolutions for the speedy termination of the apprenticeship, supporting them by a speech worthy of his brightest fame, and whose immediate publication produced a deep impression upon the country. I cannot forbear quoting the closing paragraph of the peroration.

Said Lord Brougham :

"So now the fullness of time is come for at length discharging our duty to the African captive. I have demonstrated to you that everything is ordered—every previous step taken—all safe, by experience shown to be all safe, for the long-desired consummation. The time has come, the trial has been made, the hour is striking : you have no longer a pretext for hesitation, or faltering, or delay. The slave has shown, by four years' blameless behavior and devotion to the pursuits of peaceful industry, that he is as fit for his freedom as any English peasant—aye, or any lord whom I now address. I demand his rights ; I demand his liberty without stint. In the name of justice and of law, in the name of reason, in the name of God, who has given you no right to work injustice, I demand that your brother be no longer trampled upon as your slave ! I make my appeal to the Commons, who represent the free people of England, and I require at their hands the performance of that condition for which they paid so enormous a price—that condition which all their constituents are in breathless anxiety to see fulfilled ! I appeal to this House. Hereditary judges of the first tribunal in the world, to you I appeal for justice ! Patrons of all the arts that humanize mankind, under your protection I place humanity herself ! To the merciful Sovereign of a free people, I call aloud for mercy to the hundreds of thousands for whom half a million of her Christian sisters have cried aloud ; I ask that their cry may not have risen in vain. But first I turn my eye to the Throne of all Justice, and devoutly humbling myself before Him who is of purer eyes than to behold such vast iniquities, I implore that the curse hovering over the head of the unjust and oppressor be averted from us—that your hearts may be turned to mercy—and that over all the earth His will may at length be done."

On the 29th of March, Sir George Strickland brought forward a motion in the Commons, for the termination of the apprenticeship on the 1st of August following. Ministers resisted, and it was lost. While the motion was pending, two large anti-slavery conventions met in London, and soon afterwards five thronged meetings were held in Exeter Hall, in whose proceedings Brougham, Buxton, O'Connell, and other distinguished men, played a prominent part. The obstinate course of the Cabinet had not only exasperated public opinion at home, but had produced a feverish excitement amongst the apprentices in the Colonies.

In the midst of this furious contest, whose issue was shrouded in darkness, light suddenly broke in from an unexpected quarter. Lo! a ministerial dispatch, dated the very day after the November convention met, appeared in the West India newspapers, addressed to the Colonial Governors, in which Lord Glenelg informed them that agitation had again commenced, and would no doubt go on as before, and urging them to impress on the Legislatures the necessity of doing for themselves, and in season, what the people of England were seeking to compel the Parliament to do for them. Thus the Cabinet, while presenting a bold front at home, was saving its life by indirectly and secretly doing the work Abolitionists were forcing it to perform.

Simultaneously with the arrival in England of the journals containing copies of the dispatch, came the news, that the two small islands of Montserrat and Nevis had yielded to the ministerial solicitation, and resolved to emancipate their apprentices on the 1st of August. Other small islands soon copied their example. Barbadoes, with her 83,000 apprentices, followed in the train. Then came Jamaica, with her 330,000. This settled the question. Other Colonies now gave way, and ministers pledged themselves that all should be completed by the appointed day. It was done—the Cabinet averted an inglorious defeat—the planters escaped a hurricane of violence in a dark night of negro insurrection—and, on the first day of August, 1838, the friends of emancipation assembled in all parts of the Empire, to render thanksgiving to God for the final overthrow of British negro slavery.

The great work of 1834 and 1838, which we have hastily scanned, was accomplished by the People, and not by the Government; by the Democracy, as distinguished from the Aristocracy—the latter moving only when impelled by the former. Of political parties, the large share of Abolitionists came from the liberals. Of religious sects, the most active were the Friends, the Baptists, and the Independents. The cry occasionally heard in this country, that the abolition of West India Slavery was intended to be an indirect blow at American republicanism, is the shallow cant of owlish ignorance or demagogical hypocrisy. The Englishmen who bore a prominent part in the Abolition cause, generally admire our free institutions, and are now efficient laborers in those reforms which aim to cripple the power of the privileged orders, to prevent class legislation, and to secure the equal rights of the masses of their countrymen.

The conduct of the emancipated negroes during the last ten years has justified the eulogium pronounced upon them by Lord Brougham, in the last of the two quotations from him. The magistrate has driven out the overseer; the school has taken the place of the whipping-post; the press has supplanted the tread-mill. It is said that the large landed estates are diminishing in value; that the quantity of sugar, coffee, and rum, annually produced, decreases; that the negroes are reluctant to labor upon these large properties, preferring to set up little shops, or work at trades, or cultivate small grounds on their own account. In the mass of conflicting testimony, it is difficult to get at the precise facts. I presume that, to a large extent, these reports are true. Monopolies in the flesh of man, and in the soil he tills, are at war with Nature and with God. If they have been long continued, a change will produce some bitter fruits. But they will be the growth of the evil rather than the remedy. The tropics belong to the colored race. The Saxon must abandon the West Indies. His huge landed estates must inevitably continue to diminish in value till they are broken up into small freeholds, each being cultivated by its individual owner. Such a consummation will be deprecated only by those who believe that the chief end of poor men, in hot climates, is to work as day-laborers, on small wages, for bloated capitalists, in the production of large quantities of cotton, coffee, sugar, and rum.

CHAPTER XIX.

Notices of some Prominent Abolitionists—T. Fowell Buxton—Zachary Macaulay—Joseph Sturge—William Allen—James Cropper—Joseph and Samuel Gurney—George William Alexander—Thomas Pringle—Charles Stuart—John Scoble—George Thompson—Rev. Dr. Thomson—Rev. Dr. Wardlaw—Rev. Dr. Ritchie—Rev. Mr. James—Rev. Messrs. Hinton, Brock, Bevan, and Burnet.

Sir Thomas Fowell Buxton was the Abolition leader in the House of Commons during the Anti-Slavery conflicts of 1832 and 1833. His life is a beautiful illustration of Solomon's saying, "Train up a child in the way he should go, and when he is old he will not depart from it." At six years of age, Thomas lost his father; but there was left to him that most valuable of blessings, a vigorous-minded, well-educated, virtuous mother, who watched his young days with pains-taking solicitude. He was naturally of a sportive, roving disposition, and, when at school or college, made rather greater proficiency in the practice of hunting and fishing than in the study of mathematics and the languages. Though his juvenile tastes led him to scatter large quantities of that erratic grain called "wild oats," the teachings of his mother inclined his maturer years to the cultivation of the more profitable fields of Humanity and Philanthropy. The training of the child was shown in the actions of the man. Mr. Buxton's public life was devoted to meliorating the condition of the unfortunate classes of society. Especially was he the friend of prisoners, criminals and slaves While a young man, he took a lively interest in Prison Discipline—published a work on that subject in 1816, being the result of observations in the prisons of France and Belgium—and having taken his seat in the Commons in 1819, joined Mackintosh in his efforts to limit the death-penalty, and soften other severe features of the criminal code.

Surrounded by a strong Quaker influence from his youth, his mother being a Friend, which was subsequently increased by his marriage with a sister of the Gurneys and Mrs. Elizabeth Fry, (he had been accompanied by J. J. Gurney and Mrs. F. in his continental tour,) Mr. Buxton's mind was early turned toward the state of slavery in the Colonies. In 1821, (I think,) immediately after he had delivered an able speech in the House on Prison Discipline, Mr. Wilberforce wrote him an earnest letter, alluding to his own services in abolishing the slave trade, and requesting Buxton to join him in "a truly holy alliance" for meliorating the condition of the negro slaves, and ultimately advancing them to the rank of a free peasantry; and, in view of his advancing years, solicited Buxton to become his successor in "the blessed service," when increasing infirmities should compel him to relinquish the lead to younger hands. Mr. Buxton at once threw his mind and heart into the work, and his subsequent ability and devotion to it justified the compliment of Wilberforce, a few years afterward, when he called him his "Parliamentary Executor."

The resolutions of 1823, which have already been mentioned, were moved by Mr. Canning, as an amendment to a more radical proposition introduced by Mr. Buxton. To him, therefore, humanity is indebted for the first important ministerial step towards Abolition, which was the precursor of all that followed till the end was attained. It is with reference to the debate on this occasion, I believe, that the anecdote is told of "Brougham helping Buxton, and Buxton helping Brougham." Buxton was to move the proposition, and Brougham was to second him. Due notice had been given, and the West India interest was in commotion. Buxton anticipated that an attempt would be made to cough and scrape him down—not an unusual practice in this "assembly of the first gentlemen in the world." Just as Buxton was rising, Brougham whispered to him, "I will cheer *you* with all my might, and then you must cheer *me*." "Agreed!" responded the agitated brewer, who, in the suppressed mutterings and growlings, saw a storm was brewing. But he went on, Brougham crying "Hear! hear! hear!" so vigorously, and stamping and cheering so lustily, that the West Indians were dumb with wonder, and permitted Buxton to finish his speech without much interruption. Mr. Canning replied in his adroit and elegant style, moved his amendment, and resumed his seat under cheers from all sides. Brougham sprang to his feet, full of excitement with the great theme. Members cried, "Divide! divide!" in deafening tones. But Harry stood firm, lifted his voice above the tempest, and began to roll out long sentences crowded with big thoughts, while Buxton's shouts of "Hear! hear! hear!" finally silenced the clamor, when, his cheers of the matchless eloquence of his colleague becoming contagious, Brougham wound up a great speech amid "thunders of applause."

It has already been stated, that in May, 1832, on motion of Mr. Buxton, a committee was appointed in the Commons, to inquire and report upon the most expedient measures for the extinction of slavery throughout the British dominions. His labors as chairman of this committee, of which Lord John Russell, Sir Robert Peel, and other distinguished statesmen, were members, whose sittings did not terminate till August, were indefatigable, and worthy of the highest praise. His permitting the reins of leadership in this measure to slip into the hands of the compromising Colonial Secretary, the next spring, was censured by some Abolitionists. But no man strove more earnestly than he to remedy the defects in the ministerial plan. He repeatedly divided the House on amendments, and succeeded in reducing the period of apprenticeship one-half. And any ground which he might have lost by the transactions of 1833, was nobly redeemed by his subsequent services in bringing to an end a system, which, at the outset, he had denounced as "unjust in principle, indefensible in policy, and anomalous, unnatural, and unnecessary."

After the abolition of the apprenticeship, Mr. Buxton turned his attention to the slave trade. In June, 1839, he instituted the "Society for the Extinction of the Slave Trade and the Civilization of Africa," and was appointed its chairman. The same year, he brought out an elaborate work on "The Slave Trade and its Remedy," which was followed the next year by an enlarged edition, extending to some 600 pages. It is the most valuable and authentic publication extant on that subject. The facts it detailed, as to the extent of the traffic, astonished all who paid any attention to what Mr. Pitt had denominated "the greatest practical evil that ever afflicted mankind." While for a quarter of a century "the triumphs of humanity in the abolition of the African slave trade" had rounded the periods of orators in the British Senate and on the rock of Plymouth, Mr. Buxton proves that in 1840, and for a long period before, the victims of the traffic were more numerous, and its features more grim and gory than when Clarkson entered upon his philanthropic work in 1786. If Mr. Buxton had done nothing more, during his life, than to open the eyes of deluded Christendom to the present extent of this atrocious piracy, he would be entitled to the thanks of mankind.

The publication of his volume stimulated the British Government to greater efforts for bringing the traffic to an end. Though his main remedy, the civilization of Africa, showed a comprehensive and benevolent mind, the African expeditions undertaken in accordance with his plan were less successful than he fondly anticipated; and many of the best-informed persons became firmly fixed in the opinion, that the only effectual remedy for the slave trade is the complete abolition of slavery itself, and that anything short of this is amelioration, and not extermination. While it is believed that Mr. Buxton never abandoned his favorite plan, yet, till the close of his laborious and philanthropic life, he was the steady friend of all efforts for the overthrow of slavery and the slave trade throughout the world.

Mr. Buxton possessed large wealth, which he liberally devoted to the promotion of benevolent enterprises—had a clear and capacious mind, well stocked with useful knowledge—was ever under the influence of a liberal heart and catholic spirit—and his majestic form, he being about six feet and a half in hight, gave impressive dignity to the lucid style in which he presented his subject, whether pleading for justice and mercy before an adverse House of Commons, or surrounded by applauding thousands in Exeter Hall.

Next to Mr. Buxton, if indeed he was not in advance of him, Mr. ZACHARY MACAULAY exerted as wide an influence in marshaling public sentiment for the victory of 1833–4, as any other person in the kingdom. His services were not of an ostentatious kind, being confined chiefly to the committee room and the editorial chair. Having resided both in Africa and the West Indies, his practical acquaintance with the matters in controversy imparted rare value to his counsels, while his acute and powerful pen was in constant requisition, to prepare reports of committees, memorials to Parliament, pamphlets for general distribution, and articles for the periodical press. The self-sacrificing spirit in which he wore out his life in the cause received additional luster from the rare fact that he coveted none of the glory of his good works.

Mr. JOSEPH STURGE deserves a high place, not only among the Abolitionists, but among the reformers of Great Britain. Having taken an active part in preparing public opinion for negro emancipation, he recorded his protest against the apprenticeship. When contradictory statements as to its operation were confusing the English mind, he determined to investigate the matter for himself. Accordingly, in 1836 and 1837 he made a tour of the West Indies. Satisfied of the pernicious character of the scheme, he wrote home, advising an earnest movement for its abolition. On his return, he published the results of his observations—the demand for repeal reverberated through the British Isles—the days of the apprenticeship were numbered. To him, more than to any other man, this consummation is attributable. Soon afterward, he conceived the plan of a General Convention to promote the universal abolition of slavery and the slave trade. The result was, "the World's Convention" of 1840, composed of delegates from many nations and both hemispheres, over whose deliberations the patriot Clarkson presided, and which contributed to the overthrow of East Indian slavery, and gave an impulse to the cause throughout the world.

Mr. Sturge has been an assiduous laborer in other fields of reform. Among the first to embark in the movement for the total repeal of the corn laws, he participated in it till victory crowned the exertions of its friends. During this controversy, he became thoroughly convinced that a more radical and comprehensive reform was requisite to break up the system of class legislation, which bore so heavily on the working masses of the country. The Chartist enterprise had arrested his attention and enlisted his sympathies from its beginning. A firm believer in the second, if not the first line of Mackay—

"Cannon balls may aid the Truth,
But Thought's a weapon stronger"—

he could not countenance the violent measures of some leading Chartists, and would fain infuse into their counsels a more pacific spirit. Advocating their cardinal doctrines, but wishing to base his opinions on actual observation and experiment, he visited the United States in 1841, to inquire into the working of universal suffrage, voting by ballot, equal representation, and frequent elections. Returning to England, he published the results of his investigations, which had convinced him of the practicability of applying the main features of our

Congressional system of representation and election to the House of Commons. At a meeting of anti-corn law deputies, held at Manchester, in November, after the business for which they had assembled was finished, Mr. S. brought forward the subject of "complete suffrage." His lucid and practical views begat a general desire among the deputies for the commencement of a movement for a thorough reform in Parliament. In December following he issued a "Declaration," embracing the outlines of his plan, which ultimately drew to his views a portion of the Chartists, who, throwing off the old name, united with others in adopting that of Complete Suffragists.

In February, 1842, a meeting of delegates was held in London, on the call of Mr. Sturge, cotemporaneously with an immense anti-corn law convention, which had assembled to protest against Mr. Peel's proposed new law. After a full discussion, in which many members of the latter convention participated, the basis was laid for a union between the Corn-Law Repealers and the Complete Suffragists. In April following, a conference was held in Birmingham, mainly through his influence, composed of delegates from England, Scotland, and Ireland. The proceedings of this important body, over which Mr. Sturge presided, gave new energy to the movement commenced at the previous meeting in London. "*The National Complete Suffrage Union*" was formed by this conference, and Mr. Sturge was chosen its first President. In the course of this year a vacancy happened in the representation of Nottingham, a town containing some four thousand electors. Mr. Sturge was requested to stand as the Radical candidate, merely as an experiment, no one expecting him to succeed. In his address to the electors, he avowed himself in favor of universal suffrage, the severance of the Church from the State, and the total repeal of the corn laws; declared he would not spend a farthing in electioneering purposes, (i. e., bribing and treating,) nor countenance any efforts in his behalf, not sanctioned by the precepts of morality; and urged his friends to employ only such measures, during the canvass, as would make defeat honorable, and add luster to victory. His opponent, Mr. Walter, the proprietor of the London Times, stimulated the exertions of his supporters with a purse of £15,000. At the close of the poll, Mr. Sturge lacked but seventy-four votes of an election. He would have succeeded, but for the extensive bribery and intimidation of his opponent, who, on this account, was unseated on the reässembling of Parliament.

During the last six years, Mr. Sturge has devoted himself, with his characteristic ability, zeal, and munificence, to the promotion of general education, complete suffrage, church reform, corn-law repeal, slavet-rade extermination, universal peace, and cognate reforms.

On the summoning of a new Parliament, in 1847, he reluctantly consented to contest Leeds. In the course of his speech at the hustings, his proposer, the venerable Edward Baines, who had long represented the town, said: "I have to propose for your choice, as one of your representatives in Parliament, my friend and your friend, the friend of his country and of the human race, Joseph Sturge. With his principles you are well acquainted. They are the principles of liberty, of humanity, of economy, of equal rights, of freedom of trade and of thought, of voluntary education, of universal peace, and of justice to all mankind, of whatever color and of whatever clime. There are in Parliament an abundance of merchants, of manufacturers, of bankers, of lawyers, of soldiers, of sailors, of ecclesiastical patrons, of peers, and of bishops; but there is a deplorable deficiency of such men as Joseph Sturge." In his address to the electors, Mr. Sturge gave a thorough exposition of his political views, in the face of frowning Whigs and hissing Tories, both of whom brought forward candidates, and made him the object of their common hostility. After a hot contest, he was barely defeated by the concentration of a part of the Tory votes upon one of the Whig candidates; but the result was a moral triumph for Mr. Sturge and his cause.

Mr. Sturge is a member of the Society of Friends, and his beneficent life and amiable deportment are a beautiful embodiment of the principles of that sect. Till within a few years, he was extensively engaged in the corn trade, and has long been one of the most wealthy and influential citizens of Birmingham. Not satisfied with devoting liberal sums and remnants of time to philanthropic objects, he withdrew from a profitable mercantile connection, that he might consecrate all his energies to the advancement of civil and religious liberty. With no pretensions to literary or oratorical excellence, he is able to express his clear and vigorous ideas with terseness and point, both with pen and tongue. His plans, like his mind, are eminently practical; and he goes straight to the subject-matter, stripping off the husk, somewhat regardless of its texture and hue, and piercing at once to the kernel. His mercantile training has given him business habits of the first order, making him as efficient in executing plans as he is shrewd in their formation. A little apt to push aside, not to say push over, obtuseness and sluggishness, yet he mingles his unostentatious activity with such purity of intention and suavity of manner, as not to offend colder and more timid natures, while doing in a day what would occupy a month in their hands. Should he ever enter the House of Commons, he would be found, not among its brilliant, but certainly among its most useful members.

In this chapter it would be impossible to name all who bore a prominent part in the cause now under review. The Society of Friends alone kept an army in the field during the war. And no soldiers did better service than the household troops of George Fox. I may name William Allen, to whose many virtues the Duke of Kent gave the highest evidence, by appointing him one of the guardians of his daughter Victoria—and James Cropper, the munificent Liverpool merchant—and

Joseph and Samuel Gurney, the London bankers, the former of whom traveled over the Continent to investigate the state of its prisons, and made the tour of the West Indies, to examine into the condition of the emancipated negroes—and George William Alexander, who has visited France, Denmark, Holland, and Spain, to arouse them to the duty of abolishing slavery.

I can only allude to Thomas Pringle, one of England's sweetest and most graceful poets, who officiated as Secretary of the London Anti-Slavery Society in its infancy, its vigor, and its victory—and Captain Charles Stuart, one of the purest and bravest of mankind, whose voice and pen were sacred to Freedom—and John Scoble, who twice visited the West Indies, and whose chaste oratory on the platform, and terse productions as Secretary of the British and Foreign Anti-Slavery Society were of signal service to the cause. Of George Thompson, whom Lord Brougham pronounced one of the most eloquent men either in or out of Parliament, I shall speak at greater length, in connection with the abolition of East Indian Slavery.

I will close this chapter by briefly noticing a few of the many clergymen who rendered important services to the Anti-Slavery cause.

North of the Tweed, was Rev. ANDREW THOMSON, D.D., of Edinburgh, a leading minister of the Kirk of Scotland. He has been dead several years. Posthumous fame tells wondrous tales of his overpowering eloquence. The reports of his speeches, which I have read, show him to have been a son of thunder. He did not polish the angles of his sentences so much as Dr. Chalmers, but he possessed in large measure the comprehensive views, argumentative power, and splendid imagination, which distinguished that great divine; while, in directness and point, and ability to arouse and sway the passions of men, he undoubtedly excelled him. Robert Hall never said of Andrew Thomson, that he was a massive door, always turning on its hinges, but never moving onward. A speech of three hours length, delivered by him, in 1830, before the Edinburgh Anti-Slavery Society, in vindication of the principle of immediate as opposed to gradual abolition, and which was widely published, brought over the great body of Scottish Abolitionists to the new doctrine, chiefly through its intrinsic merits, partly, no doubt, because of the high standing of the orator. Its influence crossed the Border, and among its English converts was the celebrated Mr. George Thompson, who soon afterward became a lecturing agent of the London Committee.

The perfect opposite of Dr. Thomson, was the eminent dissenting minister, Rev. Ralph Wardlaw, D.D., of Glasgow. His tall person is the fitting embodiment of his large mind ; and his benignant countenance is the index of the purity of his heart. No one ever attended his chapel without pronouncing him a model for the pulpit. One of the best readers that ever opened the sacred Volume, his mellow voice, musical cadence, and chaste delivery, give to the precept or parable he has selected for the exercise a force and reality that never appeared to the hearer before. And his sermon—how harmoniously do strength and simplicity blend, to give vigor and transparency to the argument ; and how his felicitous similes and pointed tropes illustrate and adorn it, without confusing the reason or sending off the fancy in a chase after mere imagery.

But, though justly celebrated as a preacher and a divine, he is more widely known for his able advocacy of Voluntaryism, in opposition to Church Establishments, his early and steady services in behalf of negro emancipation, and his devotion to the general cause of civil and religious liberty. Probably no chapel in Scotland has opened its doors to so many secular meetings for the improvement of the human race as his ; and usually the venerable pastor is present to give his countenance and voice to the work.

We cannot linger longer on Scottish ground; though if we did, we should certainly be attracted by the erect form and elastic step of Rev. John Ritchie, D.D., of Edinburgh, whose Quaker-cut coat, ample white cravat, jaunty hat, and dangling cluster of watch-seals, would make you assign him now to membership in the Society of Friends, and then to membership in some sporting club, but never to his proper place, at the head of the Secession Church of Scotland. He is an old soldier in the ranks of Freedom; has fought many a hard battle with Negro Slavery and the State Church: is an ardent free trader, universal suffragist, and, in a word, a thorough radical reformer, who can instruct the reason or arouse the feelings of an auditory with capital effect.

We will hasten to English ground, and spend a few moments with a clergyman who, in mental characteristics and oratorical peculiarities, is a cross of the thunder of Dr. Thomson, and the sunshine of Dr. Wardlaw—Rev. John Angell James, of Birmingham. Of Mr. James' course in the early stages of the anti-slavery movement, I cannot speak with certainty. But, during the controversy growing out of the apprenticeship, and in the later efforts for the overthrow of slavery and the slave trade throughout the world, the contributions of his pen and voice to the cause received additional influence from his position as one of the most conspicuous leaders of the Congregational body of Great Britain. He has also been among the foremost of the dissenting clergy in advocating the principle of Voluntaryism, in its application to ecclesiastical affairs and the education of the people. Perhaps, at the present time, he stands at the head of the denomination which he adorns by his talents and virtues. Mr. James has a high reputation as a writer and preacher on both sides of the Atlantic. It was not my fortune to hear him in the pulpit, but I can bear testimony to his power over audiences on the platform. He has the external qualities, the physical embellishments, of an orator: a well-proportioned person—a voice of great compass, and as flexible and rich as a flute—a singularly expressive countenance, polished manners, and a graceful gesticulation. These are the frame and border of that grand and beautiful picture which his strong mind and glowing imagination paint before admiring assemblies. He captivates and converts more by winning grace than conquering power; more by the charms of his rhetoric than the severity of his logic. Let it not be inferred from this that his speeches are devoid of argument. Far from it. They abound in that ingredient, without which all public addresses become the mere sounding brass and tinkling cymbal of an unbridled imagination, or the sound and fury of hollow declamation, signifying nothing but the emptiness of the mere word-spouter. I only mean to say, that his reasoning is not sent into the world bald, but is embellished with artistic skill, and that his speeches bear the hearer onward to conviction in a mixed current of strong argument, elevated sentiment, witty allusions, and happy hits. His appeals to the nobler feelings of the supporters of the cause he is advocating, are fully equaled by his adroitness in sweeping away the objections its opponents have strewed in his path, leaving prostrate antagonists to admire the skill and courtesy with which the victor waved rather than hurled them to the ground. In the select social circle he is as attractive as when eliciting public plaudits on the rostrum; and though an ecclesiastical leader, and ready to defend his religious tenets on suitable occasions, his liberal sentiments and courteous bearing toward all sects, have won him troops of friends in every denomination and class of Christians, from Bishops in lawn to Quakers in drab.

Even an incomplete list of clergymen who bore conspicuous parts in the contests detailed in the last chapter, would be unpardonably defective if it omitted to name Rev. JAMES HOWARD HINTON, an able Baptist preacher, and the author of a history of this country—and Rev. WILLIAM BROCK, an eloquent divine of the same denomination—and Rev. WILLIAM BEVAN, of the Congregational church, whose pamphlet on the Apprenticeship did much toward terminating that system—and Rev. JOHN BURNET, of the same church, one of the keenest debaters the English pulpit affords.

CHAPTER XX.

British India—Clive and Hastings—East India Company—Its Oppressions and Extortions—Land Tax—Monopolies—Forced Labor and Purveyance—Taxes on Idolatry—Amount of Revenue Extorted—Slavery in India—Famine and Pestilence—The Courts—Rajah of Sattara—Abolition of Indian Slavery—British India Society—General Briggs—William Howitt—George Thompson as an Orator—Lord Brougham's Opinion—Mr. Thompson's Anti-Slavery Career—His Visit to India—His Defense of the Rajah—Advocates Corn-Law Repeal—Is Elected to Parliament.

NEAR the close of the seventeenth century, English ships occasionally skirted the coast of Hindostan, anxious to exchange a roll of flannel or a pack of cutlery for a case of muslins or a bag of spices. A surgeon from one of these vessels was called to attend upon the daughter of the reigning Prince, and succeeded in curing her of a dangerous disease. Being asked what reward he would have for his services, he refused to receive any gift for himself, but solicited commercial privileges for his countrymen. They were granted ; and English trading factories were established at Madras and Calcutta. These purely trading posts became the germs of a power which, shooting out its gigantic branches, ultimately spread over the largest and most fertile portion of the peninsula of Hindostan. Robert Clive, a clerk in the Madras factory, laid the foundation of British empire in India. Warren Hastings, a clerk in the factory at Calcutta, erected upon this foundation a towering superstructure, whose blighting shadow now covers a million square miles of territory, inspiring awe in the breasts of a hundred millions of people. The dominion of Britain over this immense area and population is justifiable neither by the mode in which it was obtained, nor the manner in which it has been exercised. Obtained by force, fraud, and cunning, it has been exercised in a spirit of avarice which might tingle the cheek of a Shylock with shame, and of oppression which gives verity to the fabulous tales of Oriental despotisms in the olden time.

The whole of Anglo-India is ruled primarily by the Government of Great Britain, but a large portion of it is governed practically by the English East India Company. These sovereigns in Leadenhall street execute their mandates through a small body of Directors, who acknowledge a slight allegiance to a Board of Control in Downing street. They derive their authority from the Charter of the British Crown, and rule India by permission of the British people. The fundamental principle of their government is, to make India subservient to their pecuniary interests, regardless of its own. Proceeding on the plan of realizing as large a profit as possible on the capital invested, they have taxed the land to the utmost limits of its capacity to pay, making every successive province as it fell into their hands a pretext and a field for higher exactions, and boasting that they have raised the amount of revenue beyond what native rulers were able to extort. They have monopolized every branch of trade that could be made productive, employing in the prosecution the smallest number of laborers, at the lowest rate of wages. The instructions of the Company to their Indian agents have been to make as large remittances as possible. This done, little concern has been felt as to the means employed by the thousand or twelve hundred Englishmen sent thither to enrich their employers and amass private fortunes by plundering the country. The periodical invasion of these hordes of needy adventurers has been like the march of the locusts of Egypt—before them was fertility and beauty; behind them was barrenness and desolation. For the Company to listen to the complaints of the natives, was a sickly sentimentality unbecoming a great mercantile association; to demand inquiry, was an impertinence; to redress grievances, no part of the obligations imposed by the charter. The Hon. F. J. Shore, who spent fifteen years in India, part of the time as a judge of one of the higher courts, says: "The British Indian Government has been practically one of the most extortionate and oppressive that ever existed in India; one under which injustice has been and may be committed, both by the authorities and by individuals, (provided the latter be rich,) to an almost unlimited extent, and under which redress for injuries is almost unattainable." All unprejudiced authorities agree that Anglo-Indian rule has been worse than that of either of its predecessors, the Hindoos and Mahometans.

From a mass of documents before me, I will select a few items in support and illustration of these general statements.

The great curse of India is the *Land Tax*. The principle on which the Government acts is, that it is the owner of the soil, and that the occupiers are only tenants at sufferance, though their titles can be traced backward till lost in the haze of antiquity. While under Hindoo rule, the people paid to the Government an annual tax equal to one-sixth of the produce of the soil. The Mahometans, having partially subdued the Hindoo Princes, increased the tax to one-fourth of the produce. Then came the civilized and Christianized English. Asking as a boon the permission to erect two or three warehouses on the coast, they pursued for many years the humble occupation of factors, dealing in silks, muslins, rice, spices, and precious stones. Growing rich, insolent, strong, and rapacious, they overrun the finest provinces, bribing, swindling, butchering the native Princes. Well secured in their regal seats, trading became a secondary occupation, subservient to the arts of diplomacy and the strategy of arms. Having conquered, they resolved to plunder. They apportioned the soil among surveyors and collectors, whose duty it was to levy and collect the land tax. The cupidity of the conquerors increasing by what it fed upon, they ultimately directed the tax to be fixed at a money value, before the crops were ripe, and to be rated at the highest capacity of the soil in the most fruitful seasons. The result is, that in the most favorable years it absorbs one-third of the produce; in medium years, two-thirds; in years of scarcity, and in unproductive localities, the whole, and more than the whole—the deficiency in the latter case being made up from neighboring farms or districts, or by selling personal property. The average of this tax is variously estimated at from two-thirds to three-fourths of the annual produce. The Company instructs the collectors, that "if the crop be even less than the seed sown, the full tax shall still be demanded. If the occupier be unable to pay, the deficiency is to be made up by assessing it on the entire village or neighborhood. If these be unable to pay it, then on an adjoining village or district—limiting, in such cases, the assessment to ten or twelve per cent. of the value of the land, lest it injure the next year's revenue!" The immediate consequences of this extortion are appalling. Thousands of all classes, ages, and sexes, are turned out of their homes, and wander about in nakedness and want, begging and plundering, selling their children into slavery or giving them to those who will feed and keep them as servants, while other thousands perish of hunger in the jungles and the highways, or are swept off by diseases incident to such squalor. In a single year, famine alone has carried away a million of the population of a land fertilized by a thousand rivers, and fecund of vegetation under the warm blushes of a tropical sun.

Next to the land tax, the most noxious fruit of British rule is a system of Government *Monopolies*, covering not merely the luxuries, but the necessaries of life. The chief of these are in corn, rice, salt, indigo, and opium. The district washed by the mouths of the Ganges produces immense stores of corn and rice. The sea, in the contiguous district of Madras, throws up large quantities of the most beautiful salt. But, though the one district furnishes a surplus of what the other is destitute of, they cannot interchange commodities without paying a monopoly tax to the Government, which amounts to a positive prohibition. Even the owner of a plantation bordering on the ocean, whose liberal waves line it with salt, cannot gather in the product without subjecting himself to heavy fines and imprisonment. It is all seized by the Government, and doled out at such prices as to create an annual revenue of from £2,000,000 to £3,000,000. The opium monopoly is still more odious. On the finest corn-lands of Benares, Behar, and part of Bengal, the inhabitants are compelled to grow this pernicious drug, and this alone. The poppy is planted amid curses, its produce is purchased by extortion, carried forth by violence, and sold to work the ruin of millions. The opium being manufactured, the East India Company takes it all, giving the growers such prices as it pleases. Not long ago, while selling it at Calcutta at sixty shillings per pound, it allowed but two shillings per pound to the miserable cultivators. In 1839, it exported to China alone £2,700,926 in value; and for many years past its annual profit from the opium monopoly has been estimated to exceed a million sterling. Other monopolies might be mentioned; but these will suffice as a specimen.

Another branch of British extortion is what is termed *Forced Labor and Purveyance.* In procuring supplies for camps; cattle, sheep, and other food for European soldiers; carriage for troops or civil functionaries; provisions for jails and implements for convict laborers; trains of workmen for the Government and for privileged persons—in short, in any levy for civil or military exigencies, whether in peace or war, the most cruel exactions are practiced. Out rush the myrmidons of Government, or privileged Europeans, and seize cattle, camels, sheep, carts, corn, fruits, and whatever is needed, and wherever found. On highways, at fairs, on farms, they seize on men, horses, and carriages, to transport their loads, throwing the effects of the owners into the roads; and entering shops and dwellings, they carry off what pleases their fancy, gratifies their appetites, or supplies their necessities. When one of these military or civic cavalcades is passing over the country, it scatters terror far and wide. An eye-witness says: "As soon as the people perceive the *cortège* approaching, accompanied by a police officer, they run and hide themselves. You may see, sometimes, half a village scampering over the fields, pursued by one or more officers in full hue and cry." As long ago as when Hastings traveled in state from Calcutta to Benares, to plunder Cheyte Sing of his treasures and his territories, he expressed his astonishment to see the inhabitants flying at his approach, shutting up their shops, and escaping to the woods. Seventy years have scarcely modified the rigors of the conquering Briton, or abated the terrors of the subdued Indian.

The rapacity of the English rulers cannot be better exemplified than in the fact, that while British societies have sent missionaries to convert the natives to Christianity, and on the first Monday of every month tens of thousands in two hemispheres invoke Divine blessings on "India's coral strand," the East India Company has levied taxes on travelers who would visit the Temple of Juggernaut or bathe in the waters of the Ganges, taxing the devotee before he threw himself under the wheels of the idol, taxing the widow before she leaped on the funeral pile of her husband, taxing the mother before she offered her offspring to the crocodile on the banks of the sacred river, and taxing Hindoos for becoming Christians, and on their refusal to pay, torturing them with thumb-screws, and with standing in the burning sun, bearing heavy stones on their shoulders.

By these and like means, England wrings from this wretched people an annual revenue of more than twenty millions sterling. Besides this amount, there are numerous incidental drains upon the resources of the country, of which no account is rendered or kept, and untold sums extracted by the unlicensed extortion of individuals and squads, making the naturally fertile and beautiful peninsula that stretches from the snows of the Himalaya mountains to the sands of Cape Comorin, the plundering-ground of England.

And more than this: during ten years of English boasting, immediately following the abolition of slavery in her West India Colonies, that in whatever part of the world her flag floated in dominion, there the air was too pure to be inhaled by a slave, the chattel bondmen of British India were to be counted by millions, held in servitude by permission of British laws, which British power could have revoked at any moment by a dash of the pen.

The calamitous consequences of this long-continued system of oppression and extortion can hardly be overrated. The ancient public works have fallen into decay. Public improvement has languished. The roads, bridges, and canals, are in the most deplorable state. Education and the arts are neglected. Native property-holders are ruined by taxation. The laboring poor sink into the arms of beggary, while surrounded by foreigners who riot in plenty. The earth refuses to yield her natural increase in return for niggardly culture. And the country has been wont to relieve itself of its redundant squalor by famines which sweep its table lands, and by pestilences, which, having depopulated its towns, take to themselves wings, invade distant nations, cross wide oceans, and scourge every part of the world.

In return for all these inflictions, and for a trade which crowds her ports with the richest products of Asia, one would suppose that Great Britain, which boasts of its judicial and municipal institutions, might give to India a tolerable internal government. Not so. It could hardly be more wretched. Its internal affairs are conducted for the same ends for which its taxes are collected—enriching and aggrandizing the rulers.

Indians are excluded from every honor, dignity, and station, which the meanest Englishman can be induced to accept. A writer of probity and experience informs us, that the public offices are sinks of every species of villainy, fraud, chicane, favoritism, and injustice. The courts are a libel on the very semblance of justice. Practically, there is no law for the multitude. Often but a single magistrate can be found in a district as large as the State of Connecticut. He cannot hear a tenth of the causes demanding his attention. The distance, the expenses, the hopelessness of getting a hearing, deter thousands from seeking it. Those hardy enough to attempt it, on arriving at many of these tribunals, find them conducted, not in the Hindostanee language, which the suitor understands, nor in the English, which the judge speaks, but in the Persian, which neither suitor nor judge knows a word of. Justice, or rather *judgment*, is sold to the wealthy, and denied to the poor. If an influential native, in the pay of the Company, or an Englishman, is prosecuted, the prosecutor may deem himself fortunate if he and his witnesses are not seized and imprisoned by order of the Court. If the Government prosecutes for a fine or a tax, torture is sometimes applied to extort confession and payment. Judge Shore denounces the inferior courts as sinks of villainy. As to the Supreme Court, sitting at Calcutta, it has been regarded with an undefined and unintelligible horror since the day when Impey, at the instigation of Hastings, sentenced to death Nuncomar, the head of the Hindoo race and religion, on a trumped-up charge of forgery —a venial offense in the code of Indian morals.

And this is a feeble picture of England's government of India, a picture that all the plausible and brilliant extenuations of Macaulay, in his sketches of Clive and Hastings, do not obscure.

I will give an illustration of the mode by which England has extended her territory in India.

In the vicinity of the holy city of Benares, on the banks of the sacred Ganges, resides Purtaub Sing, an illustrious Hindoo prince, better known as the RAJAH OF SATTARA. He once sat on the throne of Sattara, but for ten years has been the captive of the British Government, subsisting on its charity. He is descended from the renowned Sivajee, whose skill and courage, in the seventeenth century, delivered the Mahrattas from the Mahometan yoke of the successors of Tamerlane, and founded the mighty Mahratta empire. This warlike people, so long the terror of the English in India, made their home in the fastnesses of those mountains whose blue summits watch the distant coast of Malabar, and on the rich table lands stretching eastward from their tops, and the alluvial valleys which slide westward from their base, into the sea of Arabia. In 1817, after a checkered contest of thirty years, during which the cavalry of the Mahrattas often carried dismay and havoc among the white villas sprinkled around Madras, and the rice fields clustering among the mouths of the Ganges, their empire fell before the superior military skill and political intrigues of the British. At that time, Purtaub Sing, a youth of eighteen, was the rightful possessor of the Mahratta throne. By treaty with his conquerors, a small portion of the territory he had lost was allotted to him; he was placed on the throne of Sattara, and made tributary to the Government of Bombay. The mind of the prince was liberal and acute; his habits frugal and temperate; his character humane and noble; and for twenty years his just and beneficent rule rendered his dominions among the happiest and most flourishing in India. For his many virtues and wise administration, the Directors of the East India Company, in 1835, presented him a rich gift and a eulogistic vote of thanks. The neighboring Government of Bombay had long had its greedy eye on this prosperous principality. Having exhausted the arts of flattery and chicane to induce the Rajah to relinquish his throne in favor of a fawning creature of its own, it fastened a quarrel upon him in respect to certain revenues arising under the treaty of 1817.

He appealed to the Board of Directors at London. They decided in his favor, and sent their decision to the Governor of Bombay. This was in 1835. The decision was withheld from the Rajah, and he was kept in profound ignorance of the result. The Governor now had recourse to the blackest crimes, to convict him of treasonable designs against the British power in India. Charges were preferred, and he was brought to trial before Commissioners appointed to determine his case. It was in vain that he denied the jurisdiction of the tribunal, and offered to submit the matter to the Board of Directors. He was pronounced guilty by a majority of the Commissioners, on evidence since proved to have been perjured and forged. General Lodwick, the English Resident at his Court, who sat on the Commission, denounced the testimony, as a mass of perjury and forgery. The honest soldier was removed from his post, and Colonel Ovans, an unscrupulous agent of the Bombay Government, appointed in his place. Not daring to punish the Rajah on the strength of such a trial, the new Resident was instructed to spare no pains to entrap the unwary Prince. After two years of vexatious dispute, and fruitless efforts to inveigle him, desperate measures were employed to accomplish the rapacious purposes of the Bombay Government. The Prince was dragged from his bed at midnight, torn from the palace of his ancestors, carried nine hundred miles across the country, and imprisoned in Benares. His estates were confiscated, his private treasure seized, his entire territory secured to the East India Company, and one of its creatures placed on the vacant throne. Twelve hundred of the Rajah's subjects, with tears and lamentations, followed their Prince into exile, leaving their wealth to their persecutors, and bestowing on them their blistering curses. This black crime was perpetrated in 1839. The principal witnesses against the Rajah have since confessed their guilt, disclosed the names of their suborners, and the sums paid for their villainy. In vain has the deposed Prince appealed for justice to the authorities of the Company, both in England and India. And this is the way that England extends her dominions in India—the England that lifts her red hands in holy horror at Texan annexation and Mexican invasion.

But it would be unjust to suppose that all Englishmen have looked with indifference, much more with approval, on the administration of Indian affairs. From the day when Edmund Burke made the old oaken arches of Westminster Hall ring with his thundering philippics against Warren Hastings, whose splendid administrative qualities for a time dazzled and drew the public eye from his gigantic crimes, down to the day when George Thompson shook the India House by his lightning eloquence in defense of the deposed Rajah of Sattara, a few jealous eyes have watched the rulers of India. It is only within the past ten or twelve years that any considerable portion of the British people has uttered a hearty protest against English oppression in the East, and demanded justice for its Oriental brethren. Some palliation for half a century's indifference may be found in the profound ignorance in which the mass of the English people were steeped in relation to their Indian empire. Till a late period, even men of intelligence supposed the functions of the East India Company were chiefly commercial, and never dreamed that it marshaled an army in the field three times as numerous as that which conquered at Waterloo; that its agents reigned over a population seven-fold that of England, with a power and splendor equaling Roman proconsuls in the days of Cæsar; that it deposed and crowned princes at pleasure, giving away thrones erected by the successors of Tamerlane; that the Great Mogul himself, reposing under the mere shadow of his ancestral greatness, was in reality but the titled pensioner of a Company, whose arms, intrigues, and extortions had scattered terror, strife, and poverty from the pine forests of Afghanistan to the cinnamon groves of Ceylon. But a better day has dawned for India. A people which, in the stormy times of Clive and Surajah Dowlah, of Hastings and Maharajah Nuncomar, hardly knew the locality of the island that sent out their oppressors, and which, in milder days, found it impossible to waft their complaints across 15,000 miles of ocean, now breathe their petitions in the ears of a listening Parliament, and through generous champions make even the great court of the India House echo the utterance of their wrongs. Many improvements in Indian affairs have already been secured. The eye of an influential party in England is fixed upon Hindostan, never to be withdrawn, till British rule ceases to vex the peninsula, or ceases wholly to exist. Tens of thousands of the best minds in the kingdom would prefer to see that rule instantly shivered in atoms, and the army, with the cowardly plunderers that throng in its train and hide behind its bayonets, driven in defeat and disgrace from India, than that it should exist for a single day, except to make atonement for past offenses. And to no man is this change in public opinion so justly attributable as to George Thompson.

It has already been stated that a better day has dawned on British India. The first purple streaks of the morning were seen when Earl Grey's administration abolished the last remnants of the maritime monopoly of the East India Company, and opened the Indian trade to the whole commercial marine of the kingdom—an important step in a line of policy, which, for many years, had been gradually circumscribing the ancient powers and privileges of the company.* The full-orbed sun arose when, ten years later, chattel-slavery ceased in all the vast regions stretching from the highlands whence spring the sources of the Indus and the Ganges, southward to where "the spicy breezes blow soft o'er Ceylon's isle," elevating millions of serfs to the condition of men, and verifying the words of our Whittier, that

* Since 1813 all British subjects have been permitted to trade to the East Indies under certain restrictions, which were wholly removed in 1833-4.

——"Every flap of England's flag
Proclaims that all around are free,
From farthest Ind to each blue crag
That beetles o'er the western sea."

This great boon, out of which the slaves of India were defrauded six years by a political trick, in which the Duke of Wellington bore a dishonorable part, was a consequence rather than the cause of a broad and comprehensive movement among the Abolitionists of Great Britain, set on foot by the benevolence of Joseph Pease, and the eloquence of George Thompson, for redressing the wrongs of India. In July, 1839, "The British India Society" was formed, in the presence of a large audience, in Freemason's Hall, Lord Brougham in the chair. Soon after, auxiliary societies were organized in Manchester and Glasgow. Lord Brougham, and Messrs. Clarkson, O'Connell, Cobden, Bright, William Howitt, Joseph Pease, Gen. Briggs, Dr. Bowring, and George Thompson, were among the officers of these associations.

The main objects of the British India Society were declared to be, to inform the public of the history of the British acquisitions in India, and the character of the British rule therein; to make known the condition of the natives; to introduce more extensively the cultivation of cotton, and to develop the resources of the country; to abolish slavery, and put an end to injurious monopolies; to stay the march of famine, and quench the lust of conquest; to mitigate the land tax, and secure for the inhabitants a practical recognition of their claims to the soil; and to awaken in behalf of that distant people the sentiments of a genuine sympathy, and a proper sense of national responsibility in the empire which claims to govern them.

These noble objects have been kept steadily in view during the past ten years. The soul of the enterprise has been Mr. Thompson. He has been greatly aided by Major General John Briggs, a generous and gallant soldier, who spent thirty years in India, traveled over most of the Peninsula, administered the

Government in several provinces, and has published two able works on the Land Tax, and on the Cotton Trade of India Mr. William Howitt, so favorably known in our country as a writer of taste and research, has given many of the best productions of his pen to the same cause. Numerous public meetings have been addressed by Brougham, O'Connell, Bowring, Thompson, Briggs, and others; valuable pamphlets issued; and a great amount of startling information spread before the public eye. A radical change in the administration of Indian affairs is demanded by a body daily increasing in numbers and influence, whose advocates have found their way into the Board of Directors, the Court of Proprietors, and the Halls of Parliament.

I will now speak more particularly of Mr. Thompson. At the close of his speech on the occasion of the formation of the British India Society, Lord Brougham said: "I have always great pleasure in listening to Mr. Thompson, who is the most eloquent man and the most accomplished orator whom I know; and as I have no opportunity of hearing him where he ought to speak, inside the walls of Parliament, I am anxious never to lose an opportunity of hearing him, where alone I can hear him, in a public meeting like the present." This is high eulogy, but it will not be deemed extravagant by those who have listened to its subject in his happiest moods.

Mr. T. was bred in a mercantile house in London. While a clerk, business could not prevent the gratification of his fondness for books, nor the cultivation of his remarkable native powers of elocution. He devoured libraries, and mingled in the debating clubs of the metropolis. In 1830, having read the great speech of Rev. Dr. Thomson, of Edinburgh, in favor of immediate emancipation, he embraced the doctrine, and soon after was invited by the London Anti-Slavery Society to traverse the country, and bring its objects before the people. His addresses in Liverpool, Manchester, Glasgow, and other large towns, drew throngs of hearers; and so great was their influence, that the West India body, taking the alarm, employed Mr. Peter Borthwick (afterward, like Mr. T., elected to Parliament) to meet him, and present the slaveholding view of the question. This was the very stimulus needed to bring out all the powers of Thompson ; for Borthwick was an able, ardent, and accomplished advocate. They measured swords on many a field in the presence of thousands, their encounters often extending through several successive evenings. Most unflinchingly and right gallantly did Borthwick bear himself in these conflicts. He was a foeman worthy of the glittering blade of his antagonist, and many a time did he feel its piercing point and excoriating edge. But the advocate of Slavery was not an equal match for the champion of Freedom ; and he could hardly have been, had their relative positions been reversed. As it was, he was invariably overthrown. Thompson shook him from the point of his weapon, quivering and bleeding, at every crossing of swords. Many of Mr. Thompson's speeches were reported. They are crowded with passages of power and beauty. Master of the facts of his case ; skilled in its logic ; expert in the arts of attack and defense ; apt in quotations and allusions ; fertile in illustrations ; singularly perfect in the command of language, still his *forte* lay in the power of his appeals to the humanity, the sense of justice, the hatred of oppression, the innate love of liberty, of his hearers. When rapt with his theme, his frame throbbing with emotion, the perspiration dripping from his forehead and hands, his voice pealing like a trumpet, his action as graceful and impetuous as that of a blood-horse on the course, the hearer who, for the moment, could stifle the sentiment that Slavery was the most atrocious system under heaven, might be trusted to sleep quietly on his knapsack in the breach, when it spouted a torrent of fire.

The next year after the passage of the West India abolition act, Mr. Thompson visited this country, where he remained till driven from our shores for advocating the natural equality of man, and his inalienable right to liberty. We would not permit a foreigner to interfere with our institutions—it was offensive, indelicate, impertinent. Probably Nicholas, the Sultan, Ferdinand, Victoria, Louis Philippe, and Metternich, thought just so when we interfered with Poland, Greece, South America, Ireland, France, and Germany. Not knowing the particulars, I shall not go into the details.

Returning to England, Mr. T. joined his old associates for the overthrow of the West India apprenticeship. When victory crowned their exertions, his brilliant services, with those of the more sober but not less efficient Joseph Sturge, were specially commended by Lord Brougham in one of his great speeches in the House of Peers.

Mr. Thompson now turned his attention to the affairs of British India. Having formed the British India Society, and established auxiliary associations in various parts of England, he, in 1842–3, visited India. His fame as the advocate of the rights of the natives had preceded him. In several parts of the country, he was greeted with long processions of richly-caparisoned elephants and camels, with cymbals and trumpets, and the gorgeous pomp customary in the festivities of orient climes. But he visited India for business, and not for show. He traveled through the upper provinces, held conferences with the people, gathered a store of important information, and, having been personally solicited by the Rajah of Sattara and the Emperor of Delhi, to present their claims before the British Parliament, he returned to England.

On a murky afternoon, in the dingy hall of the Court of Proprietors, in Leadenhall street, which was filled by merchants and speculators in India stocks, eager to pocket the spoils wrung from a people whom they had first conquered and then plundered, a tall man, personally unknown to but few present, rose from one of the back benches, and, with a pile of dog-eared documents before him, proposed to bring the case of the deposed Rajah of Sattara to the consideration of the Court.

At this announcement, a few members, not so dozy as the majority, turned their heads to see who this intruder could be. It was not long before he had thoroughly roused these free and easy gentlemen to a full sense of consciousness. Mr. George Thompson (for he was the man) began to spread out the unmitigated rascality of the transactions I have detailed. He was soon interrupted. His right to be there was questioned. But he was the proprietor of a sufficient amount of stock to entitle him to be heard. He went on. He was called to order. He would not come, but still went on. They proposed to take down his offensive words. He begged them to be patient, and he would soon give them something worth taking down. He was declared impertinent. He insisted that his speech was decidedly pertinent. Clamor was tried. His voice pierced the din, with the defiance that "he *would* be heard." He was denounced as the feed agent of the Rajah. He repelled the charge in a passage of cutting power. He was threatened. But he rode on the surges of too many mobs, in the turbulent days of the West India discussion, to be frightened at a tempest in the East India House. He still held his ground, and kept up a heavy and well-directed fire. The excitement was intense, the turmoil continuing till three o'clock in the morning. It was one of the stormiest sessions which had ever taken place in that stormy hall. It revived the recollection of the days when Lord Clive, the founder of the Anglo-Indian empire, encountered Sullivan, the prince of London merchants, and the chairman of the Company, who had tabled infamous charges against him; or the days when Warren Hastings, laden with rupees and flushed with triumphs, measured powers with his deadly foe, Sir Philip Francis, the author of Junius. Above the war of this tempestuous night, the trumpet-voice of the gallant Thompson was heard, cheering on the band that rallied to the defense of the dethroned Rajah. It was an era in the history of the Indian Court of Proprietors. Justice, humanity, right, honor, were strange words to be echoed from arches which had so long looked down on fraud, cruelty, oppression, and avarice. Thanks to George Thompson, these words are becoming more and more familiar in that temple of Mammon.

When the Corn-Law struggle was approaching its crisis, Mr. T. yielded to the solicitations of the League to again advocate its cause before the country. He had been an agent of the League previous to going to India, and his peculiar eloquence contributed essentially to the rapid change of public opinion during the years 1841–2. In the last year of the Corn-Law contest, he fought shoulder to shoulder with Cobden, Villiers, Bright, and Wilson, and no Free Trade chief carried over that triumphant field a brighter blade or a stouter shield than he.

As a testimonial of their regard for his many services in the cause of civil and religious liberty, the Lord Provost and Magistrates of Edinburgh presented him, in June, 1846, with the freedom of their venerable city. A higher honor awaited him. At the general election in 1847, Mr. Thompson was returned to the House of Commons for the Tower Hamlets, by the largest majority, over a popular opponent, obtained by any member of the new House.

In addition to the reforms already mentioned, he is the advocate of Universal Suffrage, of a dissolution of the union of Church and State, of Free Education, of Retrenchment in all departments of the Government. In a word, he is a radical democrat.

I have already spoken of his powers as an orator. His logic is not of the firstly, secondly, thirdly sort—a didactic, pulpit sort of logic—but a sort in which all the numerals are combined, and confounded, and sent home with the accelerated momentum of geometrical progression. His rhetoric is not so systematic as Campbell's, nor so stiff as Blair's, but leaps spontaneously from a fruitful mind, from an observation of men and things active and broad, from a sympathy with the grand in nature, and the beautiful in art. He attacks an opponent with a general pell-mell of argument, fact, appeal, sarcasm, and wit, not the more easily repelled because this onset of "all arms" is not arrayed according to the precise rules of art, but comes from unexpected quarters, and in unanticipated forms. He deals seriously with the great facts of his subject, and specially addresses himself to the higher parts of man's nature—the reason, the conscience, the affections. Yet can he gambol in playful humor, throwing the galling arrow of sarcasm, scattering the *jet d'eau* of wit, or with a stroke of his crayon, drawing the ludicrous caricature, imitating to the life any peculiarity in the tone or manner of his antagonist—gliding from grave to gay, from lively to severe, with charming grace. His speeches might be set down merely as rare specimens of elocution or declamation, but for one peculiarity. They deal largely with the facts, the details of the case in hand. He *reads up* on every topic he discusses. His stores of facts are relieved of all dryness or repulsion in the presentation, by the panoramic style in which he marshals them before the eye, all clad in the garb furnished forth by a rich elocution and lively fancy. Here lies his strength; for a single apposite fact outweighs, with the mass of men, a whole volume of abstract reasoning or florid declamation. His story charms like a well-acted tragedy or well-written novel.

If India shall ever enjoy a Government which protects its rights and promotes its prosperity, its happy millions will pronounce no name with more grateful accents than that of their early friend and advocate, George Thompson.

CHAPTER XXI.

Cheap Postage—Rowland Hill—His Plan Proposed in 1837—Cmparison of the Old and New Systems—Joshua Leavitt—Money-Orders, Stamps, and Envelopes—The Free Delivery—London District Post —Mr. Hume—Unjust Treatment of Mr. Hill by the Government—The National Testimonial.

A SKETCH of recent British Reforms, even as imperfect as that I am attempting, would be defective without some notice of one of the greatest blessings of the age—CHEAP POSTAGE. Not only Britain, but Europe and America, (for they have in some degree partaken of its benefits,) are indebted to Mr. ROWLAND HILL for this measure of human improvement and enjoyment. There are two aspects for contemplating this reform. The one, to go into heroics on its vast social, political, commercial, and moral advantages ; the other, to go into tables of figures. The former may be called the poetic, the latter, the mathematical, view. I shall avoid both of these extremes.

The high rates of British postage, down to 1840, and which were adjusted much on the same scale as ours, were a dead weight on correspondence. For thirty years previous to that time, the gross receipts of the post-office had remained nearly stationary. Thus, the amount of correspondence by mail continued about the same during a period in which the population of the country increased fifty per cent., commerce and wealth in a nearly equal proportion, and knowledge among the masses, and the facilities of transmission, to even a larger degree. These facts arrested the attention of many minds. But the sagacious Rowland Hill probed to causes and devised remedies. He published his scheme for postal reform in 1837. Its outlines were these. The controlling idea of the post-office establishment should be, the convenience of the people, and not Governmental revenue. It was extortionate for the Government to tax as much for carrying a letter from London to Edinburgh, as a merchant charged for transporting a barrel of flour. The chief labor being expended in making up, opening, and delivering mails, therefore the fact, whether a letter was carried one mile or one hundred miles made comparatively little difference in the expenditures of the department. The number of pieces of which a letter was composed should not regulate the rate of postage, but weight should control. As much postage was lost on letters which were never called for, therefore there should be a distinction between prepaid letters and others ; and in large towns there should be a free distribution of prepaid letters, by postmen. There should be no privileged class, with permission to use the post-office free ot charge. Guided by these principles, Mr. Hill recommended a uniform rate of postage for all distances—a postage of a penny per half ounce, on letters, if prepaid, irrespective of the number of pieces, and two pence if not paid till delivered, the rate increasing as the weight advanced—a free delivery of prepaid letters in large towns—total abolition of the franking privilege. His scheme embraced great improvements in other respects, such as envelopes, stamps, post-office money-orders, &c. He also insisted, that the increase in the number of letters under his scheme would be sufficient in a few years to carry the net income as high as under the old system.

Now, all this seems very simple and plain—so simple and plain, that those who hourly enjoy its benefits never think of the times when it absorbed a day's wages of a poor Irish laborer in London to send a letter to his wife in Cork, informing her that he was well, and hoped these few lines would find her enjoying the same blessing—when a commercial house in

Liverpool paid a yearly tax to the post-office sufficient to discharge the salaries of its clerks—when an editor, happening to be absent from the metropolis, wrote his leaders, to avoid triple postage, on very thin folio post, with very close lines, to the great disgust and vexation of compositors and proof readers—when love letters and money letters were peered into by gossiping and rascally postmasters, to see whether they were double—when a manufacturer, who could send a ream of paper a hundred miles for six pence if it went in the coach box, must pay a shilling per sheet if it went in the coach bag—when a luckless neighbor, about to take a journey of business or pleasure, must conceal his departure to the last moment, or be laden with a portmanteau full of letters, to "save postage"—when—but there is no end to the absurdities, annoyances, and extortions of the old system. And who thanks the genius and perseverance of Rowland Hill for exposing and exploding this relic of the times of the Stuarts, and introducing a reform worthy of the noon of steamers, railways, and electric telegraphs? It is so simple! Columbus is almost as sure of immortality for teaching a bevy of courtly buffoons how to make an egg stand on end, as for giving a new world to Ferdinand and Isabella. It looked very simple—especially *after it was done*. So did the discovery of the magnetic needle and the new world. It is the capacity which conceives how simple things, which produce great results, can be *done*, that is entitled to be called genius. He is both a genius and a practical man who can first conceive and then execute. And such a man is Rowland Hill.

His pamphlet, of 1837, soon attracted the attention of the nation. The next year, several hundred petitions in favor of his plan were presented to Parliament—a select committee was appointed to collect facts—a hundred witnesses were examined—and a report, embodying a great variety of important information, was published, filling three volumes of the Parliamentary papers. After much deliberation, his scheme, having suffered considerable mutilation, was adopted in 1839, to take effect early in 1840. In its actual workings, though crippled by half-hearted officials, it has exceeded the expectations of almost everybody except its sagacious originator, working out, during nine years, before millions of eyes, the problems he solved twelve years ago in his closet.

In 1839, the last year of the old system, the letters passing through the British post-office numbered about eighty millions. The average postage was seven pence per letter. The first year of the new system, the number reached one hundred and seventy millions. It steadily advanced, till, in 1848, it had risen to three hundred and fifty millions. The gross receipts of the department in the latter year about equaled those of 1839. The net income of 1839 was about a million and a half sterling ; that of 1848, about three-fourths of a million. The increased expense, and consequent diminution of net revenue, under the new system, are owing to the increase of business on old post routes, the opening of new routes, and great improvement on both. The net revenue increased from 1840 to 1848, a period of eight years, one-fourth of a million. Hence, it is safe to presume, that in a few years more, it will equal that of 1839. What a demonstration have we here of the much controverted proposition, that a great diminution in the cost of that which the public needs will so increase consumption, that revenue will not be the loser, while convenience will vastly gain? But, discard the principle of revenue, and make the post-office simply support itself, and England might probably in a few years reduce the rate of postage one-half, while transmitting a mass of letters which would almost defy enumeration. This more than realizes the brightest visions of Mr. Hill.

But, the money view of this great reform is a paltry view. It is well said by Mr. Joshua Leavitt, in his admirable American pamphlet on Cheap Postage: "The people of England expend now as much money for postage, as they did under the old system; but the advantage is, that they get a great deal more service for their money, and it gives a spring to business, trade, science, literature, philanthropy, social affection, and all plans of public utility."* Probably the corn laws were repealed two years sooner, because of cheap postage.

Nothing can exceed the convenience of the money-order, the stamp, and the envelope branches of the system. The money-orders are drafts by one post-office upon another, for sums not exceeding £5. They are a sort of post-office bill of exchange, and are largely employed in the transmission of small sums by mail. In 1847, the number issued in England alone was 810,000, amounting to £1,654,000. The department charges a trifling commission for the order—say 3*d* for £2. In a country where the brokers are Jews, and the smallest Bank of England notes are £5, this arrangement is very beneficial to the poor. The label stamps, which prepay letters, are convenient to all classes. They are of all rates, and, being first prepared by the department, are kept on sale, not only at all the post-offices, but by shop-keepers of all sorts. They are used, not only to pay postage, but as small change. Indeed, they are used as a kind of circulating medium. The number sold in a year is counted by millions. The envelopes, stamped by the department, and sold like simple stamps, are used not only to enclose letters, but by all sorts of persons and associations, for circulars, advertisements, &c., these being printed on the inside of the envelopes after they are stamped. The great majority of letters are prepaid, because of the diminution in the rate of postage. *Gentlemen* everywhere always pay their own postage, when writing on their own business. In England, they also enclose a stamp to prepay the answer. Large commercial houses cause their address to be printed on stamped en-

* Mr. Leavitt is probably better acquainted with this subject than any other man in America, and his valuable writings are doing much to prepare the public sentiment to demand the full measure of this reform.

velopes, and then send packages of these to their correspondents, to be used when needed.

The free delivery of prepaid letters in the large towns is astonishingly perfect. Almost a stranger among the two millions of London, I once received a letter at my lodgings, from a correspondent to whom my city address was unknown, in three hours after its arrival at the post-office. The postman, when I was in London three months before, had delivered letters to my address, and he now recollected the name and number. Besides the "General Post," which delivers letters coming from the country and foreign parts, there is connected with the department in London, a machine of curious contrivance, and great exploits, called the "District Post." It covers a circle of some twelve miles, from the center, and delivers letters which originate and end within the circle, ten times a day, at dwellings, shops, and offices. In 1848, the number delivered by this post was nearly fifty millions. To these must be added at least a hundred and twenty millions for the General Post, making an aggregate of a hundred and seventy millions of letters delivered in London annually, by the post-office department, a large proportion of which, being prepaid, are delivered free! But there is no end to these statistics, and I leave them.*

The committee, when presenting to Mr. Hill, in 1846, the National Testimonial, had ample grounds for pronouncing his reform "a measure which has opened the blessings of a free correspondence to the teacher of religion, the man of science and literature, the merchant and trader, and the whole British nation, especially the poorest and most defenseless portion of it —a measure which is the greatest boon conferred in modern times on all the social interests of the civilized world." The veteran reformer, Joseph Hume, in a letter to Mr. Bancroft, then our minister at St. James, dated in 1848, says: "I am

* I have not attempted in this chapter to do more than give *statistics* in "round numbers," nearly approximating to precision.

not aware of any reform, amongst the many reforms I have promoted during the last forty years, that has had, and will have, better results toward the improvement of this country, morally, socially, and commercially."

And how has the benefactor of a great and powerful nation been treated by the British Government? He has shared the general fate of useful inventors and reformers. At the outset he was ridiculed as a dreamer, an enthusiast. After a conviction of the utility of his plan had penetrated the masses of the people, Parliament mutilated it, supplying the exscinded parts with uncongenial inventions of its own. When even thus much of his plan was adopted, he was permitted to have but slight influence in working it out in practice. He should have been appointed Postmaster General; but that station belonged, by prescription, to the nobility—to some Lord Fitztoady or Earl Muttonhead, who could hardly tell a mail bag from a handsaw. Liberal Whig though he was, the great reformer was placed, by a Whig administration, in a minor place, where he could exert only a subordinate influence over postal affairs. And after six years of incessant labor and anxiety, which had impaired his health and wasted his fortune, the Peel government turned him out, though he entreated the Premier to allow him, at any pecuniary sacrifice to himself, to remain and aid in working out his plan. Being now embarrassed in his circumstances, a national subscription in his behalf was started, the net proceeds of which amounted to £13,360. It was presented to him, in 1846, at a public dinner, accompanied by many honeyed words. The reply of Mr. Hill was modest. He gave ample credit for the aid he had received from others in carrying his plan through Parliament, and specially named Messrs. Wallace and Warburton, members of the committee of 1838, Mr. Baring, the then Chancellor of the Exchequer, and Lords Ashburton and Brougham. He delicately alluded to his proscription by the Peel administration, and pointed out the improvements necessary to give complete efficiency to his reform.

Thirteen thousand pounds, for devising and introducing a measure which has carried blessings to every princely mansion and peasant cabin in three kingdoms! Why, if Rowland Hill had patented a first class washing machine, he could hardly have made less money out of it. Thirteen thousand pounds from a people that smothered the "Divine-Fanny-show-her-legs," as George Thompson called her, with bouquets and bank notes. But if his cotemporaries do not requite his services, posterity will do justice to his memory.

CHAPTER XXII.

Disruption of the State Church of Scotland—Its Causes—The Veto Act of the Assembly of 1834—Mr. Young Presented to the Church of Auchterarder—Is Vetoed by the Communicants and Rejected by the Presbytery—Resort to the Civil Courts—The Decision—Intrusionists and Non-Intrusionists—The Final Secession of 1843—The Free Church—Dr. Chalmers—Dr. Hill.

One of the most important ecclesiastical occurrences of our times is the disruption of the State Church of Scotland. We see a venerable establishment, founded in the religious affections of a great people, sustained by the arm of secular power, rent in twain, and five hundred of its ministers, possessing a moiety of its talents and piety, and drawing in their train a proportional share of their congregations, secede in obedience to the dictates of conscience, and, under the leadership of one of the most learned, eloquent, and celebrated divines of the age, assume the position of Voluntaries. The difficulties which caused this result arose somewhat in this wise:

In consequence of some controversy as to the right of "patrons" to "present" pastors to churches, a majority of whose members were unwilling to receive them, Lord Moncrieff, in the General Assembly of the Church, in May, 1834, moved a resolution declaring that the disapproval of a majority of the male heads of families, being communicants, should be deemed sufficient ground for a Presbytery rejecting any person presented as a clergyman to a parish in Scotland. After a warm debate, it was carried, 184 to 138. It was sent down to the

Presbyteries, and, being sanctioned by a large majority of them, was confirmed by the General Assembly of 1835. This was known as the *Veto Act*. It was intended to declare the existing law. Whether legal or not, (for on this point, when the trouble arose, lawyers and judges of course differed, and the books, as usual, furnished precedents on both sides,) the veto had generally been acquiesced in for a long period.

In October, 1834, Lord Kinnoul presented Mr. Young, a licensed probationer, to the Church of Auchterarder. Of the heads of families, being communicants, 287 out of 330 protested against the admission of Mr. Young to be their pastor. The Presbytery of Auchterarder, in obedience to the resolution of the Assembly of 1834, rejected him. A suit was commenced in the civil courts, by Lord Kinnoul and Mr. Young, against the Presbytery. After great displays of learning and acrimony, the Court of Session, in 1838, by a majority of 8 judges to 5, decided that the rejection of the presentee was illegal, and that the Presbytery was bound to take Mr. Young "on trials."

Presbyterian Scotland, from John O'Groat's to Gretna Green, was violently agitated with the question. It divided into parties known as Intrusionists and Non-Intrusionists—Doctors Macfarlane, Cook, and Hill, being conspicuous among the former, and Doctors Chalmers, Welsh, and Candlish, among the latter. Every Presbytery was rent with discussion, while the debates in the venerable General Assembly were hardly less violent than in the East India Company Court of Proprietors, when Mammon strives with Mercy for the rule of Hindostan, or when political chiefs in the House of Commons struggle for mastery in the councils of Europe.

The majority of the Assembly having sustained the Presbytery of Auchterarder, the Presbytery appealed from the decision of the Court of Session to the House of Lords. In 1841, I believe, the Lords dismissed the appeal—thus, in effect, affirming the judgment of the Court below, and pronouncing the Veto Act illegal. Upon this, the Court of Session made a further order, directing the Presbytery to take Mr. Young on trials. Whereupon, the Assembly, after a violent debate, in which the Veto was sustained by a power of Caledonian eloquence that John Knox would have gloried to hear, resolved, by a majority of 49, that the principle of Non-Intrusion could not be abandoned, and that no presentee should be forced upon a parish contrary to the will of the congregation. Acting under this vote of the Assembly, the Presbytery still refused to receive Mr. Young; and, thereupon, the Court of Session gave damages to Lord Kinnoul and Mr. Young in the sum of £10,000, and prohibited the Presbytery from settling any minister over the Church of Auchterarder, though he were to be maintained by the Non-Intrusion portion of the congregation.

Matters had now reached a point from which there seemed to be no retreat for either party. The Non-Intrusionists, though they had prevailed in the assembly of the saints, had altogether failed in the court of the unbelievers. In the mean time, other similar cases had arisen, especially those of Strathbogie, Culsalmond, and Glass, where obnoxious pastors, who had been obtruded upon churches, were marched into the pulpits on the Sabbath, guarded by police and soldiery, and the people compelled to receive the gospel with batons over their heads and bayonets at their hearts. These spectacles aroused the spirit that fired the same people a century before, when, in the piquant language of Sydney Smith, the persecuted Scotchman, "with a little oatmeal for food, and a little sulphur for friction, allaying cutaneous irritation with the one hand, and holding his Calvinistic creed in the other, ran away to his flinty hills, sung his psalm out of tune his own way, and listened to his sermon of two hours long, amid the rough and imposing melancholy of the tallest thistles." The same spirit, in 1842–3, refined by a higher civilization, and tempered by a more liberal learning, made the same people prompt in deciding, that when the decrees of the Lord Jesus Christ and the Lord

Chancellor of England came in conflict, the latter must be repudiated and the former obeyed. The interdicts of the Courts were not merely disobeyed—they were literally torn in pieces and trampled under foot by incensed assemblies, amidst the applause of multitudes.

But, though other instances of intrusion had arisen, that of Auchterarder was the case on which the question turned. That question, stated in its simple form, was, whether the will of the patron or the will of the communicants should prevail, in making the presentee the pastor of the parish; and whether the members of a Presbytery were liable to damages to the patron for rejecting his presentee on the veto of the people. But the points involved penetrated far deeper. They touched not only the right of the Church of Scotland to be supreme in her ecclesiastical affairs, but they involved the whole subject of a union of the Church with the State. They reached beyond this. They raised the question of the right of the people to be supreme in religious affairs. They stopped not here. They leaped the boundary that divides spiritual and civil authority, and mooted the question of the supremacy of the popular will—the question, whether the people are the legitimate source of all power—an inquiry which stops not in its researches till it has explored the foundations of human government in their broadest aspect. Not only, then, were the rights of the communicants of Auchterarder, of the Presbytery of Auchterarder, of the Church of Scotland at issue, but the decision of this case involved principles which might shake the minarets of the Metropolitan Cathedral, the towers of Parliament House, the walls of the Throne Room of St. James.

Looking to the possibility of such consequences, it is no wonder that the "Moderates" attempted to soothe the irritation by that dernier panacea of conservatives and cowards—a compromise. The Scotch Church question had already found its way into Parliament. In 1840, Lord Aberdeen had introduced a bill to settle the difficulties. It slept in the archives of the Peers till the Tories came into power. Dr. Chalmers was now consulted by the Government. He gave his opinion as to what would satisfy the Non-Intrusionists. He was promised a bill that would justify a Presbytery in rejecting a presentee on even the most frivolous objection—as red hair or a black skin, for instance. But, instead of this, a bill was introduced which did not allow the Church judicatories to reject unless on grounds satisfactory to the civil court. The tergiversation of the Government wrung from Dr. Chalmers the exclamation, that "the morality of politicians was the morality of horse-jockies."

The General Assembly of May, 1842, met. It was opened by the Lord High Commissioner of Her Majesty, with unusual pomp, blandness, and hypocrisy. All hope of reconciliation had not fled. The friends of the Veto cherished the delusion that purity and peace, that non-intrusion and non-resistance might yet walk hand in hand; and, not being prepared to break with the Government, they suffered the Assembly to adjourn without taking any decisive action. During the ensuing summer and autumn, Sir James Graham, the Home Secretary, endeavored to cajole the Non-Intrusionists, and succeeded in inducing 40 or 50 conservative clergymen of that party to express their approval of a settlement of the question on the basis of a compromise, which should give a great deal of power to the people and the Kirk, and a little more to the Court of Session. The battle was fought, on popular grounds, in the House of Commons, in the winter and spring of 1843. A deputation of Non-Intrusion clergymen was present. Remaining in London till hope had abandoned them, they returned to Scotland, and prepared for the final disruption of the Church. An act was subsequently passed—such an one as would have been gladly accepted in 1840—but it came too late.

The General Assembly of 1843 met on the eighteenth of May. An immense throng crowded the floor, the galleries, the aisles of the edifice, eager with expectation. The Lord

High Commissioner went through the ceremony of opening the Assembly, in a style of chilling pomp. Dr. Welsh, the Moderator of the last Assembly, rose, read the solemn protest of his brethren, and the disciples of John Knox quietly left their seats, and shook the dust from their feet on the threshold of the church of their fathers. When the crowd outside saw the venerable forms of Chalmers, Welsh, and their followers, emerging from the ancient edifice, they lifted their hats and bowed their heads, with bosoms too full for the utterance of a cheer. But, as the ejected presbyters wended their way toward the high rock in the vicinity of the Castle where glittered the spires of the New Assembly Hall, thousands of acclamations rent the air, mingled with the waving of hats and handkerchiefs, from streets, windows, roofs, and balconies. They entered the house, followed by a throng, in which emotions of enthusiasm and solemnity struggled for the mastery. The Assembly immediately organized, by placing its great founder, Dr. Chalmers, in the chair. Having uttered a sublime prayer, he gave out the psalm, "God is our refuge in distress," so often sung in the bloody days, in the glens of Scotland, by the hunted Covenanters, when

"Leaning on his spear,
The liart veteran heard the word of God
By Cameron thundered, or by Renwick poured
In gentle stream."

The Free Kirk was now launched. The crew was zealous, but untried; the pilot, though skillful, was about to explore an unknown and tempestuous sea. But a voice was heard above the raging of the elements, saying, "Peace! be still!" The Assembly vigorously entered on the work of bringing order out of confusion, symmetry out of chaos. The five hundred clergymen who soon rallied round its altars, made noble sacrifices for conscience' sake. They had to leave the greater part of their churches, their glebes, their manses; many, literally, abandoning their *livings*. Their flocks followed them to their cost; for new church edifices were to be erected, and salaries to be raised, not from tithes, stipends, and ecclesiastical funds—for these had been left behind in the Exodus—but out of the pockets of those who, for the first time, found themselves Seceders in fact, and Voluntaries in position. They were prepared for this. Congregations met in groves, in barns, in lofts, in halls, and heard the Word. They raised funds, and built churches. They appealed for aid to their brethren in England and America. They soon amassed a fund of £300,000, for the support of poor pastors and parishes. They encountered great difficulties in obtaining sites for churches. Many of the Intrusion landlords would neither give nor sell them building spots. They would lease or sell lands for cockpits, horse-races, gambling-houses, dram-shops, and even for Methodist or Baptist places of worship; but they would not permit a chapel of the Free Kirk of Scotland to pollute the soil. In process of time, Parliament and public opinion brought these refractory landlords to their senses. Excluded in a great measure from the current public newspapers, they established journals of their own. Denounced by Blackwood, looked coldly upon by the Edinburgh, though the Westminster gave them two or three able and hearty articles, they set up the North British Review, which at once took rank with the first quarterlies in the kingdom. Shut out from the theological schools of the old Kirk, they founded a seminary of their own, placing Dr. Chalmers at its head, as professor of divinity. During the six years of the existence of the Free Church, it has drawn to itself a large share of the numbers and vitality of the Presbyterian body of Scotland. The Old Kirk has a great deal of wealth, a great many churches, and a great deal of pomp. It also enjoys a great deal of languor, a great deal of vacancy, and a great deal of chagrin.

Yet it must be confessed that this secession, so extraordinary in its immediate results, so congenial to the liberal tendencies of the times, so far-reaching and powerful in its remote and collateral consequences, has never excited that enthusiasm in the mass of ecclesiastical reformers in Great Britain, which might have been anticipated. The reasons given for this apathy are, that a body which had so long wielded ecclesiastical power over others, by virtue of State laws, ought in its turn to yield obedience to those laws—that the Seceders had held on upon their power so long as they could exert it in their own way—that, in the exercise of spiritual authority, they had been far from tolerant of Dissenters—and that, at the very moment of their egress from the Kirk, they repudiated Voluntaryism as a principle, and offered incense to State-church establishments.

There was, no doubt, solid ground for some of these charges. As to the course of the Seceders, while members of the State Kirk, many of their acts were no doubt oppressive. The deeds of May, 1843, are broad enough to cover a multitude of such sins. As to the repudiation of Voluntaryism, while in the very act of Secession, it was a concession to that tempting expediency which, in a crisis when principle and numbers are both important, yields some of the former to gain more of the latter. The Free Church has outgrown this folly of its infancy, and in riper years has repudiated the repudiation. It is now, both in position and profession, a Voluntary body. Learning wisdom from experience, and acting on the maxim, alike pure and profitable, that honesty is the best policy, long may it bless the land of Knox, Renwick, and Chalmers!

To attempt a sketch of the talents, genius, and virtues of Dr. Chalmers, would be a work of supererogation. It is ample eulogy to say, that he was the Moses of the Exodus, the Luther of the Reformation, I have faintly described. The sublimity of that position dims even the splendor of those productions of his pen and tongue which have made his name familiar in two hemispheres. His memory lives on memorials more enduring than monumental brass or marble—the hearts of a whole people.

I have somewhere seen a portrait of REV. DR. HILL, Professor of Moral Philosophy in Glasgow University, and a leader of the Intrusion party, sketched in the General Assembly of 1840, which I transcribe from memory, bearing witness to its faithfulness to the subject. Dr. Chalmers had just resumed his seat, after a powerful speech, when a tall, thin gentleman, on the other side of the house, distinguished for an uncommon length of neck and face, with a complexion inclining to sallow, and an imperturbable gravity of countenance, caught the eye. Never before had there been seen so prodigious an extent of white neckcloth, a figure so immovably rigid, an expression so inveterately grave. He sat so bolt upright, that the spectator was curious to know whether he ever shifted his position or moved a feature. He rose to address the assembly. He opened his mouth, and his words came marching out, dressed in the somber hues and with the melancholy tread of a funeral procession. It was evident that great truths were for the first time to be communicated to mankind. He laid down his premises. They reminded one of the lawyer in the farce, who, when pressed for a definition, thundered out, "Law is—law!" "Judgment," exclaimed Rev. Dr. Hill, "judgment is an act of the mind." There was a suppressed laugh from the Non-Intrusion side of the house. The Doctor drew himself up more stiffly, and looked across the house in dignified astonishment, as if desirous to single out the men who disputed first principles. "I am in the right," he solemnly reiterated—"judgment, Moderator, is an act of the mind!" He went on with his speech. It was a dead skeleton of logical phraseology, divested of the muscle, flesh, and blood of living argument; the speech of a man whose father, perhaps, could argue, and who, without a particle of causality, tried to argue too, sheerly through the exercise of filial imitation. As he spoke, a nervous torpor crept over the Assembly—the spectators began to nod—the reporters dropped their pens—the older divines, sinking under the weight of their dinners, rested their heads on the front boards—the very gas seemed to burn with a rounder and a dimmer flame—and when, after a long infliction, the last sentence of the peroration died away in the far galleries, and the spell was broken, there was a stretching of limbs and jaws, and a raising of hands over the benches, and a straining to collect and concentrate scattered thoughts, till by and by the members seemed to realize that they were actually sitting in a General Assembly; whereupon, a gentleman moved an adjournment, and all retired with the conviction, that whoever might doubt whether Dr. Hill was a profound philosopher and ecclesiastical historian, he possessed most astonishing *mesmeric* qualities and powers.

CHAPTER XXIII.

The Established Church of England—Its Revenues—Its Ecclesiastical Abuses—Its Sway over Political Parties—Rev. Dr. Phillpotts—Rev. Dr. Pusey—Rev. Mr. Noel—Anti-State Church Movement.

THE Established Church of England is one of the foulest sores on the body politic of the kingdom. I shall examine it mainly in its political bearings.

The King is the "Supreme Head of the Church," and appoints, through the chapters, the bishops, besides a great number of lesser dignitaries. The bishops license and ordain the inferior clergy. The owners of estates charged with the payment of the salaries of pastors, have the right to nominate or "present" them to the parishes. There are some 12,000 parochial churches under the control of the Establishment Of these the crown presents to 952; the bishops to 1248; the deans and chapters to 787; other ecclesiastical dignitaries to 1851; the Universities of Oxford and Cambridge to 721; the nobility and gentry to 5096; and the residue are disposed of by others.

The annual revenue of the whole body of the clergy is more than $42,000,000; a sum greater than is received by the Established Clergy of all the world besides. The income of the twenty-eight bishops amounts to about $800,000. The Archbishop of Canterbury receives $75,000, and of York $50,000 The Bishop of London $50,000, of Durham $40,000, of Winchester $35,000, and so on. Previous to the act of 1837, the income of the sees mentioned was much larger.

Said the late Rowland Hill, himself a clergyman of the Establishment, at a missionary meeting in Exeter Hall, a few years ago: "Would, my lord, that I had the bishops of this realm tied up by the heels to that chandelier, and could direct the stewards to hold the plates under their pockets and catch the falling guineas; what a collection we should raise!" One of the worst features of this institution is the gross inequality in the distribution of its favors. Of its clergy, fifteen hundred receive an average annual income of about $5000 each; while another fifteen hundred (and they are the working and valuable portion) receive only an average of about $400; and many of these last do not get $200. Sydney Smith has aptly asked, "Why is the Church of England nothing but a collection of beggars and bishops? the right reverend Dives in the palace, and Lazarus in orders at the gate, doctored by dogs and comforted by crumbs?"

The revenues of the Establishment are mostly drawn from tithes. But large sums are realized from other sources. And in addition to these, the clergy (whose numbers far exceed those of the parochial churches) hold all the professorships, tutorships, masterships, and fellowships, of the universities and public state schools; all the chaplainships in the embassies, army and navy, and corporate and commercial companies; worm their way into nearly all the profitable offices in educational and charitable institutions, as librarians, secretaries, treasurers, and trustees; are constant waiters upon Divine Providence and the Public Treasury; standing candidates for all places of light work and heavy pay; and show their zeal for the Crown and the Miter by promptly furnishing recruits for the great army of sinecurists in the realm.*

* A commission instituted some years ago by the House of Commons, to inquire into the abuses of charitable trusts, found a clergyman at the head of a school, with a salary of £900 a year, and *one* pupil. Another received £500, had not a single scholar, and rented the school-room for a saw-pit.

It is not my purpose to speak particularly of the religious character and influence of the Establishment. But, a few facts in this department may be given to show that Paul the tent-maker, and Peter the fisherman, are not very closely copied by some of their English successors. It is a notorious fact that a large body of the clergy do not compose their own sermons, but purchase them in manuscript at depots in London, and other large towns, as they do their stationery and wines. There is no very serious objection to this, provided the sermons are better than they could write themselves. A good purchased sermon is preferable to a bad home-made one. But, it is equally notorious that they are often written as marketable commodities by grossly irreligious men. Here is an advertisement from a newspaper, which will serve as a specimen of its class. "MANUSCRIPT SERMONS. To clergymen who, from ill health, or other causes, are prevented from composing their own sermons, the advertiser offers his services on moderate terms. Original sermons composed on any given texts or subjects. N. B. A specimen sent if required. Address L. S. W., Post-Office, Winchester."

The Church "livings" being property, they are, of course, marketable articles. English newspapers frequently contain advertisements offering them for sale. In describing their desirable qualities it is often stated that "the income is large and the duties light," or, that "the present incumbent is very aged," or, "in very feeble health;" and I have seen them represented as being in the midst of a fine sporting country, surrounded by a most agreeable society of nobility and gentry, &c. I select an advertisement from a number lying before me. "ADVOWSON. Perpetual Patronage and Right of Presentation to be disposed of, subject to the life of an incumbent, now sixty-eight years old. The benefice consists of an excellent rectory-house, lately built at a considerable expense; abounding with conveniencies, and capitally fitted, good out-offices, pleasure-grounds, garden, &c., farm-yard, and forty acres of glebe. The tithes are commuted. Annual value upward of 600*l.* per annum, independent of surplice fees, and is well situated in a pleasant and luxuriant country, four miles from a large town, to which there is railway conveyance."

Now, all this simply means, that Lord John Broadacres, being hard pushed by his gambling debts, will sell to anybody, Turk or Mormon, and his heirs forever, the right to quarter a dapper young student from Oxford on this parish, to occupy this comfortable and elegant house and grounds, and collect £600 per annum out of Episcopalians, Baptists, Methodists, Independents, and Quakers, in return for reading to a handful of people fifty or sixty sermons a year, purchased at a book-stall in London.

It needs no "Black Book" to tell us, that $40,000,000, extorted annually from the people by such an institution, and to a large extent from those who dissent from its ritual, and never listen to its clergy, is a prolific source of vexation and oppression, and tends powerfully to debauch the morals and corrupt the politics of the kingdom. The Established Church exercises unbounded sway over the politics of the country, holding in vassalage great masses of the Tory and Whig parties. The nobility and gentry find the Establishment a profitable and dignified retreat for such younger branches of their families, as are too dull for the learned secular professions, and too cowardly and puny for cutting their way to promotion in the army and navy. They send to this snug asylum their indolent and imbecile offspring, where they may receive emoluments and pensions without burning the barrister's midnight lamp, or treading the thorny road of politics, or encountering malignant fevers while filling civic stations in tropical colonies, or braving death on the deck of a line-of-battle ship in the Mediterranean, or in the spouting breach of a fortress in Hindostan. The owners of advowsons and livings, wielding a capital whose yearly income is $40,000,000, keep constantly under pay, all over the kingdom, 16 000 clergy, who, with many noble exceptions, are the ordained and licensed enemies of political progress and ecclesiastical reform.

I by no means intend to say, that there are not a large number of most worthy, pious, and faithful ministers, in the English Establishment, and especially among the poorer clergy. Nor, that its doctrines are not Biblical, and its service beautifully impressive. But, in its political tendencies, the institution stands arrayed against progress and reform.

Among the most conspicuous champions of the Established Church, and who has recently distinguished himself as the persecutor of Rev. Mr. Shore, is DR. PHILLPOTTS, THE BISHOP OF EXETER. Entering the House of Lords, the eye of a stranger is instantly arrested by the bench of bishops, whose white robes and flowing wigs give them such an old-womanish appearance, that he conjectures they must be "peeresses in their own right," and by some one of the convenient fictions of the common law are entitled to seats with the male barons. Sitting gravely among them, with rigid muscle, compressed lip, and knit brow, is Dr. Phillpotts, who conceals under his ample lawn an amount of intellectual acumen and power which are able and ready to grapple with the pamphlet of any schismatic in the diocese of Exeter, or the speech of any lord in the House of Peers. A spectator can hardly believe that those pale, icy features, cover a mental volcano. The tones of his voice give point to words that pierce to the marrow of the subject under discussion, while his cool, crafty, and dexterous style of argument shows that a trained master of debate is on the floor. Delighting equally in exposing the fallacies of his opponent, and placing him in a false position, his assaults are to be shunned rather than provoked. One of the most adroit and keen logicians in the House, he is skillful in making nice distinctions, and in setting the arguments of his adversary to devouring each other. The cold suavity with which he flays his victim, and the sweet malignity with which he sugars over his bitterest denunciations, and the apparent candor and sincerity which sit serenely on his visage when uttering the most repulsive opinions, only make him the more provokingly intolerable. This crafty prelate countenanced the Oxford Tractarians, till their open advocacy of Popish doctrines and rites alarmed his more timid brethren, when he veered off in a graceful curve, and has since made haste to divert suspicion as to his orthodoxy, by persecuting the evangelical clergymen of his diocese.

Spite the efforts of the bench of bishops, a violent intestine war has been waged within the walls of the venerable Establishment for many years. Two parties have sprung up, one of which would make the Church essentially Roman Catholic, while the other would make it more thoroughly Protestant and Evangelical. Dr. Pusey may be regarded as the head of the Catholic, Mr. Noel of the Evangelical party. Both are the immediate descendants of noble families, both possess superior attainments, are accomplished preachers, and able controversialists. The style of each in the pulpit is calm, logical, persuasive, and one cannot listen to either without imbibing the conviction that he is uttering the honest impulses of his understanding and heart. Dr. Pusey is one of the founders of the association at Oxford which issued the celebrated "Tracts for the Times." Mr. Noel has recently published a volume on "the Union of Church and State," remarkable for its research, meditative tone, and Christian spirit. It must exert a powerful influence upon the ultimate overthrow of this institution. Dr. Pusey's writings have driven several of his disciples over to Romanism; among the most distinguished of whom was Mr. Newman; and he himself came very near accompanying his associate. He still remains in the Establishment. Mr. Noel, having thrown his able testimonial into the bosom of the Church, has withdrawn from it, and united with the Baptist denomination.

The nature of the union of the Church with the State, and its influence upon the religious and political interests of the country, have been frequent topics of discussion ever since the Commonwealth of Cromwell. The repeal of the corporation and test acts, the emancipation of the Catholics, and the disruption of the Church of Scotland, have given increased intensity to these discussions in our own times. The persecution of the amiable and heroic Mr. Shore, by the Bishop of Exeter, the publication of Mr. Noel's work, his rigorous treatment by the Bishop of London, the acknowledged purity of his motives, and the dignity and excellence of his character, have kindled into a flame the agitation for the separation of the Church from the State. At no period within a century has the anti-state-church party been as strong in England as now. It counts in its ranks some of the ablest debaters, and keenest controversialists in the kingdom. Mr. Burnet leads the Independents, Dr. Cox the Baptists, Mr. Sturge the Quakers, Dr. Wardlaw the Scotch Congregationalists, Dr. Ritchie the Secession Church of Scotland, and Dr. Candlish the Free Church of Scotland. Behind them rally the whole body of the Dissenters, the great majority of the Irish Catholics, the main strength of the radical reformers, while no inconsiderable portion of the liberal laity of the Establishment sympathizes with them. These elements will continue to increase in volume and power, till they sever a union offensive to God and oppressive to man.

CHAPTER XXIV.

The Corn Laws—Their Character and Policy—Origin of the Anti-Corn-Law Movement—Adam Smith—Mr. Cobden—"Anti-Corn-Law Parliament"—Mr. Villier's Motion in the House of Commons in 1839—Formation of the League—Power of the Landlords--Lord John Russell's Motion in 1841—General Election of that Year—Mr. Cobden Returned to Parliament—Peel in Power—His Modification of the Corn Laws—Great Activity and Steady Progress of the League during the Years 1842, '3, '4, and '5—Session of 1846—Sir Robert Peel and the Duke of Wellington—Repeal of the Corn Laws.

A PLEASANT little story is told of Queen Victoria and the corn laws. During the second year of her sovereignty, and while yet a maiden, she was one day skipping the rope as a relaxation from the pressure of official duties. Lord Melbourne, the Premier, was superintending the royal amusement. She suddenly stopped, and, turning to him with a thoughtful look, (the cares of State no doubt clouding her brow,) said, "My Lord, what are these corn laws, which my people are making so much noise about?" Said the courtly Premier, in reply, "Please your Majesty, they are the laws that regulate the consumption of the staff of life in your Majesty's dominions." "Indeed," rejoined the Queen, "have any of the staff officers of my Life Guards got the consumption? Poor fellows!" Her Majesty then resumed the skipping of the rope.

Perhaps some American maidens are as ignorant of what the British corn laws were as Queen Victoria.

Lord Stanley came within a few hundred years of the truth, when he said that the principle of landlord protection had existed in England for eight centuries. In 1774, the corn laws received the impress which they retained till their repeal in 1846. They were revised in 1791, in 1804, in 1815, and in 1828. The revisions of 1815 and 1828 produced the system more generally known as *the* corn laws. The object of the system was to afford as complete a monopoly in breadstuffs to the home agriculturists as possible, and yet allow the introduction of foreign grain whenever a bad harvest, or other causes, produced a scarcity of food. At every revision, down to that of 1828, the duties were made more and more protective. The price to which wheat (for instance) must rise ere it could come in from abroad, at a nominal duty, was fixed in 1774 at 48*s*. per quarter ; in 1791, at 54*s* ; in 1804, at 66*s*. ; and in 1815, at 80*s*.—the quarter being 8 bushels. The liberal policy of Mr. Huskisson slightly prevailed in 1828, and the maximum price was fixed at 73*s*.

The system was a compromise between protection and starvation, the umpire being a " *sliding scale* " of duties. By this scale, the duties fell as the prices rose, and rose as the prices fell. The act of 1828 had 20 or 30 degrees in its scale, three or four of which are given as illustrations. When the average price of wheat in the kingdom was 52*s*. per quarter, the duty on foreign wheat was 34*s*. 8*d*. When the price reached 60*s*, the duty fell to 26*s*. 8*d*. When the price rose to 70*s*., the duty sunk to 10*s* 8*d*. When the price attained 73*s*. and upward, the duty went down to 1*s*. The price which regulated the duty was ascertained as follows: The prices of grain (wheat, for instance) on Saturday of each week, at 150 of the principal markets in the kingdom, were ascertained by returns to the Exchequer, and these were averaged. To this average were added the averages of the five preceding weeks, and then " the general average " of the whole six was struck, and this, on each Thursday, was proclaimed by the Government as the price for the regulation of the duty for one week. Wheat, flour, &c., from abroad, might be stored or "bonded," without paying duties, to await a favorable turn of the market, then to be entered or reëxported at pleasure.

The act of 1828, after being modified in 1842, was totally repealed in 1846—the totality to take effect in February, 1849. During the seven years immediately preceding the repeal, matter sufficient to fill a thousand quarto volumes was printed in Great Britain on the Corn Laws. I shall not touch this mass, but confine myself to a notice of the movement typified by the name of Richard Cobden.

The history of Voluntary Associations does not furnish a triumph so signal as that achieved by the Anti-Corn-Law League. In seven years it revolutionized the mind of the most intelligent nation of Europe, bent to its will the proudest legislative assembly in the world, prostrated an aristocracy more powerful than the oligarchies of antiquity, and overthrew a system rooted to the earth by the steady growth and fostering culture of centuries. It may not be uninteresting to trace the rise and progress of such an Association.

From the days of Adam Smith downward, a school of political economists have contended that free trade is the high commercial road to national wealth. This was a favorite doctrine with the brilliant *coterie*, whose opinions were reflected by the Edinburgh Review, and it mingled in the discussions upon "national distress," with which Parliament so frequently resounded from the breaking out of the French revolution to the passage of the Reform bill. But the landlords proved too strong for the schoolmen. The beginning of 1837 saw a fearful commercial collapse in England, which was aggravated by a deficient harvest in the ensuing summer. The summer of 1838 brought in its train another deficient harvest, which plunged the country deeper into suffering and gloom. Many sagacious minds regarded the corn laws as a fruitful source of these disasters. In September, Dr. Bowring and Colonel

Thompson, two distinguished Benthamites, started the Anti-Corn-Law crusade, by forming, in a small meeting at Manchester, an Anti-Corn-Law Association. Shortly after, a large assembly of the merchants and manufacturers of that town, in which Mr. Cobden bore a leading part, resolved to aid the Association with £3,000. In December, the Manchester Chamber of Commerce adopted a petition to Parliament, praying for an immediate and total repeal of the laws. Thus encouraged, the Association convened a meeting of delegates from all parts of the kingdom, at Manchester, in January, 1839. This body empowered the Association to assemble a meeting of deputies in London at the opening of the approaching session of Parliament. They met in February, and petitioned the House of Commons for leave to present evidence at its bar in regard to the injurious effects of the corn laws, and selected Mr. Villiers to bring forward a motion to that end. It was negatived with contempt, and the delegates separated. A month elapsed, and they again met at Brown's Hotel, in Palace Yard—the Protectionists, in derision, giving them the name of "The Anti-Corn-Law Parliament"—a name which they at once adopted, and which they ultimately taught the landlords to fear, if not respect. Their organ, Mr. Villiers, moved that the Commons take into consideration the act regulating the importation of foreign corn. He spoke in defense of his motion amidst coughings and hootings, when a large majority of members, shouting, "Divide! divide!" rushed into the lobbies, silencing for the moment the demand for cheap bread. They had yet to learn the character of the men they were dealing with.

On motion of Mr. Cobden, the Palace-Yard Convention now organized "THE NATIONAL ANTI-CORN-LAW LEAGUE," with a Central Council, to be located at Manchester. In that hour, the landlords of Great Britain insolently boasted of their ability to cope with all the other property-holders of the kingdom combined. There was cause for their boasting. Their possessions were vast, their union was perfect, their power hitherto irresistible. During a period of fifty-five years, the number of land-owners in the realm had fearfully diminished. In 1774, when Mr. Burke's corn law was enacted, the estimated number was 240,000 in England proper. In 1839, 40,000* persons, acting together, with the unity and efficiency of a close corporation, owned the agricultural soil of England. With this monopoly, the League joined issue. Richard Cobden, in the name of Free Trade, threw his gauntlet in the face of Protection, and challenged the feudalists to trial by battle before the people of the three kingdoms. The struggle was one of the severest, the victory one of the completest, of the present century.

The leading principles maintained by the League were, that the corn laws were not beneficial to the whole body of agriculturists, but only to a privileged few ; that they depressed other branches of industry ; caused frequent and ruinous fluctuations in the market value of breadstuffs, greatly enhanced the price at all times, and, therefore, were injurious to the community generally, and especially to the laboring poor. The promulgation of these principles excited a discussion of the broader question of the relative merits of Protection and Free Trade in their widest aspects.

The League entered so vigorously into the contest, that, by the close of the year 1839, upward of one hundred important towns had formed kindred associations. In 1840, Manchester, which bore so conspicuous a part in originating the movement, commenced the series of large Free-Trade meetings, which made that town so famous in the corn-law struggle. In January, a public dinner was spread for the friends of the League, under a huge pavilion, at which 4,000 persons sat down.

* Our lamented countryman, Mr. Colman, estimated the number at 30,000. I think the text is quite low enough. And an enterprise is now started for the purchase of small freeholds by landless men, which, if vigorously prosecuted, will do much to break up the land-monopoly of England.

The next day, 5,000 operatives were feasted. In February, at the opening of the Royal Parliament, the "Anti-Corn Law Parliament" met in London. Mr. Villiers renewed the motion of the previous year, and was defeated. In March, the Palace-Yard Parliament again assembled; Mr. Villiers again brought forward his motion, and was again defeated. The delegates returned home to arouse their constituents. The cry for "cheap bread" reverberated through the summer from Pentland Frith to Eddystone Light—from the Giant's Causeway to the Cove of Cork. Palace Yard again swarmed with delegates in November, and the persevering Villiers again moved, spoke, and was defeated. But the warm agitations of the League were gradually ripening public opinion. Whigism was tottering to its fall. It cast about for a crutch. Early in the session of 1841, Lord John Russell, foreseeing the necessity of a dissolution of Parliament or a dissolution of the Ministry, resolved on the former; and, wishing for "a cry" with which to rally the country, gave notice of his motion for the abandonment of the sliding scale, and for a fixed duty of 8*s*. per quarter on imported wheat. He made an able speech, closed the doors of St. Stephen's, and opened the campaign for a new House of Commons.

The Tories swept the kingdom, the Whigs falling between the "totality" of the Leaguers and the "finality" of the Protectionists. Lord John faced the New Parliament, his motion was defeated, and Sir Robert Peel, after an exclusion of eleven years, returned to power. But, though the landlords gave the Queen a sliding-scale House of Commons, the operatives of Stockport gave the People "a fixed fact" in the person of Richard Cobden. And now, said the feudalists, Cobden will find his level. He may sway a turbulent mob of unwashed Manchester artisans, but he will not dare to brave the starred and gartered aristocracy of England. Little did they dream, in this hour of their exultation, that in four years and a half the Manchester calico-printer would convert the Premier to his views, who, carrying over half the Tories to the League, would give victory to its standard, generously saying, as he retired with grace and dignity from the field, "Not to the Tory party nor to the Whig party, not to myself nor to the noble Lord at the head of the Opposition, is this change to be attributed; but the People of this country are indebted for this great measure of relief to the rare combination of elements which center in the mind and heart of Richard Cobden."

To return from this digression. The session of 1842 was opened at a period of unexampled distress in the manufacturing districts. Sir Robert Peel proposed a modification of the corn laws, which considerably reduced the duties. Mr. Villiers met the Government with a motion that the laws ought immediately to cease and determine. During the debate, Sir Robert announced that he would not pledge himself to a permanent maintenance of the sliding scale, and he distinctly abandoned the principle of protection as mere protection. This foreshadowed the events of 1846. Cobden's lucid speeches in defense of the motion won him a high place in the House. Villiers was defeated by a large majority, and the Government measure adopted.

Near the close of the year, the League proposed to raise £50,000, and deputed Messrs. Cobden, Bright, Col. Thompson, and others, to traverse the country and address the people. The great Free-Trade Hall was built at Manchester, and at its consecration, in January, 1843, it was announced that £44,000 had been raised. An attack was next made on London. After filling first the Crown and Anchor, and then Freemasons' Hall, the League was invited by Mr. Macready to occupy Drury-Lane Theater. Night after night, that spacious building was more densely packed, and rung with louder cheers, than in the days when Edmund Kean burst upon the metropolis, and carried it with a whirlwind of excitement. Thus far, the meetings of the League had been held in towns and cities. Mr. Cobden now challenged the Monopolists to meet the Free Traders on their chosen ground. He attended open meetings of agriculturists in thirty-two counties, encountered the advocates of protection, and with the aid of his associates, defeated them on a show of hands in every case but one.

The year 1844 was opened with a proposal to raise £100,000, and to distribute ten millions of anti-corn-law tracts. Free Trade Hall gave a lead to the country, by subscribing £20,000 at a single meeting. In March, Mr. Cobden attacked the landlords in their farmyards. He moved the Commons for a committee to inquire into the effects of protective duties upon tenant farmers and agricultural laborers. His speech on that occasion, one of the ablest he ever delivered, gave a new aspect to the controversy, and a fresh impulse to the national intellect. And more than all, as was afterward acknowledged, that speech sunk into the soul of Sir Robert Peel, and prepared the *finale* of the corn laws. During the session, Sir Robert carried through a bill reducing the duties on several important articles; but he did not touch corn. The "pressure from without" was becoming, month by month, more difficult to be resisted. As fast as vacancies in Parliament occurred, they were filled by the candidates of the League. Early in 1845, Sir Robert proposed sweeping financial reforms, repealing the duties on four hundred and fifty articles, reducing the duty on the important article of sugar, and otherwise modifying the tariff. The corn laws still remained inviolate, but the landlords began to be alarmed. The panic was not diminished when the League placed its choicest orators on the stage of Covent Garden. For weeks, that theater was crowded from pit to dome, with audiences more earnest and enthusiastic than the muse of Shakspeare or the wit of Sheridan could command. Distinguished Parliamentarians, and even Earls and Barons, were swept into the throng, and mingled their voices in the chorus for "cheap bread," with Cobden, Bright, Fox, and Thompson. The ladies crowned the *fete* by opening a splendid Free-Trade bazaar in the theater, crowding its doors for three weeks with wealth and beauty, and adding £15,000 to the treasury of the League. Ere the autumnal months had passed away, it became evident that Sir Robert Peel's Government must soon grant repeal or yield the ghost. A new election was anticipated. "Registration" almost silenced the shout for "Repeal." Effective measures were taken to place the name of every Free-Trade voter on the lists. The close of the year 1845 saw the League busy in raising a fund of £250,000, and marshalling one hundred thousand new electors for the contest.

The session of 1846 opened. The result is known. Sir Robert Peel and the Duke of Wellington—the same men who, seventeen years before, emancipated the Catholics—repealed the corn laws. There could be no higher evidence of the ability and tact of Sir Robert, than that on both these memorable occasions he won the support of the most inflexible of men, without whose aid neither of those measures could have passed the House of Peers. Such acts pour a flood of redeeming sunshine upon the characters of both these men.

The corn laws are dead. The principle of protection has received its death-blow in England. By mingling the question of corn-law repeal with that of protection generally, the discussions of seven years carried the mind of Britain forward a quarter of a century in the direction of Free Trade in all its departments. Nobody hopes for a permanent revival of the old order of things, except two or three superannuated ladies in the House of Peers, and half a dozen young Hotspurs in the House of Commons. If the good effected by this great measure has not realized all the promises of its advocates, it has falsified most of the evil predicted by its opponents—being but another proof that public sagacity, warned by the preliminary agitation, foresees changes in existing systems, and gradually prepares to meet them, so that their actual advent heralds neither all the blessings anticipated by their friends, nor all the disasters prophesied by their enemies.*

A more particular notice of Mr. Cobden, and some other anti-corn-law advocates, will be given in the next chapter.

* It is undoubtedly true that this corn-law contest had its origin in the conflicting interests of two classes of monopolists, the manufacturers and the landlords. But, the turn which the conflict finally took made it a battle between Free Trade and Protection, and the victory redounded to the advantage of the former. The monopoly of the manufacturers will no doubt be overthrown in its turn. A great maritime monopoly has already shared the fate of the landlord monopoly in the recent repeal of the Navigation Laws.

CHAPTER XXV.

Notice of Corn-Law Repealers—Mr. Cobden—Mr. Bright—Colonel Thompson—Mr. Villiers—Dr. Bowring—William J. Fox—Ebenezer Elliott—James Montgomery—Mr. Paulton—George Wilson—The Last Meeting of the League.

THE seasonable organization, steady progress, and signal triumph of The National Anti-Corn-Law League are attributable in a very large degree to the sagacity, ability, and courage of RICHARD COBDEN. The early career of one who so suddenly acquired a European reputation is not so familiar as to render uninteresting a few incidents of that part of his life.

The leader of the Commercial Revolution of England is the son of a poor yeoman of Sussex. Commencing active life as a clerk in a London counting-house, he afterward removed to Manchester, where he became the traveling agent of a house largely engaged in the cotton trade. His intelligence, industry, and sound judgment won him the confidence of his employers, and the respect of all with whom he had intercourse. His rise was rapid, and we soon find him associated with an elder brother in a manufacturing enterprise of his own. He was highly successful. He studied public taste then as shrewdly as he afterward studied public opinion. An anecdote will illustrate this. In 1837, a gentleman visited Mr. Cobden's warehouse in Manchester, where he was shown some printed muslins of a peculiarly beautiful pattern, which Mr. C. was just sending into the market. A few days afterward, this gentleman was walking in the vicinity of Goodwood, and met some ladies of the family of the Duke of Richmond wearing these identical prints; and shortly after, while strolling through Windsor Park, he saw the young Queen going down the slopes sporting a new dress of the same pattern. Of course, this set all the ladies of the kingdom in a rage after "Cobden's prints," which immediately became as celebrated in the market as did Cobden's speeches a few years afterward.

But Cobden was never a mere calico-printer. In his manufacturing days, his capacious mind embraced large views of finance and trade. In 1835, he published, under the signature of "A Manchester Manufacturer," an able pamphlet on "England, Ireland, and America," and, soon after, another on "Russia," in which he advocated a repeal of the corn laws, free trade, peace, and non-intervention in the politics of other nations; strongly urging that England's true policy was to abolish the agricultural monopoly, open her ports to the world, stick to trade and manufactures, and not meddle with foreign controversies. The information which these pamphlets displayed was rare and valuable; the reasonings cogent; the style forcible; and the sentiments eulogistic of "those free institutions which are favorable to the peace, wealth, education, and happiness of mankind." As an illustration of his thorough mode of sifting a question, it may be stated that, before writing his pamphlet on Russia, he made a tour to the East expressly to gain information on that subject.

Mr. Cobden had now secured a reputation in Manchester and the surrounding district, and became a leading man in all public movements, especially such as related to business and trade. In 1837, he was invited to contest Stockport for a seat in Parliament. He failed of an election by fifty-five votes. In 1840, he was requested to stand for Manchester; but he declined, because he was expected to support, in all things, the Whig Administration; and, being far in advance of it on the subject of Free Trade, he was not the man to put on a chain to win a seat on the Treasury benches of the House of Commons. He was returned for Stockport at the general election the next year, and his biography has since become a part of English history. Of his services in the cause of Free Trade, I have already spoken at some length.

On the second of July, 1846, the act repealing the Corn Laws having received the royal assent, the League held its final meeting at Manchester. All the *elite* of that victorious body had assembled from three kingdoms. George Wilson, who had presided as chairman of the council during the entire struggle, called to order. Having given a rapid sketch of the rise, progress, and triumph of the Association, he requested Mr. Cobden to address the Assembly. As he rose, the multitude sprang to its feet as one man, and greeted him with cheer on cheer, cheer on cheer, cheer on cheer. There stood the brave leader, the modest man, the victor in a field more glorious than ever Wellington won, unable to utter a word for several minutes, for the rapturous shouts of his companions in arms. His speech was characteristic. He bestowed warm eulogies upon his co-workers in the League, generously complimented Sir Robert Peel and Lord John Russell for their services in the crisis of the conflict, and delicately alluding to his own labors, insisted, in spite of the thundering "noes" which greeted the statement, that far too large a share of credit had been bestowed on him. He closed by moving that the operations of the League be suspended, and the Executive Council requested to wind up its affairs with as little delay as possible. The next day, a modest letter appeared in the public prints, addressed by him to the electors of Stockport, heartily thanking them for the confidence and kindness with which they had honored him, and announcing that the state of his health induced him to seek a temporary withdrawal from public life. Then followed the European tour; the feastings and toastings at Genoa, Paris, and other Continental cities; the munificent National Testimonial of nearly $100,000 ; the reëlection to Parliament; the plans for financial reform; the motion and speech on that subject during the late session; the defeat; the girding up of the armor for another struggle.

Those who associate in their fancy great physical endowments with great political achievements, would be disappointed in the person of Mr. Cobden. His name is announced. Forward steps a pale, slender man, with grave features stamped with few of the lineaments usually coupled with greatness and energy, and with rather a weak voice, and a gesticulation no wise striking, begins to unfold his subject. But, lucid arrangement; well selected words; arguments that penetrate to the marrow; facts new and old, clearly presented and felicitously applied; illustrations that shed light without bewildering; an occasional apothegmatic expression, embodying the whole subject in a phrase that enslaves the memory; earnestness and sincerity which first enlist sympathy and soon beget conviction—these are the elements of his power as a public speaker. The League furnished half a score of more brilliant orators than he; it produced not another such advocate. But, effective as were his forensic abilities, these did not place him at the head of the Anti-Corn-Law movement. He was as wise in council as he was resolute in action; and his well-balanced mind, his sturdy common sense, made him proof against the importunities of short-sighted coadjutors, and the snares of long-headed antagonists. A radical without rashness, a leader without arrogance, he carried straight forward to victory a constantly increasing host, never committing a blunder, nor sustaining an unnecessary reverse during a long conflict of peculiar excitement and temptation.

Next to Mr. Cobden, in popular estimation, among the League champions, stood the enthusiastic, eloquent Quaker, John Bright. He entered Parliament in 1843, and, like Cobden, was from the manufacturing class. For some years, he had been distinguished among the anti-rate paying dissenters of Central and Northern England, for his vigorous support of religious freedom. He had resisted the extortions of some persecuting dignitaries of the Establishment, and subjected them, on two or three occasions, to most mortifying defeats. He brought into Parliament a high reputation as an advocate of the League before popular assemblies, and an intimate knowledge of the subject of protection and free trade. His ready, bold, inspiring style of oratory partook more of the fervor of the platform than the calmness of the forum. But shrewdness and tact soon enabled him to catch the key-note of the House, where he displayed skill and courage as first lieutenant of the League, and won as much popularity from the aristocratic sections as so radical a democrat could reasonably expect.

Colonel PERRONET THOMPSON, a liberal of the old school, was an efficient member of the League. The incidents of his life would furnish materials for a dozen novels. He had served and commanded, both in the navy and army, in two hemispheres, going through storm and flame in contests with Frenchmen in the Peninsula, South Americans at Buenos Ayres, slave-traders on the coast of Africa, Arabs around the Persian Gulf, and Hindoos among the sources of the Ganges. In the midst of moving accidents by flood and field, he mastered the French, Spanish, and Arabic languages, wrote pamphlets on Law and Morals, read the works of Jeremy Bentham, and negotiated commercial treaties, one of which is remarkable for being the first public act that declared the slave trade piracy. Retiring on half pay in 1824, he turned his attention exclusively to politics and literature. He gave full scope to his democratic tendencies, and became a leader among the radicals. For ten years he wrote many of the ablest papers on current public questions that appeared in the Westminster Review, of which journal he was for some time the joint editor and proprietor with Dr. Bowring. His style is remarkable for its originality and vigor, combining the pith of Lacon, the raciness of Franklin, and the liberality of Jefferson. His speeches are distinguished for the same sententious and suggestive qualities that mark his writings. I am tempted to quote, though I spoil it by mutilation, his definition of a radical. "What," asks the Colonel, "*is* a radical? One that has got the root of the matter in him. One that knows his ills, and goes to work the right way to remove them. Every man is a radical that shuts his mouth to keep out flies. Does any man go to a doctor, and ask for a cure that is not radical? All men have been radicals who ever did any good since the world began. Adam was a radical when he cleared the first place from rubbish, for Eve to spin in. Noah was a radical, when, hearing the world was to be drowned, he went about such a common-sense proceeding as making himself a ship to swim in. An antediluvian Whig would have laid half a dozen sticks together for an ark, and called it a virtual representation." Colonel T. had high claims—a preëmption title—to the position he occupied in the corn law-struggle; for, twelve years before that controversy begun, he wrote "The Catechism of the Corn Laws," which contained the substance of all that was subsequently elaborated by Cobden and his coadjutors.

Mr. Villiers was the Free-Trade leader in Parliament till Cobden appeared; and, indeed, on account of his early services, he was called by courtesy the leader until the victory was won. His annual motion for repeal was a thermometer to measure the rise of public opinion; and his annual speech, laden with facts and arguments, converted thousands beyond the walls, if it failed to win majorities within. The multifarious learning and diligent pen of Dr. Bowring were often in requisition. A disciple of Bentham, an early advocate of Free Trade, acquainted with the commercial systems of foreign countries beyond most men, with a mind ripened by study and enlarged by extensive travel, he rendered important aid throughout the controversy. William J. Fox, a Unitarian minister in London, a refined gentleman, a classic scholar, an original thinker, an enlightened philanthropist, added eclat to the Drury-

Lane and Covent-Garden meetings. He now represents Finsbury in Parliament.

In this summary, I must not omit the iron poet of Sheffield. Like the Ayrshire plowman, he sprung from the working class. Like him, his songs are the lays of labor. But, unlike him, his muse did not draw her inspiration from the breath of the open fields, perfumed with daisies and adorned with hawthorn, but from the hot atmosphere of furnaces, ringing with the clang of anvils and the hoarse grating of machinery. Burns was the bard of yeomen. ELLIOTT is the bard of artisans. Both have touched the deepest chords of human feeling, and waked echoes that shall vibrate till human hearts cease to pulsate. Wandering a few years ago in the suburbs of Sheffield, my eye fell upon a building, blackened with the blackest smoke of that most somber town, whose front showed a sign running, I think, thus: "*Elliott & Co.'s Iron and Steel Warehouse.*" I inquired of a young man, dressed in a frock, besmeared with iron and coal, for the head of the establishment. "My father," said he, "is just gone. You will find him at his house yonder." I repaired thither. The "Corn-Law Rhymer" stood on the threshold in his stocking feet, holding a pair of coarse shoes in his hand. His frank "walk in" assured me I was welcome. I had just left the residence of MONTGOMERY. The transition could hardly be greater than from James Montgomery to Ebenezer Elliott. The former was polished in his manners, exquisitely neat in his personal appearance, and his bland conversation never rose above a calm level except once, when he spoke with an indignation that years had not abated of his repeated imprisonment in York Castle, for the publication, first in verse and then in prose, of liberal and humane sentiments, which offended the Government. And now I was confronted with a burly iron-monger, rapid in speech, glowing with enthusiasm, putting and answering a dozen questions at a breath, eulogizing American republicanism and denouncing British aristocracy, throwing sarcasms at the Duke of Wellington, and anointing General Jackson with the oil of flattery, pouring out a flood of racy talk about Church Establishments, Biddle and the Bank, poetry, politics, the price of iron and the price of corn, while ever and anon he thrust his damp feet into the embers, and hung his wet shoes on the grate to dry. A much shorter interview than I enjoyed would be sufficient to prove, even if their works were forgotten, that of the two Sheffield poets, Elliott's grasp of intellect was much the stronger, his genius far the more buoyant and elastic. Yet has the milder bard done and suffered much for civil and religious liberty. But the stronger! Not corn-law repealers only, but all Britons who moisten their scanty bread with the sweat of the brow, are largely indebted to his inspiring lays for the mighty bound which the laboring mind of England has taken in our day. Some of his poems are among the rarest and purest gems that shine on the sacred mount. Others are as rugged, aye, and as strong, as the iron bars in his own warehouse. They break out in denunciations of privileged tyrants and titled extortioners, with sounds like the echoes of a Hebrew prophet. The genius that animates and the humanity that warms every line, carry them where more fastidious and frigid productions would never find their way. Elliott has been called harsh and vindictive. He may be pardoned for hating institutions which reduce every fourth man to beggary, while a great heart beats in his bosom. Against meanness and oppression, his muse has rung out battle-songs, charged with indignation, defiance, sarcasm, and contempt; but into the ears of the lowly and wan sons of toil, it has breathed the sweetest murmurs of sympathy, consolation, and hope. The key which unlocks his harmony he has furnished in these angry lines:

"For thee, my country, thee, do I perform,
Sternly, the duty of a man born free,
Heedless, though ass, and wolf, and venom'd worm,
Shake ears and fangs, with brandished bray, at me."

It is impossible to even name a tithe of the men of might and genius whose public services gave energy to this conflict, and splendor to this victory. Behind these stood a host whose less conspicuous, but not less efficient labors, gave aim to that conflict and certainty to that victory. Only two will be mentioned—Mr. Paulton, the able editor of "*The League*" newspaper, who was one of the earliest actors in the enterprise, and weekly sent forth from his closet arguments which, when reïterated by eloquent tongues on the rostrum, made the land echo the cry of "Cheap Bread;" and Mr. George Wilson, who officiated as Chairman of the League from its creation to its extinction. Some estimate may be formed of the extent of his services by a fact stated by Mr. Cobden in his speech at the dissolution. It appeared from the official records of the League, that, during the seven years of its existence, Mr. Wilson had attended its meetings one thousand three hundred and sixty-one times, and had never received one penny for his labor. Such devotion bankrupts all eulogy.

CHAPTER XXVI.

National Debt of Great Britain—Lavish Expenditures of the Government—Its Enormous Taxes—Will the Debt be Repudiated?—Will it Occasion a Revolution?—Plan of Mr. Ricardo to pay the Debt—Mr. Hume's Efforts at Retrenchment.

GREAT BRITAIN is the richest and poorest nation of modern times. Her sea-sweeping commerce, her varied and vast manufactures, her fertile agriculture, the millions which flow into her coffers from her colonial possessions, are sufficient, were she free from debt, and her Government economically administered, to make her every son and daughter prosperous. But her huge national debt, and her immense annual expenditures, crush her laboring masses between the upper and nether millstones of remorseless taxation and hopeless poverty. Her debt sits upon the body politic like the nightmare of Erebus, almost stopping the circulation of the vital fluids. Like other high-born bankrupts, she is proud, as well as poor. She maintains the most lavish and expensive Government in the world. Though the interest of her public debt eats out the substance of her people, and the army, the navy, and the church, cling like leeches to her monetary arteries, she annually throws away immense sums in the shape of pensions and sinecures to worn-out heroes and civilians, to generals, admirals, ex-chancellors, judges, and diplomatists, to decayed nobles and knights, and every kind of titled nondescript noodle and nonentity.* She lavishes munificent gifts on dilapidated

* A writer in a recent number of the *London Times,* says: "There are various classes of pensions, but they all agree in this,—namely,

hospitals, schools, and charitable institutions, whose sole recipients of the bounty are the dryer branches of noble families, with long titles and short purses, whose control over the empty establishments is a sheer sinecure. She heaps bounties on numerous squads of imbeciles, whose blood is of that pale, watery kind supposed to indicate royalty, spending, in a recent year, more than £100,000 upon the nurseries, stables, and kennels of her Majesty's babies, horses, and puppies.* She

that they are for the most part undeserved, and that the recipients do nothing for their money. There are pensions given under the pretense of supporting the peerage, in consideration of parties' circumstances, and to compensate for abolished sinecures. Others there are that may be called 'mysterious pensions,' that no man knoweth the origin of. Of the first sort, Lord Bexley's pension of 3,000*l.* is an example. This man was found unfit for the office of Chancellor of the Exchequer some years ago, and therefore was hoisted into the house of incurables. Lord Allen receives a good fat pension in consideration of his pecuniary condition. The Honorable Jane Carr receives 1000*l.*, nobody knows for what. But the pensions for abolished sinecures are the most flagrant. Thus Lord Ellenborough receives 7700*l.* a year as compensation for the abolished nominal office of chief clerk in the Queen's Bench!—nearly as much as the Lord Chief Justice's salary!! There are even worse than this, however. J. C. Beresford receives between 4000*l.* and 5000*l.* as compensation for the abolished sinecure of storekeeper of the Customs, Dublin! The Reverend J. Burrard receives as compensation for the abolished sinecure of searcher of the Customs, Dublin, 1100*l.* a year!

* The writer in the *Times* gives this "royal" list:—

	Per ann.
The Queen eats and drinks	£63,000
Ditto pocket money	60,000
Prince Albert	38,000
Queen Dowager	100,000
Natural children of William IV., about	3,000
King of Hanover	21,000
Leopold, King of the Belgians	50,000
Prince of Mecklenburgh Strelitz	2,000
His wife, the Duke of Cambridge's daughter, Augusta Caroline	3,000
The Royal Dukes and Duchesses, about	100,000

The following are a few miscellaneous items:

The repairs to the Pimlico Palace, *estimated* at	150,000
The Royal Yacht	20,000
Windsor Castle has cost within the present century	3,000,000
The repairs to St. James' Palace were about	30,000
Buckingham Palace, before the present repairs	34,000
The Kitchen Garden at Frogmore	23,000
George IVth's natural children have cost the country	100,000

pays large annual tribute to her universities, that the sons of her nobility and gentry may riot on good living and bad Latin. She quarters at death's door a myriad army of starving paupers, that her landlords may maintain monopolies in the soil, the grain, and the game of the kingdom. Fond of fight and feathers, she hires the sons of her poor at thirteen shillings a month, to sail and march round the world, and bully and kill all who oppose their progress, while she keeps their fathers at home to work out the expenses at a shilling a day. She lays open the whole kingdom as foraging grounds for a ravenous Church Establishment, whose wardens tithe not only mint, anise, and cummin, but all "weightier matters;" and whose "wolves," clad in broadcloth, hunt foxes at £5,000 per year, and hire curates to look after the sheep, at £50. In a word, the pockets and patience of the larger share of British subjects are so heavily taxed by these imposts and impositions, that loyalty itself cries out in tones of vexation and agony, "Though kings can do no wrong, they have a very expensive way of doing right."

At the accession of William and Mary, in 1689, the national debt of Great Britain was £664,000. At the close of the French war, in 1763, £138,000,000. At the close of the American war, in 1783, £250,000,000. At the commencement of the Continental wars, in 1793, £240,000,000. At their close, in 1815, £840,000,000. Thus, it cost England £600,000,000 to put down Napoleon and restore the Bourbons. Some £40,000,000 having been paid off during the last thirty years, it now stands at £800,000,000. The population of the United Kingdom is 26 or 27,000,000. Consequently, the average debt of each man, woman, and child, is upwards of £30, or $150. The adult male population, with such females as are independent property-holders, does not probably exceed 7,000,000. To discharge the debt, it would be necessary that these persons should pay, on an average, nearly $600. This debt may be repudiated; but can it ever be paid?

Looking only to the records, the debt is owing to some 300,000 persons. It would seem, then, that 27,000,000 of people are enormously taxed to pay the interest on this vast debt to this small number of creditors. The British Government is always laying anchors to windward. Forty years ago, when this debt was rapidly accumulating, it saw that if a revolution should occur, and the issue be made up between the tax-payers and the tax-receivers, the former could easily trample down a class with whom they had no sympathy, and repudiate the debt. Accordingly, it has been the policy of the Government during these forty years to induce the middling and poorer classes to invest money in the public funds, through the medium of savings banks, charitable institutions, and friendly societies. Not long since, there was found to be standing in the names of the commissioners of those associations some £25,000,000 of the public debt, belonging to about 800,000 individual depositors and 16,000 associations—the latter representing probably 1,000,000 of people. Thus the debt is actually owing to 2,000,000 of people, three-fourths of whom are of the middling and lower orders of society—the very class that would be likely, if any, to foment a revolution of the Government. So long as this state of things exists, it is safe to presume that the public debt of Great Britain will never be repudiated, even by revolution.

The taxes upon the people of that kingdom equal those of any other nation on earth. The annual average of direct tax paid to the Government by each man, woman, and child, exceeds £3. It is paid by less than one-fifth of the population, making about $100, on an average, for each tax-payer, rich and poor. Nearly the whole, ultimately, comes directly and indirectly from the poorer classes, not in money solely, but in hard work, high rents, mean fare, and low wages. These taxes are levied on land meats, drinks, glass, malt, soap, spirits, windows, servants, horses, carriages, dogs, newspapers, stamps, &c., to the last syllable of the record of human wants and uses.

Sydney Smith, in the Edinburgh Review, gives a graphic sketch of this all-pervading system of taxation. He says it involves "taxes upon every article which enters into the mouth, or covers the back, or is placed under the foot. Taxes upon everything which is pleasant to see, hear, feel, smell or taste. Taxes upon warmth, light, and locomotion. Taxes on everything on earth, and the waters under the earth; on everything which comes from abroad or is grown at home. Taxes on the raw material; taxes on every fresh value that is added to it by the industry of man. Taxes on the sauce which pampers a man's appetite, and the drug that restores him to health; on the ermine which decorates the judge, and the rope which hangs the criminal; on the poor man's salt, and the rich man's spice; on the brass nails of the coffin, and the ribbons of the bride. At bed or board, couchant or levant, we must pay. The schoolboy whips his taxed top; the beardless youth manages his taxed horse with a taxed bridle on a taxed road. The dying Englishman pours his medicine which has paid 7 per cent., into a spoon which has paid 15 per cent.; flings himself back upon his chintz bed which has paid 22 per cent.; makes his will on an eight pound stamp, and expires in the arms of an apothecary who has paid a license of a hundred pounds for the privilege of putting him to death. His whole property is, then, immediately taxed from 2 to 10 per cent. Besides the probate, large fees are demanded for burying him in the chancel; his virtues are handed down to posterity on taxed marble, and he is then gathered to his fathers, to be taxed no more."

The annual Government expenditures of Great Britain are nearly $400,000,000. The heaviest appropriation goes to pay the interest on the public debt, which requires $150,000,000. The army and navy absorb $75,000,000.

There are 2,000 pensioners, who receive annually $5,000,000 or $8,000,000. The Queen and royal family get some $5,500,000 to supply the royal tables and stables, the royal babies and lap-dogs. Full $2,000,000 go to sinecures, such as the lord groom of the stole, the lord keeper of her Majesty's buck-hounds, the lady sweeper of the Mall, the lords wine-tasters, store-keepers, and packers, not omitting the chief justices in Eyre, who have done nothing for a century, and the Duke of Wellington, who seems likely to live forever. To these governmental expenditures must be added the income of the Established Church, whose Archbishop of Canterbury, pocketing, until recently, his $100,000 per year, mourns over the modern degeneracy which gives her clergy only 42,000,000 dollars annually.*

With these facts before us, we may form some estimate of the condition and prospects of the poor of a country where labor is abundant at twenty cents per day. Out on the inhuman policy which would prevent these hungry millions from emigrating to our broad American acres, which stretch westward almost to sundown, and on that remorseless policy which would exclude them from these acres, by blasting the soil with the sirocco of chattel slavery!

Should the number of public creditors in England become limited to two or three hundred thousand, its enormous debt, its immense annual expenditures, and its consequent excessive taxation, might become the occasion of a revolution of its Government. Three of the most important political revolutions of modern times are, that of England in 1644, that of America in 1775, and that of France in 1789. Each happened when an attempt was made to levy taxes upon the people, to relieve the burdens upon the national treasury. That subject is so mixed up with the first demonstrations of revolt, that, from being the mere *occasion* of the outbreak, it has been

* I have often been obliged, in this chapter, to get my statistics by striking *the average* of a mass of contradictory authorities.

often, if not generally, regarded as its *cause*. But, to assign the resistance to the levying of poundage and ship-money by Charles I, without authority of Parliament—to assign the refusal to pay a tax on tea and paper by the American Colonies, because imposed by a legislature in which they were not represented—to assign the extraordinary assembling of the States General, by Louis XVI, to supply a treasury exhausted by the foreign wars and domestic profligacies of previous monarchs—to assign these as the causes of the mighty convulsions which immediately followed, is assigning as *causes* those *events* which proved that the revolutions had already begun. It is referring the terrible explosion solely to the spark which ignited the train which a century had been accumulating—is mistaking the cataracts over which the popular currents fell, for the remote fountains from which they rose. The people were discontented with their Governments—they refused to contribute to their support—coercion drove them to revolt. A people ripe for revolution are apt at making up an issue with their oppressors, and seizing an occasion to smite off their chains, and are quite as likely to avail themselves of an odious tax, which reaches all classes, as of greater outrages, which press only upon single individuals or a limited portion of the community. If England is convulsed with a revolution, it is quite as probable to be occasioned by excessive taxation as any other event.

Anxious to avert dangers, as well as to relieve burdens, the great problem which British financiers have set themselves to solve, since the peace of 1815, has been to devise some means of paying off the public debt and reducing taxation. The boldest proposition to this end was brought forward by Mr. Ricardo, a gentleman of the liberal school of politics, an Edinburgh reviewer, celebrated for his controversy with Mr. Malthus, the writer on the laws of population and national wealth. For the ten years subsequent to the peace of 1815, the financial embarrassments of England more than once drove her to the borders of national bankruptcy. Mr. Ricardo, then being a member of the Commons, proposed, as the best mode of extricating the kingdom from those embarrassments, to tax its capital and property to the amount of, say £800,000,000, and pay the public debt off at once! He defended this scheme on the two-fold ground of justice and economy, contending that what a debtor owes ought always to be deducted from his property, and regarded as belonging to his creditors, and therefore should be given to them—that all estimates of the wealth of the debtor, till such deduction and payment are made, are false and delusive—that the then present generation had contracted nearly the whole of the debt, and therefore ought not to entail its payment upon posterity—and that, by immediately discharging the debt, the expense of managing it, and raising the revenue to pay the interest upon it, would be a large saving to the nation. These propositions he maintained with that vigor of reasoning, fullness of detail, and clearness of illustration, for which he was remarkable, and which won him a high place among the politico-economical philosophers of his time. But his scheme fell of its own weight, having few supporters except himself. It was in advance of an age which never thought of paying, but only of borrowing. Though its author did not convince the Commons of its practicability or expediency, he pretty thoroughly alarmed the capitalists and property-holders of the kingdom.

After many years of labor on the part of Mr. Vansittart, Mr. Robinson, Mr. Peel, Mr. Huskisson, and others, to *cipher* the public debt into non-existence, the hope of ever seeing it paid off seems to have given place to despair, to be followed by apathy. No sane Englishman now looks to see it discharged till huge monopolies which oppress the industry of the country are abolished, the system of Government entirely remodeled, and its expenses cut down to the lowest point of republican simplicity and economy. To talk of paying a debt of $4,000,000,000, whose annual interest is $150,000,000, whilst $117,000,000 is annually wasted on three blotches of the body politic, the Army, the Navy, and the Church, and 40,000 men own all the land of the kingdom, and every sixth man is a pauper or a beggar, is simply an absurdity.*

Taking this view of the subject, the radical reformers of England have struck at the root of the evil—a remodeling of the institutions of the State; and, in the departments of finance and taxation, have confined their efforts chiefly to the work of retrenching the Government expenditures. Foremost among these, and especially in the latter field, has stood the robust JOSEPH HUME. According to the forms of the British Constitution, the annual appropriations for the supply of the bottomless gulf of expenditure must take their rise in the House of Commons. And there, before they commence their line of march to that bourne whence no shilling returns, they have to encounter the severe scrutiny and determined opposition of clear-headed, honest-hearted, open-mouthed Joseph Hume. He contests all money-bills item by item, fastening upon them like a mastiff upon a gorged bullock.

I was listening, a few years ago, to a debate in the House of Commons on the civil list. Lord Stanley (then a member) had just closed an impetuous speech, when a broad-shouldered, rather rough-looking man, rose, and deliberately taking off his hat, which seemed to be filled with papers, commenced marshaling lazy sentences, under the command of bad rhetoric, to the music of a harsh voice. A pile of parliamentary documents lay on the seat by his side, and he held a bit of paper in

* The author of the "Comic Blackstone," first published in "Punch," says:—"The only method of getting rid of the debt would be for the sovereign to file a petition at the Insolvent Court in the name of the nation, and solemnly take the benefit of the act, in the presence of the fund-holders." About eighteen months since, Professor Newman, of the London University, published an able pamphlet, proposing that the interest on the debt should be paid for sixty years longer, after which it should cease. There is a growing disposition in England to get rid of the debt by some other mode than payment.

his hand, covered with figures. My friend informed me it was Mr. Hume. He realized the portrait my mind's eye had drawn of the man who, by dint of tireless ciphering, had convinced the masses of England that they were the mere working animals of the privileged orders. His brief, plain speech was aimed at some measure supported by Stanley, by which the people were to be cheated out of a few thousand pounds, to pamper some titled feeder at the public crib. Stanley was racy and flowery. Hume's speech resembled his lordship's as little as Euclid's problems do Milton's Paradise Lost. He explained the figures on his paper, and drove the digits into Stanley by a few well-directed blows at "treasury leeches," and sat down. Mr. Hume is a walking bundle of political statistics. No other man will so patiently pursue a falsehood or a false estimate or account, through a wide waste of Parliamentary documents, till he drives it into the sunlight of open exposure, as he. But as to eloquence, he knows no more about it than a table of logarithms. He rarely makes a speech that does not contain a good deal of bad rhetoric, and an equal amount of arithmetical calculations. Entering Parliament thirty years ago, he immediately placed himself at the door of the national treasury, which he has ever since watched with the dogged vigilance of a Cerberus. He has been the evil genius of Chancellors of the Exchequer, worrying them more than the national debt or the public creditors; whilst sinecurists, pensioners, and fat bishops, have received an annual Parliamentary roasting at his hands. Delving among the corruptions of Church and State, he has laid bare the slimy creatures that fatten on the roots of those institutions, and suck out their healthful nourishment. Bringing every proposed expenditure of money to the test of utility and the multiplication table, he has opened his budget of statistics, night after night, and measured off columns of damning figures by the yard and the hour, contesting the sum totals and the details of the appropriation bills, backed sometimes by the whole force of the liberal party, often sustained by only a few radical followers, and not infrequently left wholly alone. Of course, he is occasionally felt to be a bore. But nothing deters him from pursuing the line he has marked out. Sarcasm is lost upon him. Wit he despises. Threats have no terrors for him. Abuse only rebounds in the face of his assailant. The House may try to scrape or cough him down—Lord John Russell's reproaches may salute his ears—Sibthorpe's clumsy abuse may fall on his head—Stanley's fiery shafts may quiver in his flesh—Peel may shower contempt upon him—but there stands clear-headed, honest-hearted, unawed Joseph Hume, entrenched behind a pile of Parliamentary papers, gathering up the fragments of his last night's speech, and displaying fresh columns of figures, for a renewed attack on some civil or ecclesiastical abuse, which has been hidden from everybody's sight but his, by the accumulated dust of a century. Under any other Government than one scandalously extravagant, and whose people are taxed to the last point of human endurance, such obstinacy as he has sometimes displayed, in obstructing the passage of financial measures, would be wholly inexcusable. But every expedient which the wit or pertinacity of man can devise, to defeat or diminish such plundering of the masses as he witnesses every session of Parliament, is not only tolerable, but a sacred duty. The objects of his guardian vigilance gratefully appreciate his services, knowing that no other man has done so much to expose monetary abuses, and pull gorged leeches from the national treasury, and turn them out to get their living from their native earth.

Let it not be supposed that Mr. Hume has devoted himself exclusively to exchequer budgets and appropriation bills. He has taken a leading share in all liberal measures, advocating Catholic emancipation, Parliamentary reform, West India abolition, and has long been an able champion of Free Trade. Nor do I mean it to be inferred from the "free and easy" style in which I have spoken of him, that he is not highly re spectable, both as to talents and character. He is one of the best "working-members" of Parliament, and by constant practice and perseverance he has obtained a position amongst its able debaters. He was chosen Chairman of the Reform League, which was organized by Cobden and others, in the present House of Commons, to obtain equal representation and an enlarged suffrage, and he is the nominal if not the real leader of the present movement for Parliamentary reform.*

* Intimately associated with the subject of this chapter, is the recent unsuccessful, but by no means abandoned movement of Mr. Cobden, to reduce the government expenditures £10,000,000 per annum. His speech on that occasion was worthy of the anti-corn-law leader. Those who know him will need no assurance, that he will not give over till he has carried a far more radical measure of retrenchment. He bides his time.

CHAPTER XXVII.

Defects of the Reform Bill—Origin of Chartism—The "People's Charter" Promulgated in 1838—The Riots of 1839 and 1842—The Vengeance of the Government falls on O'Connor, Lovett, Collins, Vincent, J. B. O'Brien, and Cooper—The Nonconformist Newspaper Established by Mr. Miall—Mr. Sturge—Organization of the Complete Suffrage Union—Character of the Chartists.

THE old-fashioned Tories declare that the Reform Bill inscribed "Ichabod" on the British Constitution. Though it ushered in a better era, an experience of seventeen years has proved that power has not yet departed from the privileged few.

A few examples of its defects are given. For instance, Glasgow, with a population of 270,000, Manchester of 200-000, Birmingham of 160,000, Leeds of 130,000, were allowed two members of Parliament each; while Cricklade, with a population of 1,600, Shoreham of 1,500, Retford of 2,400, Wenlock of 2,400, were also allowed two members each. Finsbury, Lambeth, Mary-le-bone, and Tower Hamlets, with an aggregate population of 1,100,000, had two members each, whose eight votes were balanced by the members from Huntingdon, Marlborough, Dorchester, and Truro, with an aggregate population of 12,500. The entire metropolis, with more than 2,000,000 of inhabitants, received sixteen members, whose power in the House was nullified by the sixteen members of eight boroughs, with a total population of less than 24,000. Fifteen of the principal cities and towns in the kingdom, containing 3,500,000 people and 160,000 electors, were allowed thirty-two representatives, while the same number was assigned to twenty-seven boroughs, containing 170,000 inhabitants and 6,900 electors.

The inequalities in the distribution of the suffrage are not less striking. The number of males in the United Kingdom, of the age of twenty-one years and upward, is about 7,000,000. The number of registered electors is a little over 1,000,000. Thus, but about one-seventh of the adult males is entitled to vote. The suffrage is most unequally distributed amongst this one-seventh. The House of Commons consists of 658 members, which gives an average of full 1,500 electors to each member. But, 15 members are returned by less than 200 electors each—50 by less than 300 each—100 by less than 500 each—and so on, till careful calculations make it apparent that a clear majority of the House is returned by 200,000 electors, or one-fifth of the entire body, which body consists of only one-seventh of the adult male population.

In the distribution of members, reference was had to the supremacy of the landlord interest. Thus, South Lancashire, which swarms with a manufacturing population of more than 1,000,000, and has 25,000 electors, was balanced by aristocratic Lymington, with 3,300 inhabitants, and 150 electors, whom any lord can buy. West Yorkshire, the seat of the woolen interest, with 1,200,000 people and 40,000 electors, was given the same weight in the House as any two of numerous boroughs, with a joint population of 6,000, whose 400 or 500 electors were the cowering vassals of some great landed proprietor. In Lancashire and Yorkshire, whose skies are blackened with the smoke of their manufactories, there is one member for every 55,000 inhabitants, while rural Rutland has one for every 9,000, and corn-growing Dorset one for every 13,000. Manchester and Salford, the center of the cotton interest, with 300,000 people, send three members, and agricultural Buckinghamshire, with less than half that amount of population, sends eleven.*

The usual complexion of the House is alike caused by and aggravates the evils that spring from unequal representation and partially distributed suffrage. In the House previous to the present, there were 205 members closely related to the peers of the realm; 153 officers of the army and navy; 63 placemen; and 247 patrons of church livings. Of the 658 members, there were only about 200 who had not either title, office, place, pension, or patronage. And the same is substantially true of the present House.

These details, which might be multiplied indefinitely, will enable a very ordinary arithmetician to answer the question, which the CHARTISTS have rung in the public ear of England: "Does the Reformed House of Commons represent the people of Great Britain, and Ireland?"

The meager fruits brought forth by the Parliament elected under the reform bill, convinced a large mass of the enlightened working men, that Labor must look for relief to a radical change in the constitution of the popular branch of the legislature. They agreed upon a fundamental law for Parliamentary reform, to which they gave the name of "The People's Charter." Hence their name, "Chartists." The Charter, having been adopted by large numbers of Workingmen's Associations throughout the country, was ratified and promulgated in August, 1838, by 200,000 persons of the laboring classes, assembled from all parts of the kingdom, at Birmingham.

The outline of the Charter was mainly the work of Mr. William Lovett, a London cabinet-maker, one of God's nobility. It was perfected by Messrs. D. O'Connell, Hume, Bowring, Roebuck, Wakely, P. Thompson, and Crawford, then members of the Commons, who prepared the draft of an act of Parliament embodying its provisions. The leading points in the Charter

* Entire precision has not been aimed at in the foregoing statistics, "round numbers" being sufficiently accurate for my purpose.

are six, viz: Universal Suffrage, Voting by Ballot, Annual Parliaments, Equal Electoral Districts, No Property Qualification of Representatives, and Payment of Members for their Services. It is remarkable that these identical reforms were proposed forty years before, in an elaborate report by a committee of the "Friends of the People," of which the illustrious Charles James Fox was chairman.

And this is the essence of Chartism. Its principles, which fall like household words on the American ear, filled the heart of British aristocracy with dismay and wrath. Nor were the terror and indignation abated when their promulgation was followed by laying the "Great Petition," in favor of the People's Charter, bearing one million two hundred thousand names, on the tables of the House of Commons.

The Chartists were chiefly laboring men, dwelling in cities and towns. They justly expected countenance and aid from liberal Whigs who had protested against the aristocratic features of the Reform bill. They received neither. The cause of national representation was regarded as only the poor man's question, and as such it was left exclusively to the poor. The poor, thus abandoned to fight the battle single-handed and alone, nourished a fatal resentment against all above them. Far-sighted and pure-minded men among them urged the superiority of intellectual and moral means over brute force, in promoting their objects. Keen-eyed demagogues were not wanting to fan their resentment, and remind them that in their swart arms dwelt the physical strength of the country. Deprived of political power, (for the great majority were non-voters,) the mass lent a greedy ear to these wily counselors. Chartism being a knife-and-fork question to the laboring poor, starving men were easily induced to seize the pike and the torch under a promise of bread. Preparations for a rising were made. It was attempted in 1839. A few riots occurred, a few houses were gutted, a few wheat-ricks fired, a few cart-mares shot, and some human blood shed. The vengeance of the Government descended upon the deluded men—the military crushed the embryo insurrection—the courts imprisoned and transported the leaders—the noble principles of the Charter were involved in the stigma which fastened upon a portion of its advocates—the middle classes, who might have averted the disaster, were, for a season, frightened into a renunciation of the principles they had maintained during the discussions on the Reform Bill. A similar outbreak, stimulated by similar causes, and followed by similar consequences, occurred in 1842.

Governmental vengeance fell alike on the men of peace and the men of violence. Feargus O'Connor, a hot-headed bully and coward, who had stigmatized the pacific doctrines as "moral-force humbuggery," was sent to York Castle. William Lovett and John Collins, two noble specimens of the working classes, spent a year in Warwick jail. The young and brilliant Henry Vincent was lodged in a dungeon two years, for making the Welsh mountaineers "discontented with the Government." J. Bronterre O'Brien, a legitimate son of the land of Emmett, suffered twelve months in Lancaster Castle. Thomas Cooper, who dropped the awl, took up the pen, and wrote the celebrated poem, "The Purgatory of Suicides," was imprisoned two years and a quarter in Stafford jail. Other less conspicuous persons were incarcerated at home, or banished beyond the seas.

The election of 1841 returned a large Tory majority to Parliament, dissolved old party connections, and drove the radical reformers of the middle and working classes once more together in opposition to the common foe. *The Nonconformist*, a weekly newspaper, just then established in London, and conducted with marked ability by Mr. Edward Miall, took up the subject of a reform in Parliament, in a series of articles which powerfully argued the right of the working men to the franchise, and the necessity of an equalization of the representation. These essays were subsequently printed in a pamphlet and widely circulated. Their calm and cogent reasonings, their hearty and fervid appeals, arrested general attention. Mr. Miall gave to his scheme the name of "Complete Suffrage." It only remained for a practical man like Joseph Sturge to give to what was so far but a happy theory, the form and vitality of an organized movement.

After some preliminary meetings, Mr. Sturge, who had recently returned to England from an investigation of the electoral system of the United States, assembled a National Convention, or Conference, at Birmingham, in April, 1842, composed of delegates favorable to the main points of the "People's Charter," but opposed on principle and policy to all resort to intimidation or force in the accomplishment of their objects. Many of the best and brightest minds of the kingdom were present. During its four days' session, the debates were animated; the feeling earnest and warm; but the excitement glowed rather than flamed. The Chartists were represented by Lovett, O'Connor, Collins, Vincent, and O'Brien, while Sturge, Miall, Rev. Thomas Spencer, and Rev. Dr. Ritchie, represented the Complete Suffragists. After full discussion, the six points of the Charter were adopted, and an association, called "The National Complete Suffrage Union," was formed.

The cause was now on a good foundation, and under wise control. The same month of the Conference, Mr. Sharman Crawford, a judicious friend of the non-voting millions, divided the House of Commons on a motion in favor of complete suffrage. Among the sixty-nine members who voted with him were Messrs. Bowring, Cobden, Duncombe, Gibson, Napier, O'Connell, Roebuck, Strickland, Villiers, Wakely, and Ward, all of whom held prominent positions in the House.

It would transcend my limits to detail the progress of the Complete Suffrage movement since its organization in 1842. During these seven years of Corn-Law and Irish agitation, so unfavorable for fixing the public mind upon the question of an organic reform in Parliament, the Complete Suffragists have discussed their great proposition before the people, have returned several able advocates to the House, deepened the conviction that a thorough reörganization of the Legislature is a *sine qua non* to future radical reforms, and aroused a determination to place that subject on the Parliamentary "cards" so soon as matters that now occupy them are disposed of.

In the mean time, the Chartists proper have increased their numbers, as their Monster Petition of many millions, presented to Parliament during the last year, proves; and with the increase of numbers has come an abatement of their belligerent spirit, as their law-abiding conduct on that occasion shows; thus inspiring the hope of all good men, that when the great battle between the laboring many and the governing few shall be fought, Chartists and Suffragists will unite in a common struggle to make the Commons House of Parliament the representative of the common people of the realm.*

It would be doing injustice to some of the clearest-headed men in England to suppose that they for one moment regard the most radical reform in Parliament as the final remedy for the enormous evils that make one-eighth of the people of the realm absolute paupers, and one-fourth of the entire population paupers in all but the name. They look to the establishment of such a reform only as affording to the depressed classes an essential means for remodeling, on a basis of equality, the whole Governmental structure. They seek it, not as an end, but as an instrument to attain an end—a John the Baptist to herald the times and the men that shall make the crooked straight, the rough smooth, the inequalities level.

Scarcely any body of men have been regarded with more unintelligent horror, or subjected to more unreasonable denunciation, by the higher classes of England, than the Chartists.

* One or two recent divisions in the House of Commons are no criterion for determining the strength of the Free Suffragists and Chartists. That subject is not now on the "cards."

And yet, no section of British reformers are more worthy of admiration for the principles they avow, or of sympathy for the persecutions they have endured. It has been my good fortune to make the acquaintance of several of these men, to attend some of their meetings, and read many of their publications. I have never taken by the hand nobler members of the human family, nor listened to speeches that glowed with more eloquent devotion to the rights of man, nor perused papers more thoroughly imbued with the democratic sentiment, and which inculcated lofty principles in a style of more calm and lucid reasoning. Their publications dwell with emphasis upon the blessings of peace, the superiority of moral over physical means in the attainment of ends, the importance of education, of industry and economy, of self-reliance without arrogance, and of an independent and manly bearing in their intercourse with the world. Bad men are among them, who have often imposed upon their ignorance or inflamed their passions, goading them to violence and crime. But the mass are as far removed from the state of barbarism and brutality, which their traducers have assigned to them, as *they* are from the utterance of truth or the practice of charity.

It stirs the blood not a little to see such men as Lovett, Collins, Vincent, O'Brien, and Cooper, suffer through long years, in dark and filthy cells, for teaching the people to be "discontented" with a Government that first denies them any voice in its administration, and then taxes them down to the starvation point, that it may pamper a bloated priesthood and an overbearing aristocracy at home, and build navies and equip armies to scour the seas and scourge unoffending tribes in the uttermost parts of the earth. However, those who know John Bull best say the only way to manage him is to mingle a little threatening with a good deal of blarney, when the conceited old bully, after a fearful amount of bluster, will yield a point —as witness Catholic Emancipation, Parliamentary Reform, and Corn-Law Repeal. Perhaps these pacific counselors are right; though a James Otis, or a Patrick Henry, with the cry of "No taxation without representation!" on their lips, would recommend that the towers of Windsor, and the minarets of Lambeth, be pitched instantly into the Thames.

A more particular notice of some of the persons who have acted prominent parts in the transactions above detailed, will be given in the next chapter.

CHAPTER XXVIII.

Chartists and Complete Suffragists—Feargus O'Connor—William Lovett—John Collins—Henry Vincent—Thomas Cooper—Edward Miall—Reverend Thomas Spencer.

In this chapter, I will give brief notices of some of the more prominent Chartists and Free-Suffragists.

Feargus O'Connor has been styled "The Great Chartist Leader." In advocating the cause, he has suffered for his imprudences, if not for his principles. He is made up in about equal degrees of the braggart and the coward, the demagogue and the democrat—a legitimate product of the rotten institutions and turbulent times in which he was born and has flourished. With many good qualities and many bad ones, he had not the moral bravery to lead a reformation, nor the physical courage to head a revolution. Aspiring to do both, and wanting capacity for either, he failed in each. Respect for an impulsive man who has proclaimed good principles in bad times, and sympathy for a weak man who has felt the thorn of persecution from worse hands than his own, induce me to forbear further remark on the foibles and follies of one who is shorn of his influence to do much future good or evil. Better for Chartism if he had lived and died a Tory ; though, with all his sins, he will be kindly remembered when Toryism rots in contempt.

William Lovett's manly virtues and vigorous sense adorn a noble enterprise. Born in extremest poverty, he has struggled upward against the crushing weight of factious systems, to an influential position in society. While a young man, he was drafted into the militia—refused to be degraded into a machine to kill men at the word of command—was arraigned before a magistrate for the offense—terrified the justice by the boldness and ability of his defense—and was discharged from the service after seeing his little property confiscated and his family reduced almost to beggary. This petty tyranny fixed him in the purpose of preparing himself to aid in remodeling institutions that taxed him to the marrow, without allowing him any voice in the selection of his rulers. He worked at his trade of cabinet-making by day, and cultivated his mind by night. Throwing himself into all movements for the improvement of the laboring classes, he first attracted general notice by his connection with the London Working Men's Association, established in 1836. The many able addresses which this central body issued to the working men of the kingdom, and to the laboring classes in Belgium, Poland, and Canada, were prepared by him. These led the way for the Chartist movement. In 1838, he assisted Messrs. O'Connell, Roebuck, and other members of Parliament, in preparing "The People's Charter;" his part of the work consisting in drafting, theirs in revising, this noble and painfully celebrated document.

One of the main originators of the Chartist enterprise, he now gave to it his whole energies; and well would it have been had his pacific disposition controlled its direction. The National Convention of Chartists was in session in Birmingham in 1839. The people of that town, as was their wont, were holding a meeting in "The Bull-ring," to discuss questions of reform. The police, part of whom had been specially sent from London, were ordered to break up the meeting. They rushed upon the assemblage, and, with their bludgeons, knocked down men, women, and children, and dispersed the meeting. Mr. Lovett, who was secretary to the Convention, drew up and presented to that body a manly protest against these outrages. It was printed and circulated through the town. For writing that paper, he and John Collins (who had carried the manuscript to the printer) were arrested for sedition, thrust into a dungeon, indicted, tried, convicted, and sentenced to a year's imprisonment in Warwick jail. On the trial, Lovett defended himself with skill, and his address to the jury commanded general admiration. While in prison, Lovett and Collins published a pamphlet of 130 pages, entitled "Chartism: A Plan for the Education and Improvement of the People." It is able and eloquent, filled with the noblest sentiments, and contains suggestions for the instruction and elevation of the masses, which would, if acted upon by the government, place England a century in advance of her present position. Near the close of their confinement, they wrote another paper, which I transcribe entire. The Melbourne Administration, "which meant but little, nor meant that little well," became ashamed of its treatment of Lovett and Collins, and offered to release them on their entering into bonds to keep the peace. Here is their reply. Read it, and see how contemptible a nobleman looks in the hands of a cabinet-maker and a tool-maker:

"WARWICK JAIL, May 6, 1840.

"*To the Right Honorable the Marquis of Normanby, Her Majesty's Secretary of State for the Home Department:*

"MY LORD: The visiting magistrate of the county jail of Warwick having read to us a communication, dated Whitehall, May 5, and signed S. M. Phillips, in which it is stated that your Lordship will recommend us to Her Majesty for a remission of the remaining part of our sentence, provided we are willing to enter into our recognizance in £50 each for our good behavior for one year, we beg respectfully to submit the following as our answer. To enter into any bond for our future good conduct would be an admission of past guilt; and however a prejudicial jury may have determined that the resolutions we caused to be published, condemnatory of the attack of the police, were a violation of the law of libel, we cannot bring ourselves to believe that any criminality attaches to our past conduct. We have, however, suffered the penalty of nearly ten months' imprisonment for having, in common with a large portion of the public press, and a large majority of our country-

14

men, expressed that condemnatory opinion. We have been about the first political victims who have been classed and punished as misdemeanants and felons, because we happen to be of the working class. Our healths have been injured, and our constitutions seriously undermined by the treatment we have already experienced; but we are disposed to suffer whatever future punishment may be inflicted upon us, rather than enter into any such terms as those proposed by your Lordship.

"We remain your Lordship's most obedient servants,

"William Lovett,

"John Collins."

Having been confined to a narrow, filthy cell, and fed on the meanest fare, Mr. Lovett's health was so seriously impaired, that he did not recover his wonted vigor till nearly two years after his release from prison.

Mr. Lovett was a member of the Birmingham Complete Suffrage Conference in 1842, and his well-balanced mind and lucid speeches gave him a leading position in that body. For a few years past, he has been engaged in publishing works adapted to the wants of the laboring classes, and his pen has been active in their cause. He was the publisher of "Howitt's Journal," and contributed some of the best papers that appeared on its pages. In person he is tall and gentlemanly, has an intellectual countenance, and, take him all in all, is a rare specimen of the rich ore that lies embedded under the crust of British aristocracy.

John Collins, like William Lovett, came up from the ground tier of British society, and has brought along with him more of the marks of his "order" than Mr. L. He has rode out a good deal of rough weather in defense of Chartist principles. On his release from Warwick jail, he was received with the warmest enthusiasm by congregated thousands of his Birmingham neighbors. He afterward made a tour of Scotland, addressing audiences in the principal towns. I listened to one of his speeches. My mind having been filled with prejudices against him, I was prepared to see a monster. But there stood before me a stout, bold man, uttering the loftiest truths in a practical and pointed style, and with a tone and bearing conciliatory but firm—a man earnest in vindicating the depressed classes, who had shown courage in peril, endured persecution without repining, and now received applause without vanity—a nobleman by nature, a tool-maker by trade, but who never tried to make a tool of others, and was the last person who would submit to be made one himself.

The name of the young and eloquent Henry Vincent thrills the hearts of millions of Britain's laboring poor. While an apprentice in a London printing-office, he aided by extra work during the day in supporting a destitute mother and her children, while midnight generally found him absorbed in some book adapted to expand his mind. His intellect outran his years, and he became a radical reformer when yet a boy. At the age of 14, he made a speech to his juvenile companions on the then engrossing subject of Catholic Emancipation. The French Revolution next possessed his enthusiastic soul. He stood dumb with emotion when he first saw the handbill at the door of the newspaper office, headed "Revolution in France!" He rushed home, got his sixpence, bought the paper, and run through the streets announcing the event to all whom he met. Soon followed the Reform Bill excitement, which absorbed his energies. Although but 16 or 17 years old, he was chosen a member of a Political Union, and participated in its proceedings. Arriving at his majority in 1836, he resolved to consecrate his powers to the elevation of the laboring and disfranchised classes of the people. He joined with Mr. Lovett in the Chartist movements of 1837–8, traveled the country as a lecturer, and was immediately ranked among the most vigorous and brilliant advocates of The Charter. Such was his success among the hardy mountaineers of Wales, that the Government became alarmed, marked him for its victim, and, on his coming to London to visit his widowed mother, dragged him from her dwelling at dead of night, on a charge of sedition, thrust him into a dungeon, tried him, convicted him, and sent him a year to Monmouth jail. The crime proved upon him was, using violent language and making the people discontented with the Government! Just before the close of his term of imprisonment, he was again arraigned on a similar charge, and doomed to another twelve months' incarceration. While in prison, he was treated with such barbarity that fears were entertained of a rescue by the Welsh, with whom he was highly popular, and he was removed to London. His journey thither was a triumphant procession, crowds gathering and cheering him at several of the principal towns on the route. While confined in a solitary cell in the London penitentiary, Mr. Sergeant Talfourd brought his case before Parliament, eulogized his character and talents, and arraigned the Government for the harsh treatment inflicted upon him. This woke up Lord Normanby, the Home Secretary, who visited Vincent, heard some very plain talk, had him removed to Oakham jail, and furnished with decent lodgings, and pen, ink, and paper. After suffering twenty-two months, (the Government having remitted two,) this pure-hearted young philanthropist was released, and the same day partook of a complimentary dinner, when he made a speech in defense of his principles and conduct, worthy of the theme and the man.

Soon afterward, at the general election in 1841, Mr. Vincent was invited to contest the borough of Banbury for a seat in Parliament, the whole body of non-electors, and a large minority of the electors, being in his favor. On the morning of the election, (the result being very doubtful between the Whigs and Tories,) a committee of the former offered him a large sum of money to withdraw from the contest. He had scarcely spurned the proposal, when a Tory deputation offered him £1,000 to abandon the field. He refused the bribe with scorn. He was defeated, but he retired with honor, leaving hundreds of converts to his principles behind him. He subsequently, on special request stood for Ipswich and Tavistock, having failed of carrying the latter borough by only 44 votes, against the combined power of the House of Bedford. At the general election of 1847, he polled a very large vote in Plymouth. His chief object in yielding to the solicitation of his friends to mingle in these contests was, to improve the opportunity they afforded him for bringing thorough democratic principles before the people.

Mr. Vincent united with the Free Suffragists in 1842, and during the past seven years he has traversed England and Scotland, addressing multitudes in favor of Peace, Temperance, Education, Free Trade, and Parliamentary Reform, winning a high place among the advocates of radical reform. His speeches are a continuous flow of rapid, fervid eloquence, that illuminates the reason, kindles the imagination, and fires the heart. In person, he is below the middle size, symmetrically formed, with very handsome features, graceful and elastic in his action as a deer, and his voice thrills the blood like a war-trumpet.*

Thomas Cooper is another original genius, who has forced his way into sunlight through the thick shell of British caste. Eating the bitter bread of poverty during childhood, he contrived, by means that throw fiction into the shade, to gratify a native taste for reading, drawing, and music. Laboring on a shoemaker's bench from the age of fifteen to twenty-three, he snatched from toil the opportunity to acquire a respectable knowledge of the Hebrew, Greek, Latin, and French languages, and of Algebra and Geometry—to commit to memory considerable portions of Shakspeare and Milton—to peruse the works of Hooker, Cudworth, Stillingfleet, Warburton, and Paley—and to compose some poetry and essays of his own. This he did by robbing sleep of its wonted hours, and while

* The trials of Lovett, Collins, Vincent, and others, are reported briefly in the 9th volume of Carrington & Payne's reports. The legal points raised on the trials chiefly make up the reports.

his miserable wages afforded a pittance barely sufficient to keep him and his mother from starving.

At the age of twenty-three, he dropped his awl and hammer, and emerged into the world. For ten years he buffeted a sea of troubles, dividing his time between teaching country schools and writing for newspapers; now accumulating a choice library of 500 volumes, and then parting with it, volume by volume, for bread. In 1841, while engaged as a reporter for the *Leicestershire Mercury*, he was directed to report a Chartist lecture. It was the first he had heard, and its principles found an echo in his bosom. He commenced a lecturing tour in support of the Charter, visiting, among other places, the Staffordshire potteries. While in that region, in 1842, occurred those serious disturbances which for weeks tossed the Midland counties on a wild tempest of riots. At first, the object was to raise the wages of the operatives by a general "strike." Demagogues fanned the flame, till it broke loose in arson, pillage, and other violent acts, resulting in a few instances in loss of life. Cooper was arrested, and finally arraigned on four indictments for riot, sedition, and arson. He was tried, and, though acquitted on the more serious charge, was convicted of the minor offenses, against every principle of law or reason. He was sentenced to two years and three months' imprisonment. One of the trials lasted ten days. Cooper defended himself with great ability, proving no unworthy antagonist for Sir William Follett. The barbarous treatment he received in prison gave him rheumatism, neuralgia, and other diseases; but it gave to the world "The Purgatory of Suicides." This poem appeared soon after his liberation, in 1845, having been composed in Stafford jail. It was highly eulogized in the Eclectic, Britannia, and other literary periodicals, and met with immediate success. In the preface, the author proudly says:

"I am poor, and have been plunged into debt by the persecution of my enemies; but I have a consolation to know, that my course was dictated by heart-felt zeal to relieve the sufferings and oppressions of my fellow-men. Sir William Follett was entombed with pomp, and a host of titled great ones, of every shade of party, attended the laying of his clay in the grave. They propose now to erect a monument to his memory. Let them build it; the self-educated shoemaker has also reared his, and, despite its imperfections, he has a calm confidence that, though the product of poverty, and suffering, and misery, it will outlast the posthumous stone block that may be erected to perpetuate the memory of the titled lawyer."

Mr. Cooper subsequently published other works, assisted in editing Douglas Jerrold's Magazine, contributed to Howitt's Journal, and delivered courses of lectures before various literary and scientific institutions in London; but, under all circumstances, giving his heart and his hand to all efforts to elevate the class of society in which he is proud to have had his origin.

The bare names of those who have borne a prominent part in the Chartist movement would fill pages. I must leave them, and have time to notice two men only who may be classed as Complete Suffragists proper, they never having acted with the Chartists.

Mr. EDWARD MIALL has been for several years the editor of *The Nonconformist*. He formerly officiated as a dissenting minister. Competent judges have pronounced this newspaper one of the ablest of the English journals; its conductor one of the ablest of English editors. Undoubtedly it stands in the front rank of *religious* newspapers. It has a clear comprehension of the mission of a religious journal in the current crisis of English affairs, and fulfills it with courage, integrity, and ability. It is the organ of no sect, but reflects the views of radical reformers of all denominations. It is the organ of no party, but utters the sentiments of the friends of progress. While it gives much attention to ecclesiastical affairs, it discusses all political matters that occupy the public mind, probing subjects to the core, laying bare corruption, and excoriating evil-doers in Church and State, without fear or favor, ranting or cant. The leading characteristic of its editorials is their searching and philosophical style of argument; while the hue of the rhetoric, the texture of the composition, are lustrous and compact, equaling in beauty and grandeur the essays of the first class of periodicals. It occasionally indulges in the most pungent sarcasm and lively wit, all the more biting and inspiring for being exceptions to the general rule. Every line breathes a deep earnestness for truth, and a warm sympathy with humanity. The writings of Mr. Miall are models of English composition.

At the last general election, Mr. Miall contested Halifax as the radical candidate; and his speeches during the canvass were only surpassed in strength and acuteness by the emanations of his own pen. In the outward semblances of the orator—the mere frame and gilding—he falls below the expectations of those familiar with his writings. An attenuated frame, a thin voice, a stiff demeanor, a monotonous gesticulation, seem too slight a frame-work to sustain the operations of so mighty a mental machine as his. Glorious dawn of England's better day, when the seats of her Parliament are thickly sprinkled with such men as Miall, Cobden, Sturge, Thompson, and Vincent.

Having stopped a moment to look at the plain garb of a Nonconformist minister, we will glance at a hardly less radical reformer, arrayed in the canonicals of the Church of England, "as by law established"—Rev. THOMAS SPENCER. As this gentleman has traveled and spoken extensively in our country, it will not surprise Americans to be told that, though a clergyman of the Establishment, he is also a thorough teetotaler, the enemy of commercial monopolies, a complete suffragist, and almost a democrat. Possessing superior talents, a rich flow of eloquence, a commanding and graceful person, Mr. Spencer has been eminently successful in instructing and delighting large audiences of his countrymen, and commending to their judgments and tastes themes that would have been repulsive in the hands of men of less aristocratic associations. He took a prominent part in the Birmingham Conference of 1842, which organized the National Complete Suffrage Union, and was elected a member of the General Council of that association. He has mingled much with the poor of England, feels deeply for their wrongs, and boldly advocates their rights. How beautiful and cheering is the light reflected upon the wide-weltering chaos of surrounding darkness, by such clergymen as Thomas Spencer and Baptist Noel. They, as well as many kindred spirits of the Establishment, and the great mass of dissenting ministers, do not esteem it incompatible with their dignity, nor unbecoming their sacred calling, to take an active part in all questions, whether political or ecclesiastical, which vitally affect the interests of their fellow-subjects. I have never heard that their labors for the people in the forum diminished their influence over the people in the pulpit. Nay, it rather increases that influence by convincing the people that, in becoming ministers, they did not lose their interest in anything which concerns the well-being of their fellow men.

CHAPTER XXIX.

Ireland, her Condition and Prospects—The Causes of her Misery—The Remedies for the Evils which afflict her.

The "Irish Question" is environed with peculiar difficulties. An American might shrink from discussing what has puzzled and baffled Irishmen on both sides of the Atlantic.

The poetic, fancy view of Ireland is a mountain nymph, with flowing garments, wavy ringlets, glowing countenance, enrapt eye, and Venus-like fingers, thrilling the strings of a harp. The prosaic, real view is more like a mother, seated on the mud floor of a bog cabin, clad in rags, with disheveled hair, pinched features, eyes too hot and dry for tears, and skinny fingers, dividing a rotten potato amongst a brood of famishing children. Thanks to some of her orators, they have ceased to rave in fine frenzy about "the first flower of the earth, and the first gem of the sea." All friends of Ireland, native and alien, should stop ranting about "flowers," "gems," "Emerald Isles," "Tara's Halls," "St. Patrick," and such rhapsodies, and come down to the things of time and sense. Potatoes, as a standing dish, may grow stale; but to a starving people they are "roast beef and two dollars a day," compared with a surfeit of antiquated heroics. And yet, take up the report of a meeting for the relief of Ireland, whether held in Dublin or Washington, and half of it will be filled with such shining scum. Orators and writers addicted to such whims should be indicted for murdering the Queen's Irish.

The prime cause of Ireland's misery is the oppressive rule of England. For centuries she has been governed by and for the alien few, and not by and for the native many. England first wantonly subdued Ireland; then planted there an alien race and a rival church, to hate, worry, and plunder her; then, by the Catholic Penal Code, steeped her in ignorance and debasement; and finally, by bribery, and against the national will, abolished her Parliament, destroyed her nationality, and reduced her to the condition of a dependent province. Since the days of Cromwell, the ruling English have absorbed the wealth of the country, and carried it away to be expended in other lands. They have annually eaten out the substance of the people, and fled, leaving misery and poverty behind, and casting reproach upon the national character, and offering insult to the national spirit.

Since the Union, the legislation of the British Parliament, in respect to Ireland, has been an almost unbroken series of insults and injuries. I will mention two instances; and they are the very two that England always cites as proofs of her liberality. In 1828–9, the people of Ireland demanded Catholic Emancipation. The boon was granted; but it was accompanied by the disfranchisement of the whole body of forty-shilling freeholders; thus, in revenge, striking from the electoral body two hundred thousand names, which had aided in wringing the gift from the oppressor. Emancipation, granted on such ungracious terms, exasperated rather than appeased the Irish people. And in that other day, when England felt peculiarly liberal, and was ready to "give everything to everybody," she made Ireland an exception. The Reform bill made an odious distinction in the case of Ireland. England and Wales, with a population of about fourteen millions, were allowed 500 members of the House of Commons. Ireland, with a population of about eight millions, was allowed but 105. Bearing the same ratio as England, Ireland should have had 290. Scotland has two millions four hundred thousand inhabitants, and 53 members. In the same proportion, Ireland would have been entitled to 177. Thus, of the two most benign instances of English legislation over Ireland, during this century, one was accompanied by a positive outrage ; the other by a most unjust disparagement.

The Established Church of England, planted by force in Ireland, has done little for it, except to unjustly tax and cruelly treat those who dissent from its ritual, and to foment and aggravate religious feuds. Of the eight millions of Ireland, six and a half are Catholics. Of the remaining one and a half million, not half a million belong to the Establishment. And yet, to take care of this half million, the Establishment has had 4 archbishops, 18 bishops, and 2,000 clergy—drawing annually from this potato-eating people £1,500,000 ; while the income of the clergy of the seven and a half millions of all denominations has not exceeded £500,000. The whole income of the Irish Establishment, from all sources of revenue, is nearly £2,000,000 annually. An attempt was once made to modify this enormous abuse. After four years of contention in Parliament, during which two ministries were turned out, the bill was shorn of its effective features, in order to pacify the Tory peers, and passed, still leaving the revenues to the Church of England, and the people to the Church of Rome.

But the English Church is only a blotch. The great sore is the Irish landlord system. The misgovernment of the country has conspired with landlordism to drive out capital, and destroy commerce, trade, mining, fishing, and manufacturing, thus throwing the mass of the population upon the land for subsistence. This has increased competition for the hire of the soil to an extent unknown in any other country, and has stimulated a grinding scale of rents, which has descended from the landlords to the middlemen, and from them to the small farmers, and from them to the poor laborers, growing more extortionate as it goes down, till the soil has been cut into minute pieces, which are held by short and uncertain tenures, precluding permanent improvements, driving the mass of the people to the raising of potatoes, because they are cheap in the cultivation, and prolific in the crop, and yearly turning thousands out to beg, starve, rob, die of disease, or shoot their lessors at the expiration of their terms. One-third of the people of Ireland live (if they live at all) on potatoes, and the addition of a sprinkling of salt is a rare luxury. Two and a half millions are beggars, and Mr. O'Connell estimated the paupers in 1846–7 (the years of famine) at four millions. The main reliance of nearly half the nation, for food, is potatoes. God have mercy on them when that source fails!

With many noble exceptions, the large landed proprietors of Ireland are heartless, reckless, thriftless men. Nearly one-third of the country is a bog, three-fourths of which might be drained. Nearly five millions of acres, capable of cultivation, lie waste. An acre of potato land rents for from £5 to £10 per annum. Labor is abundant at the lowest rates. Yet these landlords have done little toward draining these bogs, enclosing these wastes, and improving their estates. Grant that for the four or five past years of pinching famine, attended with loss of rents, they have been unable to make improvements. It was just so before these years came, and has been so time out of mind. These landlords are generally *absentee* proprietors, who feel no abiding interest in the prosperity of a soil which they forage but do not inhabit, which they own but do not occupy. Half of the very money voted to them in 1846–7, by Parliament, for the improvement of Ireland, they spent the next season at Paris, Florence, and Baden-Baden, there to swell the pomp of British aristocracy, while millions at home, whom it was intended to assist, ate garbage that an English pig would hardly nose over, or starved in hovels that the royal stag-hounds would not skulk into from a pelting storm.

The energies of the masses in Ireland being absorbed in a hand-to-mouth struggle for existence, they have neither time nor means to stimulate the industry of the country by establishing manufactories, opening mines, carrying on fisheries, increasing trade, laying out roads, &c., nor to elevate and expand the national mind by founding common schools and seminaries of learning. The wealthy landlords and capitalists—the Besboroughs, the Lansdownes, the Devons, the Fitzwilliams, the Hertfords—who might do all this, will not; but, looking on from afar, cry to their stewards and agents, "Give! Give! Give!"

The result of this complicated system of bad government and bad management is painfully obvious. Ireland is nigh unto death of a chronic disease of famine, pestilence, agitation, despair, and insurrection.

And what is England's remedial process for this disease in one of her members? As a panacea for the miseries that she herself has to a great extent inflicted, England, at stated periods, administers to her victim-patient coercion bills and cold steel, blotching her surface with police stations and military camps. Sending her tax-gatherers instead of schoolmasters, dotting her soil with cathedrals instead of workshops, sowing her fields with gunpowder instead of grain, England affects to wonder that the crop should be famine and faction, misery and murder, improvidence and insurrection; and when the harvest is dead ripe, she sends over police and soldiery, armed with coercion bills and cannon balls, to cut and gather it in.

Sometimes England varies the prescription, or makes different applications to various parts of the body politic. Sir Robert Peel, for instance, prescribes bullets for Repealers, and guineas to a cloister of priests at Maynooth, to stop the mouths of the latter and the wind of the former, and the clamor of both. Then comes Lord John Russell with the Whig nostrum —money to carry the landlords to Baden, and a steamer to transport Mitchell to Bermuda—projects of railways to furnish hard work for laborers and fat jobs for contractors—a patch or two on a worn-out and inefficient poor-law, and packed juries for O'Brien and Meagher. So these Tory and Whig quacks administer—inflicting wounds and doling out palliatives—never probing the ulcer, but striving to skim over its surface—while there stands John Bull, robbing the naked and half-dead patient, at the same time affecting to do penance, by paying the doctors, and giving alms to the victim.

What, then, is the remedy for these evils? Having been very imperfect in detailing their causes, I must be equally imperfect in pointing out remedies. Looking on from afar, it seems to me that some of the things that Ireland needs are these:

And first, as to a few temporary measures. Ireland needs a just and beneficent poor law. The present law is a mockery and a shame. The principle of the law should be, that every man who wishes for work shall have it, or be fed by the poor rates. Government owes bread or work to all its subjects. The rates should be mainly laid on the land, where *it* is able to pay them, even if it be by sale under the hammer. This done, those landlords who apply to Parliament for money on which to live in improvidence, and in many instances in extravagance, would feel the pressure, awake to a consciousness of their condition, and, knowing that if they did not provide the laboring poor with work, they must furnish them with food, would either abandon their estates, or commence draining and planting the bogs and wastes. In either case, the laborer, for whose use God said, "Let the dry land appear!" would be restored to his inheritance.

The mass cannot wait for the meager relief of poor laws. Tens of thousands must emigrate by their own means or Government aid. The country is too densely populated for the present state of things. America should open wide her gates, to welcome the sons and brothers of those who have fought our battles, dug our canals, and built our railways, and, pointing to the unoccupied plains that stretch from the great lakes to Astoria, from the Rocky Mountains to San Francisco, say, "Go in and possess the land."

Associations should be formed, of true-hearted Irishmen, to reclaim the wastes, develop the resources, and revive the industry of the country—thus giving scope to capital and employment to labor.

The middle and lower classes should be more provident and careful, less wasteful and indolent, using thriftily the little they have, and adding to the stock by economy and enterprise. After traveling through half the island, I never was able to understand why a middling-man should waste his substance in riotous living, or a poor man should live in a hovel dirtier than a pig-sty, when pure water was abundant; or year after year let the rain drive through his thatched roof, when straw was rotting around him, merely because England would not grant a repeal of the Union.

The ignorant should, of course, be educated. But general education, it is to be feared, is a long way off. In the mean time, the better informed should instruct the people in their social duties, as well as their political rights, while such as are not utterly debased should exhibit more personal independence in opinion and action, do less of their thinking by proxy, show less subserviency to priests of all sorts, and less tolerance of demagogues of every shade of party.

But these things are only provisional remedies—mere clippings of the branches. The axe should be hurled at the root of the evil.

The Established Church should be driven out, and, if need be, by a whip of small cords, such as was applied to those money-changers in the Temple, who had set up their *desks* where they had no business to be. This done, complete ecclesiastical independence, both of England and of Rome, both of the Archbishop of Canterbury and the Pope of St. Peter's, should be declared, bringing with it less servility among the clergy, less abjectness among the people, less gathering in of parochial tithes, and a more liberal diffusion of Christian charity. In a word, less "religion," and more Christianity.

The landlord system should be broken up; all taints of feudalism abolished; primogeniture and entail destroyed; and traffic in the soil be made as free as in the potatoes it yields. "Ireland for the Irish," was the watchword of Daniel O'Connell; and when translated "The Land of Ireland for the People of Ireland," it is just and equitable. "Absenteeism" should be no longer tolerated. To strip foreign landlords of soil that they will neither cultivate nor sell, is justifiable on every principle of property and Christianity. Every farm in America is held by a title based on the doctrine that land is given to man to be occupied and cultivated, not wandered over and made a waste. We displaced the aboriginal hunters on this principle, and inclosed farms and built cities. The means used to effect this were often nefarious; the object sought was righteous. The landlords of Ireland, in regard to one-third of the soil, neither cultivate nor occupy it; and such is the dire necessity of the case, that the Government would be justified in taking the land from every such owner, and giving it to the people, so that it might bring forth its natural increase of bread to the sower. Every man owning land in Ireland, who prefers to live in England, and habitually lets the soil lie waste, or, being cultivated, draws the substance from it to be expended abroad in extravagance, should be compelled to restore it to the people of Ireland, to be used, not for purposes of luxury, but to save the dwellers thereon from starvation. This is not confiscation, but restoration. Famine-stricken Ireland, and not full-fed English aristocracy, is the owner of the soil of Ireland. The great mass of these alien proprietors hold their lands by titles derived from wholesale confiscation. Cromwell and other English rulers took them by force from the native, and gave them to the foreigner. Force, if need be, should compel their restoration. Property in the soil has its duties to discharge, as well as its rights to enjoy; and if it willfully refuse to discharge the former, then it should not be allowed to enjoy the latter. The people of Ireland have a God-given right to live upon and by the soil on which His Providence has planted their feet. Coercion bills *may* be necessary for Ireland. If they be, they should be impartially enforced on both landlords and tenants, compelling each to discharge their respective duties. If the owners of Irish estates are incapable of learning that property has its obligations as well as its immunities, they should be made to give place to more tractable scholars.

And finally : more than all this, and including it all, IRELAND SHOULD GOVERN IRELAND. This is the tender point in this much vexed and most vexatious "Irish Question." England has never brought her unbiased judgment to its investigation. The truth simply is, John Bull dare not look it steadily in the face. He knows he has no more right to govern Ireland than he has to govern Pennsylvania—no more right to govern it in the way he has since the Union, than to put its every man, woman, and child, to the sword. Conceived in sin and brought forth in iniquity, his government of that people has been one series of crimes and blunders. It was sheer usurpation in the beginning, and neither time nor the mode of its administration has changed its character. Three-fourths of the genuine, unadulterated Irish desire a separation from England. But England refuses to relinquish its grasp. It pleads in extenuation of its hold on the national throat, that Ireland is incapable of governing itself. This may be. But it is evident that England is incompetent to the task. Ireland could hardly do worse for itself than England has done for it. It should be permitted to try an experiment which, in England's hands, has proved a sad failure. Let England give Ireland the rope, and, if she hang herself, it will at least be suicide, and not murder. If free Ireland continued to shiver in bog cabins, and feed on saltless potatoes, she would at least gratify that inherent principle in human nature, which makes the beggar prefer to freeze and starve in his own chosen way, rather than on compulsion. But no such doom awaits emancipated Ireland. A government, based on democratic foundations, springing from and responsible to the people, would be a government for the people. Cast off British rule, drive out the Church Establishment, extirpate the landlord system, give Ireland to the Irish, throw them upon their own ample physical and mental resources—thus creating for them a new world, and a new race to people it—and who can estimate the upward spring of the national energies ?

But, will Ireland ever obtain independence ? Will she ever become a nation ? Will Emmett's epitaph ever be written ? Did England ever relinquish her hold upon a rod of bog or an acre of sand, except at the point of the bayonet ? By voluntarily restoring independence to Ireland, dare she set an example that would bring Canada, Hindostan, and all her colonies and "Keys" in the uttermost parts of the earth to her doors, asking, yea, demanding, like restitution ? And must Ireland draw the sword, or submit ? Ah ! must she draw the sword *and* submit ? England will never dare to give freedom to Ireland, till she dare not refuse. Commotions in her own bosom, that shall blanch her cheek, and make her knees smite together, may bring Ireland's "opportunity." If she should, in that hour, smite her chains, would not the blow quicken the pulses of every free heart in the world ? "There is no sufficient cause to justify a revolution," says some coward or conservative. The case of George Washington *vs.* George Guelph, decided that question, wherein it was ruled by the whole Court, that "Resistance to tyrants is obedience to God." The stamp act ? It was the little finger to the loins. England, by a thousand acts, has stamped the life out of eight millions of people. But, unless light beams from unexpected quarters, there is not a shadow of hope of successful resistance to British oppression for years to come. If Ireland were three thousand miles away, she could break her chains with one united blow. But the shadow of her towering conqueror crosses the narrow channel, and fills her with awe. And worse than all, her councils, which should breathe only the spirit of harmony, are rent with domestic feuds. No true son of the land of Hancock and of Henry blames O'Brien, Meagher, and the "rebels" of Forty-Eight, for striking a blow for their country's independence. The hour was unpropitious. The preparation was defective. The means were wholly inadequate to the end. But, the motive which inspired the deed was noble. Whether the graves of these patriotic men be made at the foot of an Irish scaffold, or on the soil of a penal colony, regenerated Ireland will seek out their resting-places, and her grateful tears

> "Shall sprinkle the cold dust in which they sleep
> Pompless, and from a scornful world withdrawn;
> The laurel which its malice rent shall shoot,
> So watered, into life, and mantling shower
> Its verdant honors o'er their grassy tombs

CHAPTER XXX.

Life, Services, and Character of Daniel O'Connell.

Every page of Ireland's history during the present century bears the name of Daniel O'Connell. In many important respects he is the greatest of Irishmen. He occupied a first place among the persons who have recently figured in European affairs, and was one of the most celebrated orators of our times. For the last twenty years, few men exerted so powerful an influence on the politics of Great Britain, while his sway over his immediate countrymen has probably never been equaled His death produced a profound sensation in two hemispheres. Though his character, like that of all men who leave a deep impress on their age, has been variously estimated by those who, on the one hand, received his warm sympathy and powerful support, or, on the other, encountered his fierce reprobation and vigorous opposition, yet all classes of friends and foes concurred in the sentiment that a master spirit had ceased to influence human affairs.

Mr. O'Connell was admitted to the Dublin bar at a time when Curran, one of the most witty, graceful, and brilliant advocates that ever swayed a jury, and Plunkett, one of the most eloquent lawyers that ever addressed a bench, were in the zenith of their fame. It is sufficient proof of the ability and skill of young O'Connell to say, that he had been at the bar but a year or two before he was surrounded by a large circle of clients, and had won victories over each of the eminent barristers I have named. But it was not possible for a mind composed of such fervid elements as his, to be confined within the purlieus of the courts, looking after the minor interests of John Doe and Richard Roe; and it soon became evident that he was to mingle with the sober duties of the lawyer the more exciting and less profitable toils of the politician. He came to the bar at one of the most memorable periods of Irish history—the year Ninety-Eight—when the "United Irishmen" struck an unsuccessful blow for the independence of their country The leaders of the rebellion were arrested for high treason. The life-blood of the chivalrous Robert Emmet was poured out on the scaffold. Several of his compatriots, after suffering cruel imprisonments, and wandering, as exiles, through Europe, reached America, where they were received with open arms by the friends of freedom. Among these, were Thomas Addis Emmet, the eloquent Attorney General of New York; Counselor Sampson, one of the acutest lawyers and keenest wits that ever excoriated a brother advocate at the bar of New York, and whose father, a dissenting minister, was hanged as a rebel; and Dr. Macneven, who rose to eminence in the medical profession in that city. The rebellion of Ninety-Eight resulted in the legislative union between Great Britain and Ireland. Against this measure Mr. O'Connell, in company with a majority of his countrymen, uttered a solemn protest. His first political speech was made in opposition to the proposed act, the repeal of which occupied so prominent a place in the efforts of his declining years. This speech, pronounced before the congregated thousands of Dublin, is said not to have been surpassed for power of argument, severity of invective, and splendor of declamation, by any of his later displays on the same subject. His young soul welled up from full fountains as he portrayed this final degradation which England was about to inflict upon Ireland; and when the deed was done, and he saw the emblems of national independence borne away by the conqueror, Hannibal-like, he swore eternal hostility to the oppressor. And most religiously did he perform his vow!

Mr. O'Connell now turned his attention to the civil and ecclesiastical disabilities of the Roman Catholics of the kingdom. Of the extent of his services in procuring their removal, I have spoken in another place. To this work he gave up twenty-five of the prime years of his life. To him, not the Catholics only, but the Dissenters of every name in Great Britain, are much indebted for the enlargement of their privileges during the last thirty years. This endeared him to large bodies of Christian men, who widely differed from him in religious opinion, giving him a strong hold, Catholic and agitator though he was, upon liberal Baptists, Congregationalists, and Quakers, who, while repudiating his creed, cherished the principle of toleration for which he contended. Mr. O'Connell regarded Catholic Emancipation as the great achievement of his life; and it was that which won for him the title of "The Liberator of Ireland."

During the Catholic controversy, of the bitterness of which Americans can scarcely conceive, Mr. O'Connell for once departed from the pacific policy which was the guiding principle of his excited life. Dublin was the central heart whence he sent out agitating pulsations through every artery of the Irish body. The corporation of that city was a high Tory municipality, of the most bigoted and vindictive class. The leader of the Emancipationists was often in collision with its members, many of whom encountered his severest attacks. In 1815, Mr. D'Esterre, a member of the corporation, at the instigation of its leading officers, challenged Mr. O'Connell to personal combat. The parties met, and at the first fire D'Esterre fell, mortally wounded. The successful duelist saw his antagonist stretched on the grass at his feet, gasping in death. The awful spectacle left an abiding abhorrence of blood on the sensitive mind of O'Connell. Twenty-five years later he inscribed on the Repeal banner his memorable saying, "No political change is worth the shedding of one drop of human blood." His remorse for the D'Esterre tragedy brought forth fruits meet for repentance. During their lives he contributed liberally to the support of the widow and children of the man whom he had slain.

After the death of Grattan, Ireland had no champion in the British Senate, to give utterance to the emotions that swelled her full heart. The Emancipation Act of 1829 opened the doors of the House of Commons to Mr. O'Connell. Born and cradled in Ireland, he had grown up with her people, an Irishman of the Irishmen. He landed on the eastern shore of St. George's Channel the same man as when the spires of Dublin faded from his eye in the western horizon. He carried with him a name endeared in every cabin from Coleraine to Cork, and familiar to statesmen in England and throughout Europe. Widely as he was known, he was known only as an Irishman; and his reputation was, in its kind, purely Irish. To his dying day, he gloried in the epithet early bestowed upon him in Parliament, and which, though intended as a reproach, he converted into a talisman—"The member for all Ireland."

A new field was now opened before him. Grattan, alluding to Flood's failure in the English Parliament, said: "An oak of the forest is too old to be transplanted at fifty." Though O'Connell was fifty-four when he entered that body, his parliamentary career, covering eighteen years, was of the most sturdy growth. His speeches in support of the Reform Bill rank with the ablest which that controversy called forth. He threw his soul into the cause of Negro Emancipation, fighting side by side, in and out of Parliament, with Wilberforce, Clarkson, Buxton, Brougham, Lushington, till the slave became a man. He early embraced the doctrine of immediate and unconditional emancipation, and was among the few members who voted against the delusive scheme of apprenticeship. He united with Sturge, Wardlaw, and Scoble, in the subsequent movement that restored to the apprentices the full rights of British subjects. At the outset of the enterprise, he gave his voice and vote in favor of the leading principles of the Chartists, and was among the earliest advocates of Rowland

Hill's plan of cheap postage. He joined George Thompson in portraying the wrongs of British India and denouncing the crimes of its oppressors, and was an able supporter of the doctrines and measures of the Anti-Corn-Law League.

The member for all Ireland gave a large share of his thoughts to Irish affairs. Regarding the abolition of the Irish Parliament as one of the chief sources of the national suffering, he consecrated the last ten years of his life to efforts for the Repeal of the Union. The means employed were the same as those by which he obtained Emancipation—Popular Agitation. The Repeal excitement, which was soothed for a time by the conciliatory course of the Melbourne Government, broke out with increased intensity when Sir Robert Peel rose to power in 1841–2. In the latter year, "Repeal!" resounded from every parish in the island. The next year saw the "Monster Meetings," when the assembled populace, which swayed to the inspiring eloquence of the Liberator, was measured by acres. The Government was alarmed. Just previous to a grand demonstration at Clontarf, O'Connell, and five others, were arrested for conspiring to change the laws of the realm by intimidation. The trials, which consumed nearly the whole of January, 1844, resulted in the conviction of most of the defendants. O'Connell, when brought up for sentence, pronounced an able and dignified protest against the proceedings. He was adjudged to pay a fine of £2,000, be imprisoned one year, and give sureties to keep the peace for seven. He brought a writ of error to the House of Lords. In the mean time he was sent to the Richmond Penitentiary. The Lords reversed the judgment. After spending three months in a prison, where his "cell" was fitted up and filled like the presence-chamber of a king, and his "confinement" consisted in walking among arbors and parterres that "a Shenstone might have envied," he was released, and, mounted on a triumphal car, rode in state to his residence in Dublin, attended by uncounted thousands of his shouting countrymen. In the frenzy of its joy,

Conciliation Hall declared that "The Liberator had driven the car of Repeal through the Monster Indictment."

Darker skies were gathering over O'Connell. The pacific tenor of his agitations had thwarted the government. The magic of his name had prevented any overt act of violence by vast assemblies of his excited countrymen. The sub-leaders became impatient of delay, assumed a defiant tone, and demanded that the non-resistant doctrines of O'Connell be repudiated by the National Repeal Association. Then arose "Young Ireland." Then came strife and division, one party clinging to, the other separating from, the great leader. The alienation of large numbers of his friends overtaking him when his powers were impaired by years of exhausting toil, broke the spirit of the old man, undermined his constitution, and compelled him to repair to the Continent to resuscitate his waning health and drooping heart. But he left the field of exertion too late. His energies rapidly declined; death overtook him while on his weary pilgrimage; his eye saw the sun for the last time in a foreign sky; and he slept his final sleep far from the land which gave him birth, and from that ocean by whose side his cradle was rocked. The stroke that felled him to the earth sent a pang through many a heart in every country where humanity has a dwelling-place; for his sympathies, like his reputation, were world-wide. He had delivered his own countrymen from the bonds of ecclesiastical tyranny, and had plead for the victims of a hellish traffic on the shores of Africa, for the swarthy serfs of British cupidity on the banks of the Ganges, for the persecuted Jews of ancient Damascus, and for the stricken slaves in the isles of the Caribbean Sea and in the distant States of America.

No impartial and well-informed mind doubts the sincerity of Mr. O'Connell in demanding a Repeal of the Union. But it is equally unquestionable that, in his estimate of the benefits to flow from that measure, he either was deceived himself, or misled his followers. Probably long contemplation of that object, as the one remedy for the ills of Ireland, betrayed him into the errors of all disciples of "one-ideaism," while he was not exempt from the common infirmity of political leaders, in unduly magnifying before the eye of their partisans *the* measure of the party. Ineffectual as Repeal must have proved in producing a radical cure for Ireland, it would have been a preliminary stage in her restoration to complete independence, and therefore was important.

In respect to Mr. O'Connell's general course as a public man, it may be said that he did not belong to the ascetic school of politicians. He was not exempt from trick and artifice in attaining his ends, and was lavish in promising to do for his followers what he must have known he could not perform. Indeed, he was something of a demagogue. In honesty of purpose, he ranks with the better class of great public leaders; and if this be not saying much, it is saying more than can be uttered of the body. He is a rare man who is worthy to be ranked among the exceptions to bad general rules. The objects to which he devoted his political life were the noblest that can move the hearts of men. He that has never employed questionable means to secure even such ends may cast the first stone at Daniel O'Connell.

It only remains that I refer to his personal, social, and mental characteristics. Mr. O'Connell had a massive frame, capable of enduring great fatigue, and he was one of the most industrious and laborious of men. His manners were cordial and frank; his social qualities genial and winning; and he was singularly affectionate as a husband and a father. It was only in the fierce conflicts of partisan strife, when challenged by some strong provocation, that the unlovely and almost vindictive traits of his nature were displayed. Then, the man who, an hour before, had been all gentleness and good humor—caressing his grandchildren with womanly fervor, or, in his seat in the Commons, affectionately holding the hand of his son for a half hour together—now opened that terrible battery of invective which he so well knew how to employ, and covered his foe with a storm of fire.

He possessed a mind of uncommon native vigor, trained by a complete education, and enlarged with a knowledge of men and things varied and ample. The versatility of his genius, his extensive information, and his capacity to adapt himself to the matter under discussion or the audience before him, were surprising. I have heard him exhaust topics that required for their elucidation an intimate acquaintance with the Constitution of the United States, with the condition of barbarous tribes in the interior of Africa, with the wrongs inflicted by the East India Company upon the dwellers in Hindostan, with the commercial tariffs of European nations, with the persecution of the Jews in Asia, with the causes of the opium war in China, with the relative rights of planters and laborers in the Western Archipelago—and he was at home in each. I have seen him hold the House of Commons spell-bound, call shouts from the *elite* of British intelligence and philanthropy in Exeter Hall, lash into fury or hush into repose acres of wild peasantry gathered on the moors of Ireland—and he was at home with each.

As a popular orator, before mixed assemblies, our age has rarely seen his equal. So good a judge as John Randolph pronounced him the first orator in Europe. Every chord of the human bosom lay open to his touch, and he played upon its passions and emotions with a master's hand. He could subdue his hearers to tears by his pathos, or toss them with laughter by his humor. His imagination could bear them to a giddy hight on its elastic wing, or he could enchain their judgment by the strong links of his logic. He could blanch their cheek as he painted before their eye some atrocity red with blood, or he could make them hold their sides as he related some broad Irish anecdote fresh from Cork. He used to say he was the bes-tabused man in Europe. But he was able to liquidate all such scores with most usurious interest. He could excoriate an antagonist with invective, or roast him alive before a slow fire of sarcasm. When his indignation was fully roused, he boiled like a volcano ; yet there was no excess of action or noise, but an eruption whose lava consumed all before it. His recital of facts charmed like a romance, and his appeals to the sympathies, uttered in a musical voice and the richest brogue of his native island, were tender and subduing.

No actor ever excelled him in reflecting the workings of the mind through the windows of the countenance. He *looked* every sentiment as it fell from his lips. I have seen a deputation of Hindoo chiefs, while listening to his detail, before an assembly, of the wrongs of India, never take their eyes off of him for an hour and a half, though not one word in ten was intelligible to their ears. His gesticulation was redundant, never commonplace, strictly *sui generis*, far from being awkward, not precisely graceful, and yet it could hardly have been more forcible, and, so to speak, illustrative. He threw himself into a great variety of attitudes, all evidently unpremeditated. Now he stands bolt upright like a grenadier. Then he assumes the port and bearing of a pugilist. Now he folds his arms upon his breast, utters some beautiful sentiment, relaxes them, recedes a step, and gives wing to the coruscations of his fancy, while a winning smile plays over his countenance. Then he "stands at ease," and relates an anecdote with the rollicking air of a horse-jockey at Donnybrook Fair. Quick as thought, his indignation is kindled; and, before speaking a word, he makes a violent sweep with his arm, seizes his wig as if he would tear it in pieces, adjusts it to its place, advances to the front of the rostrum, throws his body into the attitude of a gladiator, and pours out a flood of rebuke and denunciation.

Like most other rare men who have acted conspicuous parts in turbulent times, he had great faults, eminent virtues, crowds of enemies, troops of friends. His flatterers have rarely called him a statesman. In truth, he was neither a good statesman, nor a bad statesman, but simply a bold and generally successful political agitator. He grappled with questions that shook empires; led the van in many a contest against despotism; was indebted in no small degree for his victories to the rottenness of the institutions he assailed. All right-minded and liberal-hearted men will ascribe his defects partly to the evil times in which he lived, partly to a hasty temper and an indomitable pride of opinion, while to a large extent they will be attributed to a generous and impulsive nature, impatient of unmeasured abuse and unreasonable opposition. Impartial history will record that his fury was usually poured out on the heads of meanness, fraud, injustice, and oppression; that he was the friend, the champion, the brother, of depressed and outraged manhood, irrespective of clime, color, or creed; and that wherever Humanity writhed under the heel of Tyranny, there were found the glowing heart and trumpet voice of Daniel O'Connell, sympathizing with the victim and rebuking the tyrant.

CHAPTER XXXI

The Temperance Reformation—Father Mathew.

THE Temperance Reformation in Ireland, one of the most surprising moral phenomena of this century, is attributable, under Providence, to the zealous and discreet labors of one man.

The 10th of April, 1838, begun a new era in this philanthropic enterprise. On that day, Rev. THEOBALD MATHEW signed the pledge, took the lead of the Cork Temperance Society, and entered upon those labors which have sent his fame over the earth like sunshine. For a year afterward he held semi-weekly meetings in Cork, for administering the pledge to the people. Feeble in its beginnings, the popular feeling gradually rose in favor of the movement, his meetings were crowded to overflowing, his house was besieged night and day, the roads leading to Cork were, on "pledge days," thronged with multitudes, eager to take the vow from the lips of "the good Father;" and at the close of the year, the number of names enrolled exceeded 150,000.

No doubt the reverential element, which constitutes so prominent a trait in the Irish character, contributed to the early success of Father Mathew. A priest and a friar, respected for his purity of life, remarkable for the winning simplicity and kindness of his manners, solemnly pronouncing the pledge to a convert, kneeling devoutly at his feet, and he, in the presence of listening thousands, repeating the vow as it fell from the lips of his spiritual teacher, and receiving a medal as a token of his plighted faith, and rising from the ground while the Father pronounced the benediction, "May God bless you, my son, and help you to keep your promise," was adapted to sink into the soul of even a less susceptible people than the Irish.

Near the close of the year 1839, Mr. Mathew visited Limerick, and was greeted by such an outburst of popular feeling as has not been equaled except by some of the Monster Repeal Meetings of O'Connell. Every street and lane of the city exhibited a dense mass of human beings. When the "Apostle of Temperance" arrived, a shout went up that was heard for miles around. Provisions rose on that day three-fold, and at night, though every house, hall, and cellar even, was filled, thousands upon thousands were unable to find a lodging or a shelter, and were compelled to shiver in the open streets till morning. He remained four or five days in Limerick. At one time, and in one street, 20,000 persons might be seen kneeling to receive the pledge, after which they arose and retired in order, and made room for other thousands. The thrilling shouts, as Father Mathew moved from place to place, the serried ranks of kneeling recipients, the solemn stillness that prevailed while the pledge was given, the press of eager thousands to fill the places of those who withdrew, were scenes that bankrupt description. The number of persons who took the pledge at this time in Limerick was upwards of 150,000. Leaving Limerick, he visited Waterford, and administered it to 60,000. In the spring of 1840, he repaired to Dublin, which rose *en masse* to receive him, while the neighboring counties sent their thousands to the city to take the pledge and obtain his blessing.

During the succeeding three years, he visited all parts of Ireland, grateful shouts everywhere heralding his approach, thanksgivings attending on his steps, and successes which a Howard might have envied, and triumphs which a Cæsar could not have won, following in his train. In five years from the commencement of his services, he had obtained the pledge of five millions of persons in Ireland alone, to the practice of total abstinence. The fame of his good deeds having long before crossed the Channel, he yielded to invitations, and visited Scotland and England in 1842–3, administering the pledge to half a million of people. During the following six years, this remarkable man has prosecuted his work with all the constancy which the famine-stricken condition of his fellow-subjects would permit. He has raised up a myriad throng of emancipated men to call him blessed.

This great Irish reform, mildly winning its way through all the avenues of society, has done wonders in elevating the social condition of that unfortunate people. Even if this truly good man had not visited America on his errand of mercy, but merely as a traveler on a tour of observation and pleasure, the rich blessings he has showered upon his country and mankind would entitle him to the warm greeting, alike honorable to us and to him, which a generous nation tenders to a devoted philanthropist.

CHAPTER XXXII

International Peace—European Military Establishments—British Establishment—Mr. Cobden—Peace Party in England—Peace Congress in Paris—Elihu Burritt—Charles Sumner.

My limits forbid such an extended notice of the sublime enterprise of International Peace as its importance demands, and my own feelings dictate.

At the present hour, about two millions of Europeans, in the prime of manhood, are withdrawn from the arts of peace, to bear the sword and the musket, and hold themselves ready, at the beck of diplomatic chicane and the tap of the drum, to slaughter other millions, in defense of arbitrary or aristocratic governments. To maintain these two millions, on ship and on shore, costs directly and indirectly two hundred millions sterling per annum.

Great Britain has been a severe sufferer for naval and military "glory." From 1793 to 1815, her public debt increased £600,000,000, the greater part of this sum being expended in contests with Napoleon and his allies. Since the peace of 1815, she has spent an average of full £15,000,000 per year for warlike objects. Paying her sailors and soldiers at the meanest rates, she gives large salaries to their officers, lavishing incredible sums on many of them for doing literally nothing. There are in the army sinecure colonelcies alone to the amount of £200,000 per annum, and Prince Albert, who never saw and never will see a shot fired in anger, pockets yearly £8000 for sporting a Field Marshal's uniform, on court days, in the drawing-room of St. James'. The pay of the soldiers and marines is plucked from the pockets and stomachs of the laboring poor. No wonder that Cobden, Sturge, Gurney, Lee, Hindley, Ewart, Conder, Miall, Burnet, Vincent, and their associates, think this anti-christian system should come to an end. The Peace party in England is rapidly becoming so influential that it will soon make itself felt in the National Councils. MR. COBDEN's motion (which is postponed rather than defeated) to reduce the national expenditures £10,000,000 per annum is aimed at the army and navy. It will ultimately triumph, and with usurious interest for all delays. A large share of the Complete Suffragists, of the Free Traders, of the Financial Reformers, and, indeed, of the radicals generally, if not technically "Peace-men," are hostile to the existing military and naval establishments. Mr. Cobden, from his eminent talents, his distinguished services, and his firm hold on the popular mind, may be regarded as the leader of the Peace movement in England.

The Peace Congress, held in Paris, during the past summer, in whose proceedings so many eminent philanthropists of various countries participated, has given an impulse to the pacific enterprise in Europe.

From the list of American names that have aided this cause, it will not be invidious to select two, as worthy of special commendation: the philanthropic and indefatigable ELIHU BURRITT, who has done so much during the last three years to arouse the attention of England to the horrors of war and the blessings of peace; and CHARLES SUMNER, the accomplished lawyer, classical scholar, and eloquent orator, whose writings and speeches, alike instructive and brilliant, have greatly assisted in commending this noble reform to public favor both in our own and foreign States.

CHAPTER XXXIII.

Mrs. Elizabeth Fry—Mrs. Amelia Opie—Lady Noel Byron—Miss Harriet Martineau—Mrs. Mary Howitt.

It would do injustice to my own feelings and the facts of history, to leave it to be inferred, from my silence, that the Women of England have not furnished some of the brightest names in the galaxy of Modern Reformers.

Looking ever so casually in this direction, what figure so promptly meets the eye as that of Elizabeth Fry—the friend of the prisoner, the bondman, the lunatic, the beggar—who has been aptly named "the female Howard"? Mrs. Fry hardly deserved more credit for the benevolent impulses of her heart, than for the dignity and urbanity of her manners. They were natural, for they were born with her. The daughter of John, and the sister of Joseph and Samuel Gurney, could hardly be else than the embodiment of that charity which never faileth, that philanthropy which embraces every form of human misery, and that amenity which proffers the cup of kindness with an angel's grace. In youth, her personal attractions, and the vivacity of her conversation, made her the idol of the social circle, and severe was her struggle in deciding whether to become the reigning belle of the neighborhood, or devote her life to assuaging the sorrows of a world of suffering and crime. Happily, she resolved that Humanity had higher claims upon her than Fashion. Her resolution once formed, she immediately entered upon the holy mission to which, for nearly half a century, she consecrated that abounding benevolence and winning grace, which, in her girlhood, were the pride of her parents and the delight of her companions.

Though her eye was ever open to discover, and her hand to relieve, all forms of sorrow, it was to the inmates of the mad-house and the penitentiary that she mainly devoted her exertions. Wonderful was her power over the insane. The keenest magnetic eye of the most experienced keeper paled and grew feeble in its sway over the raving maniac, compared with the tones of her magic voice. Equally fascinating was her influence over prisoners and felons. Many a time, in spite of the sneers of vulgar turnkeys, and the positive assurances of respectable keepers, that her purse and even her life would be at stake if she entered the wards of the prison, she boldly went in amongst the swearing, quarreling wretches, and, with the doors bolted behind her, encountered them with dignified demeanor and kindly words, that soon produced a state of order and repose which whips and chains had vainly endeavored to enforce. Possessing peculiar powers of eloquence, (why may not a woman be an "orator?") she used to assemble the prisoners, address them in a style of charming tenderness all her own, win their assent to regulations for their conduct which she proposed, shake hands with them, give and receive a blessing, return to the keeper's room, and be received by him with almost as much astonishment and awe as Darius exhibited toward Daniel, when he emerged from the den of lions.

In this way, Mrs. Fry made frequent examinations of the prisons of England. She pursued her holy work on the Continent, visiting prisons in France, Holland, Belgium, Denmark, Germany, and Prussia. In the early part of her career, she encountered both at home and abroad some rudeness, and many rebuffs. But her ever-present dignity, tact, and kindness, at length won the confidence and plaudits of the great majority of her own countrymen, and of many philanthropists and titled personages in other lands. She was a favorite of the Kings of Prussia and Denmark—the former, when in England, paying her a complimentary visit at her own house. She sought frequent occasions to press, in person, the subject of her mission upon the attention of crowned heads and ministers of state. She accomplished a great work in the cause of Prison Reform, in ameliorating the Penal Code, and improving the condition of convict ships and penal colonies. Her special mouthpiece in Parliament was her brother-in-law, Mr. Buxton—her measures were supported by Mackintosh and other illustrious Senators—and it is the highest tribute to the dignity which her rare excellences threw over her enterprises, that they got the better of Sydney Smith's love of ridicule, and drew from him two or three articles in their favor in the Edinburgh Review. This greatly useful and greatly beloved woman died in 1845, at the age of sixty-six. To her may be applied with equal propriety Burke's beautiful tribute to Howard:

"She visited all Europe, not to survey the sumptuousness of palaces, or the stateliness of temples; not to make accurate measurements of the remains of ancient grandeur, nor to form a scale of the curiosities of modern art; not to collect medals, nor collate manuscripts; but to dive into the depths of dungeons, to plunge into the infection of hospitals, to survey the mansions of sorrow and pain; to take the guage and dimensions of misery, depression, and contempt; to remember the forgotten, to attend to the neglected, to visit the forsaken, and compare and collate the miseries of all men in all countries. Her plan was original: it was as full of genius as of humanity. It was a voyage of discovery; a circumnavigation of charity. Already, the benefit of her labor is felt more or less in every country."

Mrs. Fry having been a member of the Society of Friends, we easily turn to Mrs. AMELIA OPIE, also belonging to that venerable body. As Mrs. Opie wrote the celebrated work on *Lying*, we must tell the truth if we say anything of this excellent lady. When I saw her, though the sun and shade of more than sixty years had flitted across her path, her conversation and manners retained much of the sprightliness of youth, and would have been *very* agreeable, had she not affected more juvenility than she really possessed. Nearly half a century before, she had sent to press a volume of poems, marked by graceful versification, sweetness, and pathos; and a domestic tale, "The Father and Daughter," which was distinguished, amongst the mass of sentimental nonsense which floated all around, by lively narrative, and a high moral tone. This novel run through several editions, and still holds its place in libraries. Since then, numerous works of fiction have flowed from her pen, which bear the same literary impress, are elevated in their moral aim, and tend to soften the heart, and make us love mankind better than before. Some of Mrs. Opie's best gifts have been laid on the altar of humanity. She has been the warm friend, both in youth and in old age, of enterprises for the improvement of man, without respect to clime, creed, or color.

I have said that Mrs. Opie was a Quakeress. In doctrine, she belongs to the straitest of the sect, while she talks of Barclay's Apology and Byron's Childe Harold, of George Fox's preaching and Walter Scott's novels, in the same sentence, and with equal delight. Suppose her *thee* and *thou* did sound oddly in such company, and her tongue trip occasionally when repeating some of Tom Moore's champagne jokes at Lord Holland's dinners; and suppose her dress is juvenile in style, and fastidious in arrangement, dazzling the eyes as it throws back in disdain the envious brilliancy of the blazing chandelier, showing that no belle in the room has toiled more hours at her toilet this evening, than she ; still she is good Mrs. Opie, is not "a birth-right member" of the plain-speaking and plain-dressing sect, but joined them "on convincement," while far advanced in life, with habits firmly fixed, and after passing the line when it is easier to change one's creed than one's manners Under that glossy satin dress, there beats a heart whose every avenue is open to truth, and whose sympathies gush out in streams that return not to their fountain, till they have swept the entire circle of human want and woe. Suppose this worthy Christian philanthropist is rather fond of telling her auditors (and are they not fond of hearing?) the fine things Sir Walter Scott said to her in Melrose Abbey, or the flat joke that some flatter earl cracked in her ear when leading her into the drawing-room of Lord Fitzfoozle, or what Campbell said to her at her own house, when she was participating in a discussion with Wordsworth and Sir Thomas Lawrence, about the relative merits of poetry and painting, or how she used up all her stock of French the day she dined with Lafayette—she is only one of a great crowd of book writers and book readers on both sides of the Atlantic, who are fond of insinuating that they have shone as conspicuous spangles in more than one comet's luminous tail.

In her declining years, Mrs. Opie has occasionally sent into the world some effusion of her benevolent pen, on religious and charitable subjects—lives in a neat style at Norwich—shows her visitors rooms lined with rare paintings, partly the product of her husband's lively pencil—is active in all works of love and mercy—was on familiar terms with the late warm-hearted Bishop of Norwich—and delights to guide her friends through the long aisles of the aged cathedral, when the organ sounds its sweetest notes.

The circumstances under which I first saw Mrs. Opie remind me to say a few words of Lady Noel Byron, the widow of the poet. She appeared as mild as the blue sky of an Italian summer evening. Edified by her intelligent conversation, and charmed with the softened grace of her manners, one could not but say to himself—Can it be that that mild blue eye, that mellow voice, that bland mien belonged to *the* Lady Byron, the wife of the wild genius, whose erratic fire, while it startled the round world with its glare, withered all that was sweet and lovely within its own domestic circle, nor paled till it had consumed its owner by the intensity of its own volcanic hell? Hidden under that pale cheek and quiet countenance, there *may* lie the smoldering embers of passions that once shot their flames through the very veins of the bard, and made him the mad suicide he was. But they now slumber so profoundly, that one must disbelieve they ever existed. The mystery must die with the parties.

There is a sprightliness in the conversation of Lady Byron that wins the listener, and a common sense that edifies him, while the tinge of sadness which flows through it gives a serious and sincere hue to the vein of pure morality that pervades much of this unfortunate woman's discourse. Decidedly plain-looking—for, even in the bloom of youth, she could not have been handsome—her countenance when in repose is rather dull and uninteresting, but it kindles up when excited by the contact of kindred minds, and is set off by an address and manners familiar and easy.

Lady Byron has found occasional relief from the cloud which memory hangs over her, by participating in enterprises of charity and philanthropy. Indeed, she seemed to be quite a reformer, apparently holding firmly, while uttering cautiously, the liberal political sentiments which constituted the redeeming feature in her husband's character. As might be expected, she is sensitive to all allusions in her presence to him, seeming desirous that the thick veil of oblivion should hide all traces of their lamentable union and separation. It is not so with her daughter, Ada Augusta—the "gentle Ada" —since Lady Lovelace, who loves to talk of her father, and glows with delight when you tell her that his works are universally read, not only in the seaboard cities of America, but among the far-away woods and prairies of the New World.

Who that can appreciate a happy blending of philosophical acumen with philanthropic devotion, illustrated in writings profound and poetic, and conversation rational and racy, could fail to be pleased with Miss Harriet Martineau—in spite of her tin trumpet? And well would it be for their own reputation and the comfort of society, if many authors and talkers used a trumpet to gather up the responses of their readers and auditors, rather than to blow private griefs or fancied merits in the averted face of the public. Descended from one of the families exiled from France on the revocation of the Edict of Nantes, Miss Martineau inherits the fondness for philosophical speculation and the vivacity of spirit of the people whence she traces her lineage, mingled with the hatred of tyranny and love of toleration which the event that drove her forefathers to England was calculated to inspire. These French Puritans, wherever scattered up and down the world by the bigotry of Louis XIV, if they have had less of iron in their character and marble in their aspect than the Huguenots of Plymouth, they have displayed, under persecutions equally severe, as heroic a defense of their own civil and religious freedom, while exhibiting in their treatment of others a larger measure of that charity which suffereth long and is kind.

Miss Martineau became a student in extreme youth. While a girl, delicate health prevented her mingling in pastimes usual to her sex and years, and she sought society in books. Subsequently, an embarrassing deafness threw her upon her own mental resources for amusement and instruction. Gifted with ready powers of writing, and the needed motive for "trying her hand" being found in pecuniary necessity, she naturally turned from reading books to making them, and became an author at the age of twenty. During the next twenty-five years, she sent to press numerous works, ranging over a wide field of topics, from verses and stories adapted to the nursery and the school, to volumes on political economy and poor-laws, after the order of Bentham and Malthus. She has written tales, novels, prayers, hymns, illustrations of political economy and pauperism and taxation, sketches of travels in Europe, Asia, Africa and America, and numberless papers for reviews and magazines, exhibiting high powers of reflection and rare graces of composition, and aiming at the great and good end of instructing, amusing, and elevating mankind. Two of her most interesting publications, and they are among the most recent, are "Life in a Sick Room" and "The Holy Land"—the former, a beautiful record of her own experience and reflections while suffering under deep-seated disease; the latter, a vivid and graphic picture of her lingerings around the sacred scenes of Palestine.

The works of Miss Martineau that produced the greatest sensation, and most widely extended her reputation, are those on political subjects. In politics, for she is a politician, she must be classed with the radicals of the school of Bentham, Cobden, and Hume. This fact, uniting with the class of topics she handled, have not vouchsafed to her exemption from the canons and hot shot of criticism to which the writings of the other sex are exposed. And she is too much of a woman to plead her sex in bar of the operation of any legitimate rule of literary warfare. She is able to give as well as take in the arena of authorship. Her works, or rather tales, (for she dressed her disquisitions in the drapery of fiction,) on political economy, poor-laws, and cognate subjects, drew down upon her the sneers and maledictions of the High Tory Quarterly Review—the former being aimed at her sex, the latter at her doctrines—which only resulted in proving that the critics had very slender claims to be regarded either as gentlemen, philosophers or statesmen. So novel was her undertaking, that she encountered great difficulty in getting a publisher for her "Illustrations." She first offered them to the generally astute and always liberal Society for the Diffusion of Useful Knowledge The managers declined to issue them, prophesying that the project would prove a dead failure. At length a bookseller was found, hardy enough, or wise enough, to send into the world essays on political economy, poor-laws, and taxation, dressed up in fiction by the hand of a woman. The success of the experiment was immediate and complete. The numbers were eagerly bought as they came out, the advent of each link in the series being looked for with as much interest as Dickens' Nickleby or Dombey; new editions followed new editions; Germany and France translated and sent them over Europe; till the most driveling specimen of Britain's old-womanish legislation received a shock from which it has never recovered, and looked at one time as if it might fall a sudden victim to the exposures of a comparatively young damsel.

Mrs. Mary Howitt has walked gracefully over a portion of the same field of literature as Miss Martineau, gathering flowers not seen by or not congenial to the eye of the more matter-of-fact disciple of the great Utilitarian. She has more poetry and less philosophy in her temperament than Miss Martineau, is more domestic and rural in her tastes, grapples less with themes that agitate senates, and has a heart more susceptible to the *individual* joys and sorrows of mankind. She is equally bountiful in her contributions to the every-day reading of the times; gives her writings a high moral aim; makes her readers good-humored, and overflowing with *bonhommie;* and if she does not set them to thinking so hard about the causes of human misery, stimulates them to as much activity in alleviating the effects.

In 1823, soon after her marriage with Mr. Howitt—and two more congenial spirits never closed hands at the altar—they jointly published "The Forest Minstrel," a volume abounding in lively pictures of rural scenery, and filial reverence for the poetry of the olden time. They made a tour of Scotland, traveling more than a thousand miles over highland and moorland, half of which they performed on foot, drinking at the storied fountains, and holding familiar converse with the spirits that haunt the old castles and battle-fields of a country whose novelists and bards have associated

"With every glen and every stream,
The romance of some warrior dream."

This tour, taken when their minds were alive to the sublimities and beauties of the scenery, and when their poetic eye threw its young glance upon each filament of the drapery that song and story have spread over every spot between Tweed-dale and Loch Ness, gave form and color to all the subsequent writings of the Howitts. Returning home, they published another volume of poetry, which, like the first, was warmly eulogized by the public press. They were now fairly launched on the stream of English literature. For several years Mrs. Howitt gave much time to the preparation of works for the young. Being first enlisted in this department by the wants of her own rising household, she subsequently wrote for the public, throwing off scores of stories, which were bought, read, and admired by "the million" of her own country, are found in "morocco and gilt" on marble tables in American cities, and in yellow covers in the log huts beyond the mountains, while some, through the medium of translations, have found their way into the nurseries of Germany and the forest-homes of Poland.

After a variety of literary adventures in England, Mr. and Mrs. Howitt visited Germany, about 1840, where they resided some three years. Here they acquired a knowledge, among others, of the Swedish tongue. The result of their continental sojourn was the translation into English by him of the celebrated "Student Life in Germany," and the publication of his "Social and Rural Life in Germany," and her translation and introduction to British and American readers of the now widely known Swedish novels of Frederika Bremer. Deeply sympathizing with all efforts to elevate the mind and condition of their countrymen, and feeling the need of a weekly periodical that should combine high literary qualities with radical political doctrines, they started, in 1846, "The People's Journal." Mrs. Howitt was a large contributor to its pages, both under its original name and that of Howitt's Journal. Some numbers of the latter for the closing part of the year 1847 are now under my eye, and I am struck with the great amount, varied character, and benevolent aim of her contributions. Stories for children; translations from Hans Christian Andersen; poetic gems; a sketch of Laura Bridgman; translations of Swedish and Hungarian tales; a sketch of "the Deserter in London," which kindles indignation against war; "Love passages in the lives of every-day people;" a most eloquent petition to the Queen, for commuting the sentence of a woman then lying in Newgate, whose execution had been postponed that she might give birth to a child—these, and such papers, scattered through the Journal, exhibit the mode in which Mrs. Howitt has spent her life of late years. And, her husband being witness, she is not only an industrious authoress, but a model wife and mother.

While the Journal gave an impulse to the cause of freedom, it was most disastrous to the pecuniary interests of the Howitts They have had their full share of the joys and sorrows, honors and perplexities, profits and losses of literary life. They have encountered their checkered lot with as hopeful a brow as anybody can be expected to exhibit, that attempts to get a living by writing "books which *are* books," in this age of "*cheap* literature." In prosperity and adversity, they have given hand, heart and pen to progress and reform. Should they ever accomplish their purpose of visiting America, the friends of pure and pleasing literature would unite with the friends of social and political reform, to give them welcome hands with hearts in them.

CHAPTER XXXIV.

The Literature of Freedom—The Liberal Literature of England—Periodicals—Edinburgh Review—Its Founders—Its Contributors—Its Standard and Style of Criticism—Its Influence—London Quarterly Review Started—Political Services of the Edinburgh—Its Ecclesiastical Tone—Sydney Smith—Decline of the Political Influence of the Edinburgh—Blackwood's Magazine—Tait's Magazine—Westminster Review—The Eclectic—The New Monthly—The Weekly Press—Cobbett's Register—Hunt's Examiner—Mr. Fonblanque—Mr. Landor—The Spectator—Douglas Jerrold—Punch—People's and Howitt's Journals—Mr. Howitt—Chambers's Journal—Penny Magazine and Cyclopedia.

In the times of the Commonwealth, when the mind of England was set free, Milton was the center of a constellation of intellects that exemplified in their writings the value of his own saying—"Give me the liberty to know and to argue freely, above all other liberties." After his sun set, liberty without licentiousness hid behind a cloud, which was not fully cleared away till the storm of the American and French revolutions. While the literature of England depended for sustenance upon the patronage of the great, it was marked, with occasional exceptions, by the brand of servility; and so long as authors looked for remuneration to the munificence of the lord or lady to whom they dedicated their works, they laid their choicest gifts at the footstool of power and title. As education became diffused, enlarging the circle of readers, writers began to look to the public for patronage, and adapted their works to the popular taste. Then the publishers and booksellers became the agents, the middle-men, between the author and the reader. Long after this change, however, it was hazardous for a writer to lift his pen against existing institutions in Church and State ; and he who run a tilt against these, were he able to make sale of his works, might deem himself fortunate if he escaped a prosecution for libel or sedition, that emptied his purse of its guineas, or planted his feet in the stocks. Even so late as the beginning of this century, the instances were not a few where writers, who doubted the divinity of the royal Guelphs, and questioned whether all the religion in the kingdom emanated from Lambeth Palace, were fined, cropped, branded, and shipped beyond seas. The impulse given to European intellect by the first French revolution, was not confined to statesmen and warriors. It stimulated thought in all classes. As in politics, so in letters, fetters fell from men's minds, and reason, imagination, and utterance were emancipated. The Fox school of politicians encouraged the growth of a literature in England favorable to freedom. It immediately started up, rank and luxuriant ; and though bearing every variety of fruit that could delight the eye, or regale the appetite, or poison the taste, the decided preponderance of the product has been congenial to rational liberty, healthy morals, and sound learning.

In estimating the literary influences which have contributed to the cause of Progress and Reform in Great Britain, during the present century, a high place should be assigned to the Edinburgh Review.

This celebrated periodical appeared at an era when independence of thought and manliness of utterance had almost ceased from the public journals and councils of the kingdom. The terrors of the French revolution had arrested the march of liberal opinions. The declamation of Burke and the ambition of Napoleon had frightened the isle from its propriety. Tooke had barely escaped the gallows through the courageous eloquence of Erskine. Fox had withdrawn from the contest in despair, and cherished in secret the fires of freedom, to burst forth in happier times.

Previous to 1802, the literary periodicals of Great Britain were mere repositories of miscellanies, relating to art, poetry, letters, and gossip, partly original and partly selected, huddled together without system, and making up a medley as varied and respectable as a first class weekly newspaper of the present day. The criticisms of books were jejune in the extreme, consisting chiefly of a few smart witticisms, and meager connecting remarks stringing together ample quotations from the work under review. They rarely ventured into deep water on philosophical subjects, and as seldom pushed out upon the tempestuous sea of political discussion. Perhaps one or two journals might plead a feeble exception to the general rule ; but the mass was weary, stale, flat, and unprofitable.

The Edinburgh appeared. It bounded into the arena without the countenance of birth or station, without the imprimatur of the universities or literary clubs. Its avowed mission was to erect a higher standard of merit, and secure a bolder style and a purer taste in literature, and to apply philosophical principles and the maxims of truth and humanity to politics, aiming to be the manual of the scholar, the monitor of the statesman. As in its advent it had asked permission of no one *to be*, so as to its future course it asked no advice as to what it should *do*. Soliciting no quarter, promising no favors, its independent bearing and defiant tone broke the spell which held the mind of a nation in fetters. Its first number revived the discussion of great political principles. The splendid diction and searching philosophy of an essay on the causes and consequences of the French revolution at once arrested the public eye, and stamped the character of the journal. Pedants in the pulpit, and scribblers of Rosa-Matilda verses in printed albums, saw, from other articles in the manifesto, that exterminating war was declared on their inanities and sentimentalities. The new journal was perused with avidity, and produced a sensation in all classes of readers, exciting admiration and envy, love and hatred, defiance and fear. It rapidly obtained a large circulation, steadily rose to the highest position ever attained by any similar publication, reigned supreme in an empire of its own creation for a third of a century, accomplishing vast good mingled with no inconsiderable evil.

The honor of founding this Review belongs to Sydney Smith. He suggested the idea to Messrs. Jeffrey, Brougham, and Murray—he, a poor young curate of Salisbury Plain, "driven in stress of politics" into Edinburgh, while on a voyage to Germany—they, briefless young advocates of the northern capital. They all subsequently rose to eminence; all becoming lords except Smith, who might have been made a lord bishop if he had not been created the prince of wits. The four adventurers, who met in the eighth or ninth story of Buccleugh Place, and agreed to start a Review, provided they could get the first number published on trust, they not having money enough to pay the printer, could not have dreamed that the journal would be eagerly read for half a century, from London to Calcutta, from the Cape of Good Hope to the sources of the Mississippi, and that Brougham would become Lord Chancellor of Great Britain, Jeffrey Lord Justice of the highest court of Scotland, Murray also Lord Justice of Scotland, and Smith Canon of St. Paul's Cathedral, firing hot shot at Pennsylvanians for not paying interest on a small loan from his surplus of £70,000.

Did space permit, it might be interesting to attempt to trace the causes of the great power which this periodical exerted over public opinion. The temper of the times when it appeared in respect to politics, and the Dead Sea of dullness in literary criticism that spread all around, gave novelty to an enterprise which proposed to combine the highest literary and scientific excellences with the boldest discussion of public men and affairs. The execution of the plan came up to the lofty tone of the manifesto. In its infancy, and onward to its maturity, the Edinburgh surrounded itself with a host of contributors whose names have given and received celebrity from its pages. Smith, Jeffrey, Brougham, Murray, Scott, Playfair, Leslie, Brewster, Stewart, Horner, Romilly, Stephen, Mackintosh, Brown, Malthus, Ricardo, Hallam, Hamilton, Hazlitt, Forster, McCulloch, Macaulay, Carlyle, Talfourd—and these are but a tithe—have given it their choicest productions, ranging through the fields of polities, finance, jurisprudence, ethics, science, poetry, art, and letters, in all their multiform departments. The contributions of many of these writers have been extracted and published in separate volumes, which, in their turn, have challenged the criticism of celebrated reviewers on both sides of the Atlantic.

Nor was less zest imparted to its earlier pages because ability was not always accompanied with candor, and attacks upon distinguished authors and statesmen were no less fierce than assaults upon popular works and venerable institutions. Persons and principles were alike mixed in the melee. Nobody, nothing was spared that opposed the march of the literary Tamerlane. In the department of literary criticism, its standard was just, lofty, or capricious, according to its mood; its style, by turns and by authors, grave or sarcastic, eulogistic or saucy, argumentative or sentimental, chaste or slashing, classical or savage. A man-of-war of the first class, and of the regular service, when civil and ecclesiastical abuses were to be discovered and destroyed, in literary contests it often run up the flag and used the weapons of the buccaneer. Not only did it exterminate the small craft of penny-a-line novelists and poetasters, but it pursued Wordsworth, Southey, Coleridge, Byron, Montgomery, Lamb, and all with whom they treated or sympathized, with a spirit akin to that of the "Red Corsair of the Mozambique," when chasing

——"Argosies with portly sail,
Flying by him with their woven wings,
Rich with Barbaric pearl and gold."

The very temerity of the Review, sustained by such rare learning, ability, and brilliancy, gave it currency with friends and foes. It was admitted by its enemies that no similar publication displayed so many rich veins of thought, uttered so many acute observations, or arrayed its offspring in such graceful drapery ; and they found fault, not so much with the standards set up, or the principles inculcated, as with their alleged unjust application to their favorite books and authors. The answer of the reviewers was short and characteristic. If they used the stiletto or the scalping-knife when they ought to use the scimitar or the broad-sword, why, that was according to the canons of criticism they had in such cases made and provided, and the friends of the slain might resort to reprisals.

A specimen of the mode in which it drowned in ridicule pedantry and stupidity, is found in the first number, in a review, by Sydney Smith, of Rev. Dr. Langford's "Anniversary Sermon of the Royal Humane Society." After giving the title of the publication in the usual form, the reviewer says: "An accident which happened to the gentleman engaged in reviewing this sermon proves, in the most striking manner, the importance of this charity for restoring to life persons in whom the vital power is suspended. He was discovered with Dr. Langford's discourse lying open before him, in a state of the most profound sleep, from which he could not, by any means, be awakened for a great length of time. By attending, however, to the rules prescribed by the Humane Society, flinging in the smoke of tobacco, applying hot flannels, and carefully removing the discourse itself to a great distance, the critic was restored to his disconsolate brothers. The only account he could give of himself was, that he remembers reading on regularly, till he came to the following pathetic description of a drowned tradesman ; beyond which he recollects nothing." Then follows a paragraph from the sermon, dropsical with dullness ; and here the article ends.

A specimen of the style in which it pronounced sentence of

contempt on an author is found at a later date, and is perfect of its kind. It is the introductory paragraph of Macaulay's review of Gleig's Life of Warren Hastings. "This book," says Macaulay, "seems to have been manufactured in pursuance of a contract, by which the representatives of Warren Hastings, on the one part, bound themselves to furnish papers, and Mr. Gleig, on the other part, bound himself to furnish praise. It is but just to say, that the covenants on both sides have been most faithfully kept; and the result is before us in the form of three big bad volumes, full of undigested correspondence and undiscerning panegyric." Macaulay then goes on through seventy pages, giving his own brilliant portrait of Hastings, never noticing the author except at long intervals, when he turns aside for a moment to give him a blow in the face with his brush.

The Review gave an impulse to periodical literature, and elevated the tone of literary criticism and political disquisition. Grub street made a stand against the invader, worthy of its ancient garrets. It issued fifty pamphlets in a single year, explaining, extenuating, defending, defying. But dullness and insipidity at length gave way, and retreated rapidly to the trunk-makers and green grocers. Much evil was mingled with the good. The excellences of the new journal were not alone imitated. Ferocity and fire blazed out from the pages of cotemporaneous publications. But, they were the rush-light to Vesuvius. At length, soldiers of higher mettle and brighter armor than Grub street could muster took the field. Byron had shivered a lance with the Edinburgh. Southey, whose scalp it had mangled, was stung to madness, and vowed vengeance. Scott denounced its politics as rash, radical, and revolutionary. The great Whig rhinoceros from beyond the Tweed had ravaged the softer landscape of England, and tossed Tory politicians and poets on its horn for six years, when Brougham's celebrated article on Don Pedro de Cevallos and Spanish affairs appeared, avowing ultra-democratic doctrines.

Scott, who had some time before ceased to be a contributor, now ordered his subscription stopped, and entered into correspondence with Ellis, Southey, Gifford, and others, in regard to starting a rival periodical, that should encounter the spoiler in his own field, and with weapons of like temper and force. The result was the establishment, in 1809, of the Quarterly Review, in London. Its editor was William Gifford; and in boldness, bitterness, dogmatism, and ferocity, he was a full match for any writer in the Edinburgh; though, in comprehension of broad principles and appreciation of the beautiful, in acuteness and originality, he fell below the journal he was set up to overthrow.

But, dazzling as has been the meteoric career of the Edinburgh in the firmament of letters, it is in the department of governmental reform that its greatest and best services have been rendered. Its founder has well said, that at its advent "it was always considered a piece of impertinence in England if a man of less than £2,000 or £3,000 a year had any opinion at all on important subjects." The Edinburgh Review has taught a Manchester calico-printer how to take the Government by the beard. In the forty-six years of its existence, it has seen the British slave trade abolished—a devastating European war terminated—the Holy Alliance broken up, and its anointed conspirators brought into contempt—the corporation and test acts repealed—the Catholics emancipated—the criminal code humanized—the death-penalty circumscribed—the reform bill carried, extending the suffrage to half a million of people—West India and East India slavery abolished—the commercial monopoly of the East India Company overthrown—municipal corporations reformed—the court of chancery opened, and sunlight let in upon its doings—the common law courts made more accessible to the masses—the law of libel made endurable—the poor-laws made more charitable—the game-laws brought nearer the verge of modern civilization—the corn-laws repealed—the post-office made subservient to all who can raise a penny—the means of educating the poor increased—the privileges of the Established Church curtailed in three kingdoms—and a long catalogue of minor reforms effected, and dignity and intensity imparted to the popular demand for still larger concessions to the progressive genius of the age. And this journal may proudly say, that all these measures have received the support, and most of them the early, zealous, and powerful support of the Edinburgh Review. These measures gained advantages from the advocacy of the Review, far beyond the intrinsic force of the arguments with which it supported them; as, indeed, did the party of progress whose oracle it was. Its brilliant literary reputation shed a luster around the most radical political opinions, clothing them in bright raiment, and giving them an introduction into the halls of the learned and the saloons of the noble. Its numerous articles on liberal and general education, especially those written by Sydney Smith, are above all praise. And while it impaled bores and charlatans in literature, and scourged quacks and villains in the State, it was no less a terror to hypocrites and oppressors in the Church. But candor must admit, that if it was generally a terror to evil doers in the name of religion, it was not always a praise to them that did well.

The ecclesiastical and religious tone of the Review, during the first twenty years of its existence, was imparted to it mainly by Sydney Smith. He had a good deal more wit than charity; was not ashamed to steal his sermons from Taylor, Hooker and Barrow, that he might save time to shoot sarcasms at Wesley and "the nasty Methodists," and shower ridicule upon Wilberforce and "the patent Christians at Clapham;" and seemed to have little reverence for any part of the Establishment which he defended, except its tithes and its titles. He pleaded for toleration and emancipation, not so much because Dissenters and Catholics deserved them, but because to grant them would silence clamor, and more firmly secure the power and patronage, and exalt the dignity of "the Church." But, though it breathed a good deal of this spirit, the Review always contended for religious freedom, and, when need be, was as hearty in its assaults upon the miter of the primate, and its ridicule of the starched robes of the bench of bishops, as of ranters and patent Christians. Sydney Smith hated tyranny, but he loved money; he was a humane man, and no ascetic or bigot; and it was his superabundant wit, and the ludicrous light in which almost everything struck his mind, that gave edge to his sarcasms, and made him seem more uncharitable than he really was. Two of his articles in the Edinburgh carried through Parliament a bill extending to all grades of felons the full benefit of counsel when on trial. Previous to this, counsel, even in capital cases, were not allowed to address juries in favor of prisoners, and before a poor wretch could get half through a stammering speech in his own behalf, he was generally choked off by the judge, that he might be the more speedily strangled by the hangman. Ah! old Dean Swift humanized; few men have done more to explode error, shame bigotry, and expose abuses, than thou!

As a political journal, the influence of the Edinburgh Review has, to a great extent, passed away. Its power and glory culminated during the administration of Earl Grey. Till then, it shone in unrivaled splendor, pouring its beams in the path of progress, and shedding more light around the footsteps of reform than all other like sources combined. Other luminaries, fresher in their rising, and reflecting the opinions of the awakened mind of England, have dimmed its fires. It has grown wayward, timid, conservative, and aristocratic, touching gingerly, and with gloved fingers, topics which it once handled without mittens. From the hour it became the organ of power, it ceased to be the herald of the people. In its decline, it has occasionally roused itself, and struck a blow for freedom, which revived the memory of the glorious days before the blight of Conservatism came upon it. It has shared the fate of the Whigs, and of all Quarterlies, as the organs of political opinion. Periodical literature has seen a revolution in the public taste. Quarterlies and Monthlies hardly survived the advent of railways. The electric telegraph, which can barely keep pace with the revolutions of parties and states, has made even Weeklies seem stale. The Penny Magazine defies the Quarterly, and the Daily Press rules the hour. But, ten thousand thanks to the Edinburgh Review, for ushering in an era which has made its own existence no longer necessary to the politician and the statesman.

A brief notice of a few other liberal periodicals will close this chapter.

The London Quarterly having failed to destroy the influence of the Edinburgh, a less stately and more lively periodical was planted on the spot where the great Whig champion bore sway, to encounter its politics with the lighter weapons of wit and satire, and dispute its mastery in the field of polite letters and criticism. Blackwood's Edinburgh Magazine entered the lists in 1817. Reckoning among its contributors some of the ripest scholars and rarest wits of the times, it occupies a first place among literary journals, while able partisans sprinkle its pages with the spiciest vindications of ultra Tory politics. During the reform-bill excitement, Tait's Edinburgh Magazine was sent forth as an antidote to Blackwood. A corps of rare essayists and critics have given it a highly respectable position in the literary world, and its political articles, written with vigor and eloquence, have kept pace with the advancing step of the age.

After several unsuccessful attempts had been made to establish a permanent Quarterly journal in London, to support the liberal side in politics, Mr. Bentham and his disciples started the Westminster Review, in 1824. Leaping into the arena far ahead of the Edinburgh, it drew its blade in defense of the radicals, and proposed fundamental reforms in the Constitution of the country. Reflecting the views of its celebrated founder, it has advocated, with great ability, unqualified suffrage, freedom of trade, the dissolution of the union of Church and State, the abolition of the hereditary feature of the House of Peers, the abrogation of the court of chancery, and a complete remodeling and codification of the laws of the realm. Bentham, Bowring, Col. Thompson, and Roebuck have been among its political contributors, and many of its literary articles have been of a high order. Carlyle has published in it several characteristic essays. It exhibits more courage and soul than any of its cotemporaries, and is the most democratic Quarterly in the kingdom. The Eclectic Review, a periodical devoted rather to ecclesiastical reforms, though it indulges in literature and politics, has, under the control of Dr. Price, a distinguished Baptist clergyman, rendered good service in the cause of philanthropy. Robert Hall and John Foster, names familiar to scholars and divines in both hemispheres, used to contribute to its pages. The New Monthly Magazine, under the editorship of Campbell, and afterward of Bulwer, though chiefly devoted to literature, espoused the liberal side in politics. For a time it received the contributions of our accomplished countryman, Mr. Willis.

But, it is not the Quarterly and the Monthly that originate and guide public opinion. At best, they but follow in its wake. The Weekly and the Daily trace the channels in which its currents flow. And here we are launched upon an ocean of periodical literature. From the days of Wilkes' "North Briton," down to those of Punch's "Charivari," a constantly swelling mass of newspapers has borne the cause of the People forward from triumph to triumph. Confining our view to those standing out of the mass, on peculiar and independent ground, the eye is at once attracted by the Register and the Examiner—the greatest of their class. The former was founded by William Cobbett, the latter by Leigh Hunt; the one uttering the discontents of the lower class of radicals, the other reflecting the opinions of the higher. Of Cobbett's writings I have already spoken at considerable length. He was the best exponent of the wrongs, prejudices and hates of the subterranean strata of English society, that has ever appeared. The Examiner was established in 1809. It displayed a much higher order of literary talent than the Register, but was equally radical in politics, and scarcely less violent in its attacks on public men and institutions. Hunt was repeatedly prosecuted by the Government, and lay two years in prison for a libel on that decoction of treachery and lechery, the Prince of Wales. While in jail, he composed some of his best poems. The Examiner has always displayed marked ability and brilliancy, both in its political and literary departments. While under the editorship of Mr. Fonblanque, a writer of extraordinary vigor and taste, it ordinarily produced political articles executed in a style that would have adorned the Edinburgh Review, while their doctrines were congenial to the progressive genius of the times. Among its frequent contributors is the intrepid, proud, humane, eccentric Walter Savage Landor, a poet of keen sensibilities, an ardent lover of truth and freedom—a man, "take him all in all." Latterly, the reformatory tone of The Examiner is somewhat modified, but it maintains its place in the front rank of the weekly literary and political press. The Spectator deservedly holds a high position in this department of newspapers. At first it was strongly radical in its politics; but, like the Examiner, it has latterly abated its tone without diminishing its ability.

Belonging to the same general class as the Examiner and Spectator, are the various periodicals that have borne the name of Douglas Jerrold. Mr. Jerrold has written successful melodramas, comedies, and farces for the theaters; sparkling essays for the classic Blackwood; humorous and serious tales for the New Monthly; stories and squibs for Punch; political "leaders" for first-class newspapers; besides sketches, criticisms, and "articles" without number for the million. Abounding in wit, sarcasm, humor pathos, philosophy and fun, there runs through his writings a large vein of unadulterated humanity, which gives life and heart to the whole. He wages holy war against fustian literature, sham statesmanship, sectarian cant, legalized injustice, and titled tyranny. If England's periodical writers were of his temper and metal, the good time foreshadowed by Mackay, would soon come, when

"The pen shall supersede the sword,
And right, not might, shall be the lord.'

Having unexpectedly fallen upon Punch, in connection with Mr. Jerrold, I will say that that eccentric person deserves honorable mention among English Reformers. His unparalleled wit is tempered with love to mankind ; his sympathies are with the million ; and he displays in his weekly walk and conversation a great deal more humanity, quite as much Christian charity, (though far less "religion,") as "The Church of England Quarterly Review," the organ of High Church Toryism. Punch is too much of a man to send Mr. Shore to prison, or to excommunicate Mr. Noel.

The People's Journal and Howitt's Journal are successful attempts to mingle tasteful literary essays with radical political disquisitions, and bring them within the reach of every-day men of business and toil. Though many accomplished writers contributed to their pages, the Howitts, who originated the enterprise, were for some time its animating soul. The educated radicalism of England found an organ in these journals, whose tone harmonized with their sympathies. High as is Mr. Howitt's literary reputation, it is as a political and social reformer that his name will be the most widely known. His "History of Priestcraft," published in 1834, while he lived in Nottingham, and which met a sale of some 20,000 copies, gave him eclat in a new field, brought him some money, which he needed, and an election as alderman of that town, which he did not want at all. Four years afterward, he published "Colonization and Christianity," which led to the formation of the British India Society, to the abolition of slavery in the peninsula of Hindostan, and to efforts to relieve from oppression and stimulate to enterprise the myriads that swarm in that long-neglected portion of the empire. Mr. Howitt's writings in behalf of Complete Suffrage, Religious Toleration, and Irish Relief, are as honorable to the benevolence of his heart as are his numerous literary works to the fertility of his genius.

Still confining myself to *quasi* literary productions, I may mention in this connection a series of publications, adapted to the means and capacities of the common people, which, though not specially intended to promote social and political reform, exerted a powerful influence in that direction. Chambers' Edinburgh Journal was commenced in 1832; it consists of papers on literature, science, history and biography, and, being sold at a cheap rate, reached at one period a circulation of nearly 100,000 copies. The Society for the Diffusion of Useful Knowledge, founded in 1825, caused to be prepared, and placed at cheap prices in the hands of the working classes, numerous publications of the same general character, but of a higher order, as those of the Chambers; and it subsequently issued two weekly periodicals, the Penny Magazine and the Penny Cyclopedia, filled with entertaining knowledge, which circulated by thousands through all the workshops of the kingdom, and have found their way to the learned rich and the laboring poor on this side of the ocean. These publications imparted to the common mind of England that knowledge which is power, and, in conjunction with the political press, taught the people the nature and value of their rights, and inspired them with courage to demand and defend them.

So much for periodical literature. Another department of English letters, more strictly deserving the name of "Literature," which has rendered powerful aid to the cause of political reform during the present century, will be noticed in the next chapter.

CHAPTER XXXV.

The Liberal Literature of England—Poetry—Southey—Coleridge—Wordsworth—Burns—Rogers—Montgomery—Moore—Campbell—Herbert—Byron—Shelley—Keats—Hunt—Pringle—Nicoll—Peter—Barton—Hood—Procter—Tennyson—Milnes—Elliott—Horne—Mary Howitt—Eliza Cook—Mackay—Novels—Godwin—Holcraft—The Drama—Bage—Scott—Miss Edgeworth—Mrs. Opie—Miss Mitford—Mrs. Hall—Miss Martineau—Banim—Lever—Lover—Bulwer—Dickens—Essays—Jeffrey—Smith—Brougham—Mackintosh—Macaulay—Lamb—Hazlitt—Carlyle—Talfourd—Pamphlets—Holland House—French Literature and Louis Philippe.

FURTHER notice will now be taken of the liberal literature of England, after the French revolution. We can enter only on the borders of this large field. Since the modern "revival of letters," the *Poets* of England have furnished their quota of friends of Progress and Reform.

Among the strange theories concerning the regeneration of mankind, to which the great French convulsion gave birth, was a day-dream of Southey, Coleridge, and Lloyd, three young geniuses, then sojourning at Bristol. Having vainly endeavored to make England a republic, by writing a drama on the fall of Robespierre, delivering a course of lectures on the French revolution, and publishing two or three seditious pamphlets, they proposed to leave the kingdom in disgust, bury themselves in the aboriginal forests on the banks of the Susquehanna, and there erect a "Pantisocracy," in which property should be held in common, every man be a legislator, and a model democracy be wrought out, that should consummate the happiness of its founders, while its reflex influence cured all the ills of European institutions. Unfortunately for the human race, the three poets happened just then to fall in with and fall in love with three tempting young Eves of Bristol, the Misses Fricker, one an actress, one a mantua-maker, and one a school-teacher; and giving up their scheme of regenerating the world, they wisely concluded, with Benedick, that it was better to people it, and so all got married. Thus ended *their* "Much Ado about Nothing."

Lloyd sunk into obscurity, Southey atoned for his Susquehanna sins by spending a long life in hostility to civil and religious freedom, and Coleridge lived and died a moderate friend of liberty and reform. Wordsworth early became acquainted with Coleridge and Southey, participated in their French enthusiasm, and, like them, his first poetic dreams were of freedom. In one of his earliest productions he proposes to invoke the restorative aid of the Royal Humane Society in behalf of crowned heads, as follows:

"Oh give, great God! to Freedom's waves to ride
Sublime o'er conquest, avarice, and pride;
And grant that every sceptered child of clay
Who cries, presumptuous, 'Here their tides shall stay,'
Swept in their anger from the affrighted shore,
With all his creatures sink to rise no more"

Through his long career, the productions of the greatest of the "Lake Poets" have exerted a calm but steady influence in favor of humanity.

About this time Burns appeared, "whistling at his plouw," and teaching the world that

"The rank is but the guinea's stamp,
The man's the gowd for a' that."

He, too, caught some of his inspiration from France. By force of his genius, the Scotch yeoman opened his way to the highest rank of cotemporary poets, carrying with him the sympathies of the class from which he sprung. No writer is oftener quoted to round a period in a Reform speech. I have seen a meeting of Scotch Chartists go wild with enthusiasm under the inspiration of one of his songs. The same year that Burns became an author, Rogers sent his first volume of poems to press, of whom Lord Brougham, in his Sketch of Grattan, says: "He is one of the greatest poets whom this country has produced, as well as one of its finest prose-writers; who to this unstable fame adds the more imperishable renown of being also one of the most uncompromising friends of civil and religious liberty who have appeared in any age."

In 1794, James Montgomery, a name honorably associated with the cause of humanity, published in the *Sheffield Iris*, a newspaper edited by him, a ballad on the overthrow of the Bastile, which the Pitt Government saw fit to regard as a seditious libel. He was prosecuted, convicted, amerced in a fine, and imprisoned three months in York Castle. The next year the Government again prosecuted the amiable poet for an analogous offense, upon which he was again fined and shut up six months at York. These persecutions did not quench his zeal for human freedom; and despite a most offensive critique in the Edinburgh Review of his first volume of poems, he published another in 1807, celebrating the abolition of the slave trade, which was distinguished for vigor of expression and richness of coloring. These, and subsequent publications of kindred character, have given Montgomery an enduring place in the affections of Christian philanthropists.

At a later period, two poets appeared, who have exerted a wide sway over the mind, not of Britain only, but of every land where the English language is spoken—Moore and Campbell. The political tendency of their writings (and it has been considerable) is on the side of freedom. Moore's father was of the proscribed sect of Irish Catholics, who, in the language of the son, "hailed the first dazzling outbreak of the French revolution as a signal to the slave, wherever suffering, that the day of his deliverance was near at hand." When Moore was a boy of twelve, he sat on the chairman's knee at a celebration in honor of the revolution, when this toast was drank, with three times three: "May the breezes of France fan our Irish oak into verdure!" The poet has lived to see the foliage of the oak grow more sere and yellow, though another breeze from France has swept its branches. But, in all seasons, and when mixing in the brilliant revelries of London society, the idol of a devoted band of worshipers, he never ceased to love his native island. His "Irish Melodies" have inspired a strange sympathy in many climes for his blighted country, while they have taught Irishmen, in whatever corner of the earth they wander, to say—

"Wert thou all that I wish thee—great, glorious, and free—
First flower of the earth and first gem of the sea
I might hail thee with prouder, with happier brow,
But, oh! could I love thee more deeply than now?"

Campbell's poetic offerings to the cause of Polish liberty are in the school-books of two continents, and have fired the indignation of two generations of youthful orators at that great European felony, the partition of Poland, when

"Sarmatia fell, unwept, without a crime."

The heroic struggle for Grecian independence animated the classic soul of Campbell, and he took an active part in rousing European sentiment in her behalf. And down to the last moment of his life he was proud to give his cordial support to the cause of liberty and humanity in every part of the world.

William Herbert, a scion of the ancient houses of Pembroke and Percy, is still more illustrious as a scholar of rare attainments, and as the author of "Attila," which the Edinburgh Review has declared the most Miltonic poem since Paradise Lost. Some of his poetic effusions were offered at the shrine of freedom ; and while a member of Parliament, he coöperated with Wilberforce in the abolition of the slave trade ; and after withdrawing from politics, and taking holy orders, and reaching stations of dignity in the Established Church, he gave his influence to liberal measures, advocating Catholic emancipation and the Reform bill.

The wayward genius of Byron, though it uttered much that good morals condemn, recorded nothing hostile to political liberty, but, on the contrary, something in its favor. On the few occasions that he addressed the House of Lords, he advocated the liberal cause, once vindicating in manly tones the character and life of Major Cartwright, the father of Parliamentary Reform. The conflict for Grecian independence, in which Byron's last days were spent, throws a broad ray of sunshine across the dark horizon of his career.

But we must dismiss a galaxy of bright names more summarily—some without mentioning them, others by the briefest allusions. Shelley, the unfortunate, calumniated, generous, and supereminent son of genius—Keats, an evanescent being, whose transparent soul was clad too thin for this prosaic world—Leigh Hunt, the founder of the London "Examiner," which ought to live forever, and the Italian "Liberal," which ought never to have lived at all, a true son of the Nine, whom Gifford could not kill, though Blackwood Wilson helped him try—Pringle, who died at the desk of the Anti-Slavery Society, and whose "Afar in the Desert" Coleridge ranked among the two or three most perfect lyrics in the language—Robert Nicoll, a Scotch plowman, an ardent and sincere radical, who, dying at twenty-three, lived long enough to write "The Ha' Bible," "We are brethren a'," and other poems, not unworthy of that other Scotch Robert who has canonized plowmen-bards—William Peter, now British consul for Pennsylvania, a graceful poet, but better known as a political pupil of the Fox school, a commoner advocating liberal measures, and the biographer of Romilly—Bernard Barton, the friend and correspondent of Lamb, a "Quaker poet," whose effusions show calm reflection and refined feeling, but have none of the strangely pleasing blending of the war song of the knight templar with the pastoral ballad of the mountain shepherd, of Peter the Hermit's crusade-preaching with Virgil the heathen's classic singing, which give life and beauty to the lays of *our* Quaker poet—Hood, the prince of punsters, whose "Song of the Shirt," sung in all climes, and imitated on all themes, dignified sympathy with seamstresses, who toil twenty-four hours for twelve pence—Procter, the Harrow chum of Byron, whose "Rising of the North," "The Open Sea," and "Touch us Gently, Time," show that Barry Cornwall's harp can sound at will the highest and deepest, the wildest and the tenderest notes, and while giving volumes of "morocco and gilt" to the nobility and gentry, sends "poetry for the people" through Howitt's Journal—Tennyson, an inspired singer, whose "Princess" is a reformer—Milnes, who, though a Tory in the House of Commons, always appeared as a liberal when he entered the Temple of the Muses—Elliott, whose Corn-Law Rhymes roused a nation to arms against landlord monopoly, by kindling sympathy with the poor man's lot, and firing indignation against taxes on his bread—R. H. Horne, a true poet and sterling reformer, the author of "Orion," the editor of the "New Spirit of the Age," and a contributor to the People's and Howitt's Journals—Mary Howitt, whose sex never was permitted to prevent her doing valiant service for the right in the battles of freedom with tyranny—Eliza Cook, not unworthy, as a poetess and a reformer, to be associated with Mary Howitt—Mackay, whose prophecy of the "good time coming" has been applauded to the echo by voices that would have smothered in hisses the same sentiments if uttered in prose:—these, and a glorious company besides, have laid some of the richest gifts, where all genuine poetry is welcomed, on Freedom's altar.

In this summary, only here and there a star has been pointed out in the brilliant constellation which has shone in the firmament of freedom, during the period we are now glancing over. The catalogue of slavery's poets is not yet published. It must be rather meager. If the poetry of liberty is inspired by airs from heaven, the poetry of despotism must rage in blasts from hell. Dante and Milton have given glowing descriptions of Pandemonium, and put splendid diction into the mouths of devils; but neither the descriptions nor the diction have won admirers for the domicil or its denizens, among the inhabitants of high latitudes.

Some of the *Novelists* of this period have contributed not a little to the cause of political reform.

William Godwin, one of the remarkable men of the times, is known not only as the writer of that extraordinary tale, "Caleb Williams," but of the "Inquiry concerning Political Justice," a production whose style is as vigorous as its doctrines are radical, displaying rare originality and boldness of conception, and breathing the loftiest aspirations for the well-being of man. "Caleb Williams," which appeared soon after the "Inquiry," was intended to give wider currency to the author's views of social and political reform, by clothing them in the attractive colors of romance. Had Godwin been an ambitious politician, he might have placed himself at the head of a school of reformers. He chose to be a philosophical recluse; and in the storm of the French revolution, he sent out from his retreat breathing thoughts and burning words, that gave increased life and vigor to the heaving mass of mind around him. The friend and counselor of Tooke and Holcroft, he was obnoxious to the Government, but his retired habits saved him from the prosecutions that periled the lives of his more active associates. His numerous writings, like those of Jeremy Bentham, whom he in some respects strongly resembled, while in others no two men could be more dissimilar, have left abiding impressions on many of the noblest minds of England.

Holcroft imbibed liberal principles during the time of the French convulsions. He was the writer of several successful plays, among which was the highly popular "Road to Ruin." He published various novels, which, on account of their political sentiments, attracted much notice. As mere romances they belong not to the first rank, the plots and characters being mere frame-work to hold aristocratic doctrines up to ridicule, and democratic principles to admiration. The dialogue is often lively and piquant, and many of the portraits are skillfully drawn. And in this connection, it may be said that the dramatists of this period poured some of their rills of philosophy, wit and satire into the popular channels. Even Rolla's fustian address to the Peruvians, which sounds like Sheridan's speeches against Napoleon, always stimulated the galleries to a higher pitch of hatred to tyranny. Colman's comedies made upstart noblemen and pedantic doctors of laws shade their faces, while the pit shook its sides with laughter. William Tell launched his arrow not in vain at Gesler, for George IV came near being shot in the royal box on an occasion when it was played; and Talfourd and Bulwer, in Ion and the Lady of Lyons, having disguised democracy in classic robes, introduced it to the admiration and applause of the dress circle. To return to novelists. Coeval with Holcroft, Robert Bage, a Tamworth Quaker, not having the fear of George Fox nor the Attorney General before his eyes, published some good political novels. He, like the dramatist, had caught some of the fire of liberty at the general conflagration of the old order of things in Europe, and he bore his "testimony" against the bigotry of Guelph and the arrogance of Pitt, in the form of romances, which, though they fell below Holcroft's, received the imprimatur of Walter Scott, when he included them in his "Novelist's Library."

The works of the Godwin, Holcroft and Bage school not only introduced a new era in novel writing, by making fiction the medium of communicating radical opinions, but they aided in evaporating the rose-water style of romance, which had so diluted the public taste that "novel" and "insipidity" had come to be synonymous terms. By and by, the public appetite was prepared for a more racy and invigorating regimen. Then appeared the gorgeous but manly and natural historical novels of Scott, too prone to flatter "blood," wealth, and noble lineage, but wearing an air of the most genial *bonhommie*, and looking with a brotherly eye upon humanity in its humblest forms. About the time that Scott was beginning his Waverley, came the piquant and beautiful stories of Miss Edgeworth and Mrs. Opie, to be followed by those of Miss Mitford and Mrs. Hall, who, whether painting life and manners in the cottages of the lowly or the drawing-rooms of the great, place virtue and philanthropy in the foreground of the picture. At a later period, the philosophic and benevolent Miss Martineau, despite the maledictions of the London Quarterly, admirably succeeded in the till then doubtful experiment of conveying the principles of politico-economical science to the masses through the medium of tales and sketches. The English Miss Sedgwick deserves the thanks of humanity for putting Benthamism into clean purple and fine linen. Ireland has been prolific in delineators of her suffering and crimes, jocularities and bulls, both in poetry and prose. Banim, the author of the *O'Hara Tales*, and other stories, is the greatest of his class. He paints the times of Ninety-Eight in colors so vivid that the tragedy leaps living from the canvas. In the *Nonconformist* he depicts the evils and cruelties of the Catholic penal code in figures so graphic and truthful that the veriest bigot can hardly restrain his indignation at the Protestant oppressors. Lever places in a strong light the blarney and blunders of the Irish, and his stories generally begin in farce and end in caricature. Lover puts you at once into good humor; and, whether you read him, or hear him tell his stories or sing his songs, he makes you love the genuine Irish character, and you alternately cry and laugh at its miseries and drolleries to the end of the volume or ballad. Bulwer's world-read novels, attractive to the scholastic mind by their acute analysis of character, and to the poetic temperament by their deep coloring, though, like Byron's poems, they enunciate a good deal of doubtful ethics, drawing no very broad line between the morals of plowmen and highwaymen, yet their political tendencies are decidedly towards liberalism. But the writer of fiction who has done the most in our day for his race, is Charles Dickens. He is not merely a novelist, but a philanthropist, whose overflowing humanity surpasses even his abounding humor. No right-hearted man ever rose from the perusal of Dickens without feeling a deeper affection for human nature, a more cordial contempt for cant and hypocrisy, and a holier hatred of cruelty and meanness. His Nicholas Nickleby and Oliver Twist have done more to drown in ridicule and smother in abhorrence the absurd private schools and the diabolical parish work-houses of England, than the "works" of all the didactic authors of the kingdom.

Another class of writers have, during the present century, secured a firm footing within the pale of English literature—the *Essayists*. Indeed, at one time, it looked as if the new comers would succeed in excluding everybody from it but themselves. At the head of this class stand the leading contributors of the Edinburgh Review, of whom Mr. Whipple has aptly said, "they made reviewing more respectable than authorship." Jeffrey, for twenty-six years its editor, shed over its pages a strong, steady, and beautiful light, which tempered and irradiated the whole. His papers are a rare compend of literary criticism. Though sometimes more sophistical than philosophical, more brilliant than profound, and betraying prejudices when he should elucidate principles, he was, upon the whole, not unworthy to be called "The Prince of Critics." For a quarter of a century his fiat was law in far the larger portion of the republic of English letters. Since he left the throne, many of his canons have been disputed, and some have been totally annulled. His contributions to the Review, when published in a separate form, appear more homogeneous, more like a "work," than those of his brethren who have put theirs to press. Sydney Smith bore undisputed sway in the realm of wit and sarcasm. Papists, prisoners, poachers, paupers, school-boys, and chimney-sweepers, owe him a monument each, for he was their very friend; and if the Pennsylvanians repudiate, nonconformists might purchase a pension for his heirs with the lawn he tore from the shoulders of "persecuting bishops." Brougham glared from the pages of the Review a baleful meteor, striking terror into dunces in Grub street and charlatans in Downing street, now scorching a poetaster and then roasting a prime minister, nor quenching his fires till they had penetrated and lit up the royal harem of Carlton House and Windsor Castle. Mackintosh made the Edinburgh the medium for exhibiting to the public eye some of those philosophical disquisitions, laden with the lore of the school-men, and embellished with the graces of the poets, which justified the assertion of Robert Hall, that if he had been less indolent and discursive, he might have attained the first place amongst modern metaphysicians. Macaulay has been one of the chief literary attractions of the Review for the last eighteen years. His contributions are no more *criticisms* than are his descriptions of the state of England in 1685, or his sketch of the death-bed of Charles II, in his recent history. True, he places the title of a book at the head of a page. But his papers have men for their subjects rather than books, are essays rather than articles, panoramas of events instead of histories, living portraits of individuals rather than biographies of the dead. According to the old standards, they would have been more appropriate in the history of England than in the Edinburgh Review. But the old standards have decayed. They are read and imitated in two hemispheres. The scholar admires their learning, the philosopher their penetration, the rhetorician their art, the poet their imagery, the million their politics.

And these five are the greatest of the "Edinburgh Reviewers." Freedom in every part of the world owes them a heavy debt of gratitude.

Passing through a brilliant throng of essayists, each man of whom is worthy of special note, and stopping barely long enough to say of Lamb that he is one of the most quaint, humorous, witty, genial, and humane writers in the language, and of Hazlitt, that he is a mine of diamonds, all rich and disorderly, brilliant and cutting, but of the first water, we approach with no little awe and diffidence the strange but not stranger Thomas Carlyle, "a writer of books." He has done yoeman service in the conflict with "shams," and has made the bankrupt institutions of England echo their own hollowness, under the heavy blows of his German truncheon. The obscurity of his style is often alleged against him. In many passages, an interlined translation, or a glossary, would be convenient. But, he is readily understood by those familiar with his fanciful mode of backing up to a question, rather than going straight forward to it. His defects seem to lie deeper than the obscurities of his rhetoric. They pierce through words to things. A vein of profound reflection pervades much of his writing. But no inconsiderable portion of it is indebted to his style for its seeming profundity. Straighten some of his crooked sentences, which, *prima facie*, seem to embrace in their sinuosities some great idea too awful to be uttered in plain Saxon, and thus, as it were, having thrown out the meaning, lo, the matter turns out to be rather commonplace. This is not his worst fault; for no author is bound to be always saying original or profound things, and he may be excused sometimes for wrapping up a common idea in superfine clothing. As a writer on social and political evils—his chosen field—Carlyle whelms the reader deeper and deeper in the abyss of wide-weltering wrong—*and there leaves him*. He points out no way of escape; suggests no remedies. Read his "Chartism," his "Past and Present," his article in a recent Spectator on "Ireland and Sir Robert Peel"—and what then? He gives you clearly to understand that the governmental machine is sadly out of gear—that Poor-Laws are a "sham," and Emigration a delusion—that the "*sans-potato* Irish" are rotting under bad rule—but what then? Why, so far as Mr. Carlyle tells you, *Nothing!* Rot to all eternity, for aught he proposes by way of remedy. His writings abound in hearty expressions of dissatisfaction with existing things; in vivid pictures of human suffering, more graphic than limner ever drew, more startling than poet ever painted; but, trusting to him, you look in vain for any relief, either for your own excited feelings, or for the pitiable objects in whose behalf he has aroused your sympathies. He leads you into a foul morass, tells you it is a "sham," and as you sink out of sight, surrounded by a mass of smothering humanity, he cries, "God help you," mounts some transcendental crotchet, and soars into the clouds. It is suspected that Carlyle has a theoretic remedy for bad government, but dislikes to disclose it. He has no faith in Toryism, Whigism, Liberalism, or Radicalism. To him, they are "shams all." If he belongs to any school, it would seem to be the absolute. He don't believe in the divine right of kings, though he holds that some men are born to command. Nor would he give the governed the right of selecting their commander. He recognizes a sort of intellectual and moral "might," the possession of which confers the "right" to govern. The abstract theory may be good; the difficulty is in reducing it to the concrete. Who is to decide as to the possession of the "might?" Jefferson would refer the decision to the governed; Nichols would leave it to the accidents of royal procreation; Carlyle says it belongs to —— who knows what he says? He is a great "Hero"-worshiper, and a good many of his "Heroes" have been splendid tyrants. He despises imbecility, but idolizes power. His rather obscure chapter in "Chartism" on "Rights and Mights" can, with little effort, be turned into a special plea for absolutism. His eulogistic essay, in the Foreign Quarterly, on Dr. Francia, "the Perpetual Dictator of the Republic of Paraguay," seems to disclose the kind of government and governor he glories in. Francia was a man of intellect and decision, and he was a despot. He erected a "workman's gallows," to terrify and hang laborers who failed to do their work well—a "not unbeneficial institution," says Carlyle. A poor shoemaker made some belts for the Dictator's grenadiers. He did not like the sample shown to him, though the shoemaker "had done his best." Francia ordered a rope about the neck of the trembling wretch, calling him "a most impertinent scoundrel," (a "very favorite word of the Dictator's," says Carlyle,) and had him marched back and forth under the gallows, in the momentary expectation of being hung. He was at length released, half dead with terror. Carlyle remarks upon this, in plain English, (his admiration for the scene is too intense for a crooked sentence,) that the shoemaker worked with such alacrity all night, that his belts on the morrow were without a parallel in South America. The whole story, drawn out through a page, shows that Francia was a brute; as, indeed, does the whole article in the Quarterly. Carlyle gloats over him with wild enthusiasm. But, it is often neither just nor generous to measure others by our own standards. Every man has his *forte*, his mission. Carlyle's may be to point out existing evils, while leaving it to time and plain men to suggest remedies. His gigantic soul sits enshrouded, to common eyes, in clouds. To his own, it may bask in sunshine. Honest, humane, mystic, magnificent, the world cannot spare the great mind of the age, whose calling seems to be to set smaller minds in motion. Long live this "Writer of Books."

To relieve the picture, let us glance at the anti-counterpart of Carlyle—Thomas Noon Talfourd. He is one of the brightest and purest specimens of the *literati* of England. A lawyer, a poet, a dramatist, an orator, a statesman, an essayist, he has succeeded in each of these varied departments. The instances are not unfrequent in which persons have attained a high place both in politics and literature. Instances of marked success both in law and literature are extremely rare. The most striking English examples of the attainment of eminence by the same individual in the profession of law and the cultivation of literature, are Jeffrey, Brougham, and Talfourd. The latter has achieved this by the versatility and elasticity of his genius, unaided by the accidents of birth, family, or wealth. There is a magnetic philosophy, a classical witchery, an intoxicating enthusiasm, about his literary productions, that make him one of the most attractive and delightful of authors. As a lawyer, he is at home in the grave and studied discussions at *banc*, and in the showy and extemporaneous contests at *nisi prius*. His defense of Moxon, the poet bookseller, so foolishly and scandalously prosecuted, a few years ago, for publishing the works of Shelley, was a splendid vindication of the right of genius to conceive, and enterprise to print, some of the rarest productions of the century. His rhetoric, in the quiet retreat of letters, and his eloquence in the bustling road of politics, have been employed to instruct, delight and elevate his fellow-men.

There is a department of writing, not yet dignified with the title of "Literature," which exerts an influence over popular sentiment, second only to that of the weekly and daily press. It is peculiarly the offspring of this age, and bears the strong lineaments of its parent. I will call it the *Literature of Occasional Pamphlets*. In England, the Catholic Controversy, Parliamentary Reform, Negro Slavery, Chartism, the Corn Laws, Church and State, General Education, and all those questions which have moved and do move the nation, have called out a mass of such literature, which, in intrinsic ability and artistic excellence, will bear comparison with any cotemporaneous branch of writing. In that country, and more especially in this, he who does not stock his library with volumes of selected pamphlets excludes from it some of the most valuable literature of the nineteenth century.

I cannot close this imperfect view of the liberal literature of

England, without a brief allusion to the peculiar but powerful aid rendered to it by the late Lord Holland. The nephew of Fox inherited much of the eloquence, all the democracy, and more than all the love for learning and the fine arts, of his illustrious uncle. For a third of a century, which carried England forward a hundred years in the path of improvement, "Holland House" was the center of attraction for liberal statesmen, orators, poets, painters, wits, and scholars. Mingling in the brilliant throngs that so often filled its gorgeous drawing-rooms, elegant picture-galleries, and ample libraries, were to be seen statesmen who guided Cabinets, and orators who swayed Senates; men of letters who had reached the hights of human knowledge, and modest genius just struggling into notice; poets reposing under the shadow of their fame, and poets just plucking their first laurel-leaf; sculptors who had engraven life in the marble, and painters who had impressed beauty on the canvas; the writer of the first article in the last Edinburgh, and the author of the best comedy then acting at Drury-Lane; here a Whig Duke with a long title and a landed air, and there a Radical Editor under indictment for a seditious libel on the Government; the Duchess of Sutherland shedding grace around this circle, and Mrs. Opie diffusing benevolence around that; Buxton, the brewer, discoursing on Prison Discipline with Bentham, the philosopher; Brougham explaining to a Polish refugee his plan for educating the people, while Moore delighted a bevy of belles by singing his last Irish melody; Sydney Smith enlivening this alcove with his humor, and Mackintosh enlightening that with his learning—all these varied and diverse elements meeting on terms of social equality, and impressing upon the literary mind of the country the all-influential lesson, that, so far from losing caste by embracing liberal political opinions, the man of letters, of science, and of art, might find the profession of that faith a passport to circles where fashion displayed its smiles and power dispensed its favors.

The literature of France prostrated the Throne of Louis Philippe, and erected the Republic of Lamartine. The follies of the cowardly Louis, the errors of his vacillating ministers, the barricades of the *sans-culottes* mobs, the bayonets of the recusant guards, were insufficient to have overthrown the monarchy, had not the literature of France been gradually but efficiently preparing the national mind for the great change. During the preceding thirty years, a taste for philosophical speculation had raised up a school of bold thinkers, who had employed their rarest powers in eulogizing the rights of man, in depicting his wrongs, in displaying the merits of the masses, in painting the crimes of the Government, and in demonstrating that the throne and its institutions stood between the laboring poor and their social regeneration. Poets, essayists, novelists, dramatists, and orators brought the artillery of eloquence, the lighter and more insinuating weapons of romance, and the glittering arms of wit and satire, to bear against the acknowledged abuses in the administration of affairs, and especially the factitious institutions of the State, which sat heavily upon the middle and lower orders of society. As the crisis drew nearer, the liberal portion of the political press stimulated the popular discontent —the *cafés* and clubs were thronged with the advocates of equality—the theater and the opera gratified the public taste by adapting their amusements to the appetite for social change —the ballad-singers chanted the blessings of freedom and fraternity at the street corners, in bad verse and harsh melody— the Parisian circles of fashion, nowhere more brilliant, nowhere more influential, reflected abroad through a thousand avenues the popular sentiment, imparting to it the charms of beauty, the grace of scholarship, and the dignity of station. These influences had been silently and steadily at work all over France, and especially in Paris, the national heart of this susceptible people, for years before the mere accident of the suppression of a Reform Banquet became, in the natural order of events, the occasion of that explosion which electrified Europe.

But though the streams of public feeling had so long poured into one channel, whose currents tended toward one result—the undermining of existing institutions—Louis Philippe was blinded to his destiny, and boasted of his power to crush the rising mass, only a few hours before the tri-colored flag, bearing the talismanic motto, "Liberty, Equality, Fraternity," was displayed from the Hotel de Ville, while he leaped into a carriage, on the very spot where the blood of Louis XVI was poured out, and, with money borrowed of his guards, fled an exile from republican France

Thus the literature of France prostrated the throne of Louis Philippe, and erected the Republic of Lamartine. The literature of England can do more to change its institutions, than the clubs of Chartists or the pikes of Repealers. Without the shedding of one drop of human blood, it might, in the next third of a century, revolutionize the Government, and establish institutions that would recognize and protect the equal rights of the whole people. Will it fulfill its glorious mission ?

CHAPTER XXXVI.

Conclusion.

In the foregoing chapters, I have endeavored to trace the rise and progress of the Great British Party of Reform, which, adopting such changes in principle and policy as experience may suggest, will live and grow till every man has a voice in the election of both branches of the Legislature that governs him—till the burdens of taxation are impartially distributed among the people—till the sinecure and pension rolls are destroyed—till the public debt is paid or repudiated—till the main reliance for home defense rests with an organized militia—till the marine of a free commerce has chased the "wooden walls" from the ocean—till traffic in the land is as free as in the wheat it grows—till labor, fairly paid, becomes labor duly respected—till every sect supports its own church and clergy, and none other—till common schools, drawing nourishment from the bosom of the State, nestle in every valley—till the precepts of the law are made plain, and its admistration cheap—till Ireland becomes independent, or is allowed her just share in the national councils—till the dogma that a favored few are born booted and spurred, to ride the masses "by the grace of God," has had its last day, and the England of the times "when George the Third was King" exists only in the chronicles of History.

Since these Sketches were commenced, Europe has been the theater of a series of revolutions and counter-revolutions.

France rose, overthrew the Monarchy, and expelled Louis Philippe. In an evil hour, she thrust aside Lamartine, to make room for Louis Napoleon. Ireland, having made an attempt to break her chains, has fallen into the arms of despair. Austria and Prussia kindled a flame which, for a time, gladdened the eye of Liberty. The expiring embers have been trodden out by the hoof of the Cossack. Rome expelled her Dictator, and founded a Republic more glorious and free than that of antiquity. She died under assassin blows dealt across the Alps by a professedly fraternal hand. Hungary made a stand for Freedom which electrified the world. Her immortal Kossuth and Bem have been compelled to flee to the mountains, while the hordes of Russia lay waste her plains, and Austria, the meanest of despots, rivets chains on the limbs of her sons. From this dark and dreary prospect, the eye turns to the Radical Reformers of Great Britain and Ireland. Acting through institutions comparatively free, they will by slow but sure advances yet work out for themselves, and, by the aid of kindred spirits in other countries, for Europe, the great problem of Constitutional liberty. In the present aspect of Continental affairs, they, with the Radical Republicans of France, must be regarded as the rallying point, the forlorn hope of the struggling masses from the Gulf of Finland to the Straits of Gibraltar.

THE END.

www.ingramcontent.com/pod-product-compliance
Lightning Source LLC
LaVergne TN
LVHW020118110826
845151LV00001B/201

* 9 7 8 1 4 2 5 5 4 1 9 5 8 *